TOURISM, HERITAGE AND NATIONAL CULTURE IN JAVA

Curzon-IIAS Asian Studies Series

Series Co-ordinator: Dick van der Meij
Institute Director: Wim A.L. Stokhof

The International Institute for Asian Studies (IIAS) is a postdoctoral research centre based in Leiden and Amsterdam, The Netherlands. Its main objective is to encourage Asian Studies in the Humanities and the Social Sciences and to promote national and international co-operation in these fields. The Institute was established in 1993 on the initiative of the Royal Netherlands Academy of Arts and Sciences, Leiden University, Universiteit van Amsterdam and Vrije Universiteit Amsterdam. It is mainly financed by The Netherlands Ministry of Education, Culture, and Sciences. IIAS has played an active role in co-ordinating and disseminating information on Asian Studies throughout the world. The Institute acts as an international mediator, bringing together various entities for the enhancement of Asian Studies both within and outside the Netherlands. The Curzon-IIAS Asian Studies series reflects the scope of the Institute. The Editorial Board consists of Erik Zürcher, Wang Gungwu, Om Prakash, Dru Gladney, Amiya K. Bagchi, James C. Scott, Jean-Luc Domenach and Frits Staal.

Images of the 'Modern Woman' in Asia
Edited by Shoma Munshi

Nomads in the Sedentary World
Edited by Anatoly M. Khazanov & André Wink

Reading Asia
Edited by Frans Hüsken & Dick van der Meij

Tourism, Heritage and National Culture in Java
Heidi Dahles

Asian-European Perspectives
Edited by Wim Stokhof & Paul van der Velde

Law and Development in East and Southeast Asia
Edited by Christoph Antons

The Indian Ocean Rim
Edited by Gwyn Campbell

Rethinking Chinese Transnational Enterprises
Edited by Leo Douw, Cen Huang & David Ip

'Hinduism' in Modern Indonesia
Edited by Martin Ramstedt

The History of Tibet
Edited by Alex McKay, 3 vols.

Diasporas and Interculturalism in Asian Performing Arts
Edited by Hae-Kyung Um

TOURISM, HERITAGE AND NATIONAL CULTURE IN JAVA

Dilemmas of a Local Community

Heidi Dahles

CURZON

First Published in 2001
by Curzon Press
Richmond, Surrey
http://www.curzonpress.co.uk

Editorial Matter © 2001 Heidi Dahles

Typeset in Times New Roman by Dick van der Meij
Printed and bound in Great Britain by
TJ International, Padstow, Cornwall

British Library Cataloguing in Publication Data
A catalogue record of this book is available from the British Library

ISBN 0–7007–1520–7

Kepada:
R.L.P.
Ikan yang terbang

CONTENTS

PREFACE

Once it sat firmly in the saddle the New Order government in Indonesia deployed tourism strategically as the engine of modernization. Tourism, in particular international tourism, was supposed to contribute significantly to the development (*pembangunan*) of Indonesian society, development being defined in terms of measurable growth of the economy as well as political unity and the emergence of a national culture.

Scholars in the field of the 'politics of tourism' have developed partly converging and partly conflicting paradigms regarding the relationship between tourism, politics, and culture. While most scholars agree that tourism is a major symptom of as well as a force behind the process of globalization, they disagree about the effects of the growth of tourism in general and of international tourism in particular on local communities. Whereas some expect international tourism to bring about cultural homogenization and the destruction of local cultures, others believe that tourism development leads to the maintenance and even revitalization of local and ethnic identities. Most scholars, however, tend to underestimate the role of national governments as they believe either in transnational integration or in increasing local autonomy.

In this work, the role of the state and especially the role of the national government in local and regional tourism development will be of central concern. This book looks back on over twenty-five years of tourism politics and policies under the New Order government of former President Suharto, an era in which domestic and international tourism was booming to become Indonesia's 'first most important economic sector'. As will be argued in this book, the New Order government has been strategically promoting the expansion of tourism to implement its political agenda, i.e:

1. Polishing the image of Indonesia and obtaining international esteem in terms of an economically prosperous, politically stable, and culturally advanced country before a world audience through international tourism.

2. Promoting national unity, *pancasila* ideology and other government-orchestrated values through domestic tourism.

Both aims have cumulated in the policy of 'quality' tourism which offers carefully constructed and controlled tourist experiences provided by the Jakarta-based tourism industry under the control of the Ministry of Tourism, Post and Telecommunications. The New Order tourism policy has proved to be successful: under the six subsequent Five-Year Plans international and domestic tourism has grown considerably indeed. Tourism development has benefited from and at the same time contributed to the increasing economic prosperity and the long stretch of political stability under the New Order, both economic prosperity and political stability being important conditions for tourism to prosper.

For a long time the centralist organization of tourism in Indonesia favoured a limited number of well-defined areas for tourism development, particularly the island of Bali and the Special Region of Yogyakarta. The New Order tourism policy channelled investments to these two areas, but failed in its attempts to concentrate tourism developments there, as local small-scale and medium-sized entrepreneurs became involved and facilitated the expansion of tourism all over Indonesia. In tourism research attention has been paid to the ways in which local communities participate in these developments: how ethnic groups and villages not only benefit from but also actively re-construct and revitalize their cultural traditions in the face of increasing numbers of domestic and foreign visitors. Scholars studying local responses to tourism point out that the revitalization of ethnic and local culture within the framework of tourism is problematic in Indonesia: firstly because of the New Order government's propaganda for national unity, and secondly because of the re-emergence of ethnic conflict. To make ethnic revival through tourism even more complex, the same government that is focusing on national unity also recognizes the advantages of ethnic revival for the marketing of Indonesia as a tourist destination of 'endless diversity'. While ethnicizing processes through tourism have recently received ample attention in tourism studies, scholars have failed to analyse the differentiation and inequalities within local communities *vis-à-vis* opportunities offered by tourism development. The national government's policy of 'quality tourism' creates opportunities for large-scale and medium-sized businesses in the formal economy by establishing a star-rated tourism sector. Small-scale and micro businesses are either left out or find themselves marginalized, while participation of self-employed people that largely operate informally is discouraged through sometimes violent intervention. As a consequence, government policy generates a two-tiered tourism economy. Its constituent parts seem to form two worlds apart. On closer analysis, however, there is a myriad of interlinkages between the two, with network relations, family ties, and ethnic bonds overruling the government-orchestrated separation between star-rated and non-star-rated sectors, formal and informal businesses, large-scale and small-scale economic activities.

To present an in-depth analysis of the differentiation and inequalities within the tourism sector and the multivocality of stake holders at a local level, this book focuses on a detailed case study of tourism developments in the city of Yogyakarta in the 'heart of central Java'. Yogyakarta provides a very interesting case of tourism development in New Order Indonesia for several reasons. First, the city was one of the few spearheads of the national government policy throughout the 1970s and 1980s, generating an almost complete dependency on tourism as a source of income, entrepreneurship, and employment. Second, Yogyakarta is not at the periphery of Java-centred dominant culture (as many of the communities figuring in recent case studies), but right at its centre. Third, because of its prominent role in national history, Yogyakarta has been meticulously re-constructed as the cradle of the Indonesian culture, a place where lessons of national history are taught. Fourth, while the city seems to benefit greatly from the New Order tourism policy in terms of increasing visitor numbers, there are manifold threats to tourism development that are jeopardizing Yogyakarta's future as a major tourist destination area. The image of a booming city through successful tourism development is based on strategic marketing instead of a sound structural basis. Tourism development has different impacts on the government-controlled enterprises lining the city's main streets (the 'streetside') and the small-scale businesses and self-employed people in the neighbourhoods (the 'kampung'). While the former are organized and managed to fit in with the concept of 'quality' tourism, the latter are tucked away in low-class neighbourhoods. Government officials and representatives of the city's 'quality' tourism sector favour an image of Yogyakarta's tourism industry in terms of two different realities: 'streetside' tourism and 'kampung' tourism existing side-by-side, but establishing two different worlds, occupying separate spaces, organized in different institutions and frequented by different categories of tourists with different needs using different facilities. However, the praxis of tourism in Yogyakarta is one of partly converging and partly conflicting, but ever-changing configurations of people participating in the tourism sector, generating coalitions and cleavages between 'streetside' and kampung tourism, stifling measures to curtail kampung businesses and encroachments by kampung people on government-controlled discourses and territories in the 'streetside'.

ABOUT THIS BOOK

Methods of research
This book is basically an ethnography of tourism practice in the city of Yogyakarta set against the background of national tourism policies and politics under the New Order regime. It is in the domains of daily practice

and routines that anthropology offers its most valuable contribution to the understanding of tourism dynamics. The book is based on anthropological fieldwork adding up to twelve months of participant observation in the city of Yogyakarta and its vicinity. I approached tourism practice in Yogyakarta from different angles. My first acquaintance with the city was as a delegate attending the above-mentioned International Conference on Cultural Tourism in 1992. One year later I returned to enrol as a student in an Indonesian language course at Sanata Dharma University in Yogyakarta. At the time my hidden agenda was to find out whether Yogyakarta would be an eligible location for my intended research. During the language course I gained access to the library of Sanata Dharma University which turned out to be a treasure trove for studies of local and regional tourism projects that could not be found in any other libraries as much of the material remained unpublished. Moreover, the course for regional guides that this university offered under an assignment from UNESCO brought me into contact with Indonesian and foreign tourism experts on cultural tourism developments in the region. This wealth of material and expertise available and a vibrant tourism industry made it easy to decide that Yogyakarta was to figure prominantly in the research.

As many scholars working in Indonesia have experienced, it is difficult to obtain a research permit from the controlling body of LIPI (*Lembaga Ilmu Pengetahuan Indonesia*) and without such a permit one is not supposed to conduct any research in Indonesia. It took me over two years to obtain this much sought-after permit, not because LIPI was suspicious of my research or refused, but because I had a problem finding an acceptable 'sponsor'. After all, not just any signature will do and I lacked the proper connections in the first phase of my research. But at last the permit materialized and I was able to use the approval of LIPI for the benefit of my research in its final phase. During the first part of the research, I stayed in Yogyakarta as a counsellor and teacher for Dutch and Indonesian students, as a guest lecturer, tourist, and researcher. At that time conversations with English-language teachers who made some additional money by acting as tour guides for local travel agencies were most instructive. Most confusing, however, were the young (and not so young) men in downtown Yogyakarta who introduced themselves as 'friends' and then offered to act as my 'guide'. At first I perceived them as unwelcome interruptions to my attempts to come in contact with formal guides and other actors in the official tourism sector of Yogyakarta. While I failed to socialize with the tourism professionals, I was lucky to run into a young man who became my key informant and made a network of unlicensed guides accessible to me. I suppose that sooner or later every anthropologist has this lucky stroke meeting his or her key informant – this is how ethnographies come about. Thanks to this contact, I was able to move around the inner city without being constantly hassled and to build up a better understanding of the lifestyles, motives, and strategies of those working in the large 'informal' sector of Yogyakarta's tourism industry.

For most of the time I lived in Sosrowijayan, a Yogyanese neighbour-hood that can be classified as a popular tourist area as well as a low-class residential area. I took up residence in a local guesthouse mixing with tourists and local people alike and participated in tourist activities as well as in daily life in the neighbourhood. Through the choice of my field site I was able to observe and participate in tourism practice. However, by living in the 'international community' of Sosrowijayan and by being regarded as a foreign tourist – a 'long-termer' – my fieldwork is inevitably biased towards international tourism. Hampered by my obvious non-Indonesian identity, I was unable to experience 'domestic' tourism without having an impact on the performances of local actors and therefore changing the situation. I recollect an occasion on which I attempted to join a group of domestic tourists in the sultan's palace to gain insight into differences between the guides' discourses when catering to an international versus a domestic audience. The very moment the guide noticed me, he repeated every sentence that was addressed to the Indonesian group in English, and at the same time some of the Indonesian visitors speaking some English added facts to the guide's story, facts they considered of interest to a foreigner like me.

My data collection constitutes a true example of *bricolage* or, in academic terms, triangulation. Fieldwork started the very first day I set foot on Indonesian soil. During my first months of fieldwork I preferred to rely on my senses more than on speech. I observed, listened, tasted, and sensed what was going on around me. One of the most time-consuming activities during this phase was to write up my observations. I produced a fairly voluminous field journal distinguishing between reports of daily routine and special entries categorized according to different tourist spaces in the city and its vicinity. Wearing a modest leisure outfit and carrying a daypack and camera, I visited tourist attractions and local tourist events, joined organized excursions and guided tours. These excursions and events, like organized tours to the major tourist attractions, formed an arena where the interaction between the local population and tourists could be examined. Although the research did not focus on tourist behaviour, I considered it of importance to observe the local actors 'on the job', giving information about the attractions, telling tales, and interacting with tourists. The tourists and guides I met during these occasions assumed I was a tourist. I did not feel like revealing my academic purposes as this would have disturbed the 'natural situation' and people would have started to behave differently. It was only in the final phase of my research when many people in the local tourism industry were already aware of my research activities, that I approached a travel agent with the request to book me on a tour guided by a person who fitted in with a specific profile that I had established. As I found out later, most of the guides whom this travel agent approached (telling about my presence on the tour) refused to accept the assignment, although it was low season and guides were desperate for a tour. They felt extremely uncomfortable with the idea of being 'screened' by a foreign researcher. The one who finally accepted the tour reflected my marginal status in the Yogyakarta tourism industry: she was an unmarried, middle-aged female senior guide from outside Yogyakarta with an expired licence.

After I had visited the tourist attractions of Yogyakarta several times and felt familiar with the locations and the tourist routines, I decided to tape the stories told by the local guides. For this purpose I carried a tiny tape recorder in my breast pocket or day pack and stayed close to the guide. Although the quality of the recordings was not superb, and the transcriptions were a tiresome and time-consuming job, the material they provided were of crucial significance to this ethnography. Because of the complexity of a guided tour coupled with the impossibility of walking around with a noteblock and pencil, it would have been impossible to collect data on the guides' discourses, interruptions by tourists, and the guides' reactions. A word about research ethics is in order here. I did not ask the guides' permission for the same reason I did not reveal my identity as a researcher. If I had done so there is no doubt whatsoever that the guides would have changed their discourses knowing about them being taped; or worse they would have refused the recording, even denying me access to their guided tour. Needless to say that all these possible results of my openness would have turned out to be disastrous to my research. I do not think that my informants suffered any disadvantage from my research strategies nor will they do so in the future. Not only have I used pseudonyms, but also I changed some personal details making them unrecognizable even to other local people in the Yogyakarta tourism industry. Second, I want to emphasize that the recordings were made not to reveal any secret information. The guides' stories were performed in a public space accessible to a public audience. The purpose was to record their stories as they are routinely performed without distorting them through the process of recording. Third, the material generated in this way is not used to the disadvantage of the guides but to analyse the impact of the cultural, social, and political context on their daily work. As the detrimental effects of lack of proper training and thought control is clearly shown versus the enhancing effects of human creativity, my findings obtained through 'secret recordings' may even contribute to an improvement of my informants' situation.

The information generated by participant observation was supplemented by interviews with government representatives in the Special Region of Yogyakarta as well as in national government organizations in Jakarta, with respondents working in the tourism industry and in tourism education, and consultants and academic experts in the field of tourism. Secondary data, statistics, and case studies were obtained from government agencies, educational institutions, and consultancies. As far as the interview method is concerned, I applied two techniques, structured and informal interviews – more informal than structured – with a vast number of actors in the local tourism industry and by recording life-histories of a number of local key informants. I never used a tape recorder for the interviews. I took notes during formal interviews which were conducted on the basis of a well-prepared list of items. Informal interviews, or rather research-related conversations, took place frequently and unexpectedly. Often the most relevant information emerged only when my noteblock was closed and put away into my bag again as this was the moment when my informants began to feel comfortable with the interview situation. On these occasions I switched on my fabulous brain recorder which I acquired during years of anthropological training and practice, writing up the conversation immediately upon returning to my accommodation.

A final word about the 'Indonesian' English that is used in literal quotations. I decided to quote literally without correcting the grammar and pronounciation. After all, the language quoted here is the vernacular of local people in Yogyakarta expressing themselves in English. This vernacular is part and parcel of tourism practice in Yogyakarta, and putting Oxford English in the mouths of my informants would distort the ethnographic descriptions.

Structure of this book
This book basically consists of two parts. The first three chapters are based on an extensive literature review. Chapter 1 establishes the general theoretical perspective which is at the basis of the analysis and interpretation of my data. Chapter 2 investigates the ways in which the New Order government strategically used tourism development and tourism discourse to realize its economic objectives and promote its political aims of international esteem, national unity, and the domestication of its cultural diversity. In this chapter examples are drawn from tourism development under groups eccentric to the predominantly Javanese power holders in

Jakarta. Chapter 3 directs full attention to the area that was pivotal to the cherished Javanese identity of the New Order regime, i.e. the Special Province of Yogyakarta. The cultural heritage of this area is an intrinsic part of the core of the national culture of Indonesia. This chapter investigates the ways in which the Special Province of Yogyakarta first became domesticated and folklorized to serve the central government's needs for a common culture as displayed in the *pancasila* tourism established in this region. Secondly, the chapter shows how this tourism economy, once it was thriving, came under serious threat because of the government-induced processes of regionalization. Beginning with Chapter 4 and continuing throughout Chapters 5 and 6 is an 'ethnography of local tourism practices' offering a thorough or, in terms of Geertz (1973), 'thick' description of the social construction of Yogyakarta as a tourist destination by local actors. Chapter 4 offers an analysis of processes of differentiation that generate a multi-layered tourism sector in Yogyakarta. Large parts of this tourism sector depend on local, i.e. *kampung* initiatives that withdraw from government control, whereas government-supported 'streetside' tourism suffers serious losses in terms of market shares and popularity among tourists. Chapter 5 deals with the backgrounds to the decline of the popularity of the 'streetside' sector in one specific field, i.e. tourist guiding. While the government has imposed a comprehensive system of control on the access to and the practice of the guiding profession, it has left the guides insecure about the politically correct narratives and encourages the establishment of clandestine modes of operation among guides. In Chapter 6 the ultimate failure of the government's system of control is discussed. On the basis of an analysis of their network operations it is shown how unlicensed guides have mocked the New Order's attempts to enforce its display of national culture onto cultural tourism. They do so through their dealings in the thriving but marginalized *kampung* economy that exhibits links across the 'streetside' economy right into the centre of 'quality' tourism.

ACKNOWLEDGEMENTS

To provide a glimpse of the complexities of business practices, image building, and everyday life in Yogyakarta's multifaceted tourism industry, the author conducted anthropological fieldwork during an intermittent period of twelve months. The results of this research are presented in this book which represents a hybrid between an academic monograph and a more 'applied' account of the strengths and weaknesses of New Order tourism policy. This book addresses a rather heterogeneous audience. Academic scholars in the field of Indonesian history and culture may be irritated at being 'over-informed' at times when well-known facts and widely accepted wisdoms are reproduced and discussed at length; they may sometimes even accuse me of superficialities when it comes to complex matters like the impact of the Java War on Yogyakarta. Vice-versa, experts in the field of tourism studies (tourism policy and management) may feel irritated by the lack of more elaborate explanations about the imponderabilities of Indonesian history and culture, and in their turn they may feel bored by lengthy exposés on what they may regard as common knowledge in the field of tourism studies. In the vein of a good Indonesian tradition the author begs the patience of all of these experts, reminding them of the fact that this book is not addressed to any one of the disciplinary specialities, but instead attempts to attract the interest of a multidisciplinary audience.

The preparation for this book started in 1992 when the author visited Indonesia for the first time in her life. Repeated visits between 1992 and 1996 for the purpose of establishing vital contacts with Indonesian academics and bureaucratic institutions, language courses, field explorations, and library research involved a myriad of organizations and individuals without whose support this book would not have materialized. The author wants to acknowledge these institutions and individuals who generously supported the preparation and implementation of the research in Indonesia and provided the infrastructure and intellectual setting that were of vital importance when writing this book.

Lembaga Ilmu Pengetahuan Indonesia (LIPI) in Jakarta provided the research permit and introductory letters that made governmental bodies and academic institutions accessible for the researcher.

Professor I Gusti Ngurah Bagus of Udayana University in Denpasar generously acted as sponsor for the research project and provided the moral support to finalize the fieldwork.

Professor J.J. Spillane SJ of the Center for Tourism Research, and Drs. Th. Gieles SJ, Dean of the Economic Faculty of Sanata Dharma University in Yogyakarta, granted access to the accumulated knowledge about tourism development in Yogyakarta which is available in their research library. Moreover, Sanata Dharma University provided the author with the facilities and a pleasant work surrounding throughout her fieldwork. The author is indebted in particular to Maya Sienta, Ibu Puji, Ibu Astiah, Pak Idaman, and other staff members of the Center for Tourism Research of Sanata Dharma University for their kind assistance.

Professor Moeljarto Tjokrowinoto of the Centre for Tourism Research and Development of and Pak Sugeng Martopo (†) of Environmental Studies of Gadjah Mada University in Yogyakarta provided valuable contacts with other staff members and tourism experts of this university.

Ir. Myra Gunawan, Centre for Research on Tourism of the Institut Teknologi Bandung, has shown an ongoing interest in the author's research and has proved to be a valuable source of knowledge and a good friend.

The government bodies of Dinas Pariwisata Yogyakarta, Badan Pengembangan Daerah Yogyakarta and Kantor Wilayah Pariwisata Daerah Istimewa Yogyakarta have shown an interest in the research and provided invaluable data, as did the regional offices of the tourism organizations of the Association of Indonesian Travel Agencies (ASITA) and the Himpunan Pariwisata Indonesia (the guide association). I am also indebted to the management of the PT. Taman Wisata Borobudur, Prambanan dan Ratu Boko; the general managers of Ambarrukmo Hotel, Hotel Santika and Radisson Hotel; the directors of Academi Pariwisata Indonesia and Ambarrukmo Palace Tourism Academy; the head of the Yogyakarta Tourism Police and the director of the Yogyakarta Urban Development Project. I am grateful to Multatuli Travels for allowing me to participate in their city tours in Yogyakarta.

The Department of Leisure Studies of Tilburg University provided the bulk of the funding of the research while I was a staff member of this department. The Dutch Ministry of Education, Culture, and Sciences, The Hague, Netherlands, generously funded a language course and pilot study in the preparatory phase of the project. The Netherlands Foundation for the Advancement of Tropical Research (WOTRO) granted additional funding for parts of the research within its programme 'Globalization and the construction of communal identities.' A special thanks is due to Professor Wim van Binsbergen and Drs Cora Govers for their recommendations. The International Institute for Asian Studies (IIAS), Leiden and Amsterdam, provided the author with a Dutch Senior Fellowship and thereby enabling her to write up the fieldwork material. A special thanks is due to Professor Wim Stokhof of the IIAS for his ongoing interest in the project and to Professor Frans Hüsken for his support in a later phase of this project. Finally, the Department of Culture, Organization and Management of Vrije University Amsterdam has to be acknowledged for generously offering the author the time to finish this book.

During fieldwork and at home Karin Bras has proved to be a good pal, loyal friend, reliable colleague, and inspiring co-author of many joint projects and publications. Without her this project would have been a lonely venture. While writing the first draft of this book, Freek Colombijn's critical but encouraging comments, scribbled in the margin of the first version of the manuscript, have provided me with the intellectual feedback I badly needed. I am also indebted to Peter Nas and his KLU and the participants of the monthly meeting of the WOTRO group 'Globalization and the construction of communal identities' for commenting on earlier drafts of a number of chapters.

I am greatly indebted to Professor Michael Hitchcock and Professor Geoff Wall for their constructive reviews of the first complete version of this book. Thanks to their meticulous comments the author was able to improve the manuscript considerably.

For their intellectual support, letters of recommendation, warm hospitality and precious friendship I want to thank:

Maya Sienta, Richarda Yuddi and the teachers of the Sanata Dharma Language Course; James Spillane; Bea Erlina and the staff of Ella Homestay; Ibu Ferida Fida; Ibu Sisca Vembriarto; Britta, Tanto and the the staff of Bladok Losmen; Roy Pardede; Ibu Dewi of Setia Tours; Wiwik Pratiwi; Wiwien Tribuwani; Alice and Fred Bunnell; Lance Castles; Ettore Amato (†); Pak Mariatmo; David Hough; Piet Preuss; Freek ten Broeke and Multatuli Travel in Amsterdam; Janine van Kalmthout and Margit Jokovi for 'letters to the fieldworker'; Albert and Margot Trouwborst; Huub de Jonge; Jojada Verrips; Jeremy Boissevain; Greg Richards, Leontine Onderwater, Theo Beckers and my students Esther van Genugten, Hanneke van Gemert, Saskia Peeters and Jolanda Urru who contributed greatly to my understanding of tourism in Yogyakarta.

Final words of gratitude are addressed to Mrs. Rosemary Robson for her meticulous work improving my English and Dick van der Meij for his critical editing of the final version of the manuscript. Thanks are also due to UvA Kaartenmakers for the excellent maps they provided for this publication.

Heidi Dahles, Amsterdam 2000

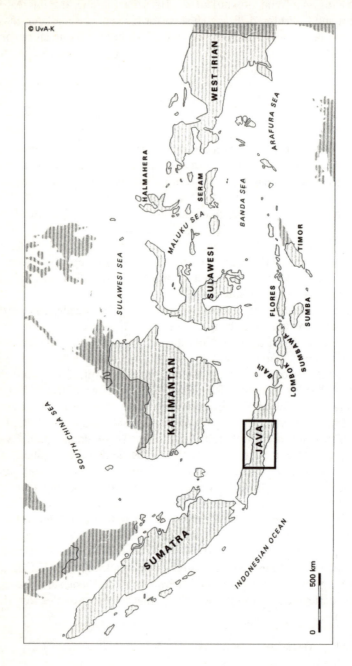

Map 1: Indonesia

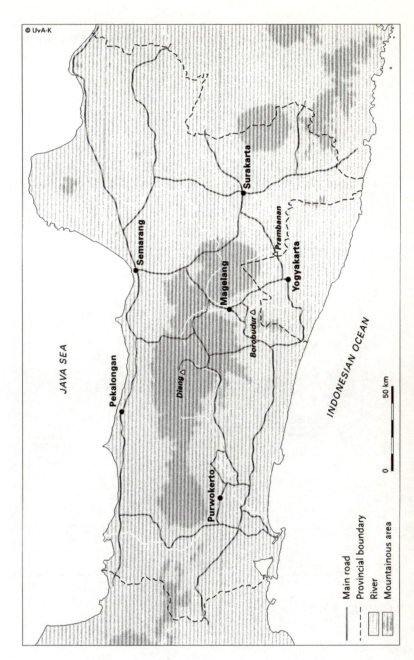

Map 2: Central Java and Yogyakarta's Special Province

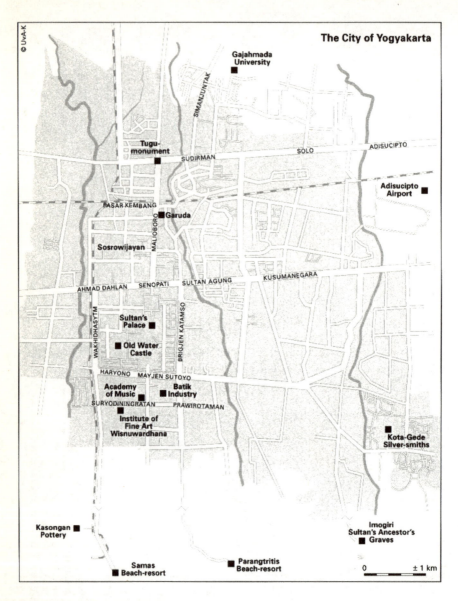

Map 3: Citymap of Yogyakarta

CHAPTER 1

TOURISM, POLITICS AND THE PARADOX OF CULTURE

CULTURAL TOURISM POLICY IN INDONESIA UNDER THE NEW ORDER GOVERNMENT

INTRODUCTION

In 1992 the first International Conference on Cultural Tourism in Indonesia was held in Yogyakarta, a middle-sized town 'in the heart of central Java,' as tourist guide books usually extol this place. On the surface the focus of the conference – cultural tourism – reflected changes in the advanced economies leading towards the formation of a consumer society in which the consumption of culture has become a major asset of economic growth in general and of tourism development in particular (Richards 1996:3-4). However, the hospitality offered to the conference and its delegates by the Indonesian government revealed a hidden agenda. The conference was organized and sponsored by the Ministry of Tourism, Post, and Telecommunications, UNESCO and the United Nations Development Project (UNDP) and supported by the World Tourism Organization (WTO), the Pacific Association of Travel Agencies (PATA) and others. This conference was attended by almost 400 delegates, a quarter of whom came from outside Indonesia. After two days of plenary presentations discussing subjects like tourism and cultural heritage, religious belief systems, the role of women, village tourism and tourism marketing, the organizing committee, chaired by Joop Avé (then Director-General of Tourism), launched the 'Yogyakarta Declaration on National Cultures and Universal Tourism' which was signed by the delegates. This declaration – the complete text of which is presented in Appendix 1 – has been strongly grafted onto the struggle for national unity that characterized Indonesia – and especially the New Order government of former President Suharto – since independence. The motto 'Unity in Diversity,' which was the major point of reference of many a distinguished speaker, was closely intertwined with the principles designed for global cultural tourism developments as outlined in the Declaration.

What we wish to encourage is the richness and diversity of the many cultures, and to inquire how the tools and technology that makes globalization possible can not only preserve and protect the cultures they

> make accessible but much more than this, to rather encourage a cultural renaissance, a renewal and an enriching of those cultures. We are not seeking uniformity among mankind, we are encouraging *Bhinneka Tunggal Ika* – Unity in Diversity,

writes Joop Avé in the Introduction to the Conference Proceedings (Wiendu Nuryanti 1993:xi). What may be regarded either as a mode to propel Indonesia into the transnational bodies that promote cultural tourism, or as the empty rhetoric of Indonesian state ideology, actually revealed the political programme which lay at the basis of the New Order's espousal of cultural tourism. Under the New Order cultural and tourism policies merged into a political programme. A state ideology celebrating cultural diversity, based on the *pancasila*, i.e. literally 'five pillars,' addresses the problem of national culture and supports the lucrative tourism industry (Kipp 1993:105). The New Order's catchphrase became *kelestarian kebudayaan nasional*, i.e. the preservation of national culture (Kipp 1993:113). What is at stake here is the impact of tourism not on culture – the anthropological concept defining the human condition of forming meaningful arrangements of co-habitation – but on *national cultures*, i.e. territorially and politically defined cultural entities. In his speech delivered at the opening of the Yogyakarta conference, then Minister of Education and Culture, Fuad Hassan, expressed his fear about cultural loss that may emanate from culture contact through 'global tourism.' Therefore he pleaded for 'cultural awareness and cultural resilience' to counteract the homogenization of culture. The appeal made by Fuad Hassan and the organizers to respect national cultures and to protect, preserve, and revitalize them for the purpose of cultural tourism development, and to enhance the awareness of and educate people for cultural tourism, reflects the New Order government's strategic use of cultural tourism development.

As an archipelagic nation consisting of more than 17,000 islands that extends over more than 5,000 kilometres from east to west and comprising over three hundred ethnic groups and a multitude of religions, Indonesia faces the challenge of building a shared national consciousness and identity. How fragile a construction this nation is, has now been pitilessly revealed in the political upheaval and the ethnic and religious conflicts that followed the economic crisis which broke out in 1997. The New Order government attempted both to control ethnicity and to use it. Paradoxically while ethnic and regional secession recurrently threatens national unity, indigenous cultures provide a repository of traditions and symbols that the political leaders and the national elite can use to forge national identity and foster a sense of community (Kipp 1993:105). Constructing nationalist ideals, a nationalist sense of history, and a transcendental loyalty to the nation have been goals of both the Old Order and New Order governments in their attempts to come to terms with ethnic diversity. Not only does Indonesia consist of very many different cultures and languages, there is also a distinct imbalance between these groups. The Javanese constitute two-thirds of the population, and they predominate in the leadership elite that flocks together in the economic centre of the country which is not Java as a whole but specifically Jakarta. The capital city enjoys a disproportionate share of the county's wealth. The state policies encourage traditional cultures partly to mask these imbalances. One way the Indonesian government strives to instil a broader sense of national unity is by championing tourism, in particular cultural tourism (Adams 1997:156).

The political programme behind tourism development was envisioned by the Indonesian leaders as early as 1969, when the contribution of the tourism sector to nation-building was defined in terms of a source of foreign revenue, a way of enhancing Indonesia's celebrity on the international stage, and a strategy for fostering domestic brotherhood (Adams 1997:157). In the early 1980s, facing declining oil revenues, the Indonesian economic policy was directed towards the expansion of non-oil sectors. Deregulatory measures were intended to facilitate private sector activities, particularly in the export sector (Booth 1990). Exports were the key to earning the foreign revenues to support the New Order's modernization projects. Tourism was embraced as a vehicle to contribute to economic development in terms of measurable growth. The high priority given to tourism in national development policy generated a rapid growth in tourist arrivals and in earnings from tourism, the latter a major source of foreign exchange. International and domestic tourism has grown considerably since the 1980s. The number of foreign visitors increased by more than 200 per cent between 1988 and 1995, and the income from foreign tourism more than doubled between 1990 and 1994. Before the crisis hit Indonesia, the government estimated that in the year 2000 about 6.5 million foreign tourists would visit Indonesia, yielding US$ 9 billion of foreign exchange earnings. Growth scenarios for the turn of the century anticipated visitor arrivals to double and income from foreign tourism to triple (Parapak 1995). In the wake of the crisis official sources state a decline of about 30 per cent of international arrivals and 60 per cent of revenues from tourism in 1998 (KOMPAS 31-03-1999).

In this book, the role of the Indonesian state, and especially of the New Order government, in the development of cultural tourism and its impact on tourism practices at the provincial level will be of central concern. This book has been inspired by Linda Richter's point that 'tourism is a highly political phenomenon' (Richter 1989:2) and that countries – especially in the developing world – see in tourism a means of enhancing their economic growth and their political legitimacy, the latter conveyed by the high number of tourist arrivals (Richter 1989:5-6). With a few exceptions, scholars have failed to consider tourism in terms of the political strategies deployed by power holders. 'Such needs are not publicly articulated like economic objectives are, but that makes them no less salient in policy development, implementation, and evaluation' (Richter 1989:19). The a-political approach to tourism in academic discourse reflects the fact that tourists are seldom aware of the agency of the state in structuring the images and the experiences of travel (Wai-Teng Leong 1997). Nevertheless, the state is a major actor in tourism, not simply by providing the infrastructure for services but also by creating the images and symbolic representations that shape tourist experiences. In their introduction to one of the first volumes addressing tourism issues in Southeast Asia, the editors pointed out that

> We need more data on the relations between national identity, political image building and tourism (...). These national arenas of representation are also the focus for conflicts over identity and the contesting by various social groups of particular constructions of 'national culture. (...) The whole field of policy-making with regard to tourism is a virtual terra incognita (Hitchcock, King & Parnwell 1993:29).

As will be argued in this book, the New Order government strategically promoted the expansion of (cultural) tourism to implement its political agenda. This book looks back on thirty years of tourism policy under former President Suharto who identified tourism as a major asset in his policy of economic growth and development. On his agenda for tourism development the following points predominated:

1. The increase in the Gross National Product through tourism revenues, especially foreign revenues.
2. The polishing of the image of Indonesia to attain international esteem and status as an economically prosperous, politically stable, and culturally sophisticated country before a world audience through the advancement of international tourism and participation in a global market.
3. The domestication of its ethnic minorities and control of cultural diversity through the commercial exploitation of selected (so-called 'peak') ethnic cultures as tourist objects.
4. The strengthening of national unity, *pancasila* state ideology and other basic values of the New Order government through domestic tourism.

These four interdependent strategies resulted in carefully constructed, staged, and controlled tourist objects and destinations operated by a Jakarta-based tourism industry under the watchful eye of the Ministry of Tourism, Post and Telecommunications. As Indonesian provincial boundaries are an often overlooked factor in shaping the discourse of tourism development and

4

promotion (Adams 1997:156), this book will focus in particular on the way in which provincial governments and local actors in the tourism industry cope with, give shape to, and counteract Jakarta-initiated tourism policy guidelines. This focus answers the call for a local-level approach to tourism issues. As Hitchcock, King, and Parnwell (1993) point out local perspectives on tourism and leisure have been very much neglected, largely eclipsed by the representations of those who promote and sell the tourist product. Local people create niches for themselves to benefit directly or indirectly from the state's incapacity to organize tourism according to its own plans.

> Crucial elements are the tour agents, guides, and leaders who act as social and cultural brokers between tourists and hosts. Yet again, we do not know much about how these intermediaries convey information, organize and conduct encounters, and portray local cultures and scenes. This kind of research requires local-level anthropological fieldwork (ibid:29).

The focus of this book is the Special Province of Yogyakarta, the host of the first and then a number of subsequent conferences on cultural tourism and the gateway to the two UNESCO-designated World Heritage sites in Indonesia, the temple complexes of Prambanan and Borobudur. Contrary to popular wisdom, both temple complexes are partly (Prambanan) or completely (Borobudur) located outside the Special Province of Yogyakarta in the neighbouring province of Central Java (Wall 1997b). Despite this, as one of the plenary speakers of the 1992 conference pointed out, the region of Yogyakarta is a 'demonstration of the 'unity-in-diversity' guiding theme of Indonesia' (Gertler 1993:15). Yogyakarta has played a prominent role in the political history of Indonesia. Many of the city's current tourist resources are derived from its royal and military past (Timothy & Wall 1995). As both the vanguard of traditional Javanese culture and testing ground of nationalist forces, Yogyakarta is a place where heritage and tourism have become closely intertwined to establish a highly challenging arena in which to study processes of inventing, (re-)producing and (re-)presenting cultural identity. Images of Yogyakarta form an expression of the tensions between the global, national, and ethnic interests. This study aims to reveal the struggle between processes of globalization introduced through the transnationally organized tourism industry and the influx of large numbers of international tourists, 'Indonesianization' through Jakarta-led policies and Jakarta-based project developers, and 'indigenization' through local practices and performances of the 'tourist product.' To analyse the partly converging and partly conflicting forces at work, the following questions will be addressed:

1. How did the New Order government attempt to accomplish the objectives of economic development, national unity, and cultural diversity through tourism and how does it deal with the potentially problematic situation created by ethnic revival through cultural tourism?
2. To what extent did the *pancasila* state ideology influence the social construction of the 'national' cultural heritage and how did 'Indonesian-ness' relate to 'Javaneseness' in local tourism practice?
3. To what extent did local practices and performances representing local cultural heritage converge or conflict with government-orchestrated *pancasila* tourism? Through what institutions has *pancasila* tourism been either maintained or undermined?
4. What are the mechanisms of 'authentication' by which the New Order government attempted to control tourist discourses?
5. To what extent did 'uncontrolled' local discourses form a threat to govern-ment-orchestrated *pancasila* tourism?

Each of these questions will be addressed in separate chapters in this book.

CULTURAL TOURISM AND THE 'PARADOX PARADIGM'

The organizers of the Yogyakarta conference on cultural tourism were well aware of the global impact of tourism on culture. Hence the title of the conference: 'Universal Tourism – Enriching or Degrading Culture?' Many contributions discussed the threat of cultural loss and the emergence of a homogeneous global culture in the wake of increasing international tourism (cf. Wiendu Nuryanti 1993). Images of an emerging 'world culture' or 'global village' have a profound effect on tourism, bringing to the fore people's concerns about 'authenticity,' which appears to be receding as fast as it is approached, as well as about commercial concerns with an edge to the main chance to 'invent traditions' and promote nostalgia (Graburn 1995:159). International tourism accelerates the process of the uniformization of culture. All over the world the diversity of touristic genres is almost unlimited, but at the same time this very diversity is becoming more and more the same everywhere. This development has been described by Robertson (1990) as the process by which the world becomes a single place. The increasing uniformization has been analysed in terms of 'Disneyfication' or 'McDonald-ization' of culture. The McDonaldization thesis as developed by Ritzer views the world as growing increasingly efficient, calculable, predictable, and dominated by controlling non-human technologies (Ritzer 1993; Ritzer and Liska 1997).

The rapid growth of international tourism – international arrivals expanded seventeen-fold world-wide between 1950 and 1990 (Waters 1995:154) – indicates the extent to which tourists themselves conceptualize the world as a single place without internal geographical boundaries (ibid:155). Mass tourism, particularly its most rigidly standardized form, i.e. package tours, form a manifestation of the 'culture of tourism' that spreads all over the globe bringing in its train the same sort of shopping areas, the same fast-food restaurants, mass-produced souvenirs, and amusements. Recently voices have been heard arguing that these standardized tours have passed their heyday and are in decline, giving way to much more diversified patterns of tourism and the rise of a small-scale, flexible tourist market which marks the revival of local identities. The levelling and standardizing effects of mass tourism are countered by cultural differentiation, the accentuation of the 'authentic,' and the invention of tradition (Urry 1990, 1995).

Global tourism creates opportunities for favoured destination areas to capture a position in the global tourist market. The economic power and concomitant status that are entailed have provided a strong incentive for sites around the world to emulate their success (Britton 1991). This has resulted in the production of a new breed of attractions and intermediaries who supply culture specifically for tourist consumption, a phenomenon dubbed the 'heritage industry' by Hewison (1987). As cultural provisions shift into the market in a significant way, the test of 'success' for existing cultural institutions can no longer be a purely aesthetic one. Cultural manifestations find themselves under increasing pressure to justify themselves in quantitative terms, such as the number of visitors and income generated. These quantitative performance indicators are equally important to institutions which operate in a wholly commercial environment and for public-funded organizations which have to demonstrate the effectiveness of the subsidy bestowed on them. Cultural and arts institutions as well as regional and local governments are therefore becoming increasingly concerned about the cultural audience and its needs (Richards 1996:13).

These strategies have to be understood against the background of processes of globalization which refers to the multiplicity of linkages and inter-connections between states and societies which make up the modern world system. It describes the process by which events, decisions, and activities in one part of the world can come to have significant consequences for individuals and communities in quite distant parts of the globe (McGrew 1992:23). Giddens (1990) stresses that local transformations are part of the globalization process in as much as large-scale transnational processes shape local happenings. In terms of tourism this two-sided process would explain the cultural revival witnessed among many communities and ethnic groups throughout the world. In contrast to the homogenization implied by the

7

'McDonaldization' thesis, the globalization theory does not imply that every corner of the world must become 'rationalized' according to Western principles. The heterogenization of culture is an integral aspect of globalizing processes – a phenomenon which Featherstone (1990) has referred to as the 'paradox of culture.'

Behind this 'paradox paradigm' lurk tensions between cultural homogenization and cultural heterogenization in much of today's global interactions. In the domain of tourism these tensions emerge at the intersection of transnational tourism organizations and industries, national governments and local communities, all with their own specific interests and expectations regarding the economic and cultural benefits of tourism development. One prominent aspect of tourism is its global organization and impact. International tourism is already considered one of the primary economic activities in international exchange under the heading of external trade. According to the World Tourism Organization, tourism is destined to become a 'first world industry' and a driving force of global development by the year 2000 (Lanfant 1995a:4). Since the end of the 1960s many regions in the world have been transformed into tourism destination areas or 'pleasure peripheries' (Turner & Ash 1975) for thousands of holiday-makers from the advanced economies. Underlying this process are the politics of tourist promotion which became organized on a global scale, under the direction of international organizations and multinational enterprises, and with the scientific and technical support of international experts (Lanfant 1995a:2).

Many authors have raised the issue of how local communities cope with the consequences that emanate from their integration into global configurations (cf. Theobald 1994; Lanfant, Allock & Bruner 1995; Boissevain 1996; Abram, Waldren & Macleod 1997). Some argue that tourists are not the '"shock troops" of Western modernity as it steamrolls across the world's remaining areas of cultural diversity' (Oakes 1997:35), but that tourists are often appropriated by locals in their symbolic constructions of culture. For their part local communities are not passive, and often embrace tourism to display their existence and to establish their own power (cf. Dahles & Van Meijl 1999). Certain ethnic groups have been marginalized and excluded by central power, and they acquire recognition at the international level by participation in tourism. As Lanfant (1995a:6) points out, tourism is a double-edged sword. In certain cases it contributes towards repressing, marginalizing and neutralizing autonomous or resistance movements. In other cases it allows ethnic minorities and local communities that have been cut off from international decision-making to claim and assert their identities. In this respect, however, tourism can destroy an authentic sense of place, alienating people from their established identity as they emulate the behaviour and the norms and values of their visitors. While some authors point out that tourism brings about processes of commodification that result in a 'loss of authenticity of the place and of cultural identity of its inhabitants' (Britton quoted in Oakes 1997:36), other authors argue that the process of commercial and cultural integration associated with tourism does not necessarily break down a place-based sense of identity or render it flat and inauthentic, instead, it becomes an important factor in the ongoing construction of 'place' (Oakes 1997:36).

Lanfant (1995a:8) argues that tourism is a very particular trade which is closely intertwined with culture, heritage, traditions, and identity itself. Cultural tourism especially presents itself as supporting a return to sources, a journey towards roots and 'authentic' culture. It has often been said that the appeal of identity in traditional societies meets the demand of Western tourists for authenticity: tourists who choose to visit a place in order to rediscover in themselves an identity which they cannot find in their everyday lives (Lanfant 1995a:9). We shall return to this alleged 'quest for authenticity' below. Here the relationship between tourism and culture has to be examined more closely. The term 'cultural tourism' has been used to describe the consumption of art, heritage, folklore, and a whole range of other cultural manifestations by tourists (Richards 1996:22), or in the terms of Craik

> '[the] customized excursions into other cultures and places to learn about their people, lifestyle, heritage and arts in an informed way that genuinely represents those cultures and their historical contexts' (Craik 1997:121).

Culture in this context is related to a product-based definition, the 'sites and monuments' approach, that concentrates on describing the type of attractions visited by cultural tourists. In this approach culture is regarded as the product of individual or group activities to which certain meanings are attached. Here the concept of cultural tourism as linked to 'high culture' predominates; the concept inclines towards the consumption of cultural products rather than involvement in cultural processes. A second approach has been termed the process approach (Richards 1996:21). The notion of culture as a process is derived from anthropology, the discipline which made the concept of culture its domain and which has been concerned throughout its history to 'limit, specify, focus and contain' this concept (Geertz 1973:5). Dominated in its early days by E.B. Tylor's 'most complex whole' and later by Kluckhohn's 'learned behaviour,' the anthropological concept of culture assumed a semiotic connotation in Geertz' definition of culture as 'webs of significance' (1973:5). Culture in anthropological terms may therefore be regarded as the domain of meaning production, or the processes through which people make sense of their lives.

Within this process approach, we need to distinguish between cultural tourism and ethnic tourism. Where ethnicity is the product, we are dealing with ethnic tourism rather than cultural tourism, argues Wood (1984). In cultural tourism the role of culture is contextual, it shapes the tourists' experience in general, 'without a particular focus on the uniqueness of a specific cultural identity' (Wood 1984). Ethnic tourism focuses on 'people performing a cultural identity, the uniqueness of which is being marketed for tourists' (Wood 1984). Richards (1996:22) argues that the product and process approaches to culture overlap in the field of tourism, where there has been a certain degree of integration between the two phenomena. Culture as process is the goal of tourists seeking authenticity and meaning through their tourist experiences. However, the very presence of tourists leads to the creation of cultural manifestations specifically for tourist consumption: 'culture as process is transformed through tourism into culture as product' (Richards 1996:26). Cultural tourism is composed of both the cultural products presented for tourist consumption and the cultural processes which generate the motivation to participate in cultural tourism. As the distinctions between 'high' and 'popular' culture erode, the scope of cultural tourism expands to include elements which would previously not have been considered 'cultural.' Richards suggests that as distinctions between 'culture' and 'tourism' or 'everyday life' are also beginning to erode, so cultural tourism is gradually including activities such as simply 'soaking up the atmosphere' of a destination, or sampling the local food (1996:26).

However, places that become tourist destinations find themselves comparing and contrasting themselves to the tastes of their visitors in order to enhance the numbers of their guests and the revenues from tourism. Globalization in general and global tourism in particular requires emerging local particularisms to be legitimated in Western terms. This may imply a cultural revival, the construction and accentuation of the 'authentic' and the invention of tradition (Urry 1990, 1995; Lanfant 1995a). The quality and ambience of places are a critical element in the selling of goods, services, and experiences, and the encouragement of consumption (Shields 1990). In many parts of the world this process involves a preference for Western goods and lifestyles (Waters 1995). Yet the assumption that such goods and lifestyles will inevitably communicate the values of their culture of origin must be questioned. On entering another culture, the use and the meaning of goods become transformed in accordance with the values of the receiving culture (Howes 1996:4). Appadurai argues that as rapidly as forces from the advanced economies are brought into new societies they tend to become indigenized (1990:295). This point of view is shared by Hannerz (1992) who has coined the concept of 'creolization' to describe the process of recontextualization. This concept is concerned with the in-flow of goods and ideas, their reception and domestication. Creolization is not simply the opposite of global homogenization; it is instead the articulation of the intersection of the local and the global in cross-cultural consumption (Howes 1996:6). The establishment of new cultural identities mediated through Western goods and lifestyles within the context of tourism may be regarded as an example *par excellence* of creolization.

ISSUES OF NATIONAL CULTURE: ASIAN PERSPECTIVES

The state is of great importance as mediator between tourism and culture. In many countries the development of tourism policy at the national level usually has the twin goals of generating economic benefits and supporting culture, albeit it is usually 'national culture' which is being promoted. In Europe, culture has been used as a means of boosting feelings of national identity and cohesion since the nineteenth century (Richards 1996:63-4, 91). The globalization of culture in terms of the revival of local particularisms against the background of increasing integration into a global system is seen by many as being a threat to national culture and the nation state (Peleggi 1996). Under the circumstances, national governments would seem to have little choice but to relinquish parts of their power to transnational levels of decision making or to growing local autonomy. National culture seems to be lost to either transnational integration into the 'global village' or to thriving local and ethnic identities (cf. McGrew & Lewis et al 1992; Friedman 1990). However, as many scholars have pointed out, there may be a temptation to view the world in terms of intensifying patterns of global interconnectedness from the vantage point of the affluent West, and there is no unequivocal evidence to support the assumption that processes of globalization are generating a 'crisis of the territorial nation-state.' On the contrary, the position of the nation-state as the primary unit in world politics is itself a product of globalizing forces. Although historically only a relatively modern phenomenon, the nation-state is today the supreme territorial, administrative, and political unit.' Nationalism, the theory of political legitimacy in the terms of Gellner, 'requires that ethnic boundaries should not cut across political ones, and, in paticular, that ethnic boundaries within a given state ... should not separate the power-holders from the rest' (Gellner 1983:1). Particularly in the developing world, where memories of the struggle to achieve independent statehood is still fresh in the collective consciousness and where, at the same time, ethnic diversity within the national state boundaries is often large, the integrity of the nation-state is guarded with a certain grimness (McGrew 1992:2).

Tourism constitutes an arena where issues of cultural identity are related to the process of nation-building (Peleggi 1996). Many scholars studying local actors in tourism (see for example the contributors to Picard & Wood 1997) have pointed out that tourism offers new opportunities for identity-expression and senses of place. 'Elements of tourism are at the same time the ingredients of nationalism: the identification with a place, a sense of historical past, the revival of cultural heritage, and the national integration of social groups' (Wai-Teng Leong 1997:72). Through tourism promotion the nation is shaped as an 'imagined community,' as a culturally integrated entity, 'whether that integration is the promotion of one central culture and its values, e.g. Islam, or whether it is the blending of peripheral cultures with a dominant core, without their eradication' (Graburn 1997:199). In many Asian countries tourism accelerated the process of re-imagining nations, a process in which the core themes were chosen to present a nation's identity because they were supposed to appeal to foreign tourists (Wood 1984; Graburn 1997). The process is marked by the emergence of 'miniature theme parks' like 'Thailand in Miniature' and 'Ancient City' outside Bangkok, 'Splendid China' and 'China Folk Culture Villages' in Shenzhen (China), 'Taman Mini Indonesia Indah' in Jakarta and copies of this concept in Korea, Malaysia, and Vietnam. Some of these theme parks pretend to offer a glimpse of the lives of ordinary people, whereas others display high cultural traditions, such as Asian court culture. Most follow the cultural village format and usually comprise a collection of traditional buildings which are used to display arts and crafts and serve as venues for music and dance performances (Hitchcock, Stanley & Siu 1997). Theme parks like these have been set up all over Asia in countries that have the development of one national culture on their agenda. They all portray nations that are simultaneously ethnically diverse, but unified. These cultural displays provide Asian nations with the opportunity to come to terms with the rapid transformations brought about by modernization. In this respect they constitute an invention of tradition much in the vein of Hobsbawm. 'Elements of the past are portrayed as an integral part of the future in a rapidly changing socio-political climate. Visited by both foreign and domestic tourists, these museums provide venues for national constructions of identity derived from an exemplary past' (Hitchcock, Stanley & Siu 1997:197).

While in many Asian countries the state in terms of tourism may be lacking adequate planning (Hitchcock, King & Parnwell 1993:29), often it does play a pre-eminent role in image management. Basically, a division into three categories of state-led image management can be made. Firts, there are national identities in Asia which are virtually inventions of an authoritive state attempting simultaneously to control and benefit from its cultural diversity in their confrontation with tourism (for instance Singapore and China). Second, there are national identities that represent state-supported symbolic reconstructions to market the country in terms of its cultural diversity in the global tourism market (like Malaysia). And third, there are states that fail to tap their ethnic potential altogether, like Thailand which has hardly begun to develop ethnic tourism (Parnwell 1993; Michaud 1997). Anticipating Indonesia to rank among those countries where the state has a keen interest in keeping a firm hand on its ethnic diversity, even while parading this very diversity in front of an international audience, I shall focus on state interventions in national image management as they occur in the first two categories.

The best known example of government-led image management may well be Singapore. Here, the state displays an authoritarian paternalism obsessed with images presented both to its citizens and to the international audience (Wai-Teng Leong 1997). The city-state manages its cultural diversity in a reductionist way by organizing dozens of ethnic groups into four sub-categories: Chinese, Malay, Indian, and 'others' as a residual category comprising among others Westerners working and living in Singapore. Tourism in Singapore reflects this subdivision. Any city tour takes visitors to the Indian quarter and the neatly-restored Chinatown. However, there is no such thing as ethnic tourism as distinct from other forms of tourism. As Wai-Teng Leong points out, 'ethnic tourism in Singapore is general tourism: experiences of sights and taste are organized around the broad theme of ethnicity' (1997:85).

In China ethnic tourism is state-sponsored. It is supposed to contribute to the commercial, economic, and social integration of China. Much like the Singaporean approach, Chinese state policies towards ethnic minority cultures generate standardized cultural forms and unambiguous symbolic markers. While China is comprised of over 400 groups claiming separate ethnic identity, the state has classified them into no more than fifty-five categories (Oakes 1997:45). The Chinese state supports the idea that cultural diversity should be maintained among the officially defined ethnic groups, but it is a diversity that exists at a purely symbolic level. In promoting this symbolic cultural diversity, the 'state hopes to establish an environment conducive to national economic integration, geopolitical security, and patriotism' (Oakes 1997:47). An indispensable part of this state-orchestrated ethnic diversity are the processes of invention of traditions: '... drawing distinct boundaries around local customs, fixing them in time and space, and ensuring that they remain encased as exhibits for the modern metropolitan world to observe and appreciate' (Oakes 1997:49). Museum displays of ethnic diversity such as Shenzhen's 'China Folk Culture Villages' theme park – a display that basically addresses domestic tourists as eighty per cent of its visitors are Chinese (Hitchcock, Stanley & Siu 1997:209) – reflects the revision of the position of ethnic minorities in China's policy towards minority peoples. Whereas ethnic minorities were previously regarded as the 'unhealthy vestiges of local nationalisms' (Oakes 1997:67), at present the state – bowing to the pressure of intensified market commercialism and commodification – has come to understand that a controlled expression of 'folk culture' – even religious beliefs as the commodification of Buddhism on behalf of tourism shows (Philip & Mercer 1999) – can be supportive in building a sense of national identity. What is displayed in 'China Folk Culture Villages' – in terms of the Chinese authorities – is not the ethnic diversity of China, but 'people's customs' that 'show the harmony of the races' (ibid:206). At the same time, as Oakes observes, the state-sponsored ethnic displays offer 'much of the raw material that locals use to claim a distinct place identity' (1997:37). It is tourism that provides local minority groups with a forum for making claims about themselves and their villages.

In Malaysia ethnic diversity constitutes the reality of the state, hence its official national ideology, *rukunegara* (lit. harmony of the state), the basic tenet of which is to ensure 'a liberal approach to Malaysia's rich and diverse cultural traditions' (Kadir Din 1997:110). Given the potpourri of ethnic groups with no shared cultural themes, Malaysian culture is basically a construct of Malaysian officialdom, an *ad hoc* assemblage of beliefs and practices held by diverse populations, to serve national purposes and to assist in the promotion of tourism (King 1993:102-3). In contrast to the earlier quoted examples of Singapore and China, the Malaysian government does not attempt to enforce unity upon its cultural diversity. Instead, there are all kinds of cultural cleavages and differences between the various ethnic groups and regions, and this very fragmentation is the Malaysian cultural product. What is referred to as 'traditional' in Malaysian cultures is a symbolic re-construction, even invention, of cultural identities before, during, and after the European colonial period. Tourism, and in particular domestic tourism, is assigned a national purpose as well. It is the creation of a Ministry combining both tourism and culture which has the task to 'engender a local awareness of cultural matters and national identity and heritage, and to enhance national pride and commitments' (King 1993:109). In Malaysia the representation of its diverse ethnic groups and their cultures is a very sensitive matter, having to accommodate the delicate balance between different groups in this multi-ethnic society, and not lose sight of the significant role of Islam which frowns upon frivolities so often associated with tourism. Therefore tourism promotion tends to emphasize relatively uncontentious cultural elements. 'The role of the state is to market 'cultural meanings,' the choice of which parts of a country's cultural heritage to develop for tourism constitutes a statement about national identity which is conveyed to both tourists and locals' (King 1993:109).

INDONESIA'S 'UNITY IN DIVERSITY' IN CULTURAL TOURISM REPRESENTATIONS

Indonesia is another Asian country where the nation-state is jealously guarded against any challenge from ethnic diversity. Nas (1998:187, 189) points out that the process of globalization need not be detrimental to the state, but may even strengthen its position. The process of Indonesianization is crucial to understanding the mutual relations between the processes of globalization, nation-building, and localization. As Appadurai has pointed out, for many ethnic groups in Indonesia 'Indonesianization' may be more worrisome than 'globalization,' as 'one man's imagined community is another man's political prison' (1990:295). As the political practice of the New Order government shows, 'the many forces (and fears) of homogenization can also be exploited by nation states in relation to their own minorities, by posing global commoditization (or capitalism, or some other such external enemy) as more 'real' than the threat of its own hegemonic strategies' (Appadurai 1990:296; see also Lanfant 1995a). There is an increasing tendency in Indonesia to propagate a derivation from available ethnic roots. Before this can be done, these roots have to be stripped of 'outdated' traits and allow themselves to be adapted to the spirit of the national ideology (Schefold 1998:275). The New Order State legitimized its claim to being a nation through the 'imagination' that its inhabitants, of whatever class, represent a solid cultural community, as their manifold ethnic attachments did not establish a firm basis for national culture. Their culture is an element of great importance in the understanding of nationalism (Gellner 1983:7). As Schefold (1998:275) points out, re-evaluation of everything that has been achieved jointly in the Indonesian setting – the glorification of pre-colonial history, the struggle for independence and its heroes, the national ideology of *pancasila*, the advantages of a national language, the results of Indonesian development programmes – established an equivalent for primordial attachments without coming into conflict with ethnic loyalties. World-wide communications and the global propagation of particular values and achievements, such as great technological, sporting, and artistic feats, and international conventions and conferences turn every Indonesian success into a national event (Schefold 1998:276). Here is a strategy at work that has been described in terms of the 'invention of tradition' by Eric Hobsbawm, i.e. 'a set of practices, normally governed by overtly or tacitly accepted rules and of a ritual or symbolic nature, which seek to inculcate certain values and norms of behaviour by repetition, which automatically implies continuity with the past' (Hobsbawm 1983:1). Invented traditions are regarded by Hobsbawm as responses to novel situations that either take the form of reference to old situations or establish their own past (ibid:2). In Indonesia, the New Order regime – responding to the novel situation of

15

becoming an actor in a global society while still in the process of consolidating the nation-state – did both, referring to a common past (the great pre-colonial civilizations and the struggle for independence) and recontextualizing and reinterpreting this past. It is clear that processes of globalization were strategically exploited by the New Order government to strengthen the Indonesian nation state. However, this raises questions about how the government's eagerness to succeed at a global and national level was reconciled to the manifold manifestations of ethnic uniqueness and how it succeeded in moulding selected ethnic cultures into marketable tourist products that represent national culture. After all, the 'invention of traditions' is not exclusively generated from the 'outside' by non-participants in local culture. Local people themselves invent traditions to make their cultural expressions more attractive to tourists (Hitchcock, King & Parnwell 1993).

The marketing of ethnic diversity for tourism became a major strategy to improve the competitiveness of 'Indonesia' as a tourist product. The New Order government utilized cultural diversity: regional cultural expressions, instead of merely being tolerated, were given active support to weaken the position of any adherents of separatist ideas. This may have succeeded to some extent but this patronage is selective, reducing what are in fact ethnic ways of life to folklorist elements. In this 'aestheticized' form, oriented as it is to outward spectacle, ethnic diversity does now feature as a central element of Indonesian identity. It is not opposed to the national culture, but is merely a display of its glittering riches (Schefold 1998:276, see also Kipp 1993, Picard & Wood 1997). In Indonesia culture and art (as opposed to politics) have become an arena in which seemingly 'unpolitical' visions of national identity are stated. Applying a strategy of 'culturalization' of identity, the government is not only accommodating differences, but actually producing them. As Hellman points out, during recent decades the concept of culture in Indonesia has gone through a process of aesthetization, stylization, relativization, and standardization.

This is not a harmless exercise in semantic associations but a strategy of domination. Identity is disembedded from specific local circumstances and made into an entity regulated by the state. At the same time, people realize that 'culture' is a potentially powerful concept. They become aware of a cultural heritage and its ability to serve as an idiom which is able to formulate life experiences and political demands (Hellman 1998:11).

It is cultural tourism with its appeal to cultural heritage and its potential for the exercise of power that most suited the New Order's cultural policies. The New Order government sought and obtained worldwide support for the restoration of its ancient 'World' heritage sites and invested money and energy in the maintenance of pre-colonial and colonial buildings (mosques, churches, palaces, and governmental buildings) and the establishment of monuments and museums to commemorate the struggle for independence and other peak events in recent history. In terms of cultural tourism, the Indonesian government's approach can be characterized as the 'sites and monuments' approach to culture. In this context the concept of cultural tourism as 'high culture' predominates; the concept inclines towards the consumption of cultural products rather than involvement in cultural processes. Hence the government's investments in buildings or in orchestrated cultural performances. It does not take a vast amount of efforts to see that this product-based approach highlights the 'concrete' and 'material' aspects of culture that make culture relatively predictable and controllable. The process approach to culture does not figure in the Indonesian government's definition of cultural tourism, and poses problems of planning and control wherever it emerges, as will be discussed in detail in this book.

While economic motivations lay at the basis of accelerating tourism developments in the early 1980s, by 1988 tourism's role in nation-building was officially encoded into the mission statement of the Indonesian Ministry of Tourism:

> Development of domestic tourism is aimed at strengthening love for the country, instilling the soul, spirit and high values of the nation, improving the quality of the nation's cultural life and promoting historical sites (Departemen Pariwisata, Pos dan Telekomunikasi, quoted in Adams 1997:157).

Under the New Order the message that domestic tourism to selected cultural destinations makes a citizen a better Indonesian has generated a positive flurry of domestic travel. Young Indonesians especially have been sent on more or less obligatory trips organized through schools and employers to see the cultural highlights of their country, especially the World Heritage sites, the temple complexes of Borobudur and Prambanan. As Adams (1997:157) relates, the 'Indonesia Package Tour' was designed for domestic tourists to strengthen the bonds between Indonesian ethnic groups, while youth tourism is promoted as ideal for cultivating a love of country and a sense of national pride. This tour defines the destinations of a national pilgrimage with an emphasis on cultural continuity (Wood 1997:19).

As the discussion in this book will show, the centralist organization of tourism in Indonesia favoured a small number of well-defined and limited areas for tourism development; the capital city Jakarta, the island of Bali, and the Special Province of Yogyakarta. These areas have been designed to be so as the favoured destinations for international tourism and have been given government support for tourism development, in particular for establishing high-standard tourist resorts to accommodate and concentrate on international tourism. As a consequence, the Indonesian government has poured enormous efforts into tourism planning in general and planning for large-scale tourist resorts in particular. Indonesia's national and regional plans emphasize the construction of integrated resorts as a strategy for tourism development. This strategy has been promoted in terms of 'quality' tourism. 'Quality' tourism is not only a euphemism for attracting rich tourists (Wall 1995), it is also a safe way of protecting the elite's interests and facilitating their access to land and other resources. After all, resort development accomplished with the use of large-scale, partly foreign investments suited the Indonesian state under the Suharto regime which acted on behalf of the ruling elite. Try as it might, the state-controlled tourism industry turned out to be quite incapable of organizing and controlling international tourism. In Bali the policy of concentration failed and visitors went sprawling all over Bali and Indonesia, leading to uncontrolled tourism development in many areas (Wall 1996). Local communities and ethnic groups not only benefited economically from the uncontrolled tourism growth, but culturally as they reconstructed and revitalized their cultural identity in the face of increasing numbers of domestic and foreign visitors.

The New Order government recognized the advantage of ethnic revival for the marketing of the country as a tourist destination, both for domestic and international visitors. In the definition of the national culture, a few superior cultures – among which the Javanese culture is the highest valued – are distinguished from inferior cultures, which are excluded from contributing to the national culture (Picard 1997:193). The so-called 'peak cultures' were to furnish the shared basis provided, as was also stressed, they were advanced in such a fashion as to be able to represent a unifying asset for the new nation. No effort was made to explain where these peaks were to be found or what the advancement should look like (Schefold 1998:266). 'Peak cultures' were highlighted in the early 1990s when new tourism areas were defined in the national development plans that politically sanctioned the expansion of tourism to the 'outer islands' – as Indonesia's less-developed areas outside of Bali and Java are called.

Picard addresses a point of eminent importance when he states that the official discourse is not dealing with Indonesia's 'ethnic cultures,' but with what Indonesian officials call 'regional cultures' (*kebudayaan daerah*) (Picard 1997). More precisely, we are dealing here with 'provincial' cultures that are congruent with the boundaries of the twenty-seven (in 1996) official administrative units that constitute the Republic of Indonesia. Official Indonesian discourse speaks of 'regional cultures,' each with cultural 'peaks' suitable for being part of Indonesian national culture (Wood 1997:13).

The acceptance of the word *kebudayaan*, commonly translated as 'culture,' is at once normative and evolutionist, in that it refers to the process through which the diverse ethnic groups are expected to acquire the qualities necessary to institute the order and civilization consonant with the ideal of the Indonesian nation. Therefore we should not expect to find in this word the idea of a cultural specificity characteristic of each ethnic group or the idea of cultural relativism. The term *daerah*, which translates as region, carries an ambiguity as to the nature (ethnic or administrative) and geographic scope (local or regional) of the cultural entity under consideration (Picard 1997:198).

The term *kebudayaan daerah* implies a process of provincial differentiation. The New Order government attempted to define 'a distinctive homogeneous provincial identity, grounded on a single distinct set of unique cultural features' (Picard 1997:198) for each of its provinces. The establishment of 'provincial cultures' was supposed to divert attention from and eventually extinguish the diverse ethnic cultures enclosed within their boundaries. The emphasis on region is visually evident at *Taman Mini Indonesia*, opened in 1975 on the southern outskirts of Jakarta (cf. Chapter 2). In promoting the so-called regional cultures, remarks Picard (1997:198) 'the state is playing the provinces not only against the various ethnic groups that compose them, but also against the regions proper, which, as political entities rooted in a specific history, are considered a threat to national unity.' The folklorization of culture is compounded by a provincialization of ethnicity. In this perspective, the promotion of provincial cultural identities can be interpreted as a safe way for the state to bridge the gap between ethnic identities – regarded as being either irrelevant or detrimental to the process of nation building – and the still remote national identity. The proper term for this process is *Indonesianization* (Picard 1997:200).

Turning to the Special Province of Yogyakarta, it seems that we are dealing with the only area – with the exception of Jakarta – that is benefiting from the government's policy of Indonesianization. First of all, there is a striking parallel between the province's boundaries and its ethnic identity. The Special Province of Yogyakarta – except for its Chinese business community – is almost exclusively uni-ethnic, inhabited by Javanese people. This uni-ethnicity is equalled only by Bali. In this case local culture and identity seem to be congruent with Jakarta-orchestrated images of 'regional culture.' Second, the Special Province of Yogyakarta is in the heart of Javanese culture and, therefore, as might be expected it is part and parcel of the Javanese dominant culture. It is not suffering from 'exclusion' under Javanese domination, but is included in the circles of those executing that domination. Third, and closely related to the latter point, the Special Province of Yogyakarta is not at the periphery but in the centre of the tourism policy of the New Order. It has benefited from special government support ever since the first Five-Year Development Plan which was launched in the late 1960s. Because of its history, its court culture and its involvement in the struggle for independence, the Special Province of Yogyakarta became the cradle of the government-orchestrated *pancasila* tourism. The cultural heritage of the Yogyakarta area has shaped the (international) image of Indonesia, as government propaganda has used architectural structures like the temples and the sultan's palace and expressions of art like the Ramayana dance to promote Indonesian tourism world-wide. This is given yet another boost as a visit to Yogyakarta is a climax of the 'Package Tour Indonesia' and an obligatory place for Indonesians to visit in order to learn about national culture, history, and heritage. At first sight, then, the establishment of cultural tourism in the area of Yogyakarta in the spirit of the 'Yogyakarta Declaration on National Cultures and Universal Tourism' would not seem to elicit controversies within the context of local culture and identity. The reverse would seem to have been true. Offering a multifaceted tourism product, Yogyakarta was developed as the centre of Indonesian cultural tourism as a worthy representative of the nation *to be presented on a plate* to foreign as well as domestic tourists. Through the years there have been usually three times as many domestic tourists as overseas tourists staying in Yogyakarta (cf. Hughes-Freeland 1993). *Pancasila* tourism seemed to be a very successful strategy for Yogyakarta. Before the monetary and political crises there was rapid urban development, even a building boom in the hotel sector as the local tourism industry flourished.

However good the situation may look on the surface, the threats to Yogyakarta's tourism development are manifold. Despite the image of being the centre of Indonesian cultural tourism, the city and the surrounding areas offer a limited diversity of tourist attractions. The tourism industry is relying on a 'product' that has maintained the ingredients and meanings constructed to suit *pancasila* propaganda. Innovations have not been welcomed as they threaten the carefully planned tourist area and jeopardize the government-controlled objectives of tourism to Yogyakarta. The national tourism policy has demanded that priority should be given to the dissemination of national culture and has allowed local identity to thrive only if it fits in with national development plans. A closer look at tourism development in Yogyakarta reveals that this matter becomes complicated at the regional level as the demand for identity springs from several categories of people giving rise to controversies: 'Tensions, struggles and conflicts between interests are all characteristic in general terms of the relations between a tourist region and the central state' (Lanfant 1995b:34-5). In Yogyakarta the threat to tourism is present mainly in the government-defined 'quality' sector. The strength of the provincial tourism sector does not lie in the expensive hotels that are booming, but in the 'small-scale' businesses, the guesthouses and *losmen*, the inexpensive foodstalls, and the local transport facilities situated and operating in the *kampung* (low-class neighbourhoods) that cater to the needs of individual travelling – but not necessarily 'poor' – tourists. It could be said that – despite the concentration of 'built heritage' sites in the area – cultural tourism in Yogyakarta inclines more towards the process approach to culture than the government-favoured product approach (cf. Chapter 4). To refer to concepts coined by Patrick Guinness (1986): it is '*kampung* tourism' that is flourishing, not 'streetside' tourism. While the government promotes 'streetside' tourism, especially in terms of 'quality' tourism, the tourism industry in Yogyakarta is largely determined by *kampung* tourism. The characteristics of *kampung* tourism are small-scale, family-run businesses or self-employed people, often operating without proper licences or official recognition, offering inexpensive services and catering to the unorganized and 'uncontrolled' tourism sector. Characteristic of the local industry is the multivocality of images and meanings associated with the city and its attractions. While the 'streetside' sector is subject to all kinds of regulatory mechanisms like the enclosure of tourist areas and control on tourist discourses, *kampung*-based entrepreneurs largely withdraw from government control, and construct and sell their own tourist product. They create, and cater to, a different market from the 'streetside.' It is as if there are two different tourist realities that exist in two different spheres occupying different tourist spaces, organized by different institutions, and directed at different categories of tourists using different facilities. However, with growing pressures on tourism in Yogyakarta, both realities are increasingly dependent upon and conflicting with each other.

AGENTS OF AUTHENTICATION

The communication of the images and narratives that support this strategy is an important element in the realization of government-set aims to use tourism to obtain international esteem, to promote national culture, and domesticate cultural diversity. As Urry (1990) has pointed out, it involves complex processes of attraction building to transform a site into a sight which attracts regular, meaningful, and profitable tourist gazes. Such gazes are not left to chance. In particular in a situation like Indonesia where economic growth and political objectives are closely intertwined, images and narratives are socially organized and systematized, partly by professional experts but always under government-control. Agents of the tourism industry teach tourists how, when, and where to gaze (Urry 1990), and they usually direct the tourist gaze towards the objects they have created in glossy brochures by manipulating mythical language (Selwyn 1993). The definition, production, and representation of tourist attractions constitute a complex exchange of information and meaning between a number of agents including the site, the local community, the tourism industry, guides, and tourists; a process in which tour operators and travel agents, tourist guides and tour leaders who act as mediators between tourists and hosts become the crucial actors in the performance of tourism.

Most definitions of cultural tourism embody an educational and experiential component as well as a romanticized idea of culture and cultural communications. Some authors assume that the motivation of cultural tourists is to get more deeply into the culture itself – the history, performance, arts, and the way of life. As MacCannell suggests in his much quoted book, *The Tourist* (1976), tourists seek to encounter the 'real' life of the people they visit; tourists pursue 'authentic' experiences that reveal, or even allow the sharing of some aspect of the daily life of the host society – as tourists have lost the sense of 'authentic' experiences in their own society. He uses the term 'backstage' to describe the physical setting in which a visitor could observe, meet, or share some 'authentic' experiences. The obvious problem is that, being 'backstage,' such 'real lives' are not immediately evident for tourists. Therefore the tourist gaze involves an obvious intrusion into people's lives, which may be experienced as unacceptable by the 'objects' of this gaze. MacCannell has coined the concept of modern cannibalism to describe the impact of the quest for authenticity on host societies (1992).

Access to frontstage as well as backstage requires actors in the tourism industry to 'mediate' between the tourists' demands and 'the culture' and enhances the benefits for both tourists and hosts along the way. As has been pointed out by many tourism experts, cultural tourism demands a specific body of knowledge and a high standard of tourist guiding. In many studies the focus is on the guides' role as information-giver (Holloway 1981). As research has shown (Schmidt 1979, Holloway 1981, Cohen 1985, Bowman 1992) tourist guides are of crucial importance in cultural tourism, as theirs is the task of selecting, glossing, and interpreting sights. The guides must translate 'the strangeness of a foreign culture into a cultural idiom familiar to the visitors' (Cohen 1985:15). Sensitively guided travellers may be convinced that the experiences they gain from their visit are a rewarding way of cultural contact (Bowman 1992: 125). It may be obvious that a 'sensitive' way of guiding demands that the guides display a high level of professional skill and an intimate knowledge of local culture. Extensive knowledge is regarded as a prerequisite by which to establish the guides' professional status as a mediator of culture either as a 'pathfinder' who 'provides access to an otherwise non-public territory' (Cohen 1985:10) or as a 'mentor' who 'serves as a guru to the novice, adept, or seeker, guiding him towards insight, enlightenment or any other exalted spiritual state' (ibid: 8). The former facilitates access whereas the latter builds on that to which the traveller has access, integrating what is seen into a coherent and meaningful image of place. In either case the tourist guide is portrayed as someone who builds bridges between 'hosts' and 'guests' (Gurung et al. 1996). Guiding becomes a strategic factor influencing the quality of the tourist experience, the length of stay, and the resulting economic benefits (Gertler 1993).

Reflecting on what has been revealed about the political agenda of the Indonesian government regarding the strategic use of tourism, this approach to both cultural tourism and processes of 'mediation' seems rather naive. As I have argued elsewhere (Dahles 1998a), tourist guides should be regarded as entrepreneurs whose primary interest is their own benefit from tourism. Tourist guides are among the local tourist entrepreneurs who construct backstages in a contrived and artificial manner (Urry 1990). Tourist spaces are thus organized around what MacCannell (1973) calls 'staged authenticity.' Tourist guides take a pivotal role in the staging of these spaces: they construct tourist attractions – both frontstages and 'staged backstages' – in response to the tourists' quest for authenticity and at the same time to take advantage of the opportunities it presents for profit. Cross-cutting the distinction between 'pathfinders' and 'mentors,' another distinction has to be made: i.e. the distinction between the formal guided tour and the informal situation in which 'unqualified' locals offer their services to show tourists around, a distinction between highly structured and unstructured tourist experiences. As Schmidt (1979:449) observes, guided tours are most functional in places which have ongoing activities, such as institutions and businesses – and one may add 'political systems.' Guided tours enable tourists to observe the 'inner workings' of these institutions, but not at the expense of their efficiency; they must not be disturbed from their tasks by invasions of tourists. Guided tours ensure that tourists are channelled into the right place at the right time, doing so under the control of someone 'responsible.' It should come as no surprise that guided tours which weave in and out of everyday life so as not to be obtrusive, but at the same time do provide tourists with a glimpse of what is going on without revealing undesirable aspects, must be extremely appealing to the Indonesian government. As guided tours form highly effective instruments of controlling the tourists and their contacts with the host society as well as the images and narratives by means of which the host society presents itself before a domestic and international audience of visitors, the reasons behind the New Order government's policy of 'quality tourism' with its emphasis on guidance and control become as crystal clear.

On the 'controlled' end of the continuum are tourist guides leading package tours that entail minimal interaction with the host society. The presence of the tourist guide constitutes a buffer between tourists and the social environment, arranging transport, interpreting, and handling problems which might arise (Schmidt 1979:443). The guides' intercessionary role in shepherding the group and explaining the attractions reduces the opportunity for interaction with locals, and the group's attention becomes inwardly directed towards the guide rather than outwardly directed towards the setting (Holloway 1981:382). On a guided tour tourists not only view and interpret local sights through the words of the tour guides, they are made to experience the environment according to the way in which the tour guide constructs and represents it. However, the type of information and explanations the guides provide for certain situations may be quite different from both the information that the government requires to be disseminated about a place and the information which a local resident would provide – even though the guides are sometimes local residents. Qualified tourist guides in Indonesia are trained by government institutions and forced by their employment situation to follow the official, authorized narrative. For fear of losing their jobs, they may stick to their assignment to keep tourists away from backstages that represent the undesirable aspects of the host society that should not be displayed. Tourist guides play a pivotal role in the social construction of local identity. The quality of this important function is determined by a set of interrelated factors: professional standards, recruitment, qualifications, payment, and training. The rub is that professional organizations and training programmes only relate to a fragment of the whole domain of guiding. The world of tourist guides consists of a complex structure of formal and informal, professional and amateur, organized and unorganized, licensed and unlicensed, qualified and unqualified, permanently employed, free-lance, and unemployed categories.

Unlicensed guides, most of whom belong to the unqualified, unorganized, and permanently unemployed categories forming the informal sector of the tourist industry, are not under the obligation to tell an authorized story, as they work beyond the effective control of the tourism authorities. Instead they attempt – more than their licensed counterparts – to please the tourists and comply with their requests to make backstages accessible. It may be expected that this 'uncontrolled' informal sector offers the closest encounters with cultural backstages. In so doing unlicensed guides may threaten the carefully orchestrated images and discourses that implement *pancasila* tourism. The cultural experience they offer to tourists is as 'commercialized' and 'inauthentic' as the national government's construct may be, but it serves a purely individual economic interest instead of an ambitious political agenda. Theirs is an experience of Yogyakarta as a 'global village' with everyday encounters of the 'Hello Mister'-type that go hand in hand with the pleasures of a tourist resort, ice-cold Cokes, Big Macs, and Magnums sold by a street vendor playing the Lambada. The celebration of Western consumerism by the unlicensed guides of Yogyakarta heralds the collapse of the government-orchestrated *pancasila* tourism, and therefore, they may be the most vigorously suppressed categories in the informal tourism industry. In Chapter 6 there will be a closer investigation into how the government applies measures to banish certain groups (like *becak* drivers and unlicensed guides) from the city centre and the main tourist attractions. Public space is turned into controlled areas, the access to which is limited to people who conform to government-set rules. These rules are enforced through licensing and enclosing, and police raids occur occasionally to keep undesirable people out. In its attempts to formalize the *kampung* tourism sector of which unlicensed guides are an integral part, the Indonesian government has tried to control the growth of informal activities with the aim of maintaining and strengthening *pancasila* tourism – a forlorn hope as actors in the *kampung* economy position themselves outside the system that reinforces *pancasila* tourism. However, they do not constitute any force of political significance as their mode of operation is highly individualized and so they cannot possibly be suspected of any organized or planned subversive activities. Local people remain largely beyond the control of the authorities, while their personal networks extend beyond the artificial boundaries between the *kampung* and 'streetside' arenas as friendship, family, and ethnic ties that link actors in streetside and *kampung* tourism are stronger than government-imposed regulations. Those people who represent the government and are paid for enforcing state regulations on these premises are also willing to turn a blind eye if remunerated accordingly. In other words, *kampung* people not only withdraw from government control, they even challenge it by exposing its failures.

The conversion of heritage into a tourist product implies that its cultural value is transformed into a commercial value. In the course of this operation cultural heritage undergoes radical changes in meaning. In becoming a tourist destination a place becomes the expression of a collective memory. In an attempt to respond to an external demand for authenticity the inhabitants of such places (re-)invent cultural events 'in a new spirit of aestheticism' (Lanfant 1995b:37) to meet the wishes of tourists. Whenever these constructions are represented as true and 'authentic,' they can be regarded as a hyper-reality – a construction that is actually regarded as more authentic than any original ever could have been (Lanfant 1995b:38). In Indonesia, the New Order government has created a 'hyper-reality' in the form of its national culture that displays national unity and domesticated cultural diversity. This hyper-reality is reproduced in guided encounters between tourists under government-orchestrated *pancasila* tourism and selected aspects of the host society. However, at the local level where encounters between visitors and hosts actually materialize and are given shape in face-to-face interactions, a multitude of voices compete for the tourists' attention. Different realities emerge, of which some withdraw from government control and generate partly converging and partly conflicting, but constantly changing images and meanings of a tourist destination.

CHAPTER 2

THE POLITICS OF TOURISM IN INDONESIA

MODERNIZATION, NATIONAL UNITY, AND CULTURAL DIVERSITY

INTRODUCTION

In the national development policy of the New Order government high priority was given to tourism, a strategy that has to be understood against the background of the political and economic agenda of the regime of former President Suharto. The New Order created a political system which laid stress on political stability and economic development as two sides of the same coin (Anwar 1997:4). In the Indonesian state ideology, these two interdependent principles of the New Order regime were moulded into a more or less coherent framework, the *pancasila* (literally: 'five pillars'), which was constructed to legitimize state politics and policies. The two pillars of political stability and economic development created ideal conditions for the flourishing of national and international tourism. This sector benefited from the government policy of deregulation, i.e. measures intended to facilitate private sector activities, particularly in the export sector (Booth 1990:45-73). Examples of beneficial deregulatory measures were tax incentives for big companies, cutting tariffs, simplifying export procedures, eliminating permits, and introducing tax holidays for newly established companies. Measures designed specifically to benefit the foreign tourist sector included the partial abolition of visa requirements, the granting of additional landing rights to foreign airlines in the major ports of entry, the establishment of more international airports, the reduction of the number of licences required to build new hotels, and the designation of new tourist destination areas in islands other than Java and Bali.

Political stability is a precondition for attracting a constant flow of tourists (Richter 1989:10), as the effects of armed conflict on the number of tourist arrivals in many turbulent areas show.[1] Tourists, in their turn, contribute to economic development, directly, in terms of their expenditure, as well as indirectly, in terms of investments made by the government and the tourism industry in infrastructure and employment. In other words, the New Order regime discovered tourism as the prime touchstone for its modernization project. Tourism was assumed to contribute significantly to development; development being defined in terms of measurable economic expansion and social advancement (Dove 1988:1). At a more esoteric level, tourism was used strategically to bolster national unity. To accommodate these objectives, tourism development was orchestrated by the Indonesian government in such a way that the 'five pillars' of the *pancasila* ideology were even presented in the tourism product offered to foreign as well as domestic tourists.

According primacy to nation-building, Indonesia had to come to terms with the reality of ethnic diversity. While ethnic and regional secessions recurrently questioned the legitimacy of the New Order nation-state, the government attempted a juggling act by which it could control ethnicity and simultaneously use the ethnic diversity to promote its modernization project. The tourist industry provided an important incentive for the government to take a hand in the preservation and cultivation of traditions. Under both the Old Order and New Order governments the construction of nationalist ideals, a nationalist sense of history, and a transcendent loyalty to the nation were focal points (Kipp 1993:105), but it was only in the Suharto era that ethnic culture seems to have experienced a paradoxical revival – under Javanese control and supremacy. Quite apart from fulfilling objectives on behalf of the 'internal' agenda, tourism was supposed to provide the New Order government with legitimacy and the country with the international image of both a 'modern nation' and a 'decent nation.' In this sense, tourism could foster nation-building by reminding Indonesians of their common identity in their confrontation with foreigners (Adams 1997:175).

This chapter investigates the ways in which the New Order government strategically employed tourism development and tourism discourse to serve its political agenda. Questions will be raised about the extent to which the government succeeded in accomplishing the partially conflicting objectives of economic development, political stability, national unity, and cultural diversity through the manipulation of tourism. Questions will be asked about the ways in which cultural divisions, symbolized by ethnic markers, were selected for tourist promotion and reconciled with national integration. How did cultural and ethnic tourism, or one or the other, affect the relationship between ethnic groups and the national political economy? How did the national government deal with the potentially problematic situation created by the resurgence of ethnic revival through cultural tourism?

TOURISM AND NEW ORDER POLITICS

Tourism in Indonesia dates back to the colonial period. In 1908 the colonial government opened a tourist bureau in its capital city Batavia in order to promote the Netherlands East Indies as a tourist destination. Initially focusing on Java, the bureau extended its scope to Bali in 1914, as soon as control of the island by the army allowed it to be visited in safety (Picard 1997:190). According to Sammeng, former Director General of the Ministry of Tourism, Post and Telecommunications, the history of tourism to Indonesia began in 1914 when the first travel guidebook to Bali was published by the tourist bureau in Batavia (Sammeng 1995, Kodhyat 1996). This was followed in 1924 by the provision of a regular weekly service connecting Bali with Batavia and Makassar by the Dutch steamship line (KPM). In search of cooler climes, the Dutch developed resorts in the highland areas in Java and Sumatra, by building hotels in Bandung, Semarang, Surabaya, Medan, and Bukittinggi, places where the planters, administrators and estate holders could relax and socialize and spend their time at conferences and in meetings (Gunawan 1997b:18). In the early days of Independence, 'tourism' was related to political activities – meetings between the Indonesian and Dutch governments or among Indonesian leaders – and it was considered a very prestigious leisure activity affordable by only the very privileged few (Gunawan 1997b:18). In 1958 President Sukarno coined the Indonesian word for tourism, *pariwisata* (Kodyat 1996:66).[2] Since then, tourism has been included in the national development agenda.

To meet the economic and political objectives of tourism development, Indonesia has put enormous effort into planning. Like the other economic sectors, tourism has been targeted under the development plans, a strategy designed by the New Order after it assumed power in 1965 and was eliminating chaos and controlling all sectors of economic and social life. There were long-term development plans covering a period of twenty-five years, the first being issued in 1969, designed to develop the national economy and to bolster political stability. The long-term development policy was divided into five stages of five-year development programmes (*Rencana Pembangunan Lima Tahun*, abbreviated as *Repelita*). Besides economic growth, among the aims of the first 5-Year Plan (*Repelita* I, 1969/70-1973/74) were the development of patriotism, the strengthening of the unity and integrity of the nation, and the preservation of culture and the environment (Basuki, Sigit & Gunawan 1993:VIII-1). Ever since, Indonesia's strategic 5-Year Plans have accorded an increasing importance to national and regional development of tourism (Gunawan 1997a:47).

As Indonesia was almost non-existent on the international tourism map in the 1960s receiving less than 100,000 visitors per year (Gunawan 1997a:51), the main objective of the first 5-Year Plan was to attract more visitors, identifying Bali as the main tourist area, followed by Jakarta, Yogyakarta, Solo, and North Sumatra. In preparation for this, the major architectural remains of the past in these areas were restored, especially the temples, palaces, and colonial buildings. In the second 5-Year Plan (1974/75-1978/79), the simplistic growth scenario of its predecessor became more sophisticated and the benefits for local communities and the quality of the tourism product were specified, and the contribution of tourism to national unity became more explicit. Under the second *Repelita*, the 'Beautiful Indonesia in Miniature Park,' commonly known as *Taman Mini Indonesia Indah*, was constructed at the southern outskirts of Jakarta. In this period the government allowed the Directorate-General of Tourism to play a more active role in the management of cultural heritage, including both historical monuments and traditional folk art. A special committee was established to bridge the conflicting views on the preservation of monuments between the officials of the cultural section and those in the tourism section in the government and to promote the collaboration of both sections in utilizing cultural heritage as tourist resources (Kagami 1997). The third 5-Year plan (1979/80-1983/84) marked the era of deregulation, opening Indonesia to foreign investors and visitors by facilitating access to the country (establishing new ports of entry and reducing licence and visa requirements) and expanding tourism development plans to areas other than Java and Bali. Tourism policy was expanded to the domestic market to establish a 'better understanding of the archipelago' among Indonesian people (Basuki, Sigit & Gunawan 1993:VIII-2). By the end of this planning period in 1983, a presidential decree was issued stipulating the establishment of the Department (Ministry) of Tourism, Post and Telecommunications (*Depparpostel*) and rescinding an earlier decree that placed tourism under the Department of Transport (ibid. VIII-3). Under the fourth 5-Year Plan (1984/85-1988/89) resort development, mostly in Bali and Java, and the world-wide promotion of Indonesia as a tourist destination were the main target. The period covered by the fifth 5-Year Plan (1989/90-1993/94) was intended as a climax to tourism development, placing major events on the agenda. Even though the 1991 'Visit Indonesia Year' promotion campaign failed in terms of visitor arrivals (because of the Gulf War), it brought major events like the 'ASEAN Tourist Forum' and the 'Tenth General Meeting of the World Tourism Organization' to Indonesia. In 1992 Indonesia joined the 'Visit ASEAN Year' campaign, and after that declared the 'Visit Indonesia Decade.' In preparation for the 'Visit Indonesia Year' (1991) and the 'Visit ASEAN Year' (1992), the Indonesian government launched a national 'Tourism Consciousness Campaign' (*Kampanye Nasional Sadar Wisata*). As part of this campaign, the Minister of *Depparpostel* proclaimed the *sapta pesona*, or seven charms, to which all Indonesian groups should aspire. These tourist-pleasing charms included security (*aman*), orderliness *(tertib)*, hospitality *(ramah)*, beauty *(indah)*, comfort (*sejuk*), cleanliness (*bersih*), and thoughtfulness (*kenangan*). The campaign was widely discussed in Indonesian newspapers and lists of the seven charms were posted on plaques in villages and hotels to encourage local people to participate in tourism (Adams 1997:157-8).

Building on the success of the previous period, the second long-term development plan, commencing in 1994 with the sixth 5-Year Plan (1994/95-

1998/99), identified new areas to be developed for tourism. The eastern part of Indonesia was given priority. In this region, hampered by a lack of other resources, tourism came to be regarded as the foremost vehicle of development (Basuki, Sigit & Gunawan 1993:VIII-4). This was not the first time regionalization had been on the government's agenda, but the plans had never left the drawing board, hamstrung by a lack of money. The most recent expansion plan was backed by financial measures which channelled money into and stimulated investments in the areas to be developed. These initiatives were supported by a thorough analysis of the state of tourism developments in different areas (Sofield 1995) and by promotion campaigns like 'Bali Plus,' 'Bali and Beyond,' 'There is more to Indonesia than Bali' and 'Indonesia–A World Of Its Own' (Picard 1993, Sammeng 1995, Wiendu Nuryanti 1998).[3] These campaigns mark the emergence of regionalization processes in Indonesian tourism of which the purpose was to boost its competitiveness in the global market (Gunawan 1997b:23-7).

The basic model for provincial tourism planning has been the 'Bali Tourism Provincial Master Plan' dating from the early 1970s. The 'Bali Provincial Master Plan' emphasized the construction of integrated resorts and designated limited zones, controlled through the state-owned 'Bali Tourist Development Corporation,' for tourism development (Picard 1993:83). The most celebrated result of these government efforts to boost international tourism is Nusa Dua, an isolated area in south Bali boasting the highest concentration of carefully monitored five-star luxury resorts in Indonesia. Quite apart from this, Bali has experienced a boom in semi- and unplanned tourism all over the island, underlining the fact that the Master Plan and the Nusa Dua concept were established without consulting the provincial and local authorities. Although the Nusa Dua concept of controlled development has been found wanting in many ways (Wall 1996), this did not deter the government from using it as a model for tourism development in other provinces (Sammeng 1995). The first National Tourism Master Plan was prepared by a consortium of Indonesian consultants in 1979/80 and was continued in 1980/81 by a group from the Planning School of the Technological Institute Bandung (Gunawan 1997a). Adjusting itself to the guidelines laid down in the 5-Year Plan, this Master Plan focused strongly on large-scale developments in the areas defined as Indonesia's major tourist destinations, i.e. Bali, Jakarta, and Yogyakarta.

The oil recession and booming tourism during the second half of the 1980s necessitated a revision of the National Master Plan 'to cater to the dynamics of the international situation as well as the changing profile of the market, both international and domestic' (Gunawan 1997a:48). In other words, more tourist destination areas had to be developed to distribute the tourists to different parts of the country where tourism was expected to contribute to development-at-large. To meet this objective, Indonesia was subdivided into various tourism regions, each under a Tourism Development Corporation which leased hotel lots to investors and managed the estate (Wall 1997a:145). The main international (Medan, Jakarta, and Denpasar) and three subsidiary gateways (Manado, Ambon, and Jayapura) were appointed the distribution centres for tourism to their regions. Before these plans could be implemented, a further expansion of tourism development was recommended by a comprehensive study which had been undertaken with funding by the United Nations Development Project (UNDP), the 1991 'Tourism Sector Programming and Policy Development.' On the basis of this study, the most recent 'National Tourism Master Plan' issued in 1995 supported 'Provincial Tourism Development Plans' in most Indonesian provinces. At the time of the research, twenty out of twenty-seven provinces have 'Tourism Development Plans' (Gunawan 1997a:48). The explicit objective of national tourism policy was the reduction of regional disparities in both the quantity and quality of tourism facilities (ibid:49) by the expedient of channelling financial support for tourism development and promotion towards regions that lag behind those areas which had a well-established tourism industry. The 'Beyond Bali' campaigns imply that those destinations once favoured and pampered by the 5-Year Plans in the 1970s and 1980s (Bali and Yogyakarta) cannot count on government support and have to maintain their position in tourism development by dint of their own efforts. Although regionalization offers promising prospects for tourism development in Indonesia, it is still unclear how the new destinations will be differentiated in the marketplace so that they become complementary rather than competitive (Wall 1997a:145).

International tourism has shown considerable growth since the 1980s (for an overview of international tourist arrivals since 1969 see Appendix 2). At first sight, then, the New Order politics and policies were quite successful in generating a rapid growth in foreign tourist arrivals and concomitantly in earnings from tourism which has become a major source of foreign exchange for the Indonesian economy. Less spectacular in terms of revenues, but nonetheless impressive in terms of numbers is the growth of domestic tourism.[4] While this may have experienced a mini-boom, as Gunawan argues, Indonesia has not been able to attract a substantial proportion of the international tourism market (1997a:50). The number of tourist arrivals – comprising less than one percent of the world total – is small, considering the size of the country.[5] Some meagre comfort can be derived from the fact that Indonesia has experienced the highest growth rate in the Southeast Asian region – in the 1980s over 18 per cent annually (Booth 1992:312), in the early 1990s over 20 per cent annually on average – and as a result of the shifting market composition, enjoys the longest length of stay (Booth 1992:312).[6] Comfort is also accorded by the fact that the size of the Indonesian population, which is close to 200 million, constitutes a huge potential domestic market. This market is as yet uncertain and the actual growth potential of this market is insecure as the economic crisis of 1998 has demonstrated.

Looking back on almost thirty years of tourism development and planning in her country, Gunawan (1997a:49) concludes that tourism development is still concentrated in a few provinces, especially in Java and Bali, and to a lesser extent in South Sulawesi and North Sumatra. At present, tourism is flourishing in the most-developed areas of the six major tourism regions as defined by the Tourism Master Plan covering the whole of the archipelago,[7] and only in a few cases are tourist resorts on their feet in less-developed parts of the regions (Gunawan 1997a:54). The regional disparity manifests itself in the inability of many regions to host tourist resorts because of inadequate infrastructure and poor accessibility, poverty and a lack of human resources with the appropriate qualifications. It should be noted that national tourism planning as well as Gunawan's diagnosis are about forms of tourism that concentrate on tourism resorts, largely modelled on the Nusa Dua concept. It is in resort development that the government has invested considerable effort throughout the years. In doing so, it is hoped that 'quality tourism' will be encouraged, attracting the 'upmarket tourism customer' (Sammeng 1995).

Under the New Order the responsibility for managing tourism was distributed over two main levels of government: the national and the provincial. For the provinces, the national 5-Year Plans were adapted to the specific needs and requirements of the regions in terms of *Repelita Daerah*, or *Repelitada*. These provincial development plans exacerbated the fragmentation of decision making in the implementation of and responsibilities for tourism development. The national government was reluctant to transfer authority for programmes which promised to produce large financial benefits to provincial levels. This applied to the accommodation sector and the associated travel agencies rated in the four- and five-star category, generating the government-targeted 'quality tourism.' The concept of 'quality tourism' formed a reflection of the government's principle of economic growth and political stability. While 'quality tourism' supposedly contributed to the former through accommodating 'rich' tourists, it practised the latter through the formula of controlled tourism programmes. Government agencies and offices (*kantor wilayah*, or short *kanwil*) were established in the provinces to control the tourism industry and raise the number of tourist arrivals, particularly in the 'quality' category. The revenues generated by the four- and five-star category hotels (that add a 21 per cent service and government tax to their bills) flowed directly to Jakarta. Airlines and travel agents, hotels and tour operators based in Jakarta or overseas controlled much of the tourist sector (Guinness 1994). As a consequence, the local people in the provinces had only a fleeting acquaintance with a large percentage of the profits from tourist traffic. Procedures relating to land acquisition, tenure and utilization, and the management of star-rated hotels and resorts did not fall under the authority of the regional government (Kumorotomo n.d.). And, as the analysis of the tourism planning process has shown, tourist flows were strictly controlled through the identification of tourism development areas by the national development plans. The interesting part of tourism development for the local level materializes in those sectors that for a long time have been looked down on as 'inferior' by the national government: the domestic market and unorganized international tourism or backpackers' tourism, which is inappropriately called 'low-cost' tourism and which focuses on the non-star-rated accommodation, local facilities, the small restaurants, and tour guides. This is the domain of municipal governments which falls under the jurisdiction of the *Dinas Pariwisata*. In contrast to the *kanwil* which is under *Depparpostel*, the *Dinas Pariwisata* functions under the auspices of the Ministry of Home Affairs. The *Dinas Pariwisata* issues regulations on and licences for the small-scale tourism industry. As Timothy (1998a:61) points out, this division of tasks between national, provincial, and local levels is not based on co-operation, it is outright competition between the departments which collect parallel statistical information which represents a huge waste of time and money.

Critics point to large resort developments, particularly resort enclaves, as being major contributors to the negative impacts of tourism (Harrison 1992, Wood 1993). Not only are they often out of scale with the indigenous landscape and ways of life, it is argued, but they consume large quantities of natural resources (land and water) and capital which could be more usefully spent in other ways. The involvement of outside investors is necessary because of the large capital requirements which inhibit the participation of local people. The result is twofold: the community is deprived of its ecological and economic resources, while compensation in terms of new employment opportunities fails to emerge. Management positions often go to outsiders, for few local people have the appropriate skills. Local residents are often denied access to resources, such as beaches, which they previously used, and reap few benefits from the developments. Besides the economic costs, large-scale resorts entail environmental and social costs which can be detrimental to a country's development. The answer, critics say, lies in smaller developments which are less disruptive, have more modest capital requirements which permit local participation, are associated with higher multipliers and smaller leakages, leave control in local hands, are more likely to fit in with indigenous activities and land uses, and generate greater local benefits (Wall & Long 1996).

Generally speaking, central governments have not been successful in organizing tourism in developing countries. The market is differentiated and only coincides in part with the objectives of the state-controlled tourism industry. The needs and tastes of Western visitors are different from those of tourists from the Asian growth markets (Japan and the Newly Industrializing

Countries in Asia), not to mention the domestic markets that emerge in many developing countries blessed with growing prosperity and political stability. Moreover, there are indications that the Western market is becoming fragmented because of changing consumer tastes for highly specialized and individualized programmes and accommodation that resort tourism cannot supply (Urry 1995). Where the large-scale, state-controlled sector fails, the ever-present small-scale enterprises can make their mark, offering a vast array of consumer goods and services. This small-scale sector crosscuts the boundaries between the formal, licensed, state-controlled market and the unlicensed, uncontrolled, partially 'illegal' economic activities of local tourism industries (Dahles 1998b; Dahles & Bras 1999a).

The New Order government was reluctant to facilitate 'low-cost' tourism for several reasons. First and foremost among them was that the type of visitor who is attracted by low-cost tourism was associated with drug-taking hippies, alleged to have a detrimental effect on local communities (McTaggert 1977). Second, and perhaps more importantly, low-cost tourism involved local participation at a *kampung* and village level which was viewed by most development planners in Indonesia as 'traditional.' The rub is that traditional culture was at best seen as no asset to development and at worst a hindrance, invariably posing a problem to the national government because of its alleged backwardness and resistance to change (Dove 1988). Towards the mid-1990s, the national planners realized that the preferences and tastes of foreign tourists were changing and the government started to exhibit a different attitude towards tourism development. Large-scale resort development was questioned and the benefits of small-scale tourism were explored (Hartono 1997). In a meeting of international tourism experts in Yogyakarta in 1995, the Director General of Tourism, Sammeng, recognized that tourism trends in the 1990s indicated that many travellers were seeking alternatives to beach-oriented resort holidays. Therefore, the government agreed to encourage small-scale projects, especially in the outer islands, to support tourism developments in destination areas which were as yet underdeveloped. Local people and ethnic groups were supposed to be cast in the role of key players in tourism development so as to accomplish the development objectives of the recent national Tourism Master Plan. Local and ethnic groups were ascribed prominent positions in the promotion of tourism by the Jakarta government, which saw this as a strategy to unify and modernize the country.

THE EMERGENCE OF *PANCASILA* TOURISM

The New Order regime designed its own distinctive style of government which it chose to characterize as *pembangunan* (development), even styling itself

Orde Pembangunan and former President Suharto being officially known as the *Bapak Pembangunan*, the 'father of development' (Dove 1988:10). To achieve the ambitious projects outlined in the 5-Year Development Plans, the New Order never ceased to stress that stability and centrally directed government were essential prerequisites for progress. Seeking justification the Suharto government turned to the *pancasila* ideology to legitimize these claims. *Pancasila* as state ideology had been designed in pre-Independence days primarily by Sukarno as a foundation for what at present is known as the Old Order. It attempted to establish a compromise between the divergent social, cultural, and religious forces which were given voice in the debates that preceded the proclamation of Indonesian Independence on August 17, 1945, this disunity being most clearly shown over the issue of whether the new state would be an Islamic or a secular state. Sukarno's answer was that it should be neither. The new Indonesia should be a '*pancasila* state,' which implied belief in one supreme being, national unity, a humanitarian society, a consensus-based democracy, and prosperity for all Indonesian people (Dharmaputera 1988:150).[8] Today, Indonesia is the world's largest Muslim nation; approximately 85 per cent of Indonesia's population subscribe to Islam. However, the country is neither governed according to Islamic law, nor strictly secular. Based on *pancasila*, the New Order regime emphasized religious tolerance. As Hitchcock (1996) points out, the 'belief in one God' is the first principle of the *pancasila* state code, but which religion is not specified. Indonesian citizens must believe and in theory they can belong to any religion, but in practice the state emphasizes world religions such as Islam and Christianity, often at the expense of indigenous belief systems.

Given the historical facts that Indonesia was strongly characterized by cultural diversity in pre-colonial times and that Western influences have not eliminated but strengthened and simultaneously complicated this diversity,[9] *pancasila* has been widely regarded as a rhetorical instrument. As Dharmaputera (1988) explains, the designers of the Indonesian nation state attempted to offer the Indonesian people a 'wise' solution so that they could obviate the seemingly insoluble dilemma of becoming an Islamic state or a secular state. Besides offering a supreme compromise, *pancasila* claimed to allow all groups in Indonesian society the room not only to maintain their own identities, but also to contribute to the whole nation according to their particular beliefs. Within the spirit of *pancasila* all are treated equally in terms of rights and obligations. *Pancasila* is rooted in, and hence has to be understood in the light of, a 'common culture' based upon the notions of unity, balance, and harmony. The designers of this ideology intended *pancasila* to provide the bare bones of a national framework within which differences are neither suppressed nor allowed to be completely antagonistic to one another.

The intensive campaign of instruction in the state philosophy that the government started in 1978 may be cited as an illustration of the contrivance of this national motto. An integral part of this campaign was a programme called '*P4*,' signifying the four Ps of its Indonesian name (*Pedoman Penghayatan dan Pengamalan Pancasila*) meaning roughly, 'Guide to the Realization and Application of *Pancasila*.' The general aim of this campaign was to anchor the ideology firmly within the consciousness of the educated elite which was supposed to carry it to the rest of the society. Therefore, the first to be instructed were civil servants, the principal aim being to motivate state employees to implement the third 5-Year Development Plan with 'greater commitment and enthusiasm' (Sullivan 1991:12).[10] In 1982 all mass organizations were ordered to acknowledge *pancasila* as their basic principle, and '*Pancasila* Moral Education' (*Pendidikan Moral Pancasila*) was made compulsory in all state schools. Another component of this *pancasila* education was the organized visits to the country's cultural masterpieces like the great temples of Central Java, which will be elaborated on in the following chapters. The ideology of *pancasila* became the measure of acceptable civic behaviour – defining who was a 'good' Indonesian citizen, in other words it was an instrument to impose conformity and to legitimize government policies, a method to smooth over the cracks of social cleavages, and the promise of a prosperous future. As Sullivan (1991:14) argues, this ideology contains not so much a theory, plan, or strategy as a picture: 'a picture of the good society.' It is a picture or image that contains all the ingredients of the 'imagined political community' (Anderson 1991:6) of the fully-developed, modern Indonesian society. Above all else, this society is united: it is a 'decent' nation free from cleavages and embodying endless cultural, ethnic, religious, and socio-economic diversity but invariably undivided by it.

The challenge of governing Indonesia is not only its sheer magnitude of scale and ethnic diversity, but the very imbalances that the *pancasila* ideology attempted to blur: the imbalances caused by the cultural and political dominance of the Javanese (who comprise over 40 per cent of the population) and by the economic dominance of the Chinese. The image of national culture and harmonious co-existence of the ethnic groups created by the New Order regime was based on a very fragile unity. Despite its efforts at integration, the government was made painfully aware of some of the non-integrative measures that contributed to the existing inequalities between Java and the Outer Islands. Javanese domination of Indonesian society is hard to overlook. Not only does the number of Javanese in governmental office and the army leadership exceed a proportional share in relation to the rest of the population of Indonesia, but also the values and traditions of ethnic Javanese society have overwhelmingly contributed to the production of national symbols and influenced the political style of the elite, characterized by an excessive respect for authority and order

(Wessel 1994:40-1). This political style is the source of deeply felt dissatisfaction in the non-Javanese areas where, in addition to their ever-present dominance in the central government, a substantial number of Javanese have been settled by government-sponsored transmigration programmes. The government's policy on ethnic minorities[11] gives the task of 'bridging' ethnic differences to the dominant groups in society, like the Javanese. The latter are supposed to instigate change among isolated groups, introduce *bahasa Indonesia*, the national language, and to eliminate 'primitive' rituals in exchange for 'proper' religion, in other words, the principles of *pancasila* (Lenhart 1994). The rigorous enforcement of national unity by the New Order government has not diminished, but instead has strengthened the claims and struggles for independence in Irian Jaya, Aceh, and East Timor (Wessel 1994:41-5).

In order to shore up such a fragile unity, the founders of the state set out to forge a national identity by building a national culture based on the *pancasila* ideology (Hooker & Dick 1993:4). Theoretically, the national culture is defined as a combination of the highest cultural achievements of *all* the regions of Indonesia, a hybrid mix of the best of existing cultures in the nation. In actual fact, only the major ethnic groups, defined as 'peak cultures' (with the exclusion of the Chinese), have been allowed to contribute to the new national culture (Picard 1993). Ethnic minorities were not perceived as specific cultures, but were lumped together as if they shared an overriding common cultural pattern, that is, their alleged 'primitive' and 'isolated' nature. Therefore, in the definition of the national culture, a few superior cultures – among which the Javanese culture is the highest valued – were distinguished from inferior cultures, which were excluded from contributing to the national culture (Picard 1997:201). While the New Order can be said to have succeeded in creating a recognizable national culture, political dominance by the Javanese has inevitably led to Javanese culture being accorded greater prominence than most others in that new national culture. Despite this predominance, the New Order government realized that the richness of the plural traditions of Indonesia's ethnic groups contribute greatly to the vitality of the new national culture. In an effort to pay more attention to non-Javanese cultures, the Ministry of Education and Culture has promoted regional cultures under the spiritual resources policy of the *pancasila* approach to religion, art, folklore, and crafts (Hooker & Dick 1993:4).

The principles of *pancasila* have been expressed in the official discourse in manyfold ways. Sceptical Western academics have been inclined to dismiss *pancasila* ideology as mere rhetoric or an 'ambiguous substitution of romantic imagery for policy' (Warren 1989:48), but it has also been pointed out that the very ambiguity of the *pancasila* idiom has transformed it into an instrument for the critical re-evaluation of current policy (Warren 1989). Elements of local tradition have been reworked by the state in the *pancasila* rhetoric to become instruments for political control and ideological tools, lending the appearance of cultural continuity to state control. In this process state and local actors have both been continually engaged in the construction of 'national' tradition, in a dialogue consisting of representations and misrepresentations, in which the outcome is by no means predetermined by the state (Warren 1989:48-9).

In the case of tourism, the concern for 'national unity in diversity' was demonstrated by the policy of the regionalization of Indonesia as a tourist product. Although regionalization has become a vigorous force in tourism policy only under the sixth 5-Year Plan, the development of tourist objects in Indonesia did evolve as a basic tool for the preservation of the heritage of the imagined national community. As Pemberton (1994:9) notes, New Order politics were founded on a routine reference to 'traditional values' and 'cultural inheritance,' a routine reference that is emerging in tourism policy as well. In terms of culture, heritage refers to material forms such as monuments, historical or architectural remains, and artefacts on display in museums; or non-material forms such as philosophy, traditions, and art in all their manifestations; the celebration of great events or personalities in history; distinctive ways of life; and education as expressed through literature and folklore (Wiendu Nuryanti 1996:251). Among the items that may constitute cultural heritage, built heritage, i.e. historic buildings and structures, has taken a prominent place, along with the remains of 'high' culture (like the arts). In this respect the New Order adhered to the 'culture as product' approach, described in the previous chapter. Only recently have lifestyles and folklore been recognized as a *cultural* heritage, culture in this case being understood as 'process.' The New Order policy of cultural or heritage tourism reflected the bias in favour of historic buildings and great works of art. The first 'remains of the past' that were designated 'National Heirlooms' were the monumental Hindu and Buddhist temples of Central Java, Prambanan and Borobudur, the temple complexes of Bali (Tanah Lot and Besakih), the palaces (*kraton*) of Yogyakarta and Solo and their sophisticated court culture expressed in dance, music, philosophy, and ceremonies (Hamengkubowono X 1993, Gertler 1993). Only recently have ethnic traditions, folk art, and 'everyday life' been added to the list of national heritage, in the course of which these cultural practices have been transformed into orchestrated cultural performances.

Browsing through travel brochures issued by the Indonesian government, it is impossible to escape the sense that Indonesia as a tourist destination has been designed according to the principles of *pancasila*, mediating an image of 'endless diversity' co-existing in harmonious unity.[12] This endless diversity has been reconstructed on the remnants of material culture: archaeological and architectural treasures, of the pre-colonial and colonial eras. As many of these are temples, the politics of religion blend ambiguously with the politics of culture and tourism in their preservation and use. The temples of Java, Hindu and Buddhist, dating from the eighth to the fifteenth centuries, have been rescued from decay by extensive restoration projects which have included the construction of paved pathways leading to and around the sites, rest-room facilities, and licensed hawker stalls. A large concrete amphitheatre with elaborate lighting is located just behind the Prambanan temple complex in Central Java, in which a four-night ballet based on the Ramayana epic takes place monthly. At one level, these monuments like Borobudur and the Ramayana spectacles of Prambanan represent a national heritage, but at another level they relate to a Javanese past and, more exactly, a pre-Islamic Javanese past (Adams 1997). The restoration of the once crumbling sites made them more accessible not only to foreign tourists, but most of all for Indonesians. As is generally the case with heritage sites, these temples attract a mixture of domestic and international visitors with the domestic component representing up to ten times the number of foreign tourists (Wiendu Nuryanti 1996:254). Many Indonesians come as tourists on the 'Indonesian Package Tour' (cf. Chapter 1; Adams 1998) or on state-orchestrated visits organized by their schools or employers, but some come as devotees (Adams 1997). The delicate relationship between the 'culture as product' approach and the 'culture as process' approach may be illustrated by the issue of whether the monumental temple complexes can be used for religious purposes. Until the early 1990s the Hindu and Buddhist communities in Central Java were denied access to the temple complexes of Borobudur and Prambanan for religious worship for preservation reasons. The religious communities were highly conscious of their minority position in post-Independence Indonesia dominated by Islam and made great efforts to gain access to the temple sites for their religious activities. It was only in 1992 – nine years after Hindu new year, *nyepi*, and the Buddhist *waicak* were declared national holidays – that the new 'Law on Cultural Assets' granted permission to officially recognized religious groups to celebrate their sacred days at the temples and to access the holy sites for worship (Kagami 1997). Large religious celebrations and individual worshippers bringing their offerings have become important assets in the marketing of cultural tourist experiences at the temple complexes of Prambanan and Borobudur.

The ambiguity that characterizes the temples as place of worship as well as object of the tourist gaze is also found in attitudes to the remains of Muslim kingdoms (old mosques, palaces, and gravesites). The Hindu and Buddhist temples, Christian churches, and mosques not only represent the inspiration Indonesian culture derived from great civilizations, they also demonstrate the belief in one supreme being. Places of worship which do not comply with one the five religions defined as such in the state ideology – like the Chinese (Confucian) temples – are not displayed as tourist objects. The buildings dating from the era of European penetration, erected by the Portuguese, Dutch, and British, are not only reminders of the colonial rule, but conversely also places of political pilgrimage, where the bloody wars waged by native people against colonial governments and the victory and independence of the Indonesian people are commemorated and where powerful images of consensus and national unity are evoked. The image of Indonesia as a tourist destination being constructed in terms of civilization, monotheism, consensus, and unity unequivocally reproduces the principles of *pancasila*. Therefore, the dominant tourism discourse in Indonesia can be designated '*pancasila* tourism.' Discussing the geographical area of Central Java, Gertler (1993:15-16) identified the 'unity-in-diversity' principle as the guiding theme of regional tourism development – a significant observation which will be further elaborated in the next chapter.

The government deliberately cultivated and preserved, not the whole of what anthropologists term culture, but only a small group of selected items – the built environment, material culture, and expressions of 'high' culture. These can be marketed as tourist 'objects' (Adams 1990). It is not easy to display and market intangibles such as kinship structures and rules of land use, or 'culture as process' like the etiquette of interpersonal interaction. Where the local traditions have not included marketable elements such as elaborate dances and costumes, enthusiastic officials have sometimes invented them. The Ramayana performances at the Prambanan temple open air theatre serves as an illustration of 'invented tradition.'

The Indonesian state's discourse on nationhood has sought to downplay ethnicity not only in favour of region. Picard (1993:93) argues that the discourse of regional culture implies 'its decomposition into discrete cultural elements, to be sieved through the filter of national ideology and sorted out: those deemed appropriate to contribute to the development of the [national culture] should be salvaged and promoted, whereas those deemed too primitive or emphasizing local ethnic identity should be eradicated.' As Wood (1997:14) demonstrates, this regionalization is visually evident at *Taman Mini Indonesia Indah*. Aimed mainly at domestic tourists and promoted through school textbooks as the place to learn about all of Indonesia, the park contained twenty-seven pavilions, each representing one of Indonesia's provinces, with a representative 'customary house' as its centrepiece. It was the province, not the ethnic group(s) living within its boundaries that became the source of culture under the New Order (Hitchcock 1998). *Taman Mini Indonesia Indah* has come to represent Indonesia's 'peak cultures' as frozen images, showpieces of the Suharto era, but failing to reflect Indonesia's changing social and cultural realities.

TOURISM AND ETHNIC REVIVAL

The Indonesian government under Suharto attempted to control ethnicity and to use it. The negative aspect is that ethnic and regional movements have recurrently threatened national unity and the establishment of a national culture, but undoubtedly indigenous cultures have provided a source of traditions and symbols that can be used to construct national identity. The policies of the state, especially the tourism policy, encouraged traditional cultures partly to mask these imbalances. The tourism industry, being mostly Jakarta-led, constituted a vital force imposing the *pancasila*-based values and structures of modern Indonesian society on to those ethnic groups which were fated to be 'developed' on behalf of tourism (Adams 1998). As has been observed by Picard (1997:196), ethnicity has become the fashion in Jakarta, to the extent that the media were even talking about an 'ethnic revival.' Exhibitions of ethnic arts and crafts, dance and music performances by troupes and orchestras from the outer islands, and government-sponsored television programmes which show the variety of Indonesian peoples provide constant manifestations of the celebrated cultural diversity (Graburn 1997). Rather than denying the appeal of ethnicity, the New Order resorted to the strategy of disempowerment and incorporation. Not only were ethnic identities domesticated by the state, they were also being enlisted to contribute to the process of nation-building. While the expression of ethnic identity appears to have been officially sanctioned, it will have only for as long as it remained at the level of cultural display (Kipp 1993) – and even then, the kinds of cultural differences that could be displayed were strictly defined by the state. What has emerged is a folklorist vision of ethnic cultures, targeting two audiences: first and foremost, Indonesians themselves, who were expected to endorse a state-contrived version of their national cultural heritage and, second, foreign visitors who were expected to admire the country's famed tourist objects. Picard remarks:

> Needless to say, this showcase vision does not acknowledge that which forms the core of a culture – language, religion, legal system, economic practices, social organization, and so on – and that which sustains the sense of identity of the participants in this culture. On the contrary, the destruction of traditional economic patterns, the plundering of the environment, and the depreciation of local knowledge that ensue from the policy of national 'development' are conducive to the deculturation of religion and the erosion of the ritual function of the arts (1997:198).

What we have actually been witnessing, is a policy emphasizing provincial differentiation against the background of national unity. This process is not synonymous with cultural regionalization that emerges against the background of homogenizing impacts of globalization (cf. Chapter 1), but with government-led 'provincialization' which is a form of nationalization, i.e. imposing national structures and values upon ethnic groups and converting them into administrative units and one of the manifestations of national culture. Provincialization masks the ongoing 'Indonesianization' which is effectuated through the domestication of ethnic cultures and construction of a contrived regional identity (Picard 1997:200).

CASE STUDIES

The effects of state-directed regionalization, however, can vary greatly among and between regions. It may be obvious that tourism development – although generally expected to be economically beneficial to many dislocated areas – is quite problematic in terms of ethnic revival posing the threat of segregation. State-led tourism development in terms of Indonesia's 'endless diversity' has strengthened the ethnic identity of, for example, the Toraja of South Sulawesi in relation to their close neighbours, the Bugis, not to mention state and church authorities (Adams 1997). The prestigious image of their island as a tourist paradise has empowered the Balinese economically and culturally (Picard 1990, 1993, 1995, 1997), but without bringing them more political autonomy and at the cost of becoming a colony of the Jakartan rich as some scholars have argued (Aditjondro 1995). However, detrimental tourism has undeniably made the Balinese self-conscious of their culture (Picard 1995:60). Among the Toba Batak the touristification of their rituals has generated fears of losing their identity and authenticity (Hutajulu 1994), while large-scale resort development on Lombok has led to the expropriation of Sasak landowners and the destruction of their tourism enterprises by Javanese developers who were supported by military force (Kamsma & Bras 1999).

Although the pressures exerted by 'Jakarta' to conform to the set standards of '*pancasila* tourism' may have been strong and, additionally, the process of touristification may have led to the production of a more simplified and serialized version of local culture, the native populations are never passive victims of 'external' demands (Wood 1997:14). As Picard (1995:46) argues, the question of which ways the new meaning a culture acquires for its bearers by being promoted as a tourist attraction alters the view that a society takes of itself should be raised. It is highly possible that communities could turn tourism into a new power source to position themselves on the diversified map of Indonesian tourism areas. To investigate the spectrum of experiences and reactions to tourism development in Indonesia, I shall briefly discuss a number of cases which I found well-documented in the literature: the Balinese, the

Toraja of South Sulawesi, the Toba Batak of North Sumatra and the Sasak of Lombok, drawing largely on the work of other scholars who have conducted detailed studies on the impact of tourism on these ethnic groups.[13]

The Balinese

Picard's (1990, 1993, 1995, 1997) analyses suggest that tourism development in Bali has contributed significantly to the central government's effort to channel ethnicity in non-threatening ways: first, by delimiting the realm of ethnic culture to artistic display and, second, by subordinating ethnicity to regional and religious identity. In the process, Balinese culture has been fundamentally transformed. Having served as a model for future development of tourism in the archipelago for a long time, Bali enjoyed a privileged position in the New Order government's goals. First, as the prime tourist destination of the country, its arts symbolized Indonesia as a whole and were used to enhance the prestige of Indonesian culture abroad; second, as the acknowledged heirs to the Hindu heritage of the great Hindu-Javanese kingdoms, Balinese arts benefited from the *pancasila*-based cultural politics of the New Order. As one of the 'peak cultures,' Balinese culture shared the position of Javanese 'high culture' (Picard 1997:201).

Tourism policy in Bali had been taken out of the hands of the provincial government and vested in the hands of the central government (Kumorotomo n.d.). The Balinese authorities retained little say in the Jakarta government's decision to trade Bali's charms to fill the coffers of the state, and they were not consulted about the Master Plan that restricted tourism development on the island to the Nusa Dua area. Faced with a *fait accompli*, the provincial government nevertheless attempted to appropriate tourism as a tool for regional development. In 1971, in response to the Master Plan, the Balinese authorities proclaimed their own conception of the kind of tourism they deemed the most suitable to their island – namely what they termed 'cultural tourism.' The artistic and religious traditions which had made the name of Bali famous all over the world provided its main attraction as a tourist destination, thus turning Balinese culture into the most valuable resource for the island's economic development (Picard 1995:51). In 1988 the governor of Bali scheduled fifteen areas for development as tourist zones, thereby essentially lifting the restrictions imposed by the Master Plan on the construction of large hotels and facilities outside the initial Nusa Dua resorts (Picard 1997:203).

It is obvious that tourism has boosted the economic growth of Bali. There is also a downside. The growing encroachment of foreign, and even more importantly, Jakarta-based interests, coupled with the environmental degradation remain matters of serious concern. The Balinese are apprehensive about outsiders, in particular the Javanese migrant workers and wealthy Jakarta investors, usurping their island. The tourism boom has generated a lively debate among Balinese intellectuals and the middle classes about the ability of the Balinese to maintain their distinctive culture. Despite the ongoing concern about tourism, the Balinese appear to be genuinely proud of the fame of their culture abroad and are eager to show their cultural traditions to the tourists (Picard 1995:54). By perceiving their culture simultaneously as a 'cultural heritage' which they should look after, and as 'tourist capital' which they could exploit, the Balinese turn Jakarta's decision to promote their island as an international tourist destination to their own advantage. Tourism makes their culture their main bargaining asset when dealing with the Indonesian government (Picard 1990:74).

The Toraja of South Sulawesi

The Torajans inhabit the forests of the rugged mountains of the south-western peninsula of Sulawesi (formerly Celebes). For centuries, they were raided for slaves and gold by their neighbours, the Bugis and Makassarese. Resisting Islam which established itself on the coast, the Torajans were converted to Christianity under Dutch colonial rule. The missionaries combated pagan ritual and ancestor worship. For a long time, the Torajans were regarded as poor, backward, and primitive, an image which persisted into the 1960s. Owing to increasing outmigration, however, in the late 1960s the economy improved and cultural traditions and ritual underwent a renaissance. In the early 1970s *Tana Toraja* (Toraja Land) was 'discovered' for tourism and tourist arrivals grew quickly. Domestic tourism to *Tana Toraja* was especially flourishing, outnumbering foreign tourists by four to one (Adams 1997:172). The attraction of *Tana Toraja* as a tourist destination is based largely on claims of the 'authenticity' of the pagan funeral rituals (Volkman 1990:92-4).

Toraja gained celebrity in the national and international tourist market in the mid-1980s because of a successful campaign led by then director-general of tourism, Joop Avé, declaring *Tana Toraja* the 'touristic prima donna of South Sulawesi' (Adams 1997:159). This declaration boosted ethnic pride among the Torajans, who for centuries had endured the domination of the Islamic Bugis and Makassarese, both of whose cultures featured among the few 'peak cultures in all of Indonesia' (Antweiler 1995:127). The government-supported tourism boom in *Tana Toraja* fuelled long-simmering ethnic antagonisms between the ethnic groups of South Sulawesi. While the Toraja began to represent 'the South Sulawesians' for tourists, the government felt obliged to take measures to diversify tourism and to improve the facilities largely lacking outside *Tana Toraja* and directing the tourist flows to the Bugis and Makasarese as well. Efforts to strengthen the regional profile of the province under the acronym *Sulsel* (for *Su*lawesi *Sel*atan: South Sulawesi) were manifold. In 1991, *Miniatur Sulawesi*, a cultural park with adat houses and cultural activities modelled on the lines of the *Taman Mini Indonesia Indah* in Jakarta, was inaugurated (Adams 1997, Antweiler 1995).

As Adams notes (1997:172), the Indonesian government's attempts to foster national integration through tourism have not been entirely unsuccessful. Undeniably the touristic promotion of *Tana Toraja* improved the infrastructure in South Sulawesi, making travel within the region easier and more common. Among the Torajans it fostered a sense of *ethnic pride* as their quest for maintaining their traditional funeral rites in the face of the disapproval of the church authorities was strengthened, as well as national pride in terms of gaining the position of a new 'peak culture' (Adams 1997:175).

The Toba Batak of Sumatra

As had been the case for the Torajans, the Toba Batak people in North Sumatra, who form a Christian enclave in a Muslim society, had been discouraged from continuing their pre-Christian ritual practices, first by Christian missionaries, and later by the government because it failed to fit in with one of the five officially recognized religions in Indonesia. Once the area around Lake Toba and Samosir Island had become a major tourist destination, tourism helped to revive Batak ceremonial practice, especially one of their most important sacrificial ceremonies: the *Mangalahat Hobo Lae-lae*, the buffalo sacrificial ceremony (Hutajulu 1994:2). In the context of tourism Toba Bataks were offered a chance to practise as well as promote their ceremonies without fear of being banned from the church and being made to feel ashamed in society at large.

As Hutajulu (1994) relates, the four-day ceremony of the buffalo sacrifice, which seemed to have passed into oblivion, was revived by the Indonesian government, in particular the Tourism Department of North Sumatra, in conjunction with 'Visit Indonesia Year 1991.' The Toba Bataks attempted to adhere as closely as possible to the 'old way' of performing the whole ceremony as an attraction for international as well as domestic tourists. With this goal the Batak people put enormous effort into creating as 'authentic' and as 'exotic' a performance as possible, even though this involved changes in the ceremonial structure and content, and in the end in the creation of a ceremony that was not part of the tradition it claimed to represent. The buffalo sacrifice was turned into a theatrical performance. The whole event was sponsored by the provincial government and the 'natives' were paid for their performance. To make the ceremony accessible and understandable to an audience of tourists from other Indonesian areas, *bahasa Indonesia* was introduced as a ceremonial language. Hutajulu even mentions a synopsis distributed to the audience which was written in Indonesian and English (1994:12). To adapt the ceremony even more commodiously to tourist needs, it has been shortened to one and half hours, parts that were formerly performed in the dark have had to be played with the lights on (otherwise the tourist gaze would be wasted), entertaining elements have been stressed, while the climatic 'violent' killing has been shorn of much of its rough character (Hutajulu 1994:14-15).

While the interest of the government was to stimulate the traditional ceremonial practice with an eye to benefiting tourism, while not targetting promotion of the 'unity and diversity' of the national culture, the aim of the Toba Batak was to present their cultural identity in the context of Indonesian culture. It may seem pretty obvious that both interests coincided under the New Order cultural tourism policy. In this way the new tourist context provided an opportunity for the Batak ceremonial participants to assert their Batak identity and tradition, while redefining them as Indonesians before a domestic as well as before an international audience.

The Sasak of Lombok

For a long time the island of Lombok passed unnoticed as a tourist destination overshadowed by the prominence of its closest neighbour, Bali. In the latter half of the 1980s, when developers reached out in search of new areas, the regional tourism office of Lombok started promoting the island with slogans that alluded to Bali. After all, the western part of Lombok had been under Balinese rule for a long time. In the early days of tourism, Lombok presented itself the 'Bali of twenty years ago,' claiming the status of a 'paradise lost' (Bras 1997, Kamsma & Bras 1999). While tourist promotion used to highlight the natural beauty of the island, once Lombok started to assert its own identity, the focus shifted to the local culture of the Sasak, its indigenous inhabitants. The Sasak cultural heritage, particularly the architecture of the traditional houses and life in the villages, became the centrepoints of tourism promotion. The *lumbung*, the traditional rice barn, emerged as the landmark of Lombok (Bras 1997:2). Sasak villages in Central Lombok were constructed as repositories of 'primitive, untouched culture' by the Master Plan for the province of Nusa Tenggara Barat (NTB), consisting of the islands of Lombok and Sumbawa. As Bras (1997:5) argues, these villages with high-pitched, thatched-roof huts and *lumbung*, made from bamboo, earth, woven grass, and palm leaves, were transformed into living museums, as the provincial government issued a building regulation which prohibited the inhabitants to 'modernize' their homes, by installing electricity or converting to tiled roofs.

Outside these government-approved enclaves of ethnic identity, the indigenous people of Lombok were dealt with in a different way. The Master Plan for the province NTB projected large-scale resorts to be constructed under control of the Lombok Tourism Development Corporation armed with Javanese and foreign investments. In the south of the island this corporation purchased large plots of land from the Sasak owners for little money, which the corporation promptly resold for a large profit (Kamsma & Bras 1999). In another area, Gili Trawangan, a tiny island off the north-west coast of Lombok, local Sasak entrepreneurs successfully accommodated backpackers, young tourists who came for the snorkelling and to experience the simple life and were satisfied with modest facilities. A victim of its own success Gili Trawangan attracted outside investors. Backed by the provincial Master Plan, the island was designated for resort development and the local people were summoned to clear the area – which initially they refused to do. In 1995 the provincial government sent the army to demolish the local businesses and displaced the locals to the fringe of the island. As this case shows, the Indonesian government does not eschew violence if ethnic groups get in the way of national business interests. The revival of ethnic identity is permitted as long as it does not counter Indonesian national economy or ideology.

CONCLUSIONS

As Wai-Teng Leong (1997:82) pointed out, the marketing of tourism is not unlike international diplomacy: it is a field that involves national image-management. Indonesia under the New Order regime provided an excellent example of a state concerned with projecting wholesome and 'politically correct' images to the global market and the international polity, as well as the domestic audience in its efforts to advance the process of nation-building. It may not be a pure coincidence that in New Order Indonesia tourism was placed under the Ministry of Tourism, Post and Telecommunications, revealing that it was regarded as an agent of communication, modernization and globalization. The state ideology of *pancasila* provided the framework within which its role of economic planner and developer and guardian of cultural and religious boundaries derived its legitimacy. Pre-colonial and colonial history and the struggle for independence were transformed into a national discourse through *pancasila* ideology and reconstructed through 'heritage tourism' which was marketed to foreign and domestic visitors. Being part of the national discourse, tourism both fuelled debates about the good or moral society and contributed to national unity and economic development.

While '*pancasila* tourism' generated an awareness of the national entity, it also conferred privileges on some local or specific groups. Faced with a multitude of cultural, historical, and geographical forms, the New Order state singled out a few for tourism. Such selectivity had implications for internal struggle and competition whereby a number of cultural groups were favoured, while others were forgotten, ignored, or worse, suppressed. Being among the chosen few had its price, as those selected had to gear their self presentation to the models that were provided and controlled by the state. The front stages of tourist spectacles and the back stages of the harsh facts of daily life were instances of impression management. These are the ways tourism brings the complex relations between ethnicity and the state to the forefront (Wai-Teng Leong 1997:86).

For the New Order government, ethnic differentiation was both a blessing and a constant source of headaches. Ethnic groups were celebrated largely because of an unsatiable desire for money. The exploitation of Bali as the county's primary tourist attraction serves as a cogent illustration of the basically economic orientation towards tourism. Ethnic minorities which were not counted among the 'peak cultures' and were seen as an embarrassment (because of their allegedly primitive state) or a threat to national unity (because of secessionist movements or the contesting of land rights), found themselves ranked among the 'prima donnas' of Indonesian tourist areas under New Order cultural tourism policy. The promotion of ethnic groups as a tourist attractions implies more than the boosting of income by the influx of foreign exchange, it means the domestication of their cultures and redefinition of identity in terms of Indonesian citizenship, which may be demonstrated by the development of Toraja funeral rites, Toba Batak sacrificial ceremonies, and Sasak village life as tourists attractions. '*Pancasila* tourism' was constructed to provide the legitimization for both stimulating and suppressing economic activity and expressions of ethnic identity.

NOTES

1 Armed conflict leads to an immediate collapse of travel arrangements. Affected are not only the areas involved in such a conflict, but also those which depend on visitors from countries which in one way or another feel involved. A good example is provided by the Gulf War in 1991 which is held responsible for the total failure of 'Visit Indonesia Year,' a promotional campaign designed to boost visitor numbers to Indonesia in the early 1990s. Following the outbreak of the Gulf War in early January 1991, the chairman of the Association of Indonesian Tour and Travel Agencies (ASITA) in Yogyakarta stated that there was a 50 per cent cancellation of bookings from Europe, an 80 per cent decline in bookings

from Australia, but no cancellations from Japan, Hong Kong and Korea (Yogya In A Week, January 18-24, 1991).

2   The term pariwisata means 'many visitors'; derived from *pari* (= many) and *wisata* (= vistor). Source: personal communication of the author with Mrs. Myra Gunawan.

3   This campaign was initiated by the Directorate General of Tourism in its Rencana Induk Pariwisata Nasional (RIPPN), supporting the resort development especially in Padang (West Sumatra), Lombok (Nusa Tenggara), and Biak (Irian Jaya) (cf. Jansen 1997:14).

4   Number of domestic tourists in Indonesia

Year	Number of domestic tourists in millions
1984	72
1985	742
1986	764
1987	787
1988	82
1989	845
1990	87
1991	896
1992	923

Source: Rosyidie (1995:V:52)

I had no opportunity to verify these figures. Rosyidie claims to have derived this information from the Central Bureau for Statistics without further specifying the sources. According to Basuki, Sigit, and Gunawan (1993:VI-1) data collection on domestic tourists in Indonesia has been carried out only for the years 1981, 1984, and 1991, and different definitions of travel were used in these three cases.

5   Looking at the ranking of international tourist arrivals in 12 tourist destinations in the Asia-Pacific area, Indonesia – one of the largest countries – has climbed from rank 11 in 1981 to rank 7 in 1992:

Ranking 1981	1992	Tourist destinations	Tourist arrivals (x 1000) 1981	1992
1	2	Singapore	2,829	5,990
2	1	Hong Kong	2,535	6,986
3	3	Thailand	2,016	5,136
4	5	Japan	1,583	3,582
5	10	Taiwan	1,409	1,873
6	6	South Korea	1,093	3,231

7	9	Malaysia	1,006	2,346
8	11	Philippines	939	1,153
9	8	Australia	937	2,603
10	4	China	714	4,172
11	7	Indonesia	600	3,064
12	12	New Zealand	478	1,056

Source: Hailin Qu & Hanqin Qui Zhang (1997:36).

6   The length of stay in Indonesia was 10.3 days on average in the mid-1990s. It varies widely among tourists from different countries. Singapore residents, who constitute about 25 per cent of international tourist arrivals, stay between 2 and 6 days; visitors from Japan and South Korea stay less than 10 days; Europeans stay about 29 days with people from Switzerland at the top with 45 days (cf. Gunawan 1997a:51).

7   The six regions in the National Tourism Development Plan add up to the whole of Indonesia (cf. Gunawan 1997a:55-56):
1.   Sumatra
2.   Java and beyond including the southern tip of Sumatra (Lampung) and Bali
3.   The lesser Sunda region including Bali, West and East Nusa Tenggara,   East Timor, East Java, and North Sulawesi
4.   Kalimantan
5.   Sulawesi and Northern Moluccas
6.   Irian Jaya and Southern Moluccas

8   On June 1, 1945, Sukarno delivered his famous speech, which from then on was known as *Lahirnya Pancasila* (The birth of the *Pancasila*). According to Sukarno, *Pancasila* – literally 'five pillars' – consisted of the following principles, arranged in the following order:
1.   *Ketuhanan Yang Maha Esa*: monotheism or the belief in one supreme being, specified in the world religions: Islam, Roman Catholicism, Protestantism, Hinduism, and Buddhism
2.   *Perikemanusiaan*: a just and civilized humanitarianism
3.   *Kebangsaan Indonesia*: Indonesian nationhood and unity
4.   *Mufakat/Democrasi*: unanimous consensus or democracy led by wise policies decided in a process of discussion and representation
5.   *Kesejahteraan Sosial*: social welfare and social justice for the whole people of Indonesia
(It should be noted that in my source of information the third principle was quoted as first for reasons unknown to me; cf. Dharmaputera 1988:150).
These five principles promise a communion of citizens in the equality of their religious beliefs; their shared humanity and tolerance for the infinite

differences in people; their shared nationality and willingness to unite with all other Indonesians regardless of ethnic, regional or economic background; under a political system based, in theory, on free consultation, deliberation, and consensus (Sullivan 1991:13).

9   The Indonesian Archipelago has been exposed to an enormous variety of cultural influences throughout history. As Hitchcock (1996) has shown in his study on the emergence of Bima (Sumbawa) as an Islamic outpost in a largely non-Muslim region, historical influences are complex and do not fit in with the neatly separated cultural layers distinguished by historians to constitute Indonesia's past. The image of different cultural layers, however, is extremely appealing to New Order historians. According to Dharmaputera, Indonesian culture is historically constituted of three cultural layers, namely the indigenous, the Indic, and the Islamic. Ideologues like Dharmaputera contend that these cultural layers have maintained their influence and significance down to the present moment. The following lengthy quotation may illustrate the legitimization of *pancasila* ideology in terms of historical continuity: 'None of these layers, however, can be explained independently of the influence of the others. With the exception of few in extremely remote and isolated areas, we can say in general that no layer remains in its 'pure' and original form. This means that the Indic and the Islamic elements in the Indonesian culture, very deep and real and pervasive as they indeed are, cannot be sufficiently explained solely in terms of their formal doctrines and teachings. At the same time, Indonesian culture, thus, has to be understood in terms of interaction between the three cultural layers. It is in this perspective that we can speak about an Indonesian 'common culture,' *i.e.*, the elements which are present in, and even underlie, the three cultural layers together, precisely because it is rooted in this 'common culture,' rather than being merely a reflection of one of the three cultural layers. Not only is it acceptable to all, but more than that, all of the cultural layers see themselves represented in it. ... If none of the cultural layers is dominant enough to be the foundation of the Indonesian nation as a whole, the same has to be said with regard to the influence of modern culture. The more than three hundred years of direct contact with western culture did not uproot the traditional structures of Indonesian society. On the contrary, due to colonial times in the past, it even strengthened them. This is not to say that modern influence does not exist. Indeed it does exist, and has become stronger and stronger an influence on the life of the people. It is, however, not powerful enough to form the basis for Indonesian unity. A pure modern ideology is not a viable option. And *Pancasila* is viable, precisely because it is not modern. Yet, it is not anti-modern either. *Pancasila* is an attempt to enable the traditional culture to cope with modern

problems. ... It is from these two historical realities, among others, that we can understand why *pancasila* is effective' (Dharmaputera 1988:198-9).

10   During *Repelita* III all state employees attended compulsory two-week P4 'upgrading' seminars which explained the five principles and the 1945 Constitution in depth plus the Third Five-Year Plan (Sullivan 1991).

11   Ethnic Minority affairs are under the Minister for Social Welfare of the Republic of Indonesia (*Departemen Sosial*). According to the definition of the *Departemen Sosial*, the term ethnic minority denotes 'isolated societies' on the one hand and 'complementary or dominant and sub-ordinate groups in a multiethnic society' on the other. The former are numerically small ethnic groups living in remote areas. They are regarded as remnants of an old population untouched by modern society. The latter are those ethnic groups that dominated the economic, political and social life for a long time and emerged as dominant cultures (Lenhart 1994:89-90).

12   A good example of the marketing of cultural diversity is provided by the official guidebook of the Indonesian Tourism Promotion Board, 'Discover Indonesia,' issued in 1992. Under headings like 'The Indonesian Archipelago: Destination of Endless Diversity' (p. 1) and 'Culture: The Unique Blend of Culture' (p. 31), one finds statements like: 'The Indonesian archipelago is the largest in the world to form a single state' (p. 2); 'although Indonesians are strongly aware of their unity as a nation, the country's ethnic diversity is really stupefying' (p. 8).

13   Although these cases were chosen randomly, they represent ethnic groups which adhere to non-Islamic but officially recognized religions (with the exception of the Sasak): Hinduism in the case of the Balinese and Christianity in the case of the Torajans and the Bataks.

CHAPTER 3

PANCASILA TOURISM IN THE HEART OF CENTRAL JAVA

THE MAKING OF YOGYAKARTA AS A TOURIST ATTRACTION

INTRODUCTION

New Order tourism policy has strongly favoured the Special Region of Yogyakarta and its capital, the city of Yogyakarta, since the late 1960s. Defining Yogyakarta as the second core region of tourism development[1] – second to Bali – the central government made conspicuous efforts to extend the city's communications and transportation systems, to build hotels and improve the shopping facilities, to restore historic relics, establish monuments of the 'revolutionary period' and to preserve cultural artefacts and art forms pervaded by a traditional Javanese quality (Tsuchiya 1984). The complexes of Borobudur and Prambanan, the sultan's palace, performances of gamelan music, court dances, the Ramayana ballet and shadow puppet plays, the production of batik and other handicrafts have all been promoted as 'typical' Yogyanese tourist attractions by both government agencies and the tourism industry. It was to support this promotion in an international and domestic market that Yogyakarta was re-created as the 'cultural heart of central Java' – which has become a slogan used in the marketing of the Special Region and the city to the present day. In the global tourism market, images of 'Yogyanese' cultural assets (alongside Balinese temples and dance) represent the dominant image of Indonesia which may illustrate the centrality of Yogyakarta to Indonesian identity. Although the development of international tourism has been strongly advocated by the national and provincial government, it has been the domestic market which has formed the major target for the tourism industry in Yogyakarta (see Appendix 3 for numbers of international and domestic visitors to Yogyakarta). In the domestic tourism market, the city's role in the struggle for independence became a major marketing asset. Representing the revolutionary spirit, national pride and the defeat of the colonial power – the city was the capital of the new republic of Indonesia from 1946 to 1950 – Yogyakarta emerged as the centre of political pilgrimages. The location in Yogyakarta of Gadjah Mada University, the first Indonesian university, established in 1949, along with a large number of other educational institutions, is also significant. Yogyakarta is an obligatory place for Indonesians to visit in order to learn 'Indonesianness,' national culture and history.

argued in this chapter, Yogyakarta has been re-created as the centre *la* tourism.'

arta, it seems, basked in the benevolent attention of the New Order government. The privileges bestowed upon the Special Region contrast sharply with the struggle of other areas where expressions of cultural identity are either suppressed and marginalized or selectively reconstructed and orchestrated by the central government – as has been discussed in the previous chapter. Tourism development in Yogyakarta appears to be unproblematic as the area appears to embody the 'unity in diversity' principle *par excellence*, as Gertler (1993:15) observed. The image favoured by government and tourism industry was the image of a city with a multifaceted cultural heritage: as a *historic city*, Yogyakarta represents the diverse religious and cultural traditions that have characterized the area through the ages; as a *heroic city*, Yogyakarta represents the struggle for independence and national unity; and as a *cultural city*, Yogyakarta represents the uniqueness of a 'traditional Javanese community.'[2]

Undoubtedly it has a privileged position, but being the pampered child of the New Order government has had its price. The central government – Java-based and Java-dominated – supported Javanese culture of a particular type, that of the court tradition. Images of noble grandeur and hierarchical social order served to display and confirm the authority of the state and its officials (Hatley 1993:49-50). The seemingly inextricable entanglement of politics and culture that had been institutionalized in Javanese society, became the foundation of the New Order (Vatikiotis 1993:111-12). The close integration of Yogyakarta into the national political scene, which originated with the city's role as the revolutionary capital of the young Indonesian republic, generated the politicization of artistic and cultural activities. The development of the 'tourist product' of Yogyakarta, focusing strongly on the cultural heritage of the area, illustrates the politically driven and government controlled construction of 'Javaneseness.' The recovery of tradition that occurred in Yogyakarta on behalf of tourism development has to be understood within the compass of the New Order's intensely *cultural* discourse, aimed at the preservation of a broader inheritance of 'Java' (Pemberton 1994:238). Paradoxically, Yogyakarta's function of cultural centre in the sense of producing and reproducing 'Javaneseness' was jeopardized the very moment it was designated the 'cultural heart of central Java.' The price to pay was that the city became submissive towards Jakarta, from where the new Javanese-Indonesian culture was disseminated (Mulder 1994:18). In a way, Yogyakarta experienced a process of 'Javanization' through national policies; and this process manifested itself clearly in the social construction of Yogyakarta as a tourist product. In this respect, the experience of Yogyakarta did not diverge from the experience of other Indonesian regions, the cultures of which were domesticated and folklorized by Jakarta. Having been more central physically and ideologically to the cultural discourse of the New Order regime, this process of domestication of Yogyakarta was of a longer and more intense nature than in other areas.

The loss of cultural autonomy coincided with booming tourism development. '*Pancasila* tourism' appeared to be a very successful strategy which paid off for Yogyakarta. Urbanization has been accelerated since the 1980s. While urban development projects devoted enormous efforts to the improvement of the housing conditions of the poor and to poverty reduction, the booming tourism sector left the most visible impact on the city. Until the onset of the economic crisis in 1997 there was a construction boom in high-rise buildings and the local tourism industry was flourishing. The impact of a foreign-oriented consumer culture of which international tourism is an exponent was clearly visible in the inner city (Mulder 1994). Budget accommodation, restaurants offering fast food, shops with blaring popmusic and flashing neon-lights sprung up everywhere like mushrooms. In the major tourist areas alcohol and drugs were as easily available as international tourist menus. At the same time, the number of star-rated hotels increased considerably to accommodate what the authorities preferred to call 'quality' tourism. In Malioboro Street, the central shopping area, a fancy shopping mall crammed with trendy boutiques, a large supermarket in the basement and a McDonald's Restaurant (frequented by trendily dressed local youth) offered Western amenities. Impressive bank buildings of glass and steel, more fast-food restaurants, big department stores and supermarkets and another air-conditioned shopping mall were constantly adding allure to the business area expanding east of the city centre.

All seemed booming but appearances were deceptive. Although there has been a continuous increase in the number of tourists and star-rated hotels, the future of tourism in Yogyakarta did not look as bright as might have been expected. The threats to Yogyakarta's tourism development were manifold. The increase in foreign visitors lagged behind the national objectives (as defined by the development plans) and the length of stay stagnated. Despite the image of being at the heart of Javanese culture, the city and the surrounding areas offered only a limited diversity of tourism objects. The tourism industry relied on a 'product' that had remained unchanged for more than twenty years. It maintained the ingredients and meanings constructed to suit *pancasila* propaganda. Innovations were not welcome as they threatened the carefully constructed aim of tourism. The national tourism policy demanded priority be given to the dissemination of national culture and allowed regional and local identity to thrive only within the limits of government-orchestrated displays of 'diversity.' The attractiveness of this product declined most of all for international visitors, falling victim to changing consumer preferences and tastes, and for the large share of repeat visitors who have seen the highlights and come back to Indonesia to see the rest of the 'endless diversity' promoted in the government slogans. *Pancasila* tourism may have the same effect on domestic tourism in the near future, having to cope with the diminishing appeal of New Order propaganda under the recent political transformations. Serious though these were, the most ominous threat to tourism in Yogyakarta, however, came from the national policy of regionalization that led to a withdrawal of the privileges that Yogyakarta had previously enjoyed within national policies. It was not so much the development of tourism in Sulawesi, Lombok and the other outer islands which caused repercussions in the Yogyakarta tourism industry, its major rival was the boosting of tourism development in the neighbouring province of Central Java. The historical competition and long-standing rivalries between the two provinces were refuelled by the intervention of the central government, eager to bestow favours on the province of Central Java in terms of tourism development.

This chapter discusses the double predicament in which tourism in Yogyakarta finds itself. To illuminate this dilemma it investigates the ways in which the Special Province was domesticated and folklorized to serve the central government's need for a display of the constructed heritage of the young Indonesian Republic. Then it explores how the process of regionalization came to assume the shape of a serious threat to tourism development in Yogyakarta. Describing the emergence and development of the Special Province of Yogyakarta as a tourist destination, special attention will be paid to the extent to which the Indonesian New Order government and its local representatives orchestrated the establishment and restoration of 'tourist objects' in the area. Three phases will be distinguished: first, the emergence of international and domestic tourism in Yogyakarta in the 1970s, second its heyday in the 1980s and early 1990s, and third its stagnation towards the end of the New Order regime. Questions will be raised about the ways and the extent to which the *pancasila* state ideology influenced the selection of cultural assets to be developed as tourist attractions. What, then, were the characteristics of 'cultural heritage' in Yogyakarta? How did tourism affect urban development and to what extent did the city depend on tourism for its economic growth? What were the effects of government-generated processes of regionalization? And how did efforts to put the province of Central Java on the international and national tourist map affect the prospects of tourism in Yogyakarta, and, consequently, the city's role as the 'cultural heart of central Java'?

YOGYAKARTA: A BRIEF HISTORICAL OVERVIEW[3]

Among the twenty-seven provinces of the Republic of Indonesia, Yogyakarta is distinguished by its Special Region status.[4] According to 'popular wisdom' (i.e. the dominant discourse), this status was bestowed upon the area by the government of the nascent Indonesian republic as an expression of gratitude for the support that the sultan of Yogyakarta had given to the republican troops. The sultan was installed as governor – a hereditary position – responsible only to the central government in Jakarta and not to the governor of Central Java (Selosoemardjan 1962:5). The capital city of the Special Region of Yogyakarta, bearing the same name, is located at the centre and is the only city in the entire region. Today, the city *(kotamadya)* is a separate administrative unit, while the rest of the region is divided into four *kabupaten* (sub-provincial administrative area) – Kulon Progo in the west, Sleman in the north, Bantul in the south central, and Gunung Kidul in the south and east.

Situated in the southern central part of Java, the Special Region of Yogyakarta is surrounded on three sides by the province of Central Java. To the south, it borders the Indian Ocean. The province covers an area of 3,185 square kilometres and accommodates three million people, an average of one thousand people per square kilometre. Yogyakarta is one of the most densely populated areas in the world. The population lives in small villages widely dispersed over the rural area. The city of Yogyakarta *(kotamadya)* has about 425,000 inhabitants *(Penduduk Indonesia* 1994:60). Many sources characterize the city as a big village, as the great majority of its buildings are single-storey structures and most people live in *kampung* and village hamlets scattered about the countryside in its immediate vicinity (Sullivan 1992:3). The population of Yogyakarta belongs to the ethnic group of the Javanese who live in Central and East Java and constitute by far the largest of the many ethnic groups in Indonesia. Like the other main ethnic groups, the Javanese have their own language and culture, but do not form a homogeneous group as dialects, food preferences, rituals, dress and the like vary widely (Guinness 1986).

The picture that emerges from the present-day travel guides describing the area around Yogyakarta is as follows: the area in which traditional Javanese culture thrived, known as *daerah kejawen,* extends into the Eastern part of Java and includes places like Kedu, Madiun, Malang, Kediri, Surakarta, and Yogyakarta. This area has been inhabited for thousands of years.[5] Under the rule of Hindu dynasties the world-famous religious complexes of Prambanan (Hindu) and Borobudur (Buddhist) were established in the nineth and tenth centuries.[6] These early dynasties merged into what has become known as the Mataram kingdom, a powerful and prosperous empire that ruled the entire area of central Java. In the tenth century the centre of the Mataram Kingdom was moved to East Java and fell into decay in the thirteenth century. Its position was taken over by the Majapahit empire that ruled an area larger than the island of Java for about one century. The rise of a powerful Islamic empire at the end of the sixteenth century revitalized the Mataram kingdom. In the seventeenth century one of their princes, Senopati, founded a small settlement at Kota Gede (at present a neighbourhood of Yogyakarta), which attracted traders and artists and developed into a prosperous commercial centre. Senopati's successors moved the capital of the Mataram empire several times. In the eighteenth century, the Mataram ruler completed the building of a fortified settlement in the vicinity of Kota Gede which he called Ngayogya. This name is a Javanese version of Ayodya, the mythical kingdom of Prince Rama the eponymous hero of the Ramayana. The name Yogyakarta is an abbreviation of Ngayogyokarto Hadiningrat, the name by which it was known when it was a self-governing sultanate before the Second World War.

The sultanate of Ngayogyokarto came into being after the kingdom of Mataram was divided up into two[7] separate sultanates: Surakarta and Yogyakarta in 1755. This split was brought about after years of political upheaval, punctuated by recurrent rebellions and attacks on the Dutch-controlled ruler of the old kingdom. The legitimacy of this ruler was contested by Prince Mangkubumi, a brother of the ruler, who retired to Yogyakarta where he proclaimed himself sultan. His brother was installed as the first sultan of Surakarta under the title of Paku Buwono I with the support of the colonial power. War broke out between the Dutch and their protégé on one side and Mangkubumi on the other. A treaty between the warring parties was signed in 1755, officially installing Prince Mangkubumi as ruler of Yogyakarta under the title Sultan Hamengku Buwono I. The two Javanese sultanates have been rivals ever since. Their rulers developed their courts separately. The Dutch-orchestrated partition of Java achieved permanence through the formal laws that regularized and governed the boundaries of the realms of the two central Javanese principalities (*Vorstenlanden*), laws agreed to by the rulers themselves. Within each of the kingdoms, this process of territorial regulation was accompanied by a proliferation of internal court regulations that multiplied methodically from the late eighteenth century – regulations concerning codes of dress, standards of status, and rules of conduct. In the Kratons, batik motifs, designated *keris* (ceremonial dagger) styles, and clothing fashions were defined in detail as the palace bestowed privileges of attire upon an increasingly refined, uniform gradation of courtiers (Pemberton 1994:52).

In their behaviour the people in Surakarta (also called Solo) and Yogyakarta echoed the court rivalries. They always attempted to establish an identity which was meant to be explicitly different, contrasting in every respect from the other. A cultural animosity which has persisted up to today developed between the two populations. It is revealed in subtle but distinguishable ways in the popular language, styles of dress, music, and dance (Soedjarwo 1991:230-1). This cultural animosity has even affected more modern activities, like the development of tourism – as we shall discuss below. To the present day, both courts claim to be the guardians of truly 'Javanese' traditions. Stereotypes of the cultural identity of the two cities – Solo and Yogyakarta –

are well entrenched: the austere, 'masculine' style of the court arts of Yogya-karta stands in contrast to the more refined and intricate, 'feminine' quality of those of Solo; the progressive nationalist stance adopted by the Yogyakarta sultan and his palace during the 1945 Revolution, compared with the conservatism of the Solo nobility; and the more 'dynamic' quality of life in Yogyakarta today, more closely integrated into national affairs, contrasted with the concentration on artistic activity and local issues in Solo (Hatley 1993:53). These stereotypes act strongly in favour of the promotion of the image of Yogyakarta as the major centre of Javanese culture and traditions.

Under Hamengku Buwono I Yogyakarta experienced a peaceful and prosperous period, but after his death the kingdom was once again prone to armed conflicts with the colonial powers from without and rivals for the throne from within. The British conquest of Java in 1811 brought new difficulties for the Yogyakarta sultanate. In 1812, Raffles, the Lieutenant-Governor, attacked and captured the kraton. This was the only time a Javanese court had been taken by European troops and the humiliation of the sultanate was devastating. The period that followed this defeat was characterized by increasing discontent in central Java; the aristocracy was impoverished, harvests were poor and disease spread, and the court was weakened by intrigues. In this turmoil there arose a major revolt, cultminating in the Java War (1825-50). After this war and the Dutch were re-installed as colonial power, political resistance ended and both courts, Solo and Yogyakarta, were stripped of their political power. Their role became purely decorative and, forsaking politics, they concentrated on the cultivation of the arts and etiquette. The real power lay in the hands of the Dutch Resident (the representative of the colonial power). The aristocracy was tied to the Dutch bureaucracy and depended on positions in it for their livelihood. Though the Cultivation System of plantation crops did not operate officially in Yogyakarta, arrangements existed for the production of export crops, particularly sugar cane that was manufactured into sugar in the factories that sprang up all over the area (De Graaf 1947:283). For about ninety years Yogyakarta experienced a tranquil and modestly prosperous period in which court culture blossomed and the population growth rate rose significantly. Commoners in the countryside were almost invariably farmers, primarily engaged in the production of rice, the staple food of the population. However, the extreme population density in the rural areas caused so much pressure on the land that most of the farmers lived and produced at a subsistence level. The time not spent on the land was used for petty trade or fashioning handicrafts to earn some additional income (Soedjarwo 1991).

The city of Yogyakarta has emerged as an aggregate of *kampung* (neighbourhoods inhabited by the urban poor) which have gradually spread from the residential areas around the Kraton, the Sultan's palace, to the new quarters which were established for growing numbers of state functionaries, foreigners, and those serving them (Sullivan 1992:25). In the social structure of the state the king was the centre and sole source of power, his authority reinforced by his kinsmen who as a group constituted the nobility (*sentonodalem*). This group held the top administrative positions. A core of loyal servants, the *priyayi* or *abdidalem*, recruited either from among the distant relatives of the king or from among the commoners, were there to serve him and his court.[8] The 'little people' (*wong cilik*) constituted the rest of the population (Selosoemardjan 1962:20-1). Sultan Hamengku Buwono I established a system of residential areas which reflected this hierarchical social structure. The Kraton was placed at its centre, surrounded by a walled city where most members of the nobility resided. Commoners who served the sultan and his court and who lived in the walled town did so under the system of *ngindung*. This is a system strongly influenced by the traditional values of loyalty and service to the sultan and his family. Commoners lived on the land owned by the royal family either free or for a very low rent, prepared to serve their patron whenever he required it. Often people lived in their *ngindung* place from generation to generation ready to serve the royal family. Such a system, plus the traditional values of extended families, created a very high residential and population density in the walled city encompassing the Kraton, the *ngindung* area of Yogyakarta *par excellence* (Soedjarwo 1991:6). A larger town, Yogyakarta, was built around the walled city, to function as the seat of the administration and the capital of the sultanate. In this town, but outside the walled city, were the residences and the offices of the representatives of the colonial power. Except for the plantation managers and their staff, all Dutch people lived in the city of Yogyakarta. There was a special Dutch residential area, *Kotabaru* (literally: 'new town'), which enjoyed the best buildings and the best public facilities in town, a kind of 'little Holland' in a Javanese environment (Selosoemardjan 1962:36). A new middle class which grew up under Dutch aegis occupied a place parallel to that of the *priyayi*, the administrative nobility serving the sultan. The members of this new middle class were Indonesians, the majority of them Javanese, who worked as officials in the Dutch administration and who thus became colleagues of the *priyayi*. Most members of this new class had had primary or even high school education: only few had been able to enjoy a tertiary education and from this last group sprang many of the revolutionary leaders. Besides the members of the Javanese society and the Europeans, about 10,000 'foreign Orientals' (mainly Chinese) lived in Yogyakarta before World War II, making a living as small shopkeepers (Selosoemardjan 1962:37).

In the early decades of the twentieth century a number of important social movements emerged in Yogyakarta. Undoubtedly, the emergence of these movements was closely related to the rise of Yogyakarta as the *city of education*, a status that the city holds to the present day. As early as the nineteenth century, the Europeans established schools which were eventually made accessible for the children of the Yogyanese nobility.[9] Moreover, both the Protestant and Roman Catholic churches established primary schools, seminaries, and universities for the Yogyanese population. From the ranks of the educated classes emerged the people who would later themselves play a prominent part in the establishment of schools and organizations that expressed and orchestrated increasing dissatisfaction with the colonial rule. Among the institutions that were established in Yogyakarta were (Soedjarwo 1991): the *Boedi Oetomo*, an association founded in 1908 by young Javanese intellectuals with a Dutch education; the *Muhammadiyah* (1912), a religious organization which opened primary schools and whose subsequent growth led to the opening of high schools and universities; the *Perguruan Taman Siswa* (1922), which was a teachers training programme that established schools from the primary to the university level. *Taman Siswa* was strong, influential, and grew quickly. In 1930, only eight years after it was founded it had opened fifty-two branches catering to 6,500 students.

In 1940 the crown prince, who had been educated at the university of Leiden in the Netherlands, was installed as Sultan Hamengku Buwono IX. The personality of the sultan and the historical process that unfolded during his reign go a long way towards explaining the opening up of Yogyakarta to national life (Mulder 1994:19). After World War II and the Japanese occupation (1942-5), the Dutch fought to re-establish themselves as a colonial power, despite the Declaration of Independence and the establishment of the Republic of Indonesia in 1945. During the struggle of the republican forces against the Dutch, the two courts in Yogyakarta and Solo were on opposite sites. Solo sided with the Dutch, whereas Yogyakarta sided with the independence forces and became the revolutionary capital of the nascent republic. The town maintained this position throughout the revolutionary period from 1946-50. Thousands of political leaders, military personnel, and civil servants fled from Jakarta to Yogyakarta during that period. Consequently, the population grew rapidly, augmented also by the migration to the city of civilians who felt unsafe in areas still occupied by allied troops. In 1949 the sultan offered the front section of the palace to accommodate the first university of the country, Gadjah Mada University (Mulder 1994:172). Therefore, there was no opposition to the sultan from outside the palace; the revolutionaries operated from inside the Kraton with the approval of the sultan. The role that Yogyakarta played in the struggle for Independence led to the bestowal on the city of the title of *heroic city*, an accolade which also refers back to the past when internal and external enemies of the sultanate were combatted (Soedjarwo 1991). After two centuries of rivalry, Yogyakarta emerged as the dominant court; the *susuhunan* of Surakarta lost most of his political influence and the kingdom was absorbed into the province of Central

Java. In Yogyakarta heroic battles and victories are commemorated by a number of monuments, memorials, and museums that are visited particularly by Indonesian tourists.

Soon after the transfer of sovereignty to Indonesia on 27 December 1949, the capital shifted to Jakarta again. Yogyakarta was drained of its human resources and its potential ebbed away. Many of its prominent citizens moved to Jakarta (Selosoemardjan 1962:113). The sultan's plan to restore the power and prestige of the dynasty and establish Yogyakarta as an independent sultanate in federation with the Indonesian Republic failed. The status of 'special' province granted Yogyakarta its nominal autonomy, but under direct control of the central government in Jakarta (Woodward 1989:13-14). The sultan remained involved in national politics, serving in almost every cabinet in the period 1946-53 and under the Suharto government as Vice-President for several years (1973-8). By opting for the role of a modern politician, actively propagating the New Order socio-political construction of the *Golkar* (*Golongan Karya*, literally: 'functional group'), he emphasized his national orientation. In the 1970s, the government of the sultanate had virtually ceased to function. The sultan lived in Jakarta most of the time, but nevertheless continued to be official head of the Special Region, and his Kraton was transformed into an attraction for foreign tourists (Mulder 1994:30). In addition to the braindrain after Independence, the city underwent deteriorating economic conditions in the 1950s and 1960s. Food supplies were short and crime increased (Guinness 1991:87). Yogyakarta was lacking economic and human capital to restore old and establish new enterprises that would be beneficial to the economy. There was very little private enterprise to provide jobs in the region. The few existing private enterprises were mostly family businesses that offered no employment to non-family members. Again, it was the sultan who assumed the role of entrepreneur in order to give major impetus to the economy in the region. He attempted to re-establish the tobacco plantations (Selosoemardjan 1962:291), a sugar factory (ibid:296) and a machine workshop (ibid:298). Turning to more traditional pursuits, batik production was stimulated in the region when the central government blew new life into a national federation of batik co-operatives – one of the few industries that received government support (ibid:306-7).

In the rural areas surrounding Yogyakarta, the peasants were too poor to indulge in economic innovations. An important factor which exacerbated the poverty in rural areas was the overpopulation generating pressure on land in the rural areas, bringing about disguised unemployment, low productivity of manpower, and fragmented landholdings. Leading as they did a marginal existence, one crop failure would threaten whole families with starvation. The hopelessness of their situation caused many rural poor to move to the city where they either found a place to live in the *kampung* that constituted the majority of Yogyakarta's residential areas, or established squatter houses on waste land. In the early 1950s and again in the 1960s, the local government of Yogyakarta had to establish emergency accommodation for families from the drought-stricken region of Gunung Kidul, who fled to the city to find food, water, and to earn a living (Guinness 1986:15). The rural migrants were not easily absorbed into the city's economic and social fabric. *Kampung* are fairly close knit communities that do not allow families to drift simply into these neighbourhood clusters (Sullivan 1991:53; Guinness 1986:171). In a few areas in the city, homeless street people (*gelandangan*) and new immigrants lacking *kampung* contacts tried to set up their own residential areas on marginal land. Some *kampung* in the inner city received new impetus from the advent of backpacker tourism beginning in the 1970s, as will be discussed below.

The economically unproductive nobility survived by turning their property into economic assets. They benefited from the shortage in housing and made some money by renting rooms to the increasing number of civil servants, teachers and students. Moreover, while the male members of the nobility were primarily concerned with maintaining the social status of the family, their wives were assigned the role of taking care of the economic burden of the household, a gendered division of labour in the noble household that stemmed from former times. The wives were involved in socially approved activities in keeping with the honourable position of their husbands. Trade in gold, silver, precious stones, and batik to serve the refined tastes of their high-status customers were among the best tolerated sources of additional income. Many wives of the nobility ran profitable batik factories and were experienced jewellers (Selosoemardjan 1978:255). These economic activities turned out to be fairly profitable when tourism development was boosted in the 1980s. Socially, however, the old nobility had lost its place as the upper class of society to the new elite which bore the ideals of political, social, and economic progress on its banners. The new elite owed its position to the social mobility provided by the state bureaucracy. Their characteristic is an enormous drive for more and higher education, as diplomas (coupled with good political connections) opened up career opportunities. In this respect, the new elite found itself well catered to in Yogyakarta.

Bearing the epithet *city of education* since the early decades of this century, Yogyakarta has witnessed an enormous expansion of the number of educational institutions since Independence. In the 1970s Yogyakarta gained a nation-wide reputation as a *university city*, with both state and private universities and colleges springing up on the outskirts of the city. These attracted large numbers of students from all over Indonesia, many of whom were from wealthy families. Local businessmen took advantage of this by providing the services sought by the students and by setting up tertiary colleges. The education sector is booming to such an extent that more and more private institutions, some of questionable repute, are emerging, as the existing schools, academies and universities absorb but a fraction of the applicants.[10] In the early 1990s there were four state universities and fifty-two private universities in Yogyakarta.[11] The total number of students attending these universities was about 150,000, which is 33 per cent of the city's population. As students are not obliged to register as residents, another 80,000 should be added to this official estimate (Soedjarwo 1991:C14). Education and related services have become major industries in Yogyakarta.

Unfortunately for the city employment did not expand at the same speed as the educational institutes produced graduates. Education on its own was not sufficient to guarantee a job. Competition for jobs in public administration, the single largest employer in Yogyakarta with its many provincial and municipal government offices, and the private formal sector became murderous.[12] In the early 1990s agriculture[13] was still the major economic sector in the Special Region of Yogyakarta, absorbing almost half of the labour force (48 per cent), followed by services (18.6 per cent), and trade/hotel (17 per cent). Manufacturing had a relatively low level of 11.5 percent. The per capita non-oil Gross Domestic Product (GDP) of the Special Region in 1986 was nearly one quarter of Jakarta's GDP and one of the lowest in the country (Rotge 1991:8). There were few factories in Yogyakarta – among them a cigarette factory, some copper and ironware factories, some food processing factories, and cloth weaving establishments. Large-scale industry is absent. Yogyakarta is a city of small-scale enterprises, cottage industries, and self-employed people. Given this, the economy of Yogyakarta is characterized by a low level of development of non-agricultural economic sectors coupled with a very low capacity for employment expansion within the agricultural sector (Rotge 1991), and with few trade links with Jakarta (Wiendu Nuryanti 1998:141).

In the 1960s population growth in the Special Region was fuelled by migration from rural areas, triggered off by the loss of agricultural land and insufficient rural incomes.[14] Towards the end of the 1980s this trend was reversed: the population of the Special Region was growing more slowly than that of any other province of the country (Tjokrosudarmo 1991).[15] This change has been brought about by both a sharp drop in the number of births through efficient family planning and a relatively strong out-migration to the city of Jakarta or to the outer islands, which exceeds in-migration. The out-migration is related to a job shortage in the special region. However, in spite of what continues to be a low degree of diversification of the economy and a heavy reliance on agriculture which itself remains very little diversified, the Special Region had shown surprisingly good socio-economic achievements by the end of the 1980s (Rotge 1991). The urban-rural gap had narrowed in terms of various socio-economic indicators in the Special Region, while it had widened in other areas of Java, in the wake of significant investment in public amenities and services throughout the region (Rotge 1991). As the hotel and tl travel sector in particular showed a major growth, analysts recomm Yogyakarta should put more effort into the development of tourism the spectrum of employment opportunities and to generate regional development (Rotge 1991, Sudarmadji 1991, Tjokrosudarmo 1991).

YOGYAKARTA AS A TOURIST DESTINATION

The current representation of Yogyakarta, to be found in many tourist guide books, creates the image of a village-like community seemingly unaffected by the pressing problems that modern mass tourism engenders. Although the city has been visited by a rapidly growing number of foreign and domestic tourists, adding up to far over one million visitors in 1995, lifestyles are said to be unhurried and relaxed, life to be inexpensive and crime-free, and the people to be courteous and proudly conscious of their traditions. Tourism promoters love to point out that the cultural heritage of Yogyakarta is a multi-faceted phenomenon consisting of architectural and archaeological remains, prominent persons, philosophies, norms and values, the arts and crafts, folklore, literature, and ways of life (Smithies 1986). The government-issued travel guide book 'Discover Indonesia' – which addresses international markets – describes Yogyakarta as the 'cradle of Javanese culture,' but hastens to point out that the city is the centre of traditional culture in transition:

The golden era of the sultanate is long gone, and a new era has broken. (...) Everything has become infused with the spirit of modernity (...) Although many aspects of culture are still treasured and the classical arts live on, Yogya has become a genuinely Indonesian city (1992:163-4).

While the impact of the globalization of culture, in terms of the adoption of Western lifestyles, is visible everywhere in Yogyakarta, the current tourist discourse is structured by only a few selected 'heritage sites' and 'traditional arts and crafts' performed or produced in the city itself or in its vicinity. It is in the field of 'cultural traditions' that Indonesian cultural and tourist policy merge. There seems to be consensus among the national and provincial governments and the (local) tourism industry of what constitutes the 'tourist product' of Yogyakarta, i.e. the assets of Javanese 'Grand Culture' (Final Report 1991-2). This tourist image will be briefly introduced below.

In the inner city of Yogyakarta, the Kraton area is the most important tourist attraction. It consists of the sultan's palace, the Royal Carriage Museum, the Grand Mosque, the Sono Budoyo Museum, and the *Pagelaran*, the former assembly place of the Sultan's ministers and troops, and Taman

Sari, the former pleasure garden of the sultan. The palace, as we know it today, was established by the first sultan of Yogyakarta, Hamengku Buwono I, and completed in 1757. The present Kraton consists of a series of interconnected open courtyards, with open pavilions (known as *pendopo*) of various sizes, the dwellings of the royal family, and the whole surrounded by high whitewashed walls. The principle approach to the palace is from the north through a square called the *alun-alun lor*, onto which Yogyakarta's main street, Malioboro, debouches. The palace complex is oriented along the north-south axis, having been erected at the centre in between the apex of Mount Merapi and the shores of the Indian Ocean. Both the mountain and the sea play an important role in the mythology surrounding the palace. Conceived not only as the royal residence, but also as the focal point of the entire kingdom, the Kraton is carefully constructed to form a model of the Javanese cosmos. Each gateway, each pavilion, each courtyard, tree, and field has a specific symbolic meaning (Smithies 1986). Except for the private quarters of the sultan's family in the western part, all the buildings in the Kraton are open to visitors. On specific days tourists can attend rehearsals of the royal gamelan orchestra and the traditional dances; and on Sunday mornings there is a dance performance for tourists. Guided tours are available in the central part of the palace.

The Kraton still is the centre of traditional Javanese court culture expressed by traditional ceremonies and events like the *Sekaten* and *Garebeg,* which are now attracting many visitors from Indonesia and abroad (Soelarto 1993). In the past, the purpose of the major festivals was to represent and reinforce the position and prestige of the sultan and the splendour of his court. Under the reign of Hamengku Buwono IX, partly forced by the need to cut the royal expenditure in the post-war era, the festivals have become more austere (Selosoemardjan 1962:122-3). The *Garebeg* procession, held three times in the Islamic year, originated as a pre-Muslim charity feast, redistributing food surpluses of the court among the people. Under Islam, the feast was linked with the Muslim feast days of *Maulud* and *Idul Fitri*. The *Garebeg Maulud*, also called *Sekaten*, commemorating the birth of the Prophet Mohammed, is celebrated as a big fair with night markets and folk theatre presentations held on the northern square of the Kraton. Its climax is a procession of traditionally dressed palace guards carrying the 'rice mountains' (*gunungan*) that are distributed among the people. *Sekaten* has been developed and marketed as a major tourist attraction.

South-west of the Kraton is the Taman Sari complex, known since colonial times as the 'Water Castle,' because of an imposing structure, now in ruins, that once stood at the centre of a huge, man-made lake (Periplus 1991). Literally Taman Sari means 'Fragrant Garden' (Smithies 1986:19). It was established by the first sultan of Yogyakarta. Consisting of a number of buildings – a walled compound with three bathing pools plus a tower and bedchamber, the royal sleeping quarters, the coiled well with the mosque and the 'Portuguese' fortress – the area was originally designed as a pleasure retreat as well as a defensive complex. Soon after the first sultan of Yogyakarta died, the complex was abandoned and has lain in ruins ever since (Periplus 1991). The earthquake that devastated the Yogyakarta area in 1867 may have contributed to the ruinous state in which Taman Sari now finds itself. The complex has been left to decay. A restoration project that was launched a few years ago was aborted because members of the royal family, local residents, the government, and other stakeholders could not agree on plans for the far-reaching modernization of the complex (Wijono n.d.). The area is densely inhabited and the former palace buildings are lined by narrow streets and houses, little shops and batik galleries. Many tourists pass through the area, often accompanied by informal guides leading the way not only to the historic ruins but also to the shops and galleries to capture a small commission from the tourists' purchases. At the northern end of Taman Sari lies the large and colourful *ngasem* or bird market which – besides being a regular daily market – specializes in birds and other animals.

Crossing the large square north of the palace which served and still serves as the main meeting place of the city, one enters the main area of commerce and amusement of which Malioboro Street[16] is the centre. The most southerly part is dominated by impressive buildings from the colonial past where a bank, the major post office, and government departments are accommodated. Opposite the post office is the fort (*benteng*) Vredenburg, which once housed a garrison of troops, but is now converted into a museum with dioramas showing the history of the Independence movement. Together with other museums scattered over the city, e.g. the Museum of the Revolution (a collection of photographs documenting the Indonesian Revolution), the Army Museum (a display of weapons and equipment from the revolutionary years), the house of Prince Diponegoro (celebrating the long colonial guerrilla war against the Dutch), the home of Ki Hajar Dewantara, one of the pioneers of the Independence struggle, the memorial home of General Sudirman (the commander of the revolutionary forces), and the Yogya Kembali monument and museum – Benteng Vredenburg represents Yogyakarta as the *city of struggle*, as the government-issued guide book commemorates (Discover Indonesia 1992:164). A little further up the street is Pasar Beringharjo, Yogyakarta's main market. This huge covered market offers an astonishing assortment of merchandise, including cloth and clothing, leatherwork, household and electronic equipment, foodstuffs, spices, fruit, vegetables, meat, and fish. Malioboro street forms the major shopping area with numerous pavement shops, supermarkets, department stores, and hotels with foreign names; restaurants with international tourist menus and fast-food; tall-storeyed star-rated hotels; and a new shopping-mall selling world-famous brand names.

The street grows crowded in the late afternoon and early evening when the air gets cooler. After the shops close, streetside restaurants, the *lesehan*, open along the pavements, where customers sit on mats, cross-legged, in front of low tables.

Leaving the inner city, the tourist may come to Kota Gede (often dubbed 'silver city'), about five kilometres south-east of Yogyakarta. Most tourists visit Kota Gede because of the numerous silver workshops where one can observe the production process of jewellery and works of art made of silver and these objects can be bought at an attractive price. Kota Gede is also the place where the kings of Mataram are buried. The Royal Cemetery where, according to the rules, one has to wear traditional Javanese clothes to pay respect to the deceased, may still be visited. A place of similar significance is Imogiri Village, where the tombs of the sultans and their families are located. Few foreign tourists climb the 345 stairs to reach the top of the hill where the tombs are situated, but it is a popular destination for domestic tourists who come to pray and to leave offerings. Parangtritis beach on Java's south coast, twenty-seven kilometres south of Yogyakarta enjoys great popularity among Javanese people as this coast is the domain of the goddess of the Southern Ocean (Nyai Roro Kidul) who is the mythical spouse of the sultans of Yogyakarta and Surakarta. People visit the beach not so much to enjoy the pleasures of a beach resort (the coast is rugged and the surf is savage), but to meditate and bring offerings. Only recently the provincial government has generated resort development resources to turn Parangtritis into a tourist area to attract domestic as well as foreign tourists. One tourist destination which is well-established is Kaliurang, twenty-seven kilometres north of Yogyakarta on the slopes of Mount Merapi. This little resort is located at an elevation of about 900 metres and is visited by local people and foreign tourists because of its pleasant climate and as a starting point for treks up Mount Merapi, one of Java's most active volcanoes.

Yogyakarta is a noted batik centre, home to many famous batik painters exhibiting and selling their work in the numerous galleries. Inspired by their success, a multitude of mass-production galleries (most of them are situated around Taman Sari) offer batik paintings depicting scenes from the Ramayana, but also exotic flowers, birds, and butterflies, rising moons over ricefields, and abstract paintings. In Malioboro Street, a number of shops sell batik garments and lengths of cloth, and in the Prawirotaman area batik workshops offer free guided tours of the batik process. For those who want a hands-on approach there are many batik courses and classes on offer in Yogyakarta. Other tourism-related craft industries in and around Yogyakarta include silver, pottery, leather, woodcarving and *wayang* (shadowplay) puppets. *Wayang* puppet performances and Javanese dances are performed to entertain local people and tourists. Very popular are the gamelan and classical dance rehearsals on Sunday mornings in the Kraton which are open to visitors. Tourist performances are usually organized in hotel lobbies or special theatres. They are usually shortened, with just the highlights of the epic versions, with lavish costumes and summaries in a number of foreign languages. The most famous of these performances may be the Ramayana ballet – alluding to the story which is depicted in the relief of the Shiva and the Brahma temples in the Prambanan complex – performed at the open air theatre near the Prambanan temple on four successive nights during the dry season.

The Prambanan temple on the border with the province of Central Java (*Jawa Tengah*), seventeen kilometres east of Yogyakarta is the major attraction of international allure in the area. This Hindu temple complex was built in the tenth century and was destroyed by an earthquake in the early twentieth century. Under a project which began in the early 1970s, the temple was meticulously restored. By the launching of the Visit Indonesia Year 1991, the restoration of the three main shrines had been completed (Soekmono 1991, Moertjipto & Bambang Prasetyo 1993). On the Prambanan plain are another eleven structures which are incidentally visited by tourists, the most popular being *candi* Kalasan and Ratu Boko. Borobudur, the famous Buddhist stupa built in the ninth century, is not part of the Yogyakarta attraction system in a formal sense. Borobudur, constantly referred to as a temple but actually a stupa, is situated in the province of Central Java. However, the tourism industry of Yogyakarta is the main source of visitors to the Borobudur. Though it takes a one-hour ride from Yogyakarta by tourist transport to cover the forty-two kms distance between the city and the stupa, Borobudur is the major destination for tourists visiting Yogyakarta. Like Prambanan, a thorough restoration was necessary to make the temple accessible for tourism. The Borobudur restoration was partly financed by UNESCO and partly by the Indonesian government. The restoration began in 1955 and was finished in 1983 (Moertjipto & Bambang Prasetyo 1993). On the way to Borobudur the tourist buses pass two smaller Buddhist temples from the same era, Candi Pawon and Candi Mendut. The area of all the temples exhibits the characteristics of an organized tourist trap, as a large number of food and souvenir sellers compete for the attention of the visitors. Borobudur and Prambanan were designated World Heritage sites by UNESCO in 1991.

The dominant approach to the Yogyakarta attraction system – as represented by the government and the tourism industry – is the 'classical' package of attractions comprising the Kraton area with the Javanese performing arts and handicraft industries, the actual Kraton palace and adjacent shopping area, and Borobudur and Prambanan. It may be regarded of minor importance that, strictly speaking, the attraction system of Yogyakarta stretches beyond the Special Province of Yogyakarta, as Borobudur is situated in the province of *Jawa Tengah* and part of the territory covered by the

Prambanan complex transcends across the boundary between the *Daerah Istimewa Yogyakarta* and the Klaten district of the province *Jawa Tengah*. In the eyes of most tourists it seems to be only natural that the package of attractions of the Yogyakarta area contains the most impressive architectural remains of the past. For decades, tourists presumed that the only possibility of reaching Borobudur was through Yogyakarta. Towards the end of the twentieth century, however, the route to Borobudur has become the bone of contention between the two Javanese provinces, marking the decline of Yogyakarta in the tourist market. The route that tourists travel and the package of attractions that is composed for them is not as natural and innocent as it seems. Routes and packages are based on choices which are affected by strategic and political considerations. The objects of built heritage have turned into icons of Indonesian national identity. In Yogyakarta, local culture and heritage is developed and preserved according to the principles which are designed to consolidate the Indonesian nation (Hughes-Freeland 1993:149). As Gertler (1993) states, the cultural heritage in the area of Yogyakarta gives 'historical depth' to the *pancasila* state ideology, as cultural and religious pluralism is expressed in its 'syncretic cultural kaleidoscope.' Not only do the stupa, temples and Kraton represent three of the five officially recognized religions (the first of the five 'pillars' of *pancasila*), but they are also acknowledged as *pusaka*, sacred heirlooms which are believed to confer good fortune and strength on the Indonesian people – the welfare of the nation being the fifth of the five pillars (Gertler 1993:16). The elevation of these heirlooms to World Heritage sites transcends the cultural uniqueness to the level of a common civilized humanity, the second principle of the *pancasila*. The Javanese courtly traditions and their concomitant political culture – as represented by the Kraton – translate into the 'unanimous consensus' led by wise policies. Consensus achieved in processes of discussion and representation is the Indonesian perspective of democracy and at the same time the fourth pillar of the *pancasila*. The recent past of Yogyakarta as a centre of the struggle for independence appeals to Indonesian nationhood and unity, the third of the five principles. Against this background, it is of significance to stress that the number of international tourists visiting Yogyakarta is outnumbered more than twice by the number of domestic visitors (see Appendix 3). Following Hughes Freeland (1993:149) and Anderson (1991), this domestic tourism might be compared to the kind of 'pilgrimages' which have been described as a crucial stage in the emergence of the imagined community of nationhood. The following sections describing the making of Yogyakarta as a tourist destination since the 1960s will single out the interrelationship between national politics and the establishment of Yogyakarta as the arena of '*pancasila* tourism.'

THE CONSTRUCTION OF '*PANCASILA* TOURISM':
THE FIRST DECADES AFTER INDEPENDENCE

After Independence a few hotels dating from the Dutch era, among them the former Grand Hotel Yogyakarta, were re-established. At the time, no more than a few hundred tourists per year were visiting Yogyakarta. Nevertheless, the Sukarno government anticipated a great future for tourism development under the motto of 'guided tourism' – alluding to its political principle of 'guided democracy' (Kodhyat 1996:70). In 1955 the state bank, Bapindo (*Bank Pembangunan Indonesia*), established an enterprise named *P.T. Natour* Ltd. (National Hotel and Tourism Corporation) which took over the existing 'international' hotels; Yogyakarta's Grand Hotel was renamed Hotel Garuda under Natour management (Kodhyat 1996:56). In 1957, headed by Hamengu Buwono IX, sultan of Yogyakarta and member of the Sukarno government, the *Dewan Tourisme Indonesia* (DTI) – Indonesian Tourism Council – was established to organize and accelerate tourism development in the country (ibid:63). In his capacity as president of the DTI, the sultan proposed the building of a hotel of international standards in Yogyakarta, but it was only after the political turmoil of 1965 that this project was implemented. The sultan provided the land needed for this project and the hotel was built on land owned by the Kraton on the outskirts of Yogyakarta on the premises of the *Kedaton Ambarrukmo*, a royal residence and vacation resort for members of the royal family, established in 1859. This residence has become integrated into the hotel premises and adds allure to the four-star hotel. The establishment of the Ambarrukmo Palace Hotel in 1966 is regarded as the beginning of tourism development in Yogyakarta (Tjokrosudarmo 1991). In its wake, a large number of smaller hotels and guesthouses emerged. In the neighbourhoods south of the Kraton, the local gentry started to rent out rooms in their spacious houses to visitors as an additional source of income, and so did local people in the *kampung* close to the Yogyakarta train and bus stations and central shopping area (cf. Chapter 4).

The political isolation of Indonesia under the Sukarno government and the policy of incidental tourism projects was not conducive to tourism development. For a decade no significant growth in tourism activities occurred. It was only after the new course of domestic and foreign policy was adopted by the New Order that the potential role of tourism in the process of development was envisioned (Tjokrosudarmo 1991). Tourism policy was centralized at the national level in the Ministry of Transportation, while the management of a number of tourism activities was delegated to the provincial level. The task of dealing with tourism affairs was entrusted with the Board of Regional Tourism Development (Badan Pengembangan Pariwisata Daerah, BAPPARDA) which was installed in 1974. However, it was not until the early

1980s that a regional tourism office was established in Yogyakarta (Tjokro-sudarmo 1991). Throughout the 1970s, tourism development in the Special Province of Yogyakarta was totally Jakarta-controlled. The New Order government, initiating regional development plans for the most important tourist areas in Indonesia, intended to develop the geographical area of central Java as a whole for tourism. It has to be stressed that in the early days of tourism development no sharp distinction was drawn between the Special Region of Yogyakarta and the province of Central Java. Together the cultural and natural assets of both provinces were represented as constituting the attraction value of this geographical area. Examples of this approach can be found in a travel brochure, published in 1969 by the Foreign Language Publishing Institute of the Department of Information in Jakarta. This brochure, entitled *Central Java*, was meant to promote 'Tourism – 1969: The Central Java Year.' There is no information about the background of this focus and motto, and the approach adopted in this brochure is rather confusing. The brochure opens with a description of the 'places of interest.' The first 'attraction' to be introduced is 'Semarang and environment' which fills less than half a page. After briefly mentioning a number of towns in the north (Demak, Kudus, Jepara, and Pati) and the Dieng Plateau and Surakarta, Yogyakarta 'special territory' is described as a fifth 'place of interest' in the region. The 'tourism objects' identified in the city on the one hand and in the environs of Yogyakarta on the other, are rather revealing. For the city, the Diponegoro Monument,[17] is singled out as the most important place of interest, followed by the Kraton, Taman Sari, the Sono Budoyo Museum and the Perjuangan (War) Museum. In the vicinity, Kota Gede, Imogiri, Kaliurang, Parangtritis, and Borobudur (including Mendut and Pawon) are recommended to visitors; finally, a number of 'other temples' are mentioned, among them is Prambanan. There are several striking points in this compilation. First: the choice of urban amenities strongly focuses on the *heroic city,* which suggests that the brochure was originally designed for domestic visitors and sub-sequently translated into English to appeal to an international audience. Second: the Kraton of Yogyakarta is described as a 'living museum' redolent with antiquity and grandeur where guided tours are available. Third: Boro-budur and Prambanan are classified as Yogyanese attractions, paying no atten-tion to the fact that they are (partly) situated in the province of Central Java.

In 1973 under *Repelita* I, the New Order government requested the govern-ment of Japan to grant technical assistance for tourism development planning in Central Java and Yogyakarta. The Japanese government entrusted the Overseas Technical Co-operation Agency (OTCA) with the project. OTCA conducted a survey to evaluate the tourism potential in the area. The Japanese delegation identified the archaeological monuments – the 'cultural heritage of Indonesian civilization' – as having the most important tourism potential.

Borobudur and Prambanan had been partially restored since they had been rediscovered in the nineteenth century and British and Dutch antiquarians and later archaeologists took an interest in the ruins that were covered with soil, ashes, and vegetation. In the 1960s the main temple of Prambanan dedicated to Shiva had already been restored to a degree that it could figure prominently in an ambitious project initiated by late President Sukarno, the construction of an open-air theatre at this complex specifically for staging the Ramayana ballet. When the Japanese team of experts investigated the tourism potential of the area, the Prambanan open-air theatre drew their attention to the opportunities that were hidden in the ancient temples of Java. Their survey resulted in a master plan for the development of the archaeological sites in the area as tourism attractions: the complexes of Prambanan, Borobudur and the Dieng Plateau (OTCA 1974). The basic concept was an archaeological park, 'an open-air museum nestled in nature's midst' (OTCA 1974:2), of great international allure to enhance the appeal of the region for international tourism and to contribute considerably to tourism growth. Despite the emphasis international tourism development was not regarded as the final aim of the operation. The real intention was to create the foundations for future domestic tourism which the New Order in Indonesia intended to stimulate for educational purposes. By virtue of its historical and cultural significance to the Indonesian nation, the area of Central Java and Yogyakarta provided the ideal setting for such tourism and the OTCA team recommended that the Indonesian government give priority to developing the region for domestic tourism. In 'pancasila terms' the OTCA report stated:

> It should be emphasized that domestic tourism as so defined differs from international tourism in that it will have to be planned on the basis of a comprehensive policy at the national level which embraces (...) the national policy concerning the education, health, and welfare of all Indonesians (OTCA 1974:1-2).

These recommendations were implemented through a newly established enterprise, the *P.T. Taman wisata candi Borobudur dan Prambanan*,[18] established in 1980, with its head office in Solo and a branch office in Jakarta. This government-owned organization which is under the aegis of three ministers,[19] is managed by a president director who reports to a four-member board of commissioners, prominent figures from political, economic and academic life.[20] The overall management and development of the park is the responsibility of the *Taman Wisata* corporation, its official mandate being the preservation of the cultural heritage and the generation of a profit-making scheme to make the parks financially self-supporting. These two objectives are difficult to combine which is illustrated by what became of the sites during the

1980s. In accordance with the concept of an 'open-air museum nestled in nature's midst,' the   complexes were embedded in landscaped parks with neatly trimmed lawns, flowerbeds and broad boulevards lined with lamp poles. The parks were surrounded by a fence, and fees were charged at the entrance gate. The people living in the immediate vicinity, cultivating the soil or grazing their animals, were resettled on the other side of the fence. Visitor facilities, like restaurants and rest areas, toilets, a children's playground, a museum and information centre were built in the parks. A number of local people obtained a licence to run a souvenir shop or a food stall on the premises, but it seems that there was a certain lack of control as these stalls and vending activities tended to spread. In the early 1990s a kind of slum was emerging within the fenced area (cf. Soemarwoto 1992). Although the complexes embody the *pancasila* principle of religion, the observance of the Hindu and Buddhist religions has disappeared from Prambanan and Borobudur, with the exception of the annual Waicak celebration.[21] In the 1990s a major expansion of the Borobudur guesthouse was underway, including amenities such as a swimming pool and tennis courts. *Taman wisata candi* has developed into a fun-fair devoid of the cultural and religious meaning it was supposed to transmit, but still with the clear political mission to figure as icon of 'Indonesianness.' An annual '*safari pasaran*' (marketing campaign) organized by the management aims to entice the major target groups of the organization such as schools, companies, and government departments, to stimulate a visit to the parks when they are thinking of how to use their collective leisure and recreation time.[22]

Beginning with the opening of the palace for Gadjah Mada University in the days of the Revolution, the Kraton was made accessible for visitors. Gone were the days when the royal family and the court were the remote rulers over the people. In the 1970s the palace became the most important 'tourist object' in the area, attracting more visitors than the ancient 'temples.' As statistics show, foreign tourists were significantly outnumbered by domestic tourists (see Appendix 4). After all, the Kraton represented not only Javanese tradition, but also a heroic past, the struggle for independence, and the emergence of the sovereign nation. While in the early days of tourism, special permission had to be obtained to enter the palace gates, only a few years later the Kraton was made accessible to groups and individuals seven days a week. After paying a modest entrance fee the visitors are shown around by palace guides who explain the heirlooms of the sultan's family that are exhibited in the pavilions. Only the west part of the palace is inaccessible as this is the area where the sultan's family resides – the presence of the royal family adding to the sacred character of this place for many Indonesian visitors. The popularity of the Kraton, particularly among domestic visitors, is largely to be attributed to the propaganda that was launched by the national government to encourage Indonesians to visit the objects of national heritage. To this end and in accordance with the '*P4*' principle of *pancasila* moral education (cf. Chapter 2), schools, government departments, and companies organize collective outings to these cultural objects that offer a combination of education and entertainment. Schoolchildren and students from many different regions are invited to participate in the performing arts in Yogyakarta. As a local tourist magazine rejoiced: 'Yogyakarta has also become a place to train the Indonesian youths to have the *bhinneka tunggal ika* spirit' (*Yogya-in-a-week*, November 22-27, 1991). It is at the weekends that these collective visits take place that the Kraton (and the major 'temples') swarming with domestic tourists forced the authorities to consider 'crowd control' measures.

As of the early 1970s, the Kraton of Yogyakarta and its two[23] counterparts in Solo took centre stage in the national government's cultural policy. Encouraged by New Order visions of what would later come to be thought of as a cultural renaissance, the palaces suddenly re-emerged as idealized sites of Javanese heritage recalling the authority of 'Java.' As Pemberton (1994:111) notes, within half a decade after the events of 1965-6, Suharto and his wife would turn explicitly to 'culture' as a point of reference that might override the violent origin of the New Order. Jakarta's Javanese elite imagined the palaces of central Java to contain a wealth of all that is authentic, be this material or spiritual (Pemberton 1994:161). For many Javanese Yogyakarta has always been, and will always be, a *magical city*. It is here that the 'essentials of Javanese culture, religion, and the theory of kingship have been preserved' (Woodward 1989:21). The obsession with connecting the past and the future in the form of a present 'tourist object' has been a way of appropriating and domesticating that past. After all, the Suhartos claimed royal status.[24] For many New Order Javanese not Yogyakarta but Solo is the city of Javanese origins, 'a privileged locus for much that is recalled as (...) 'authentically Javanese' (*asli Jawa*)' (Pemberton 1994: 25). Like the heritage sites of Prambanan and Borobudur, the Kraton of Yogyakarta and Solo alike underwent a further shift towards 'edutainment' when the first Kraton Festival was organized – the first large-scale co-operative cultural event between the Yogyakarta and Solo Kraton in more than 200 years in the 'Visit Indonesia Year' (1991). For two weeks the entire ceremonial and performance repertoires of both courts were mobilized. Organizers, government officials, audiences, and experts agreed that this festival was a tremendous success and should become a 'new tradition,' to be repeated periodically. A successful follow-up was held in 1995 – in honour of the fiftieth anniversary of Indonesian Independence. Even for the Kratons tourism became a vital source of income which they needed to enable them to play their traditional role in society.

In the 1960s tourism development in Yogyakarta was largely based on private initiatives with the Sultan playing a pivotal role, but in the 1970s government planning began to leave visible traces in the provincial tourism industry. The planning process was top-down, sectoral in nature, and focused on physical and spatial planning for the enhancement of tourist attractions and infrastructure (Timothy 1998b:72). The provincial master plan established with the support of Japanese consultants, strongly favoured the restoration of the built heritage sites, reasoning that they were relatively easily implemented and quickly left visible results to be reported to funding agencies and Jakarta-based policy makers.

THE HEYDAY OF CULTURAL TOURISM IN YOGYAKARTA: THE 1980S AND EARLY 1990S

In the 1980s Yogyakarta became a centre of the nation's tourist promotions in terms of 'second destination after Bali.' The tourism office (*dinas pariwisata*, or short *diparda*) of the province of Yogyakarta Special Region – operating under the auspices of the Ministry of Home Affairs – was established in 1981. The central government delegated the management of a number of tourism sites to the province, including those tourist objects which are not under the direct management of the national government – tour guides, unclassified hotels and restaurants, the tourism information centres – all undertakings in recreation and entertainment, and regional tourism promotion. The Yogyakarta tourism office set up training programmes for tour guides and for hotel owners – concentrating especially on hygiene and sanitation (Timothy 1999:383), and produced material for the promotion of the region. However, these were incidental and isolated measures. Until the latter half of the 1980s, Yogyakarta lacked a comprehensive tourism development plan. The first – and for the time being only – tourism master plan emerged in 1988 (*Rencana Pengembangan* 1987). The plan designed a long-range planning schedule for the entire province of Yogyakarta and the positioning of Yogyakarta in relation to the near-by tourism objects of the province of Central Java. Interestingly enough, the plan did not specify its temporal range and time limits by which the identified objectives should have been realized. In the master plan tourism was assigned the role of foreign exchange earner, stimulator of regional economic activities, and employment opportunities, in other words, generator of development for the whole region (Tjokrosudarmo 1991). An ambitious programme of restoration, improvement and expansion is propagated in all areas of tourism: the tourist objects, the condition and quality of services, the human resources and the population at large. The border with the neighbouring province, so significant in politics and culture, was swept away in the develop-ment plans, positioning Yogyakarta at the heart of the central Java area and designing tourist routes that would pass through central Javanese 'places of Interest' (like Borobudur and Dieng, Kudus, Jepara and Semarang, or Solo,

Tawangmangu and Sangiran) with Yogyakarta as 'home base, vertibly both the provincial master plan as well as *Repelitada* IV the need to co-ordinate efforts with Central Java for co-operative joint promotion), but there is no evidence that this ever occur~~ ~~~ 1998b:63-4).

The tourism envisioned by the master plan was basically 'organized' in nature. The focus on organized, to wit package tourism has to be understood against the background of the national government's tourism policy, which favoured the star-rated sector. The individual travellers – 'backpackers' – were defined in government terms as detrimental to Indonesian communities. Although well-established in Yogyakarta, backpacker tourism was deliberately neglected and left to private initiatives. Moreover, the master plan projected the future of Yogyakarta in terms of a centre for nature tourism and convention tourism – without elaborating on these ideas. Finally, the master plan targeted domestic tourism, especially Indonesian youth tourism, for which Yogyakarta would serve as the most important centre of education. After the publication of this master plan in 1988 and with the nationally propagated 'Visit Indonesia Year 1991' ahead, a national tourism awareness campaign – *Kampanye Nasional Sadar Wisata* – was started by the national government to make Indonesian people 'tourist minded' and to prepare them for the arrival of a rapidly growing number of international tourists (cf. Chapter 2).

In Yogyakarta the 1989 *tahun sadar wisata* (tourism awareness year) was given ample attention, widely disseminated in government propaganda and exerted important influence on the tourism infrastructure of the city. From the early 1980s the city was serviced by daily flights to Jakarta and Bali, and connected by an ever increasing number of inter-city and inter-island overnight buses to the major population centres of Java and beyond. The older and smaller hotels and guesthouses scattered around the city station were overshadowed by resplendent international hotels. Once the Grand Hotel – at present better known as the Garuda Hotel – in Malioboro Street was the only hotel with allure in the inner city. Now the Garuda has to vie with the new multi-storey Melia Purosani which belongs to an international chain financed by foreign investors. Other international hotel chains – Holiday Inn, Hyatt, Radisson, and Sheraton – have also built new hotels. The older, dusty family stores were replaced by spacious branches of national and international department store networks, car salesrooms, supermarkets, large bookstores, life insurance offices, fancy bread and cake shops, batik emporiums, and souvenir and art shops, some of them pricing their merchandise in US dollars only. Comparable developments have taken place in other Indonesian cities where such stores have been catering to an increasingly prosperous and consumer-indulgent middle class. In a tourist city like Yogyakarta, the local tourist market provided an additional clientele for the conspicuous shopping facilities.

Appearances count, and to cater to the desired image of Yogyakarta as a tourist destination, the streets of the city were widened and beautified by the city government. Squatters were evicted. Public transportation was upgraded by the introduction of mini-buses, many under private ownership, plying regulated routes (Guinness 1991). Thus, the ingredients of what urban economists call the 'informal sector' of economic production, consisting of labour-intensive but low-capital inputs – hawking, petty commodity production, cottage industries – diminished in the urban scene. The eradication of petty economic activities was – sometimes violently – supported by the local government, as police raids were conducted to arrest illegal lottery sellers and unlicensed vendors and guides. Based on the *sapta pesona*, this 'keep our city clean' campaign included the cleansing of cultural forms that were considered unappealing to tourists.

In the early 1990s, when the urbanization and 'touristification' of Yogyakarta were well under way, a number of international programmes were launched to monitor and re-direct these processes. The Yogyakarta Urban Development Project, financed by the Swiss government and implemented by a Swiss Engineering Bureau, was set up to improve housing conditions, waste handling, sanitation, public transportation, land use, and local market activities thoroughly. Tourism development was beyond the scope of the project's strategies. This area was left to another prominent initiative; the United Nations Development Programme in co-operation with UNESCO launched a project on Cultural Tourism Development for Central Java and Yogyakarta. This project was designed and implemented with the support of the Indonesian government (the Departments of Tourism, Culture and Home Affairs). From October 1991 to April 1992 a team of international and national experts on tourism conducted an extensive study of the opportunities for and restrictions to cultural tourism developments in the area. The project gave prognoses with regard to a number of interrelated areas of tourism development and made recommendations for follow-up strategies to improve and strengthen cultural tourism in Central Java. The areas were built heritage, the arts, marketing, management and organization, and tour guides. In contrast to Indonesian government policy which focused blindly on the expansion of the number of (foreign) tourists to boost revenues and foreign exchange, the UNDP/UNESCO team pleaded for a different approach. Making 'sustainable developments' their pivotal concern the team suggested not to increase the sheer numbers of tourists, but to concentrate on length of stay as the vehicle to reach the goal of tourism acting as the engine of regional development. The UNDP/UNESCO approach put 'more emphasis on the individual traveller, who has a longer 'length of stay' than the group traveller, and who is inclined towards the use of similar accommodation and facilities as the domestic tourist – that is, modest hotels and guest houses, and *becak*, and *andong* and buses – and for the same reasons is more compatible with the host community' (Final Report 1991/92:2). There were suggestions for 'urban ecotourism' which involved opportunities for tourists to meet and talk to *kampung* groups and 'to explore the less monumental and commercial sides of town to better appreciate the life experiences of ordinary people' (Silver 1994:46). It is obvious that the UNDP/UNESCO team attempted to put the lessons from Bali into use with respect to the detrimental effects of large-scale resort developments. The team recommended establishing links between tourism and the domestic economy of the area, for example by creating incentives for luxury hotels and restaurants to purchase domestic products, and on the supply side, by encouraging farmers to grow vegetables, fruit, fish, and other products with high quality standards as part of a general policy of agricultural diversification (Rotge 1991:68). While the team was in favour of involving the local community in tourism development, it strongly opposed processes of 'informalization' that emerged along with growing numbers of visitors. The proliferation of souvenir-selling activities at or near the major tourist sites, the poor quality of goods offered and the disconnection between the site and the souvenirs on offer were strongly criticized by the experts. They pleaded for more control on the quality of the products sold and for the establishment of official shops with a unique assortment of goods that were not available on the streets. They even suggested introducing the quality seal 'By Appointment of the Royal Court of Yogyakarta' (Final Report 1991-1992:44), but there is no evidence that the sultan seriously considered this suggestion.

THE DECLINE OF TOURISM IN THE 1990s

In the early 1990s the future prospects of Yogyakarta as a tourism destination seemed very bright. Tourism development was booming, cultural tourism seemed to be flourishing in accordance with the ambitious UNDP/UNESCO project, and the city hosted a number of prestigious international tourism conferences. The sultan of Yogyakarta was appointed to the board of the newly established Indonesian Tourism Promotion Board (ITPB) that aimed at propelling Indonesia into the world's most visited countries. Joop Avé, then minister of *Depparpostel*, revealed plans to make Yogyakarta one of the country's most prominent destinations for MICE tourism (Meetings, Incentives, Conferences and Events). These plans implied further impulses for the star-rated hotel sector and resort development. Despite such promise, representatives of the local tourist industry were quite gloomy about tourism in Yogyakarta when I attended a meeting of local policy makers, hotel managers, travel agents, and tourism researchers in March 1996.[25] At this meeting a number of rather disturbing facts and figures were discussed, some of which I present below.

Among the main cities in the central Javanese area – like Semarang and Solo – Yogyakarta is the major centre for tourist accommodation boasting myriad large and small hotels and guesthouses. Until the early 1990s the occupation rate was relatively high, running at over 60 per cent annually (Final Report 1991/1992:11). In sheer numbers, however, Yogyakarta's dominance in the tourist market was far from evident. While Yogyakarta recorded 600,000 visitors per year in the early 1990s, the province of Central Java welcomed about 2.5 million. When these figures are broken down into foreign and domestic components one-third of the tourism flow in Yogyakarta was foreign; in Central Java this was less than 3 per cent. The majority of tourists in both areas stayed in non-star-rated hotels – 62 per cent in Yogyakarta and 86 per cent in Central Java. The percentage of foreign visitors staying in non-star hotels was higher in Yogyakarta (30 per cent) than in Central Java (23 per cent). This suggested that international tourism generated more income for the local economy in Yogyakarta than it did in Central Java.[26] To this has to be added the fact that foreign tourists showed a longer length of stay in Yogyakarta (about two nights) than they do in Central Java (1.5 nights) (Final Report 1991/1992:17). As it was the location of the main airfield in the region, Yogyakarta had a clear market advantage over Central Java. Throughout the 1980s and early 1990s the flight frequency to Yogyakarta from/to Jakarta and Bali (the main international airports of Indonesia) was increasing, in response to rising demand for air transport from both Indonesian residents and international tourists.[27]

Towards the mid-1990s, the advantages of Yogyakarta in international tourism development began to ebb away. There were inexorable indications that its tourism industry was having a hard time. First of all, the growth of the number of foreign visitors – though still increasing in absolute numbers – declined from 60 per cent in 1989 to 6.5 per cent in 1995.[28] Worryngly, the growth rate lagged behind national objectives. The political structure and practice in Indonesia demanded local and provincial governments implement this Jakarta-designed policy. For Yogyakarta this meant a 10 per cent growth in the international tourist arrivals to be realized towards the end of *Repelita* VI (in 1998). According to a representative of BAPPEDA Yogyakarta, whom I interviewed in August 1996, the Special Province of Yogyakarta was unlikely to exceed 7 per cent growth. This estimate, of course, did not reckon with the economic crisis which brought about a considerable decrease in visitor numbers, instead of growth. Even though there was a persistent problem in keeping up with national objectives, local policy makers did not question the aims set in Jakarta. Although government plans inclined towards the development of small-scale tourism, these ideas remained vague and many local actors in tourism scorned them as 'lip service.' Strikingly, domestic tourism did not figure at all in the national and regional tourism plans. In this sector the growth by far exceeded the international arrivals, though trends are strongly fluctuating and are clearly influenced by large-scale events like the Kraton Festivals in 1991 and 1995.[29]

The disappointing growth in the number of tourists concealed a more serious problem: the declining length of stay, particularly in the star-rated hotel sector. As the UNDP/UNESCO team pointed out, the development in the length of stay of foreign and domestic visitors deserved to be given more concern than absolute growth. Official statistics showed a stagnation in the number of nights that visitors were staying in the city. In the late 1980s the average length of stay of foreign tourists was about 2.5 nights, but by the mid-1990s it had declined to two nights. As far as domestic tourists were concerned, the length of stay remained stable.[30] Similar observations could be made about developments in the hotel sector. Data on the star-rated hotel sector in Yogyakarta showed that, whereas the number of hotel rooms had doubled since 1991, the occupancy rate had fallen by 12 per cent. Though the occupancy rate in the non-rated sector seemed to be lower than in the star-rated hotels,[31] there had been a gradual growth in the occupancy in the non-rated sector up to 1994. As the UNDP/UNESCO team predicted, the over-emphasis on the star-rated sector extracted a fair amount of earnings from the region. Star-rated hotels generally attracted organized tour groups that paid prices and booked itineraries which were fixed at the point of sale in the generating country. The benefits for the host community would be modest. There is change in the air and independent travellers are constituting a growing segment of international long-haul tourism. Although very little is known about this category, a limited survey in Yogyakarta in 1991 revealed that these travellers stayed in the area for at least double the time that package tourists did and that they preferred to be accommodated in local guesthouses. Therefore, the UNDP/UNESCO team recommended more local investment in guesthouses, as these were closer to the demand of the market and more profitable to the economic development of the region. The higher occupancy rate in the non-star-rated sector and the more stable situation in that sector supported this idea.

The stagnating length of stay was also closely related to a more general problem: the limited diversity of tourism objects in the area. The representation of Yogyakarta and the 'tourist objects' on offer had not changed since the 1970s. While the infrastructure for transportation in the region was good, the area was not easily accessible to foreign tourists. There were but few special tours available locally. Tourists – travelling individually – had difficulties in finding their way in the region as soon as they left the beaten track. The biggest problem with which they had to struggle was the lack of information (Erlina n.d.). Tourists who turned to the Tourist Office in Yogyakarta were disappointed as, except for a very general city map, there was virtually no information about the tourist highlights, let alone the lesser known sites. Foreign tourists had to depend on local travel agents offering the well-known tourism objects in an 'eight-hour package.' Star-rated tour operators and travel agents and non-rated competitors alike offered standard tours, starting with a sun-rise experience at Borobudur, a Yogyakarta city tour (including Kraton and Taman Sari), a shopping spree at commission-paying shops and factories, and finally a sunset visit to Prambanan – or vice versa (cf. Chapter 4). One of the most threatening developments was the 'transit tour' from Bali, which had originally been designed for the hurried Asian tourists who flew in from their accommodation in Bali in the morning to see Borobudur, and left the area in the afternoon. Yogyakarta did not benefit from these tours, as the tourists did not spend any time in the city. They were usually taken to a hotel on the outskirts of town where they had lunch, and to a few large shops or factories to buy silver and batik. In the last few years, these transit tours have become more popular and, besides the Asians, European, and Australian tourists spending their holidays in Bali have developed a taste for these short breaks as well.[32] People in the tourism industry in Yogyakarta were worried about these developments, but adhered to the soothing idea that 'bad times will pass' and 'tourists will keep on coming to Yogya.' The hotel sector pointed the finger at the tour operators and travel agencies, accusing them of allowing this transit tourism to increase 'because of their greed.' The travel agencies indicated that they did not have any choice but to sell the transit tours; it was their survival strategy. In fact, Yogyakarta-based travel agents were subcontractors of the big Jakarta- and Bali-based tour operators. The decisions about the local attraction system were not made in Yogyakarta at all, but in Jakarta and Bali. Local agencies did not have the means – in terms of money and human resources – to develop new products. They turned to their big counterparts in Jakarta and Bali: 'let them take the risk, we are too small and vulnerable.' Yet, their bosses in Jakarta and Bali were not interested in taking risks for Yogyakarta. They sold the city as long as it was profitable. With Yogyakarta 'out of fashion,' they would turn to another – newly emerging – destination, of which there were plenty, owing to the policy of expansion and regionalization advocated by the national government. After all, New Order Indonesia seemed to have an inexhaustible supply of attractions, blessed as it was by its 'endless diversity.'

One area that vigorously pushed ahead with tourism development under the national policy of regionalization was the province of Central Java. Yogyakarta may have seen the decline of international tourism growth set in during the early 1990s, but the province of Central Java easily met the national growth objectives and even exceeded them by a 14 per cent increase in 1993. In absolute numbers, however, international tourism represented only a fraction of tourism as a whole; even more than Yogyakarta, Central Java was a domestic destination area – without having the advantage of representing the heritage and history of the whole nation. The province of Central Java posed a major threat to Yogyakarta, first because it competed for well-established tourist attractions, second because it was supported by the national government (in particular the 'first family'), and third because it benefited from the 'law of diminishing returns.' Instead of positioning itself in the market with a 'unique' tourist product, the province of Central Java contested some of the tourist sites and attractions on which Yogyakarta had been capitalizing for many years: the major 'temples' in the area, batik production and other handicrafts, and the Javanese performing arts. The 'tourist product' of Central Java – though still underdeveloped – was more diverse and shrewdly benefited from the experience in other areas. In the mid-1990s the province drew up an initial inventory of the natural and cultural assets that constituted its tourism potential (Diponegoro University 1995). It seems that the province had in mind more small-scale and 'eco-tourist' projects. Among the assets designated to be developed were the agro-tourism area of Sodong Semarang, Nusakambangan and Karimunjawa islands for marine tourism, Dieng Plateau with a temple complex dating from the eighth century and hot springs, Rawa Pening Ambarawa with its potential for ecotourism and the marina recreation park close to Semarang complete with its *Taman Mini* for the Javanese cultural areas. Apart from that, various museums were regarded as of potential interest for tourism: the Ronggowarsito Museum for architecture, Nyonya Meneer *'jamu'* museum and Jamu Jago Museum (both for herbal medicine) – all three in Semarang, the Railway Museum in Ambarawa, and the Sangiran Museum where a replica of the skull of Java Man is kept along with other prehistoric human, animal, and plant fossils. The inventory also listed events closely related to the temples (like *Waicak*), the Kraton Festival in Solo (which is held in collaboration with the royal palace in Yogyakarta) and *Sekaten*, *Garebeg* and other occasions for ceremonial offerings in Central Javanese towns. Among its built heritage the province listed the Old City of Semarang with Blenduk Church dating from the mid-eighteenth century, both palaces in Surakarta, the Grand Mosque at Demak, Sukuh Temple with its erotic relief, the temples of Dieng, the Gedong Songo temple complex near Semarang – and the stupa of Borobudur. Some documents produced by or in collaboration with the provincial government claimed that the temple complex at Prambanan constituted a provincial cultural asset (Paribud Ekoling 1995). The involvement of the Kratons in tourism is very recent – launched with the Kraton Festival in 1991. Up to that date, the Surakarta Kraton had refrained from indulging tourism development – most probably because their counterpart in Yogyakarta claimed a prominent position in tourism and Solo usually did the opposite to anything undertaken by Yogyakarta. Unlike Yogyakarta, Solo could not pride itself on any prominent role in the struggle for independence and the establishment of the national state, as the royal family of Solo kept aloof from national politics. What might have been a disadvantage in national popularity throughout the 1970s and 1980s, seemed to turn into an advantage as the 1990s progressed. As the New Order propaganda has lost its appeal to the masses, Indonesians turned en masse to both a fun mentality fed by the global processes of MacDonaldization and Disneyfication and a reconsideration of local identity. It seems that Central Java is in a better position than Yogyakarta to cater to both these needs. As far as 'edutainment' is concerned on offer it has the Kraton festivals and Kraton-related events, the fun-fair of the Taman Wisata Borobudur dan Prambanan and the Marine Park of Semarang – to mention only a few such enticements. As far as Javanese identity is concerned, Central Javanese tourism experts point out that their Java is a 'virgin area' (Diponegoro University 1995:9), and this might appeal to an audience looking for Javanese identity unmanipulated by New Order rhetoric.

In accordance with recommendations made by the UNDP/UNESCO team (Timothy 1998b:63), the national government strongly supports tourism development in the province of Central Java. Jakarta made a clear statement when assigning the new international airport that was supposed to accelerate tourism development in the entire area to Solo, and not to Yogyakarta. In 1996, Solo which is situated only forty kilometres east of Yogyakarta, opened its new international airport which allows big jets to fly in directly from Singapore, Malaysia and Australasian destinations. The government decision in favour of Solo ended ongoing competition between both cities for the airport, a competition which Yogyakarta expected to be decided in its favour. After all, its Adisucipto Airport might well have served as the new international gateway with a few adaptations and the city's booming hotel industry would easily handle increasing visitor numbers. In the early 1990s, the UNDP/UNESCO team predicted that the location of the new airport would be of crucial importance to the further development of the area, considering that the vast majority of the international tourists visiting the area come in by air. Were the airport to be established in Yogyakarta, the city's position as a centre of tourism would be strengthened and Central Java would have to receive the bulk of its visitors through Yogyakarta as the main gateway. Weighing up the situation, the team also mentioned that if the new airport were established in Solo it would be more profitable to the entire region, including Central Java. In that case visitor flows starting in Solo would go via Yogyakarta to Semarang (Final Report 1991-1992:14). Even as it was being thought out, this scenario was about to change as a consequence of a new toll road to be constructed to connect Solo International Airport with Borobudur. This road would pass the northern outskirts of Yogyakarta making a visit to the inner city a time-consuming detour. The toll-road, experts said, would enhance the number of 'transit tours' to Borobudur and Yogyakarta would become a tourist backwater. As the new airport opened its gates in 1996 – with the toll road still under construction – it remained to be seen what effects it would have on tourist development in the area.

CONCLUSION

In the early 1990s the UNDP/UNESCO team cautioned that the development of tourism in Yogyakarta should not be considered as an all-out solution. Instead, the Special Province should continue to develop its economy in a planned manner, paying special attention to counteracting the widening of the rural-urban disparities. Government intervention in tourism development should not lead to the neglect of other sectors, in particular a diversified agricultural sector, manufacturing, and health and education services. But the writing was already on the wall, dependence on tourism has increased rather than diminished during the more than three decades of New Order rule. It became clear that future prosperity would depend on the city's ability to capitalize on its rich cultural heritage – as the sultan of Yogyakarta, Hamengku Buwono X, pointed out at the cultural tourism conference in 1992 (1993). However, this cultural heritage is at stake. The protected position of Yogyakarta on the one hand and the pressure to live up to government-set goals – material (growth) and immaterial (*pancasila* ideology) – on the other hand, has resulted in a standardization of the tourist product. Yogyakarta is about to lose its position as a cultural centre, it has grown provincial since becoming submissive to Jakarta, from where the new Javanese-Indonesian culture dissemination emanates (Mulder 1994). Facing this New Order-dominated national identity and the foreign-owned tourist culture, Yogyakarta has been constructed as a package of 'classical' attractions characterized by Javanese 'high culture,' sold through Jakarta-based tour operators. Culture in the conceptual definition as 'process' did not figure in the tourist representation and marketing of the area in New Order tourism promotion. While the cultural heritage of the city was given high priority in New Order tourism policy, a perspective on how Yogyanese people actually lived their lives – how they dwelled, worked, and played – was virtually absent from the strategies of tourist marketing. Instead a purified image was 'invented': Yogyakarta as the centre of Javanese court culture and – particularly for domestic tourists – the cradle of national unity and political resistance to colonial rule. Local diversity was made subservient to *pancasila* state ideology; it was not used strategically to establish the city as a meeting place of a variety of cultural flows. This failure inevitably had its repercussions on international tourism in Yogyakarta. Tourists from Europe, Australia and America are no longer satisfied with a presentation of 'frozen images' but demand a more conceptual approach to culture (Richards 1996).

Tourism development has proved to be a vehicle of the bureaucratic, monetary, and ideological penetration of Yogyanese society. As Mulder (1994:11) observes, national schooling has altered the outlook of the new generation, orienting it towards Jakarta rather than to their own cultural environment. The national character was re-created in school: young people were urged to shape and identify with the *Manusia Pancasila*, the exemplary '*Pancasila* Person,' who embodied the true Indonesia and adhered to a lifestyle that was plain and unpretentious – hence the '*P4*' programme that was a compulsory examination subject: 'out of joint with reality, wasting a lot of valuable school time while failing to stimulate both feelings of pride in nation and also participatory citizenship' (Mulder 1994:111). Regarding the overtly unequal distribution of wealth in Indonesia, the rise of a lavishly rich and consumption-oriented middle class, *pancasila* has turned out to be a farce, 'devoid of moral content and reduced to an instrument to control the masses' (ibid:111).

Among the older generation, the lack of confidence in the nation may heighten the need for, and even strengthen, the bonds with religion and area of origin. These ties are particularistic, referring to primordial groups whose strength lies in concrete, personalized relationships. This may account for a revival of *kejawen* among the population of the central Java area. However, Mulder (1994) suggests that this may be different for the youth. Fuelled by tourism development, increased mobility, and consumer culture the orientation of youth and the newly affluent has changed. A competition is emerging between rapid Indonesianization and a revitalized Javanese cultural production, which often appeals to a more popular taste. The demands of ordinary people have prevailed over the needs of the aristocracy. The vestiges of regal rule have become folklorized, existing residually as a mere museum and tourist attraction (Mulder 1994:16). Sites like the Kraton and the people dwelling behind its walls are becoming relics of the past, museum pieces. The traditional court arts are transformed for the entertainment of tourists and folklorized as tokens of identity of a regional 'peak' culture. Many younger people are indifferent to the nostalgia of traditional rituals, ceremonies, etiquette, and language. They have acquired a distaste for hierarchical relationships and their concomitant etiquettes that characterize Javaneseness. It is this re-orientation away from *pancasila* indoctrination and towards 'democratic' forms of enter-tainment that is strongly impinging on tourism in Yogyakarta. The city finds itslef in an unenviable double predicament. As a tourist destination it is the product of the propaganda-machine of the New Order regime which is unable to offer clear markers of a Javanese identity and, therefore – as the symbol of the failing New Order government – is losing its position as the cultural centre of Java and Indonesia as a whole.

NOTES

1   In *Repelita* I and II Yogyakarta was defined as the second tourist destination in Indonesia after Bali. This privileged position became less secure under *Repelita* III and IV, when the concentration policy for tourism was lifted. Only under *Repelita* V and VI Yogyakarta's position was actually threatened because of an active policy of regionalization. In practice, however, Yogyakarta's position as second tourist destination in Indonesia remained intact until the mid-1990s. In 1992/93 Yogyakarta's growth rate in tourism arrivals in general was almost 17 per cent (the national growth rate was 11.06); in 1993/94 Yogyakarta's growth rate had fallen back to 8 per cent while the national growth rate was almost 18 per cent (information acquired from BAPPEDA Yogyakarta on 23-03-96). In Java, however, Yogyakarta maintained its position as second tourist destination after Jakarta. Jakarta is counted as a tourist destination as the biggest port of entry of the country, and many tourists spend the night upon arrival and before proceeding to their actual destination area in Indonesia (Silver 1994:45). Disregarding this logistic necessity, Nuryanti observes that Yogyakarta still is the second most important tourist region in Indonesia after Bali – in terms of 'real' tourist destination (1998:143).

2   In these terms Yogyakarta was characterized in a number of reports written on behalf of the national government and with the aim to support urban economic development in the city, like the 'Real Demand Study' (1991), produced by the Yogyakarta Urban Development Project that was implemented by a Swiss and Indonesian Consultancy commissioned to do so by the Directorate General of Cipta Karya (public works). The studies conducted by the United Nations Development Project in 1991-2, with the aim of developing cultural tourism in Yogyakarta, took the image of a multifaceted cultural destination as a starting point without questioning the appropriateness of this image. Moreover, the weekly issue of '*Yogya-in-a-week*,' an English language periodical distributed as a supplement with the newspaper *Yogya Post*, addressing foreign tourists, attempted to transmit these images to the city's international visitors. The following citation from its first issue is illustrative of this approach: 'Like an 'army of banners' is how Indonesians think of Yogyakarta, for this city above all others, bears the proud record in the recent history of the country. From 1946 to 1950 Yogyakarta was the capital of the Republic of Indonesia during the revolution, five years of uncertainty following World War II.

It was from Yogyakarta that the struggle for Independence was chiefly directed, fought and won. Yogyakarta is also one of the cultural centres with its historical traditions, and one of the educational centres in Indonesia with many universities and thousands of resident students from all over Indonesia. Yogyakarta has been known for a long time as one of the major tourist destination area in Indonesia, the second antique area after Bali' (*Yogya-in-a-week* 19-26 October 1990).

3   This paragraph is compiled from various sources. Unless quoted otherwise, the following sources have been used: Smithies (1986), Periplus (1991), Discover Indonesia (1992), Dalton (1991), Woodward (1989).

4   Yogyakarta shares this status with two other provinces, Aceh and Jakarta Daerah Khusus Ibukota (DKI).

5   The oldest traces of human presence in the area – skull fragments excavated by Eugène Dubois in the area of Sangiran, east of Solo – are about 500,000 years old.

6   In many tourist guide books and in the discourses of tour guides Prambanan is said to originate in the eighth century and Borobudur in the ninth century.

7   After the first division in 1755, there was a second minor one in 1757 giving rise to the small principality of the Mankunegaran which was closely associated with Surakarta.

8   For centuries high rank was based on the proximity of the individual to the royal court. In pre-Independence Yogyakarta, two classes derived their privileged position from this proximity: the nobility *(sentonodalem)*, consisting of those of royal blood who generally held the top administrative positions in the country, and the *priyayi* or *abdidalem*, who were officials of the administration but were recruited from among the commoners. They either had the privilege of working in the Kraton or were engaged in the administration of the state outside the palace (Guinness 1986:29).

9   The first European school was opened in 1832. In 1911, besides the European schools, there were another five public primary schools and a teachers' college. In 1924 the total number of educational institutions in Yogyakarta had risen to seventy. Among these institutions was the 'A.M.S.-afd. B.,' the first of its kind in the Netherlands East Indies, which was established as a school specifically for autochthonous children in 1919 (De Graaf 1947).

10 In 1988 the administration of Gadjah Mada University received 20,000 applications for one thousand places (Guinness 1991:93).

11 Other sources speak of seventy-two private universities in 1996 (Interview with Pak Djoko Sudiarso, head of Bidang Pariwisata of BAPPEDA Yogyakarta, August 7, 1996).

12 In 1988 the city government received 32,000 applications for 500 vacancies. There was similar competition for jobs in the private formal sector (Guinness 1991:93). In the early 1990s the Special Province as a whole had 139,373 registered unemployed, but only 29,333 vacancies (Sudarmadji 1991:16).

13 Agriculture ranked first with 29 per cent of the GRDP (Gross Regional Domestic Product), services ranked second (19 per cent) (Rotge 1991).

14 In 1960 there was 4.5 per cent annual growth, of which 1.8 per cent was due to natural growth through births, and 2.7 per cent was due to migration (Soedjarwo 1991:4).

15 Before 1960 population growth was 4.5 per cent per year (Soedjarwo 1991:4); between 1980 and 1985, the growth rate declined to only 1.27 per cent against 2.15 per cent for the country as a whole during the same period (Rotge 1991).

16 There are many different explanations for the name of 'Malioboro.' One of the most popular explanantions which is quoted by Smithies (1986:30) and repeated by local guides says that the name is derived from the Duke of Marlborough.

17 Diponegoro (1785-1855), a Yogyakarta prince, is one of Indonesia's national heroes. He revolted against the Dutch, but was betrayed and captured during a truce meeting with the Dutch in Magelang. His residence in Tegalrejo (Yogyakarta) is accessible to visitors.

18 P.T. is the abbreviation for *perseroan terbatas*, meaning Ltd., Inc.

19 The minister of Tourism, Post and Telecommunications, the minister of Culture and Education, and the minister of Finance.

20 Among the first commissioners were the former Indonesian ambassador to Britain, the assistant rector of Gadjah Mada University, a high government official of the 'Special Region Yogyakarta,' and the director of the National Archaeological Office (Final Report 1991-92:107).

21 *Waicak* or *Wesak* is the day on which Buddha's birthday is celebrated. According to Borobudur tour guides, this anniversary is observed at the stupa on the day of the full moon in June (others say in May).

22 This information was acquired in an interview with Pak Yuwana, director of the PT Taman Wisata *Candi* Borobudur dan Prambanan on August 22, 1996.

23 Ever since the eighteenth century Solo has possessed two palaces, the Kasunanan where the sunan of Surakarta resides, and the Pura Mangkunagaran, where the descendants of the disloyal prince reside. Only the Kasunanan is entitled to be called 'Kraton.'

24 This claim was not acknowledged by the Yogyakarta and Surakarta Kratons. Consequently, the enthusiastic support of the first family was directed towards 'the other' palace in Surakarta, the Mangkunagaran. The president became the leading force behind the Mangadeg Foundation, a joint cultural effort launched by the Jakarta Javanese elite and the Mangkunagaran Palace to renovate the formal gravesite of Mangkunagara I. The support accorded that palace and dynasty in Central Java might be related to the reluctance of the other palaces to acknowledge the former president and his wife as the benefactors of 'Javanese' cultural inheritance (Pemberton 1994:162).

25 This meeting was organized by the Centre for Tourism Research of Sanata Dharma University Yogyakarta and was held at the Ambarrukmo Palace Hotel on March 26, 1996.

26 Unfortunately we are short of data regarding the amounts of money spent by tourists in both areas.

27 Number of visitors entering Yogyakarta through Adisucipto Airport 1991-5.

Year	International visitors	Growth (%)	Domestic visitors	Growth (%)
1991	128,358	-9.15	169,557	25.13
1992	163,212	27.15	198,680	17.17
1993	212,542	30.22	207,211	4.29
1994	214.044	0.70	298,911	44.25
1995	212.300	-0.81	353,765	18.35

Source: KANWIL VIII Depparpostel DIY 1996, p. 86

Flight frequency to Yogyakarta per month, 1991-5:

Year	From Jakarta	from Den-pasar	from Ban-dung	from Banjar-masin	From Sura-Baya	From Sema-rang
1991	201	121	30	30	31	-
1992	221	164	31	30	56	-
1993	263	175	29	27	80	-
1994	331	230	30	29	75	29
1995	355	199	47	31	123	-

Source: KANWIL VIII Depparpostel DIY 1996, p. 88

28 Number of international tourists and annual growth rate, Yogyakarta, 1988-95:

Year	Number of foreign tourists	Growth rate
1988	113,091	-
1989	180,896	60
1990	188,549	4.2
1991	216,051	14.9
1992	256,192	18.6
1993	299,433	16.9
1994	323,194	7.9
1995	344,265	6.5

Source: KANWIL VIII Depparpostel DIY 1996.

29 Domestic tourism development in Yogyakarta, 1988-95:

Year	Number domestic Tourists	Growth rate
1988	235,716	-
1989	483,520	105.1
1990	398,636	-17.6
1991	492,048	23.4
1992	561,224	14.1
1993	610,818	8.8
1994	640,801	4.9
1995	837,265	30.7

Source: KANWIL VIII Depparpostel DIY 1996.

30 Number of nights spent in Yogya by international and domestic tourists, 1988-95:

Accom-modation	1988		1989		1990	
	Int.	Domes.	Int.	Domes.	Int.	Domes.
Non-Starrated	2.80	1.45	2.25	1.50	2.10	1.18
Starrated	1.98	1.73	1.84	1.70	1.85	1.74
Avarage	1.13	1.54	2.18	1.60	1.97	1.96

Accom-modation	1993		1994		1995	
	Int.	Domes.c	Int.	Domes.	Int.	Domes.
Non-star-rated	2.25	1.33	2.31	1.40	2.34	1.49
Star-rated	1.60	1.68	1.69	1.69	1.71	1.79
Avarage	1.93	1.51	2.00	1.55	2.03	1.64

Source: Statistik Pariwisata, Daerah Istimewa Yogyakarta, Dinas Pariwisata Yogyakarta, 1995.

31 This gap may have been caused by bad administration of overnight stays because many owners of accommodation do not list all their rooms and register only some of their guests in order to evade taxes.

32 I found many travel agents in Bali and even Lombok offering these 'Yogya One-Day Tours.' The most elaborate programme I came across was the following: departure time from Bali at 5 o'clock in the morning, the tour includes the air trip, a visit to Borobudur, Pawon, and Mendut temples, lunch in Yogyakarta and a visit to Prambanan temple. The tourists arrive back in Bali at 8 o'clock at night. There are shorter trips to Borobudur only. Prices were between US$ 200 and 230.

CHAPTER 4

PROMINENT PLAYERS IN YOGYAKARTA'S TOURISM ARENA

KAMPUNG AND STREETSIDE TOURISM

INTRODUCTION

Yogyakarta experienced booming tourism development in the wake of the deregulatory measures directed toward the government-led star-rated sector. As a major destination for both 'quality' and *pancasila* tourism, the city's economy was expected to benefit greatly from growing numbers of tourists. This scenario worked out differently, as tourism growth rates were declining in the 1990s. The proliferation of resort development and the political burden with which tourism in Yogyakarta had been charged threatened to destroy the city's tourism economy. In the previous chapter the changing tourism policy in favour of regionalization and the diminishing appeal of the *pancasila* rhetoric to the masses have been identified as important *political* factors that contributed to this decline. But these are not the only ones. There are *economic* and *social* factors that have to be considered as well. We need to establish a better understanding of the ways in which the relationships of entrepreneurs in the tourist system of Yogyakarta – which is inextricably intertwined with New Order politics – have contributed to its decline as a tourist destination.

The rapid growth of the large-scale tourism industry has changed the appearance of the city which is quickly losing its 'village-like' character, and in the process has also widened the gap between the small capitalist economic sector and the vast petty economy. Yogyakarta's economy is largely constituted of small-scale, family-run businesses and self-employed people (Soedjarwo 1991:233; Sullivan 1992:113). This was equally applicable to the tourism industry, despite of the mushrooming high-rise hotels and resorts. While the star-rated sector was Jakarta-controlled, tourism development at the local level took place in those sectors that for a long time had been regarded 'inferior' by the national government, i.e. small-scale enterprises, in particular family businesses and self-employed people. In the light of the development policy of the New Order regime, this economic sector seemed to be a remnant of the past, of underdevelopment and backwardness (Rigg 1997:48-9). Saddled with this burden, the small-scale enterprises in Indonesia had to operate under ever more stringent conditions and conform to increasing government regulations, or face destruction.[1]

As the small-scale enterprises are a vigorous and visible element in the tourism sector, employing a large proportion of the labour force they may have been down, but they were not out. Petty modes of production are not expelled by modernization, but exist alongside the capitalist economy and often even grow and become more important in the process. The same thing happens in tourism: in Indonesia, where the presence of the informal sector is well established, it continues to increase and diversify as the tourism industry develops (Cukier 1996, Timothy & Wall 1997, Dahles 1998b, Bras & Dahles 1998, Dahles & Bras 1999a). Instead of offering facilities to improve the position of small-scale entrepreneurs, the governments at both the national and local levels have taken steps to restrict their modes of operation. The tourism industry in the centre of Yogyakarta provides an interesting case to illustrate this point. Here, the domestic and the foreign independent traveller market is flourishing, contributing particularly to the small-scale tourism industry. This is the domain of the local government which is considerably less vigorous and effective than the national government when it comes to intervention. With the national government unsupportive and the local government not capable of taking measures to benefit the small-scale tourism sector, petty entrepreneurs are left to their own devices and therefore establish supportive networks of their own and operate discretely from the dominant economy.

As pointed out in the previous chapter, the threat to tourism in Yogyakarta under the new Order was concentrated mainly in the government-defined 'quality' sector. Its strength did not lie in the expensive hotels situated along the broad, brightly lit streets in the city's shopping and business centre and in the vicinity of the airport, but in the 'budget' accommodation that can be found in the narrow sidestreets and the *kampung*. In his study of value systems among lower-class urban Javanese in Yogyakarta, Guinness (1986) distinguishes 'streetside' society from *kampung* society. The first denotes the wealthier and more influential citizens living in concrete houses along the main streets of the city establishing the educated urban culture or dominant society, while the latter denotes the urban poor dwelling in ramshackle houses cramped together higgledy-piggledy behind the main streets (Guinness 1989). In Guinness' terms, it is '*kampung*' tourism that flourished in the mid-1990s in Yogyakarta, not 'streetside' tourism. The basic characteristic of *kampung* tourism is that it is defined as the opposite of government-supported 'quality' tourism: small-scale, low-budget, unorganized, 'uncontrolled,' informal, low-quality. It also entails more intensive tourist-local interaction, generates local benefits, makes use of local facilities, and involves family-businesses and self-employed people. A complex network of small entrepreneurs have tuned their business to the needs of *kampung* tourism, and diverse categories of self-employed people operate within this network and mediate between the local industry and the tourists.

Characteristic of the local industry is the enormous diversity of images and meanings associated with the city and its 'attractions,' which certainly diverge from the standardized *pancasila* rhetoric. People in the local industry construct and sell their own versions of Yogyakarta as a tourist product. In a way, they create and cater to a different market than the government-led sector does – which makes them suspicious in the eyes of the authorities. One could say that there are two different tourist realities: the official and the local; or 'streetside' reality and *kampung* reality. These two realities exist in two different spheres occupying different tourist spaces and are organized in different 'geographies' by different institutions and different people using different facilities. 'Streetside' and *kampung* tourism are also politically segregated realities, as they fall under the aegis of different ministries and departments. 'Streetside' and *kampung* tourism are socially segregated as both areas are organized by people from different class backgrounds; and economically segregated as their businesses are characterized by different entrepreneurial cultures. With increasing pressures on tourism in Yogyakarta, both realities have come into conflict with each other. The local government is putting more and more effort into the formalization of *kampung* tourism, attempting to control the growth of informal activities. Its main strategies are licensing, sweepings, training, and enclosing areas. Space becomes contested: the built heritage is converted into controlled areas and access is limited to people conforming to the government-set rules. Public space is 'policed' and raids occur irregularly, creating an atmosphere of constant distress among small business people.

Studies focusing on the politics of tourism in Indonesia have failed to analyse the multi-layered character of tourism. The bulk of the literature focuses on the large-scale tourism sector, often regarding this sector as exemplary for tourism in general. As far as any attention is paid to the local community, this is dealt with as an homogeneous entity, as if local people show consensus regarding the way tourism should be organized to benefit them all. However, to understand the significance and meaning of tourism in local communities, we cannot confine ourselves to a simple dichotomy of the government-approved 'quality' sector versus the *kampung* sector. Instead, we have to analyse the heterogeneity of the local community and address its multivocality when it comes to tourism development. We have to raise the question of whether government measures affecting small-scale tourism in general and *kampung* tourism in particular either leave room for local initiatives or suffocate them. How do these local developments affect the success or failure of tourism and the government's development schemes? Does *kampung* tourism benefit or suffer from 'streetside' tourism? Does *kampung* tourism contribute to or threaten 'streetside' tourism as many policy makers would contend? In other words, to what extent do both realities conflict or converge? To shed light on these issues, this chapter investigates the ways in which *kampung* entrepreneurs participate in the margins of the 'tourism establishment,' how these people establish themselves, form coalitions and networks, compete and combat each other and the dominant economy. On the other hand, this chapter also discusses the strategies of 'streetside' entrepreneurs who benefit from 'quality' tourism in Yogyakarta: the ways in which they position themselves in the city's tourism industry and organize themselves in order to secure their position.

KAMPUNG AND 'STREETSIDE' IN YOGYAKARTA

The bulk of Yogyakarta's urban population lives in a *kampung*. In the eighteenth century separate compounds emerged for the nobles and their retainers, the palace servants, specific groups of artisans, craftsmen, traders, and even foreigners (Guinness 1989:55). These were originally found within or adjacent to the Kraton walls, but with the expansion of the city's population during the nineteenth century the *kampung* area spread north and east of the palace. By the early twentieth century the term *kampung* had come to designate an off-street neighbourhood inhabited by members of the lower class, the 'little people' of the town. The land on which *kampung* are located is often regarded as land left over after wealthier, more influential citizens, the 'big, notable people,' have set up their homes and businesses elsewhere. Characteristically *kampung* are in the spaces behind the 'streetside' premises of this upper class, who are locally called *wong gedongan*. These people derive their name from the buildings they are supposed to inhabit (*gedong* means stone building) and which are typical of the edifices which line the city's main streets (Sullivan 1992:110-11). *Kampung* were beyond the gaze of court or colonial administrators, and without strict building laws to delineate housing blocks, public thoroughfares, and recreation space they were exposed to high levels of population migration. Therefore the *kampung* absorbed the major proportion of the population expansion of the city. The nineteenth century witnessed the vulgarization of *kampung* culture which gained a reputation for being lacking in refinement and manners, and the term *kampungan* came to be used by 'streetside' residents to indicate behaviour that was coarse, stupid, or unsophisticated, the furthest extreme from that identified with the educated, urbane 'streetside' culture. *Kampung* thus became the repository, at least according to the 'streetside' elite, of a distinctive occupational and cultural lower class, and the term was used by the elite in a derogatory sense (Guinness 1986:55). There was another side to the coin. As Guinness points out *kampung* people began to identify strongly with their community in which they felt some pride and reject the stereotype of themselves as lacking in 'culture.' In many ways *kampung* people model themselves on the culture of the palace, emulating it to whatever degree they can afford. *Kampung* society defines itself most often in opposition to the 'streetside' people who – from the *kampung* point of view – are rich, tight-fisted, inhospitable, unco-operative, unhelpful, hard-hearted, arrogant, intolerant, and inconsiderate (Sullivan 1992:110). *Kampung* people consider themselves superior to 'streetsiders,' particularly in terms of *rukun*, translated as social harmony and co-operation, of which streetside society is said to be devoid (Guinness 1986, Sullivan 1992).

It must be obvious that *kampung* accommodates a vast array of social groups and is generally diverse in social, ideological, even ethnic terms. It contains people of disparate means, professions, religions, and education (Sullivan 1992:97). Within the *kampung* social rank is an important means of ordering social relations and expectations among a heterogeneous population originating from diverse regions of Java and beyond. The significance of social rank in the *kampung* is that there is such a wide range of clearly delineated ranks marked by various indices – age, nobility, origin, landed property, and occupation (Guinness 1986:28). High rank in any or all of these gives an individual, man or woman, prestige among his or her neighbours who, at least formally, defer to him/her, addressing him/her respectfully. Given the decline in the influence of the sultan or the court on *kampung* residents since Independence and as the nobility derived their prestige from their proximity to the court, their claim to rank within the *kampung* community has also declined in importance. Many residents continue to be conscious that their immigrant status is different from that of those Yogya born (*Yogya asli*, i.e. from Yogyanese origin) or long-settled in the city. There is a continuing orientation towards court etiquette, and most inner city *kampung* accommodate a number of *abdidalem*, 'palace servant' families, as well as some *kampung* residents who hold a court title such as *Raden, Raden Mas, Raden Ayu, Raden Ajeng* (Guinness 1986:34). Those who are *Yogya asli* enjoy the respect of most *kampung* residents for their assumed mastery of refined behaviour associated with court traditions.

The *kampung* spans a wide range of income levels. While most *kampung* people are poor and engaged in low-status work, their communities may also accommodate middle-class figures: richer traders, professionals, and white collar workers (Sullivan 1992:72). Quite apart from these groups, some self-employed *kampung* members are quite well off, owning successful businesses and earning a substantial income. These are all exceptions and the vast majority of *kampung* people make a living in the informal sector. Those employed within the formal sector, as low-ranking government workers, shop assistants, and hotel staff may also be involved in informal sector activities, as their low wages and poor conditions of service only sustain sub-standard living conditions in the *kampung*. On the other hand *kampung* people look to the formal sector of the 'streetside' as the best source of income and seek to develop relations with 'streetside' patrons (Guinness 1989:64). Similarly, those in informal sector activities foster ties with 'streetside' authorities. Pedicab drivers have ties with the pedicab owner, with regular clients and 'streetside' 'sponsors' like big hotels (Van Gemert & Van Genugten 1996). Sellers of goods and food on the city pavements or within the station have contacts with officials which make such a livelihood possible (Guinness 1989:65). *Kampung* society is as concerned with relative rank as is the wider society, inspired by the traditional hierarchies of a court culture, yet it recognizes distinctions of rank quite irrelevant in the wider society. Social esteem accorded on individuals in the *kampung* may not be reflected by 'streetside' society. The distance between *kampung* community and 'streetside' society is great. There is a relationship between this distance and the relationship of the *kampung* with the city administration generally, particularly as regards the imposition of outside decisions and expectations on the *kampung* and the suppression of individual economic activities in the city (Guinness 1986:171). Most *kampung* people would deny entry to the state if it were in their power actually to keep it out of the *kampung*; instead they deny it has entered and do not recognize it as a mainstay of their communities (Sullivan 1992:170).

TOURISM DEVELOPMENT IN A YOGYANESE *KAMPUNG*

Although the *kampung* of Yogyakarta show common characteristics such as the great internal diversity and relative impermeability to outside intervention, there are differences among them in terms of social composition and culture. These differences become more marked through tourism development. There are a number of *kampung* in Yogyakarta that have been profoundly affected by tourism, like the residential quarters in the Kraton area (in particular Taman Sari) and in Prawirotaman, an old middle-class neighbourhood south of the Kraton. In this chapter we shall focus on a *kampung* area that is in the immediate vicinity of the hotspots of 'streetside' tourism: the *kampung* of Sosrowijayan.[2] Situated behind the 'streetside' buildings of Malioboro Street, Sosrowijayan is a typical *kampung* area, extremely busy and brimming over with life, with small and crowded houses clustered along the narrow alleyways, a very heterogeneous population, and a rather unfavourable reputation in 'streetside' society. In Sosrowijayan living quarters, tourist accommodation, restaurants and *warung*, nightbars, tiny shops, batik galleries and workshops share the cramped space. Cars, tourist buses, motorcycles, bicycles, and pedicabs frequent the main traffic ways in this quarter around the clock, while everyday life carries on as usual in the narrow alleyways. The residents go about their business: local women bargain for fresh fruit and vegetables sold by traders along the street, water sellers and other mobile vendors walk the neighbourhood carrying their merchandise, housewives prepare food for their family on a stove in front of their homes, children play, people hurry to the mosque, cockfights are organized, older people squat on the sidewalk and comment on the tourists passing by, lottery sellers and *jamu* sellers walk from doorstep to doorstep. Young men frequent the streets and alleys looking for newly arrived foreigners to take them to a batik gallery to earn some commission. When it gets dark, male and female prostitutes offer their services and bars are visited by young tourists and local adolescents, drinking alcohol and smoking marihuana.

Tourism development in this area started in the early 1970s with *kampung* residents catering to the 'hippy travellers' who looked for cheap places to stay. In addition to selling food, a number of *kampung* people began a batik gallery and – after earning some money through batik sales – invested their money in their homes. The owners expanded the number of rooms and improved their services and eventually turned their home into a 'homestay' which has become a very popular accommodation among backpackers. Despite efforts by the Indonesian government to ban foreign language use in public life, 'homestay' remains a very popular term for budget accommodation in Yogyakarta. But other terms are widely used as well, such as *losmen* (from the Dutch word *logement*), inn, pension, guesthouse, *penginapan*, *wisma*, and *pondok* (Peeters & Urru 1996; Peeters, Urru & Dahles 1999). Homestays are family-run accommodation in which local people take visitors into their homes in much the same way as bed-and-breakfast accommodation (Wall & Long 1996, Long & Kindon 1997).[3] The establishment of a homestay requires a relatively low initial capital outlay and this type of business is potentially accessible to any family with a spare room or the space to build one. Successful homestay owners move out of the *kampung* where they began their business and leave the management to other family members or young employees. Having originally been a source of additional income, the accommodation develops into a business managed from a distance. With cumulative improvements and renovations – exchanging the Indonesian for a Western-style bathroom, installing air-conditioning, offering more services, building more rooms – the homestay eventually develops into a guesthouse or small hotel. The facilities offered by the homestays are varied. Some offer practically nothing but a place to sleep, while others have room service and organize excursions and batik courses (Peeters, Urru & Dahles 1999). In many instances homestays have provided their owners with the capital required to expand their business and diversify their economic activities. Some of them began restaurants with tourist menus, others offered cheap transport facilities to their guests to their next destination or to one of the popular sites in the area of Yogyakarta, and this eventually expanded into small travel agencies. One entrepreneur in Sosro-wijayan was so successful that he has started a chain of franchise businesses in the *kampung* that book seats in his buses and sell his tours. The tiny offices, often run by one man, are situated next to each other offering identical products, but compete with each other by offering very keen prices. We shall discuss the business strategies within this franchise system in more detail below.

Sosrowijayan offers the cheapest accommodation, transport facilities, excursions, and most popular low-budget eating-places in town. Therefore, the area is favoured by individual travelling young tourists, mostly students. The majority of them are long-term travellers, and they stay in Indonesia considerably longer than the average (package) tourist. It is quite common that these young people use the full two months that the Indonesian tourist visa allows.[4] As research has shown, the average length of stay of these long-termers in Yogyakarta is about nine days (Mazur 1993:152). Being young and on the move for months on end means that these tourists are on a tight budget. Therefore, these long-termers stay in the cheapest category of accommodation, of which the Sosrowijayan area has an abundant supply. Far from being put out by the noise these travellers enjoy the hustle and bustle of street life in Sosrowijayan and the modest night life in the street cafes. The long-termers in Sosrowijayan – because of the time they have at their disposal and the experience they have acquired during their long trip – spend their money not only in tourism businesses, but also directly in local shops, on local transport and local food at the cheap *warung* where the locals buy their meals as well. For many, Yogyakarta is a place to take a rest on a long journey, to relax, and to live pleasantly on very little money (Mazur 1993:144-5).

In the space of twenty years, the people of Sosrowijayan have become extremely dependent on tourism for their livelihood. The vast majority of the parents of those people who now are involved in some tourism-related business were peasants (Mazur 1993:194, 210), and many older people entered the tourism economy after having worked in a traditional craft (batik or brickmaking) or as construction worker. Nowadays there are only few families who do not depend on tourism in one way or the other (Mazur 1993:202-6), and most young people look for a job in tourism directly after finishing or dropping out of school (ibid:209). In general, the income from tourism is low and fluctuates according to the season. Many *kampung* entrepreneurs complain about a permanent lack of money to pay for their children's school fees, their debts, and even for sufficient food for their family (ibid: 1993:206-7). However, the income of the owners of family businesses (accommodation, restaurants, batik galleries) and self-employed people (*becak* men, informal guides) is above the *kampung* average (especially compared to workers in non-tourism industries), while employees in tourism enterprises receive extremely low payment (Mazur 1993:240-53). But a low-paid job in tourism may often be the only job available to these *kampung* people. Research in Yogyakarta *kampung* areas has shown that the demand for tourist services significantly enhances the income of the lowest categories of workers in the urban economy (Van Gemert, Van Genugten & Dahles 1999). Tourism has created new jobs and opportunities and introduced new consumer goods to be desired and new lifestyles to be emulated. Tourists have become an integrated part of everyday life in Sosrowijayan and nobody in the *kampung* seems to feel alarmed or disturbed by their omnipresence. The next section investigates the business strategies adopted by local entrepreneurs in tourism and their mutual dependence in this busy tourist *kampung*.

LIFE IN A 'TOURIST' *KAMPUNG*

ENTREPRENEURS IN *KAMPUNG* TOURISM

Pak Djoko[5] (51) is a self-made man. In the mid-1990s he held a monopoly on the tour and travel business in two *kampung* in Yogyakarta with Sosrowijayan as his home base. There and in Prawirotaman almost all small travel agents depend for their income on Djoko's enterprise. Djoko came to Yogyakarta as an orphan and was raised by a couple in Sosrowijayan. As an adolescent he left for Jakarta where he worked in all kinds of jobs until he returned to Yogyakarta in 1985 to marry a *kampung* woman. Her parents were among those *kampung* people who benefited from the tourism boom in the 1980s: by the mid-1980s they ran a small *losmen* in Sosrowijayan Street. The accommodation was doing well and soon Djoko learned that more money could be made from tourism. The young travellers staying in his family's *losmen* were asking for cheap transport to the airport, to the tourist objects in the area, and a transfer to their next destination as far as Mount Bromo and Bali. At the time Djoko worked as a chauffeur and his network made it easy to arrange a car or a mini-bus. This is how he started in the tour and travel business. In 1987 he established his travel agency, Sosro Tours, in the *losmen* in Sosrowijayan Street, while the *losmen* was moved to another house in the *kampung* that his in-laws had bought. It turned out to be an ingenious construction: the *losmen* functioned as a permanent source of customers for his travel agency, and through his travel agency he channelled newly arrived tourists to the accommodation. He did not stop there and the radius of Djoko's activities soon expanded. Sosro Tours has grown to become the largest in the 'budget' sector of Sosrowijayan and Prawirotaman. While the travel agency has developed into his core business with about fifteen employees, additionally he runs the *losmen* which his wife inherited from her parents. Moreover, he owns a restaurant and a school of *pencak silat* (Indonesian 'kung fu'). Pak Djoko has to be regarded as a very successful business man from a *kampung* background. At present he lives in a spacious house in a new, middle-class area of Yogyakarta, but his business activities are still focused on the *kampung*.

In the early years of his business – Pak Djoko was the first to develop tours in the budget sector in Sosrowijayan – he offered the standard package that the agents in the star-rated sector were selling as well, only much more expensively than he did! He arranged tours to Borobudur, city tours with a visit to the Kraton and a shopping break at batik and silver factories, and sunset at Prambanan. He put six to eight tourists in small buses, air-conditioned transport being slightly more expensive, and provided them with a pre-packed snack and a small bottle of water. Soon other *kampung* people started to copy him: in tiny shacks along the street, right next-door to his office, identical tours were being sold. These were one-man businesses, the owners acting as intermediaries in the hiring of transport, drivers, and guides, and often the owners had to perform all these jobs themselves. Many a time they had only two clients for a trip which made their independent business unprofitable. Eventually most of these small entrepreneurs started to turn to Djoko's agency to buy seats on one of his tours. Pak Djoko likes the idea that many small agencies in town bring in customers, so he offers them a discount. The difference between Djoko's price and the money they charge the tourists is their turn-over. At present, most travel agencies in the budget areas work for Pak Djoko as subcontractors. The small offices compete with each other by undercutting each other's prices by a few rupiah which appeals to the backpackers' preoccupation with saving money.

In the course of time Djoko has diversified his product. A yellow flyer, that is distributed among the subcontracting agencies and many *losmen* in the tourist areas and through the Tourist Office, lists an impressive choice of tours in the vicinity of Yogyakarta as far as Mount Bromo and Solo to the east and Dieng Plateau to the north-west. The prices are very competitive: he charges less than one third of what his star-rated competitors are asking. Pak Djoko proudly mentions that tourists who stay at the Garuda Hotel come to his office to book excursions at his agency: 'They appreciate a good price.' Not being eligible for membership of the association for star-rated travel agencies, he enjoys his buses entering the drive of this prestigious hotel to pick up their guests. Profiting from his good relations with officials from the *Dinas Pariwisata*, the local government agency responsible for local tourist attractions, he has acquired the more or less exclusive rights to arrange the nightly trips from Yogyakarta to the open-air Ramayana ballet at the Prambanan theatre which is a popular tourist attraction during the dry season.

Although Pak Djoko never fails to stress his love for the *kampung* and his gratitude towards the *kampung* people who brought him up, it is obvious that he is a shrewd businessman who makes clever use of his *kampung* resources. The small travel agents who depend on Djoko's enterprise for their income, do not even act as subcontractors, but merely as a booking office for Sosro Tours to which they entrust their clients. In return, Sosro Tours commits itself to arranging guided tours for any client from these related agencies, even though this may oblige them to hire a car for one single tourist only. The risk is for the bigger partner. The agency is managed in an efficient way. Instead of long-term seasonal planning, Sosro Tours draws up a schedule from day-to-day. When the last bus returns at about ten o'clock at night, the booking desk closes and the available staff members sit down to arrange the schedule for the next day: they determine the number of buses to the different destinations and the guides to accompany them. At six in the morning, everybody has to be present at the office to receive the instructions, the list of names, and addresses of where to pick up the clients. In the low season some staff members have to hang around the office waiting for incidental jobs, as there are not enough tours to keep them busy. At peak season, Sosro Tours operates like a transport business as it lacks the staff to run all the tours. Then it hires additional minibuses and the tourists are taken to the core attractions – Borobudur and Prambanan temple score highest among the bookings – without a guide as these attractions offer their own guided tours.

There are only a few travel agents in Sosrowijayan and Prawirotaman that have successfully managed to establish themselves in the budget market and this is because they cater to a particular market niche, namely adventure tourism: climbing (Merapi Tour), caving, and cycling. These specialized travel agents seem to live in symbiosis with Sosro Tours: they earn the commission for bookings for Sosro Tours and, vice versa, Sosro buys seats on their adventurous trips. However, there is fierce competition between the big patron and the few small agencies that seriously attempt to operate independently. Pak Djoko accuses these competitors of 'fraud.' The bone of contention is the successful 'sunrise tours' to Borobudur stupa. It seems that the Borobudur Sunrise Tour has been developed by one of the small agencies and it became a big success in a short span of time. Even the travel agents in the star-rated sector call an early trip to Borobudur a 'sunrise' tour. However, as Pak Djoko notes, the name is misleading. Whereas it makes the tourists believe that they are going to witness the sunrise from the stupa, the sun is already high in the sky when *Taman Wisata Borobudur* opens its gates at six o'clock in the morning. Concerted attempts by travel agents in the area to convince the park management to open the gates earlier have failed. This is why Pak Djoko decided to call the morning excursions to the temple 'Beautiful Morning at Borobudur' instead of 'Sunrise Tour.' He uses this as a marketing instrument: his guides never fail to mention the difference to their clients, stressing the reliability of Sosro Tours in contrast to its competitors.

Although Pak Djoko is not a typical petty entrepreneur – his success is much too spectacular – he is typically '*kampung*' in that he spreads his business over a number of activities. There are other entrepreneurs who try to emulate his success. For Djoko, the travel agency has become the core enterprise, but a few other *kampung* people basically operate from their *losmen* or homestay. Sosrowijayan is the area with the highest density of budget accommodation in Yogyakarta. Accommodation is regarded as a safe investment which can easily be combined with other activities (transport business, restaurant, batik and souvenir workshops) by using family labour and it provides a steady flow of customers to be channelled to the other family businesses. As has been shown in the previous chapter, the occupancy rate is high in this sector, even in the low season.

Ibu Siska, the owner of Sita Homestay, is an absentee homestay owner. She is a woman in her thirties, unmarried and living with her grandmother in another *kampung*. She is *Yogya asli*, but lived in East Java for many years with her parents and siblings. In the early 1990s she bought the building in which her enterprise is accommodated in one of the alleys of Sosrowijayan *kampung*, a quiet area where few other tourist businesses are situated. It is a two-storied building rising above the low *kampung* houses and offers a great view of Yogyakarta from the top-floor balcony. Downstairs is a common room with sofas and a refrigerator, a tiny office where she keeps her computer and a couch to take a nap, and a room covered with mattresses where her young male employees sleep. She employs two young men in their early twenties to do all the jobs: clean the rooms, do their guests' laundry, receive new and check out departing guests, answer the telephone, serve breakfast and snacks, and accompany tours at times. The two have been with her from the beginning and they seem satisfied with their job. She says that she pays them well, gives them one day off a fortnight, and encourages them to make the most of their knowledge and capabilities. In particular, she wants them to become well-trained guides for her caving tours. Her homestay has been doing well over the years and the accommodation has seen several improvements, renovations, and expansions. Siska is proud to have received a favourable mention in the 'Lonely Planet' Travel Guide, which generates a steady flow of guests who manage to find her place walking the narrow alleyways with the travel guide book clutched in their hands.

So far she has done well but Siska has far-reaching ambitions. As a graduate of Gadjah Mada University, she participates in a group of 'engaged' young entrepreneurs – former fellow students – who intend to develop forms of 'alternative' tourism. Although this group is seriously involved in issues about how to develop tourism without destroying natural and cultural resources, their main concern is to create market niches to operate successfully in the shadow of the big tour operators and to earn some money. Siska has developed a number of excursions to home industries in Yogyanese *kampung*, and she is attempting to establish herself in adventure tourism. Her 'unique selling point,' as she says in marketing terms, is a tour to Cereme Cave in the Gunung Kidul area. She has been organizing this trip for a few years now mainly for tourists staying in her accommodation but she hopes that, with the help of her friends and a connection with a Dutch tour operator, she can market it in terms of ecotourism. The flyer announcing this tour on a notice board in the common room reads: 'The trip is a good way to enhance your knowledge about potential of the cave for local welfare and your awareness of conserving species with different ecosystem. (...) Take nothing but picture, leave nothing but footprint, kill nothing but time.' Siska's great concern, besides the modest competition from *kampung* travel agents, is the local government: rumour has it, a government-supported organization intends to develop the cave for domestic and international tourism.

There are many local entrepreneurs taking advantage of the curiosity about *kampung* life that many Western tourists exhibit. The interest in local life has been related to a 'quest for authenticity' that is said to characterize people from Western, 'post-industrial' countries (MacCannell 1976). It is for this category that agritourism and village tourism have been developed. In Indonesia there are a few initiatives to take tourists to villages and introduce them to local industries and rural projects.[6] While urban welfare projects are regularly visited during 'alternative' city tours – in Yogyakarta a house for homeless children attracts foreign visitors[7] – *kampung* life has not been developed as an attraction. Only the well-established tourist *kampung* with their handicraft shops and galleries are frequented by tourists for shopping, not for meeting the local people. *Becak* men, *andong* drivers, self-employed guides, and touts take tourists to these shops and handicraft industries to earn the commission on the goods that tourists buy. Other *kampung* areas accommodating industries that have not been defined as souvenir industries (yet) are not regarded as 'tourist objects.' Travel agents cannot imagine that a *kampung* can be anything except a low-class neighbourhood where living conditions leave much to be desired. Tourists, on the other hand, dare not enter the gateways that give access to the narrow *kampung* alleys and they rarely stray into Yogyanese neighbourhoods. The air-conditioned buses of the 'quality' sector hotels and tour operators pass by and leave the *kampung* unnoticed. The few brochures that promote sightseeing in the city on foot either recommend the beaten track or convey confusing and even incorrect information about the location of the *kampung* sites.[8]

Although there are no (local) entrepreneurs who structurally exploit *kampung* life as a tourist attraction, Ibu Siska has established good relations with a number of home industries and local factories where she takes visitors on request. Her initiative is unique in Yogyakarta and, if developed further, she could monopolize this market niche and be more successful than in the field of adventure tourism where she has to deal with several competitors. To promote her *kampung* trips, she has compiled some documentation that she keeps on the table in the common room of her homestay – a picture book containing photos with comments and explanations in English about the production process of cigars in a Yogyanese factory and of *bakpia*, a local snack made from beans, produced in a *kampung* home industry. When some of her guests show an interest in visiting these industries, Siska arranges a bus with a driver and acts as guide herself. Her favourite programme comprises a visit to the once Dutch-owned cigar factory in the *kampung* south of the Kraton, a *bakpia* home industry within the Kraton walls, a *tempe* (bean curd) factory, a handicraft shop run by a non-governmental organization, and a textile workshop where batik painting techniques are applied to *ikat* cloth and where 'ethnic' motifs replace the typical Yogyanese repertoire. Except for the textile workshop and the handicraft shop, the factories visited are not involved in tourism in any way whatsoever. They produce goods for non-tourist markets at a local (the *tempe*), national (the snacks) and international (the cigars) level. Tourist visitors are warmly welcomed, tea and snacks are served, but they are not treated to a rehearsed guided tour. These industries are not prepared to receive visitors regularly and they do not have their own English-speaking hostess trained in public relations and selling techniques as many of the bigger batik factories and silver shops do. Often one of their more eloquent workers shows the visitors around, telling them something about the history of the factory, the production process and the techniques applied, and perhaps the whereabouts of its workers. Their language is Indonesian and Siska acts as interpreter. In a few cases, like that of the *tempe* factory, Siska pays the factory a small amount of money for their hospitality, but mostly the hosts are compensated by the sale of their products to tourists. Siska herself encourages the visitors to have a look at the goods, taste, try, and buy. She refused to disclose their names, but there are workshops where she herself receives commission on the goods that the tourists buy as any travel agent does. We shall return to the commission system in the next chapter.

ORGANIZING *KAMPUNG* TOURISM

The proprietors of small tourism businesses in the *kampung* seem reluctant to organize themselves. The associations for the hotel, tour and travel sector that the Indonesian government has established (see below), are not accessible to them as these professional associations are exclusively designed for 'quality' tourism. The *kampung* businesses are left without any structural support from government or private organizations. Because of the fragmentation of the industry, *kampung* businesses are in a weak bargaining position *vis-à-vis* the large tour operators when it comes to marketing their product, the more so as their market is the individual traveller, not the package tourist. The 'tourism establishment' in Yogyakarta, therefore, does not regard the *kampung* as a serious competitor. Disregarding the success of a travel agent like Pak Djoko and the constantly high occupancy rates of small-scale accommodation, they predict the decline and liquidation of *kampung* tourism. This attitude is shared by many local government officials, who may be less biased towards *kampung* tourism but are truly concerned about its future as a source of income and employment. Tourism experts have strongly recommended that small enterprises should get together and market their products jointly (Final Report 1991-1992). By establishing co-operative networks and banding together, small firms could afford the diagnostic and consultancy services which are beyond their reach as individuals; they could also market their products jointly, blending sectoral co-operation with enterprise competition. Networks have become the fundamental survival route of small tourism firms because of the benefits they offer in terms of cost advantages, marketing, information access, and, ultimately, flexibility. As examples from different tourist areas in Indonesia illustrate (cf. Dahles & Bras 1999a), informal self-help organizations among small-scale owners of accommodation, restaurants, and travel agencies do emerge, but they do not (yet) represent a vigorous force. The reluctance to organize themselves and co-operate structurally seems to be related to the fear of independent entrepreneurs jeopardizing their autonomy if they get involved in any organization, including private local initiatives (Peeters, Urru & Dahles 1999). This often-quoted individualism of small entrepreneurs should not be exaggerated.

Looking at the neighbourhood of Sosrowijayan, it is obvious that there is informal co-operation among the different categories of entrepreneurs. Although economic considerations are the basis of these co-operative efforts, personal networks, family obligations, and friendship are necessary for mutual support. Homestay owners help their family members in the same branch and other tourism businesses in a particular area to market their product. If a homestay is fully occupied, newly arrived guests are escorted to accommodation run by a family member or close friend. Because of her friendly relations with a *losmen* owner on Sosrowijayan street whose establishment is often fully booked, Ibu Siska's homestay receives a constant flow of backpackers. She needs this co-operation as her homestay is in a back alley and she refuses to call in the assistance of touts to bring in guests. Every homestay features a notice board displaying the business cards of local masseurs, beauty parlours, transport services, and souvenir shops. Many homestay are visited daily by the owner's family or friends from a compatible business to check on new guests and offer their products. Homestays spread flyers containing information about excursions and trips organized by local travel agencies, mainly those that are closely associated with the establishment, as in the case of Pak Djoko and the menus of local restaurants. Sometimes they offer brochures of other homestays or *losmen* in what will most probably be the next destination of their guests. People in Sosrowijayan maintain contacts with relatives also involved in the tourism sector as far away as Mount Bromo, and even Bali.

A very important force in the marketing of the local tourist product is the category of informal guides (cf. Chapter 6). They maintain manifold relations of interdependence with local entrepreneurs. When tourists arrive at the bus or railway station, informal guides are waiting to accompany them to a homestay where they have friendly relations with the owner and staff. For the tourists this service is 'free' as the informal guides receive a commission from the owner or staff for every guest they deliver. In the Sosrowijayan area the commission amounts to about ten per cent of the room charge. Some tourist are only too happy to be guided to accommodation after a long and tiring trip, and they willingly hand over their luggage and follow the guide. Other tourists arrive well-prepared (with the 'Lonely Planet' guide book in their hands) and want to proceed to the homestay of their choice. In this case a confrontation can occur with the intrusive guides who will not take 'no' for an answer. Tourists who keep refusing the informal guide's services, even scolding and threatening them, are followed by the guide who attempts to receive the commission anyway, claiming at the accommodation that it was he who delivered the tourist. This strategy is not always successful as many homestay owners co-operate with a limited number of informal guides and refuse to pay others. Most local *losmen* owners strongly resent the practices of the informal guides, but only a few dare to decline their services fearing a loss of business and retaliatory measures. The entrepreneurs unwilling to submit to the commission system are shunned by the informal guides who attempt to dissuade tourists from renting a room there. 'Fully booked' they will say, urging the tourists to follow them to the next homestay. Ibu Siska is among those who prefer not to co-operate with the informal guides. As a consequence, her lighted sign board in Sosrowijayan Street has been destroyed several times by vengeful local touts.

Lacking formal professional organizations to unite *kampung* entrepreneurs to pursue common targets, Sosrowijayan tourism businesses have established two different networks I know of, both largely confined to entrepreneurs in a particular *kampung*. In the *kampung* of Sosrowijayan Wetan, the busiest part of the Sosrowijayan area, the self-help organization PARTSY (*Pariwisata, Akomodasi, Restauran, Transpor Sosrowijayan Yogyakarta*) was established in 1984, supported by *Dinas Pariwisata* and registered at the Mayor's Office (Pangasti 1992:57-8). PARTSY organizes twenty-five guesthouses, eight restaurants, eight travel agencies, and four art galleries (Timothy 1999:380). In the early 1990s the adjacent *kampung* of Sosrowijayan Kulon followed with a network named *Paguyuban Pengelola Penginapan Sosrowijayan* (PPPS), constituting a purely informal organization. Whereas PARTSY aims to provide a common meeting ground for all tourism-related businesses in the area, PPPS focuses particularly on owners of local accommodation. The main objective of both organizations is to make price agreements and establish some quality standards for the associated enterprises. The influence of this network is limited as only some of the local accommodation owners regularly participate. According to the founder of PPPS, it is not possible to take far-reaching decisions or settle important agreements, as the fear of formalization is deeply rooted among the local small entrepreneurs (Peeters, Urru & Dahles 1999). Independence and autonomy being their basic interest, they will be scared off and turn against the members of this network if they suspect that any regulations are to be imposed. Another objective of this network is to counteract the detrimental practices of the informal guides. The participants in the PPPS have agreed not to pay commissions and do not allow informal guides to enter the accommodation to do business. These owners are proud to inform their guests of this regulation as a means to enhance their reliability and make them feel more protected. However, it has been observed that whenever the owner is not present, the young males who run the homestay allow their friends to enter and sit with the tourists in the common room. In many cases these friends are informal guides, doing business as usual.

THE STATE AND *KAMPUNG* TOURISM

The state is largely absent from everyday life in the 'tourist' *kampung*. It encroaches on the daily routine only if licences are applied for or need renewal and taxes have to be paid. There is a ten percent government tax added to all transactions in the restaurant and accommodation sector, and owners have to show a certificate to prove that they have paid the tax. This certificate is neatly framed and conspicuously exhibited in restaurants or at reception desks. The local government sends officials to inspect the accommodation and restaurants and register the number of rooms or tables and the type of facilities. These measures have to be understood against the background of the classification system for the non-star-rated accommodation sector that has been initiated by *Depparpostel*. Its implementation is assigned to the provincial government, *Dinas Pariwisata* (Van der Giessen & Van Loo 1996, Peeters & Urru 1996). A three-tiered system has been introduced to distinguish different levels of quality among cheaper accommodation, a distinction that is made visible by the number of *melati* (flowers) awarded to an establishment. Originally intended to establish a reliable rating system to control the proliferation of budget accommodation, the *melati* system was a failure. Owners of accommodation were reluctant to co-operate on a large scale. As *kampung* people point out, registration in the *melati* system is meant to check whether the owners are evading taxes. As a consequence, many accommodation owners remain vague about the number of rooms and the quality of their facilities, and prefer not to be indexed in government-issued brochures listing 'places to eat' or 'places to stay.' Officials are bribed to turn a blind eye to an extension to a homestay, and only some of the tourists staying in the accommodation are officially registered.

The *Dinas Pariwisata* and BAPPEDA (*Badan Pembangunan Daerah*), the government agency responsible for the implementation of the guidelines defined by the national Five Year Plans, hardly show any interest at all in the small-scale enterprises that make up the *kampung* tourism sector. They follow national policies supporting the large-scale tourism industry. The head of the tourism planning department of BAPPEDA in Yogyakarta strongly favours the revitalization of the city through the establishment of theme parks and the improvement of entertainment and nightlife concentrated in the star-rated hotels.[9] *Diparda* Yogyakarta defines its task in terms of the creation of optimal conditions in which the 'quality' sector may thrive. Therefore, *Diparda* designs plans to improve the traffic flow in the inner city to make the 'quality' hotels more easily accessible for cars and buses and to minimize delays due to traffic congestion. The idea of banning *becaks* from Malioboro Street has emerged as part of the improvements to the traffic system, an idea that caused a great deal of consternation in the adjacent *kampung* of Sosrowijayan, which is home to a substantial number of *becak* drivers. To cater to the needs of 'quality tourism' *Diparda* established a 'tourist police' with an office adjacent to the Tourist Office in Malioboro Street. The task of the tourist police is to prevent petty crime perpetrated against tourists, like pickpocketing, and to assist tourists in case of the loss of travel documents. The head of *Diparda* defines the range of action of his department in terms of 'regulating the traffic' in the literal as well as metaphorical sense, in a way that obstacles to the government-set objectives of tourism growth are minimized.

The Tourist Office, situated in Malioboro Street, is symptomatic of the malaise in local tourism policy. The place looks deserted whether one enters it during high or low season. The book shelves in the office are almost empty. The official booklet that contains tourist information about Yogyakarta which was produced under the auspices of the Tourist Office, is not available. Commercial travel agents offer it free. A billboard exhibits a number of tours described on faded sheets covered with plastic. The tours are organized by Sosro Tours. Besides these, there are flyers introducing the tourist police and warning against pickpockets. In the dry season from May to October the Tourist Office advertises the renowned art product of Yogyakarta, the Ramayana Ballet, that is performed at Prambanan Temple. Like the travel agents all over town, the Tourist Office announces the event on a large billboard in front of the entrance to the office. On the table in the middle of the room lies the newsletter of the French Cultural Association which seems to be quite active, listing the French films shown by the Association, French music performances, and many advertisements for the expensive hotels and restaurants in town. On the counter there are some xeroxed flyers warning tourists not to be cheated by fake art students who sell overpriced and mass-produced batik paintings as pieces of art. Behind the counter six employees of the office are absorbed with their private conversation. There are no tourists around, so why should they worry. When I introduce myself as a tourist staying in Yogyakarta for two nights looking for some interesting sight-seeing tours, one of the employers produces a copy of the Sosro Tours programme. The employee, a woman, recommends the daytrips: Borobudur and Prambanan with batik and silver or Kaliurang instead. For bookings, she said, it would be better to go straight to the travel agent in Sosrowijayan Street which is within walking distance. She improvises a hand-drawn map of Malioboro Street with its side streets to guide me. But if I insist, I can book here at the Office as well, she says without much enthusiasm.

Broadly speaking, it is the conviction of the local government that the small-scale tourism sector in the *kampung* constitutes a world of its own with little impact on the 'quality' sector. In this sense it is tolerated. There are annual meetings with the head of PARTSY to advise the organization about health issues, safety, and business improvements, and to collect statistical material and to check on cleanliness and safety (Timothy 1999:381), but there is no government support for *kampung* entrepreneurship. Although *Diparda* has a budget for 'people's projects' at its disposal, the money is never spent on the initiatives for which it was earmarked. Instead, *Diparda* produces brochures that lie rotting in a back office as the officials fail to distribute them among the travel agents and at the tourist sites. *Diparda* organizes guiding courses (see Chapter 5) that could be better financed by the private tour and travel sector which benefits from well-trained guides. *Kampung* people are regarded as weak links in the Yogyakarta tourism industry. The alleged bad reputation of the *kampung* is supposed to reflect negatively on the city as a whole. The BAPPEDA spokesman criticizes *kampung* people for not being polite and friendly to visitors. He suggests a local campaign to be launched to make Yogyanese people tourism-minded, 'to give their smiles.' If *kampung* people get in the way of the large-scale sector, they have to move. This has been the case for *becaks* in Malioboro Street, and it could be the case in the future for the whole neighbourhood of Sosrowijayan as investors are interested in establishing star-rated hotels in this inner city area. The future of this *kampung* is insecure. The plus factor is that the land prices have gone up because of the good location close to the shopping area. Many *kampung* people are only too willing to sell their land, but others have to sell as they cannot pay the property tax. A number of local entrepreneurs benefit from these changes as they acquire land in this crowded *kampung* on which to expand their businesses. Others, the majority of *kampung* people, are afraid that one day they will be forced off their land. With the economic crisis, however, this threat seems to have been banished at least for the next few years. Despite (or because of) its disinterest, inefficiency, and inertia, *kampung* entrepreneurs regard *Diparda* as their ally. Some *kampung* business people trust that nothing will ever change as long as *Diparda* is in charge. Others are of the opinion that *Diparda* is interested in the wants and needs of the local entrepreneurs. One of its high officials is a frequent visitor to the *kampung* businesses, 'To listen to the problems of their owners,' say some people. 'To collect his bribes' say others.

KEEPING UP APPEARANCES: THE STAR-RATED SECTOR

'STREETSIDE' TOURISM

Pak Jono (thirty-five years old) is the general manager (GM) of a four-star hotel in the inner city of Yogyakarta that was opened in the early 1990s. The building faces the glamorous Solo Street, the most expensive street in Yogyakarta. At its rear a high wall, camouflaged with tropical flowers, protects the swimming pool area from outside intrusion. The sounds of the city, the mosque, *kampung* life, and traffic noise barely penetrate the hotel premises. The hotel belongs to a national chain with branches all over Java and Bali. Compared to other accommodation in this class, Pak Jono's hotel is small, counting 124 rooms (while his competitor, the Ambarrukmo Palace Hotel has 400 rooms). The hotel depends for fifty per cent of its business on international and domestic tourists and for the other fifty per cent on business travellers. The vast majority of its guests (75 per cent) are foreigners. Pak Jono is proud that his hotel has been leading the list of best hotels in town for five years and enjoys a high occupancy rate of over 65 per cent on average. Given the seasonal fluctuations in tourism and compared to his competitors which score less than 50 per cent, this is a very good result, he says. The secret of his hotel's success is the service orientation of his staff whom he recruits from the best local and national tourism schools. 'Our hotel distinguishes itself through the smiles of the staff and the quick service,' he says, 'a cup of tea is served within five minutes of ordering.'

Pak Jono is a graduate of Gadjah Mada University where he obtained a degree in political sciences. After graduation, with no prospect of employment as an intellectual, he found employment in the middle management in several hotels in Yogyakarta, Bali, and Jakarta, and three years ago he was offered the position of GM in this hotel which he gladly accepted. Reflecting on tourism development in Yogyakarta, Pak Jono's analysis is interspersed with critical remarks about local and national politics. He accuses the local government of monumental failures regarding tourism policies. The issue of the airport that has been allocated to Solo, the lack of a provincial tourism promotion board, and the reluctance to innovate the local tourism product are only a few of the points that he raised during our conversation. In his eyes, Yogyakarta has nothing to offer to tourists, perhaps except for the Kraton and Prambanan temple. For the limited number of attractions the infamous 'one-day' tours are more than enough, because there is nothing else with which to fill additional days! Places like Taman Sari – a 'crumbling ruin' – and the bird market – a 'dirty mess' – are 'stains on the image of the city.' Yogyakarta should get rid of the 'sleepy village' image and become a proper city with a quality nightlife and entertainment sector, new core attractions like theme parks, golf courses, and luxury beach resorts on the southern shores of the Java Sea. 'Act local, think global' is his motto. Tourism is the only industry in Yogyakarta to offer employment to many people and to generate prosperity for the middle classes and *kampung* people alike. The shabby *kampung* in the city should be cleared and the people should be relocated to proper housing areas to give way to attractive buildings that accommodate leisure and entertainment facilities.

Pak Jono's hotel is situated in the 'streetside' area where almost all the luxury hotels with the associated tour and travel services are situated: at the Solo/airport road and Malioboro Street. Along this axis the city's glamorous shopping malls, department stores, foreign fast-food restaurants, and all major bank buildings and government offices can also be found. It is this axis that represents the large-scale and partly international service sector that is strongly tuned to foreign 'quality' tourism, representing the carefully constructed and screened image of Yogyakarta as a centre of cultural tourism. More recently, hotel development has spread outside the 'streetside' area to the northern parts of the city, in particular in the vicinity of Gadjah Mada University, anticipating the propagated MICE tourism (cf. Chapter 4). These hotels – like the Radisson and Hyatt – are constructed and managed as resorts with a complete package of facilities: they employ 'activity managers' who are in charge of tailor-made entertainment programmes.

The star-rated hotels in Yogyakarta are first and foremost dependent on tourism as other categories (convention participants and business travellers) play only a marginal role in the occupancy because of the underdeveloped industries and modest congress activities in the city. The dependence on tourism implies that the hotels have to deal with the seasonality of tourist demand. The market of the star-rated hotels is the packaged group vacation. Therefore, this sector is strongly dependent on the airport as almost all package tourists arrive by air. As has been discussed in the previous chapter, the declining number of flights from Bali and Jakarta and the opening of the competing airport in Solo is causing a great deal of concern in the Yogyanese hotel sector. Some managers are desperate and accuse the government of Yogyakarta of having ceded local interests to smart political manoeuvres of the neighbouring province. Others expect the negative effects of the new Solo airport to be mitigated by international tourists flying directly to central Java instead of Bali and Jakarta. Only a few managers cherish the idea that the new airport will bring large benefits to Yogyakarta.

All the star-rated hotels are members of the national hotel association, the BPHN (*Badan Pusat Hotel Negara*). Membership of this Jakarta-based organization that was established as early as 1945 is obligatory, but managers complain that the meetings are purely ceremonial and ineffectual in terms of networking and co-operation. Another semi-formal organization, *Casa Grande*, has been established by and for the general managers of the big hotels. It is intended to facilitate networking activities among the 'big shots' in the local tourism industry and confines itself to this sociable function. Some of the members I spoke to were rather frustrated because of what they call the 'ineffectualness' of this organization: 'It's like NATO, all talk no action,' said one of my informants.

The GMs of Yogyakarta's star-rated hotels agree that a lot of work remains to be done for the promotion and marketing of the tourist product. Their hope is focused on special interest tourism which the European and American markets are rapidly differentiating. Yogyakarta with its large number of quality hotels could easily jump into this market if only the city had something to offer either in terms of a revitalized product or creative marketing, or both. More and more GMs feel that 'Javanese heritage' on its own is not enough to attract visitors and keep them in the area for more than one night. Ideas about how to improve the tourist product differ widely. Some have high hopes of Asian 'religious roots' tourism, by which they mean Buddhist and Hindu devotees visiting Borobudur and Prambanan. That increasing prosperity in Asian countries would accelerate this tourism was the conviction of many tourism experts before the economic crisis hit Asia. Others strongly believe in the future of MICE tourism and want to promote Yogyakarta in terms of 'city of education.' Yet others keep looking towards Bali and plead for more resorts to be developed in Yogyakarta 'to spoil and pamper the tourists in a "total environment," keep them satisfied and make them stay.' Other strategies that were suggested focused on the development of 'quality nightlife,' golf tourism, and resort building on the Parangtritis coast modelled on the Spanish Costas. Whatever the strategies favoured to enhance the length of stay, there is one strategy to which all subscribe but criticize for its deficiencies: the marketing through the 'streetside' travel agents in Yogyakarta. There is a wide consensus that the travel agents are to blame for the stagnation in tourism growth. The hotel sector accuses them of inertia, risk-avoidance, indolence, and lack of creativity. The bones of contention are their being no more than passive sub-contractors of Jakarta- and Bali-based enterprises, their reluctance to co-operate, their disinterest in 'quality' and, most of all, their selling the transit tours and 'Yogya in one day' excursions. However, many of the GMs who spout these harsh criticisms are among the most important customers for groups of transit tourists having lunch in their hotels.

The hotels are built at the 'streetside' boundary of Yogyanese *kampung* and high walls separate the lush hotel gardens from the adjacent low-class neighbourhoods. Despite the walls, hotels have to deal with the rules and needs of *kampung* people. The managements of the hotels I visited are concerned with the 'integration' of their enterprise into *kampung* life. There is the need for *kampung* approval before the hotel is built. This is accomplished by inviting *kampung* leaders to take cognizance of the fact that a hotel is planned in the immediate vicinity of their neighbourhood. This is a cosmetic excuse as there is no opportunity for objecting to these plans openly. Instead, a 'ritual' consent is expected by the investors and planners. The managers are invited to participate in *kampung* ceremonies which they are supposed to support financially and,[10] vice versa, *kampung* people are invited to the hotel opening ceremony. Playing on the concerns of the local people, the hotel is presented as an employment opportunity for *kampung* members. Indeed, in many cases some *kampung* people do find jobs in the hotel: as chambermaids, gardeners, security men, and other low-skilled and low-paid jobs; some are employed as gamelan players and artisans, provided they possess the required talents. In most cases the hotel is integrated into the *ronda malam* (night watch) of the *kampung*. While the *kampung* is regarded as a reservoir of inexpensive labour, it is not seen as a resource for product innovation. Yogyakarta's GMs do not believe in small-scale tourism developments. As far as forms of 'alternative,' 'responsible' or 'eco'-tourism cross their minds at all, they want to make these part of the 'activity programme' of their hotel. They seem to doubt that any good can emerge from small-scale developments. Tourism development requires capital investments as tourism is a global industry, therefore small-scale initiatives will be wiped out by expanding businesses. 'Even local people think big,' one of my informants said. When they do spare a thought for *kampung* tourism, the GMs are not worried at all that any serious competition is emanating from the budget accommodation sector which is mushrooming in the inner city *kampung*. Hotel managers cling tenaciously to the idea that the occupancy rate in the budget accommodation is considerably lower than in the star-rated hotels, although the official statistics (that systematically underscore the non-star-rated sector) say otherwise. Some even predict that *kampung* tourism is doomed, for as soon as this turns out to be an interesting business opportunity, the less-expensive international chains like 'Ibis' will take over and push the local entrepreneurs out of the market. In other words: 'streetside' tourism is not threatened by *kampung* tourism; instead the unorganized businesses 'down there' are threatened by 'streetside' tourism!

Although consensus and harmony mask the fierce competition within the star-rated hotel sector, there is a big difference between the relatively new, often foreign-owned and foreign-managed hotels and the older nationally-owned and managed accommodation in Yogyakarta. The former are run by GMs who are used to operating in a Western entrepreneurial culture which is characterized by negotiability and assertive behaviour. Theirs is a culture of open discussion and disagreements which are articulated and solved. In these circles the lack of consultation as well as 'ritual' expressions of harmony and consensus between the main actors in the local tourism system meet with incomprehension. They complain that hidden conflicts persist and, at the same time, nothing ever changes. There are powerful forces in favour of Yogyakarta remaining a 'sleepy little village': although tourism growth is welcomed, local stakeholders decline to put any effort into product development nor do they want to change their lives. These forces are alive and well in local politics, and also in the management of the older star-rated hotels which are now part of the Natour chain. Typical of this attitude is the Ambarrukmo Hotel on the premises of one of the sultan's former summer palaces. This hotel is described as 'looking a little tired' in the 'Lonely Planet' Travel Guide (Turner *et al.* 1995:278). Once the 'first hotel' in Yogyakarta, it has lost this position to the many new and splendid resorts that have risen in the city centre and close to the Gadjah Mada University campus. The management is proud of the historic roots of their hotel, but they do not market the place in heritage terms. They act from an aristocratic consciousness: detached and contemplative. Their confidence in the superiority of their product is unshaken. Referring to the tourists who seem to prefer other places to stay, the Ambarrukmo management comments: 'They'll come back, they will see, that we are the old one.' It is exactly this attitude that the dynamic managers of the newly established hotels, applying modern marketing techniques and exhibiting a commercial orientation, cannot cope with.

'STREETSIDE' TRAVEL AGENTS

In the south wing of the Natour-owned Garuda hotel in Malioboro Street there are a number of shops and offices including the tiny travel agency of Pak Budi, a man in his late forties. He started this travel agency only two years ago after working in the tour and travel business in Surabaya, Jakarta, and Bali for twenty-two years. Pak Budi hopes that the network he established during his long working carrer will stand him in good stead in his position as small entrepreneur. He runs his business with only one permanent employee, a young man who works as administrator, secretary, guide, and chauffeur whenever the situation requires. Pak Budi's market is the international inbound tourist, in particular from Korea and Thailand, and he is ambitious to expand his business activities to Europe. However, he sighs, the competition is murderous. He prefers to stick to the Asian market as it shows few seasonal fluctuations and is easy to manage, as Asians prefer packaged, 'conventional' vacations. Europeans are much more difficult to satisfy as they incline towards 'tailor-made' vacations: a risky market. He characterizes the product he is selling as 'classical': the standard package consisting of excursions to Borobudur, Prambanan, and city tours with a visit to the Kraton and batik factories. So much for Yogyakarta, but a look in the few brochures he has on offer shows that he sells tours to and in Jakarta, Bali, Sumatra, Sulawesi, and Lombok as well. 'I'm selling Indonesia, not Yogyakarta,' he says, 'just like all the other small travel agents in town.' The point is that the travel agents in Yogyakarta are either subcontractors or mere branch offices of large Jakarta- or Bali-based tour operators. Pak Budi's travel agency falls into the former category, working for a bigger partner in Bali. In collaboration with other subcontractors in Yogyakarta he establishes tours in the area and produces brochures that incorporate the products of colleagues in other regions working for the same Balinese partner. In these terms Pak Budi is a small entrepreneur, operating under relations of patronage in a very extended network. If required, Pak Budi sells the infamous 'Yogya-in-one-day' and transit-tours. Although he is aware of the undesirable effects of these tours on the city's tourism industry, for him it is 'better than nothing.' He explains: 'It's a reaction to the Japanese market, the Japanese book inexpensive short package tours to expensive hotels in Bali; they have no time to move around the archipelago, they stay in their resort and take one day to visit Borobudur.' There have been attempts to change the Japanese tourists' behaviour, for example by cancelling the late afternoon flights to Bali to make them spend the night in Yogyakarta. This was counterproductive as they stayed away from Yogyakarta altogether.

Pak Budi admits that his product is not distinct from what all the other small subcontractors in Yogyakarta have to offer. Indeed the opposite is true. In his position it would be foolish to explore special market niches, invest, and take risks. It has not crossed his mind to develop forms of 'alternative,' 'responsible' or 'eco'-tourism. He is playing safe, caters to a 'guaranteed' market, and leaves the innovations to 'big brother,' as he calls his partners in Bali. If necessary, he co-operates with other small travel agents. Besides his personal network that stretches across the whole of Java and many outer islands, he socializes with members of the provincial branch of the tour and travel association (ASITA – Association of the Indonesian Tours and Travel Agencies). 'It's good to be organized,' observes Pak Budi, but he hastens to add that ASITA members allow no opportunity to undercut the prices of their colleagues to slip by. While his most dangerous competitors are his ASITA associates, he thinks it impossible that *kampung*-based Sosro Tours, less than a hundred metres away from Pak Budi's office, could present a serious challenge: 'We are worlds apart, 'down there' they are catering to a completely different class of tourists who never enter this hotel,' Pak Budi contends. He conveniently seems to forget about the guests of 'this hotel' making bookings with the travel agent 'down there' to save money.

It is no coincidence that the office of Pak Budi is accommodated on the 'streetside' premises of a prestigious four-star hotel. After all, it is the star-rated market to which this travel agent is catering, like his colleagues and competitors who have their offices in hotels like that or in Malioboro Street. The members of ASITA are recruited from this category. ASITA is the national Jakarta-based organization of the star-rated private tour and travel agencies with members from the industry and educational institutions. The objective of ASITA is the enhancement of communication among its members and between the tour and travel sector and the government. Politically, ASITA is under *Depparpostel*, the Yogyakarta branch under KANWIL, which implies that there is a direct responsibility to 'Jakarta' and that the local government does not wield any authority over the association and its members. Organizing about 15,000 travel agents nation-wide, the Yogyakarta branch has seventy-three (in 1996) full members – a number that has grown through the years according to the vice-chairman, without giving concrete figures.

ASITA members are supposed to be better informed about government measures, policies, and research results through SWASITA, the news bulletin of the association, but most of all through networking, as the ASITA office and the membership meetings are only sparsely visited by regular members. The network and the access to the ASITA-compiled 'black list' of foreign tour operators who are reluctant to pay their bills are the most important benefits travel agents derive from their membership. ASITA has actually divided the market among its members along 'national' lines: tour operators specialize in one or two specific European or Asian markets labelled by the language spoken in these countries. This strategy enables agents to focus their marketing, to attract guides, and to diminish competition among the travel agents. At the time of my research in 1996, the main concern of ASITA was the government tax of 6-15 per cent charged on all trips and excursions organized by the star-rated travel agencies in Indonesia. If the agencies were to raise their prices to compensate this taxation, they lose market share. This is especially true for Yogyakarta, where the market is extremely strained. To stay in competition, the agencies pay the tax out of their own pockets. So far what concrete steps ASITA is considering taking against the government remains vague.

ASITA is very much tuned to large-scale tourism and resort development. 'Quality' tourism is seen as the panacea for the problems Yogyakarta is encountering. After all, it is the 'quality' tourists who use the services of the ASITA-travel agents. The problem is that it is this market that is subject to alarming developments. 'For example the Germans: they are attractive because of their purchasing power and because their length of stay is increasing. However, the German tourists can afford to stay longer by sleeping in budget accommodation and by travelling unorganized. Therefore this market becomes unattractive for the ASITA travel agents,' says the vice-chairman of the Yogyakarta branch, unaware that his example undermined the carefully cultivated attitude that *kampung* tourism and the star-rated sector are 'worlds apart.' With more resorts 'Nusa Dua style' he expects to compete successfully with Bali and to divert market share to Yogyakarta. 'It makes no sense building new star-rated hotels scattered all over the city. More integration is necessary to provide the tourists with all the amenities and keep them in town as long as possible.' This is what Bali resorts do and this is why tourists prefer to stay in their comfortable resort and take short trips to Borobudur, thinks the ASITA man. The idea is dawning that the quest for 'authentic' village life may not be antagonistic to a stay in star-rated accommodation: tourists prefer to be accommodated in a luxurious way while making excursions to the village: a glimpse at backstages while safely in a tourist bubble. This implies that ASITA wants to monopolize the newly emerging 'differentiated' market of special interest tourism and to counteract small-scale developments. It targets tourist categories that seem to be a potential asset of the small-scale market by offering the luxury of star-rated accommodation in combination with the 'authenticity' of village tourism.

The Yogyanese tour and travel sector consists of small subcontractors and branch offices of bigger partners in Bali and Jakarta. This dependence accounts for their supposed inertia and reluctance to innovate and co-operate. The local agencies are extremely vulnerable and the patronage of a strong partner does not guarantee a secure business position, despite Pak Budi's confident statement. During the 1997/8 economic crisis which drastically affected tourism, many small branch offices in Yogyakarta were closed as tourism outside Bali collapsed. Moreover, if a local travel agent expands to become a tour operator with many agencies depending on him, he soon moves head office to Jakarta.[11] The debate between hotel managers and travel agents regarding the effects of transit tours reflects a clash of interests: for the hotels making their money from the tourists' overnight stay, transit tours represent a financial loss, while for tour operators making money from the sale of tours, transit tours are good business.

EDUCATING THE STREETSIDE'S WORKFORCE

The 'streetside' tourism industry is provided with educated personnel who have graduated from one of the many local tourism schools. Yogyakarta does not have the most prestigious schools in the sector; the top schools are situated in Bandung, Jakarta, and Bali, but there are good schools in Yogyakarta as well.[12] The tourism schools, of which eight are accredited, train young people with at least a secondary school (SMA, *Sekolah Menengah Atas*) certificate to meet the requirements of star-rated tourism. The accredited schools offer three-year programmes at the Diploma III level,[13] which have a two-tiered division into Hospitality Training and Tour and Travel Management. Students specialize in one of the two trajectories, and generally the hospitality sector is strongly female dominated while male students prefer the tour and travel business. Most tourism schools have facilities to provide their students with practical training, such as a hotel room, a reception desk, a travel bureau, and a ticket counter. The schools are competing amongst each other for internship contracts and employment opportunities for their graduates. Generally the graduates of the accredited institutes find jobs in the middle management of Yogyanese hotels, travel agencies, airlines and in the government departments of *Diparda* and KANWIL. They face fierce competition from the many academies and programmes which are of questionable repute and lack the proper accreditation. Many students have to turn to these competitors as the accredited schools apply fixed enrolments, which leaves many young people without a chance of ever getting accepted.[14] Sometimes they are preferred because in the face of mounting financial pressures, young people prefer to enrol in short-term programmes. This explains the proliferation of institutes offering tourism education. As a consequence, more and more graduates are entering the market and potential employers lose sight of the quality of the graduates. Networking and close collaboration with ASITA is a crucial advantage if the accredited schools are to be successful in the labour market. However, the competition for jobs in the 'better' hotels is already cut throat, and there are indications that graduates either accept a job, start a business in the *kampung* tourism sector, or enter handicraft production. It seems that tourism education – meant to contribute to the professionalization of the sector – is actually contributing to informalization and de-skilling as well-educated people are prepared to accept jobs beneath their level of training.[15]

DEVELOPING 'STREETSIDE' TOURISM

While initiatives taken to develop special interest tourism by *kampung*-based enterprises are strongly resented, the 'streetside' tourism sector, headed by ASITA, is developing plans to do exactly the same. The difference is that *kampung* initiatives are already operational, while the 'streetside' sector is still in the process of 'talking.' At the root of this talk is the general dissatisfaction with the existing 'tourism product' which is insufficient to guarantee a good market position. As the president of the Yogyanese ASITA branch office explained to me: it is not enough to advertise Yogyakarta as the gateway to Borobudur, one of the world wonders. Bali lacks an attraction of comparable significance, but is considerably more successful than Yogyakarta. The tourist product has to be revitalized. ASITA is thinking of special interest tourism and has attempted to design a number of special tours, like culinary tours, educational programmes for tourists who consider taking courses in batik painting, Javanese dance, or gamelan playing. The point is that these products have to be marketed. To do so, ASITA is looking for co-operation with the Central Java branch office. On the agenda are: mountain biking, nature tourism and caving in Gunung Kidul, and diving on Karimunjawa Island, which lies off the coast of Semarang. Borobudur should be marketed not only as a stupa, but as a gateway to Javanese village life. ASITA wants to open up Javanese villages for tourism to enable tourists to witness agricultural activities, the preparation of food, traditional market activities, weddings, or a bathe in the river. The idea is to arrange unique packages which carry the ASITA quality stamp and which can be bought by ASITA members for a fixed price, to counteract fragmentation of the market and competition among the members and to prevent the 'alternative' agencies in the 'informal' sector (which are regarded as unprofessional competitors) from taking over. What we are witnessing here is an attempt to formalize and organize an emerging market: the vast array of 'alternative' tourism, agritourism, ecotourism, and adventure tourism which up to now has barely been organized and controlled, and was therefore accessible to 'informal' entrepreneurs. Although ASITA has not taken any notable steps in that direction, it is obvious that this small-scale 'alternative' market is regarded as a threat by the tourist establishment.

As ASITA members and hotel managers agree, innovation of the tourist product is essential, but not enough. The marketing of this new product is as important as the innovation itself. Some would say that the old product will do fine, provided that the marketing strategies change. Marketing Yogyakarta constitutes a major issue in the 'streetside' tourism sector. In the early 1990s, the Indonesian government, backed by the tourism industry, established the *Badan Promosi Pariwisata Indonesia* or Indonesian Tourism Promotion Board (ITPB) that is responsible for the promotion of Indonesia abroad with offices in Europe, America, and in other Asian countries. Each province contributes to the ITPB budget according to its financial capacity; the province of Yogyakarta pays two per cent of the total ITPB budget. ASITA members support the activities of the ITPB by means of the airline commission that the tour and travel branch pays with every transaction. But very much to the growing dissatisfaction of the local government and the private sector, the ITPB has turned out to be ineffectual. The ITPB, says a representative of the local government, makes promotion for Bali, the slogan: 'Bali is in Indonesia' being their latest motto. However, there is an urgent need for a specific Yogyakarta-directed promotion. Local stakeholders feel cheated as they feel they are paying their contribution for the promotion of other parts of Indonesia. More and more voices are being heard – in the public as well as in the private sector – calling for the establishment of a regional organization for the promotion of Yogyakarta to take the government-initiated regionalization one step further. The sultan of Yogyakarta, who is a member of the Jakarta-based ITPB board, supports the claims of the Yogyakarta tourism industry. In 1995 he was one of the initiators of an informal meeting with representatives of the provincial tourism industry to discuss the establishment of a *Badan Promosi Pariwisata Yogyakarta*, a provincial branch of the national Tourism Promotion Board.[16] The outcome of this initiative is as yet unclear.

The future plans of ASITA and ITPB are reflected by a new platform for tourism development, the 'Forum for the Development of Cultural Tourism' that was established in 1994 with the support of the provincial governments of Yogyakarta and Central Java. To counteract the intrinsic rivalries between both provinces, a circulation and division of tasks have been agreed on. During its first three years the Forum was to be led by the head of BAPPEDA of Central Java, while the secretariat is in Yogyakarta; after three years the situation was to be reversed with the head of the Yogyakarta BAPPEDA office chairing the Forum and the secretariat being installed in Central Java. The Forum has been established to counteract the many problems that tourism development in the area is facing (cf. Marjatmo 1996a, 1996b). Cultural tourism, widely regarded as the most promising perspective in the area, has to be developed further and to be improved to serve one central aim: to allow the tourism industry to operate to its full capacity – tourism industry being defined in terms of the star-rated sector. Spearheading the policy of revitalizing cultural tourism in both provinces are the establishment of multimedia shows at Borobudur and Prambanan[17] and the development of special interest tourism, especially those forms that are characterized as MICE tourism. As has been discussed in the previous chapter, MICE tourism was strongly promoted by former minister of tourism, Joop Avé. Prospects of becoming a major MICE destination contributed significantly to the mushrooming of the star-rated hotel sector in Yogyakarta. In addition to the traditional core attractions and MICE tourism, the Forum intends to develop new attractions that appeal to a heterogeneous group of special interest tourists. Some of the assets that were touched upon in my conversations with Forum members were: special arrangements for honeymooners; classes for meditation, mysticism, martial arts, and traditional healing; adventure tourism like rafting, climbing, caving, and horse-riding; the study of the tropical flora and a complete academic study programme for tropical medicine. This list demonstrates two things: first, the preliminary phase and non-focused state of the Forum's activities; and second, the shift that is taking place in the concept of culture, which now lies at the heart of tourism development. Culture is being approached less in terms of heirlooms (Javanese, national, or both) but in a more conceptual way, alluding to the organized diversity of local life. In other words, the product approach to culture is giving way to the process approach (cf. Chapter 1).

'STREETSIDE' TOURISM AND THE STATE

Tensions between the provincial government and the local tourism industry are almost unavoidable given the different competencies of both bodies. As far as 'streetside' enterprises are among the star-rated establishments, it is *Depparpostel* through its regional office (KANWIL) that is responsible for policy measures that define the margins within which these establishments can prosper. *Diparda* has no say in these cases. The sultan of Yogyakarta, exhibiting a dynamic approach and representing the business interests of the 'streetside' e.g. through his function as ITPB board member, is consulted in all planning and implementation of tourism development projects. The different actors in 'streetside' tourism may not agree with each other's business strategies, but they do agree that the government policy represents the major non-market threat to local tourism. Although the buoyant personality of former minister of tourism, Joop Avé, met with wide admiration among the leaders in the Yogyakarta tourism arena, the policy of his department has often been criticized. Condemnation has been directed towards the fallible marketing and promotion strategies of the government-supported ITPB and the effects of regionalization as propagated by *Repelita*. Both measures were said to deprive Yogyakarta of its privileged position among Indonesia's tourism destinations. In contrast to the private sector, the government-owned enterprise that manages two major religious complexes in the area, *PT Taman Wisata*, a big stakeholder in Yogyakarta's tourism industry, objects to the demand for an independent regional promotion body. This enterprise pleads for an improved and better-integrated promotion for Yogyakarta under the existing ITPB and more efforts to be made to appeal to the domestic market. Both points have to be understood against the background of the enterprise's status as a government-owned body and therefore fairly dependent on the massive numbers of Indonesians visiting its heritage parks. The provincial government is criticized because of its maladroit political lobby losing out to the neighbouring province of Central Java, the airport being the major bone of contention. ASITA complains about *Diparda*. The local tourism department appears to have indeed produced a brochure promoting Yogyakarta's tourist attractions and facilities, but then failing to distribute it; they did not even reach the Tourist Office next door!

Not to be outdone the provincial government has harsh words to say about the local hotel sector and the travel agencies castigating their lack of a competitive attitude and inept marketing strategies. The travel agents of Yogyakarta in particular are widely regarded as a weak link in the tourism system by provincial policy makers. While the expanding star-rated hotel sector evokes their pride, the travel agents are seen as a major obstacle to the development of an appropriate tourism product as they lack knowledge and skills in the area of promotion and marketing. Travel agents are the most important actors in the major goal of the tourism system at the moment – to induce tourists to stay longer. But they are their own worst enemies as by selling the infamous transit tours and operating 'Yogya in one day' tours, they contribute to the decline of tourism in the area. In general, the government complains about the inferior quality of the tourist product which, except for the core attractions, is short on innovation and dynamism. Government and private sector both agree that Yogyakarta needs a new image and new target groups. MICE tourism is the new magic formula on which all hopes are pinned. By boosting this form of special interest tourism the provincial government hopes to capitalize on Yogyakarta's reputation as city of education.

CONCLUSION

Government officials and actors in the star-rated tourism sector have constructed an image of 'streetside' and *kampung* tourism in which the two constitute two different 'worlds' in Yogyakarta, separated not only in terms of size and scope, but also in terms of entrepreneurial culture and power relations. In this dualist structure *kampung* and 'streetside' businesses exist side by side, but 'never the twain shall meet.' They are supposed neither to converge nor to conflict. This image reflects the structure of government responsibilities divided among the 'dominant,' 'developed,' 'modern,' and 'profitable' star-rated sector versus the 'dependent,' 'underdeveloped,' 'traditional,' and 'marginal' *kampung* sector. Counteracting this image is the increasingly articulated fear in the 'streetside' sector of serious competition emerging from *kampung* tourism. After all, *kampung* tourism is not the poor, marginal, unorganized and informal antipode to 'streetside' tourism. For many *kampung* people involvement in tourism has brought about more prosperity, a better income, better housing and health conditions, new consumer goods, more knowledge of other ways of life, a greater proficiency in foreign languages, and perhaps a better education, and new lifestyles. People like Pak Djoko have become quite rich and run relatively large businesses offering employment opportunities to many *kampung* people, even though he himself has moved out of the neighbourhood to establish himself among the urban middle class. His travel agency has no trouble competing with the star-rated sector, where one-man businesses are quite common. He is respected and envied in the *kampung* for having made it from driver to 'boss.' Ibu Siska who is a university graduate and a successful businesswoman is highly respected in the community, though she is still unmarried and childless.

The *kampung* tourism industry is characterized by the ethos of individualism and autonomy among its entrepreneurs who are reluctant to organize themselves. But *kampung* tourism is not as unorganized as it may seem. The few formal organizations that have been established operate according to the unwritten rules of *kampung rukun*: decisions are taken in a spirit of harmony and by mutual agreement and may be postponed or fail to emerge, rather than run the risk of straightjacketing individual members. Even more characteristic of *kampung* ways are the manifold forms of informal co-operation that provide jobless people with an income. Again *rukun*, in terms of social harmony and mutual help lies at the foundation of this system. Those who possess property support, and at the same time are supported by those who have none: unlicensed guides, *becak* men, and touts provide tourism businesses with clients and receive commission in return. These relationships exist on dyadic ties of mutual agreement and are expressed in terms of friendship. This is not to say that *kampung* economy is an informal economy. Most *kampung* businesses are formal businesses which make sure that they are in possession of all the required licences (cf. Timothy & Wall 1997, Timothy 1999). They may pay their taxes, though they may have been supposed to pay more according to the size and profit of their business; they may have the required licenses, though some may have expired years ago; they may employ personnel, but the bulk of work may still be cleared by unpaid household members or underpaid family members; their owners may have gone through a formal training, but not in the appropriate schools and programmes, or they may have earned academic diplomas that are not matched by their employment in the *kampung* economy; they may keep some records of their costs, income, and profit, but may do so irregularly; they may expand their businesses, but only with marginal additions and rarely change their basic product; and they may still rely largely on personal networks. *Kampung* establishments are operating under the fluctuating conditions of an unpredictable tourism market and they plan from day-to-day. Their businesses are less specialized and professionalized than 'streetside' businesses in the same branch used to be. Many *kampung* entrepreneurs practice risk avoidance by spreading their activities over a number of businesses to make them less dependent and vulnerable. Other risk reducing strategies are: to put in low or unpaid family labour, to consume instead of re-invest, to be reluctant to grow and, most of all, to imitate other more successful businesses. But that is not to say that they are marginal, backward, traditional, or in their decline. Quite the contrary. It is in the *kampung* I have encountered innovative entrepreneurship: travel agents who dare to develop adventure tourism, homestay owners who offer a glimpse of *kampung* backstages, visit home industries, and support self-help groups. All in all, *kampung* businesses are closer to the formal than the informal local economy which should be regarded as being a continuum instead of exhibiting a dualist structure.

'Streetside' businesses are quite unaware of what goes on in the *kampung*. The dominant image is that *kampung* tourism caters to poor and dirty hippies, indulges in illegal business, drug abuse, and prostitution and is steadily on the decline strangled by government measures to promote 'quality' tourism. *Kampung* entrepreneurs are equated with *kampungan*. They are denied the social esteem that they enjoy within their neighbourhood, although in terms of income and education some of the *kampung* entrepreneurs are equal or even superior to 'streetside' businessmen. 'Streetside' tourism businesses are not necessarily large-scale themselves, as we have seen in the case of travel agencies, but most of them are associated with or even dependent on foreign or Jakarta-based firms. There is a lack of co-operation and initiative within the star-rated sector of the city's tourism industry. Hotel managers, travel agents, and restaurant owners all behave as small-scale entrepreneurs: they jealously cherish their autonomy and independence and compete with each other. They underestimate the threat emanating from global competition on the one hand, and from *kampung* tourism on the other. 'Streetside' tourism is organized through state-controlled organizations, the membership of which is compulsory. These organizations, like ASITA, BPHN, and ITPB, do not function to their members' satisfaction. As a consequence, 'streetside' businesses are thrown back heavily on their networks. In this respect they do not differ from their much abused *kampung* colleagues, the difference being that the latter benefit from better developed networks. Though competition is fierce among *kampung* entrepreneurs, the existing co-operative efforts are of a local and personal nature and can easily be controlled by the stakeholders themselves. It is a different story in the 'streetside' sector. While Pak Budi is dealing with a partner in Bali who is more powerful and uncontrollable, Pak Djoko exchanges clients with a travel agent from across the street. There is another parallel between 'streetside' and *kampung* entrepreneurs: subcontracting relations are quite common in both realms. There is a difference in scale since in the *kampung* the supplier of contracts and the subcontractor are *kampung* members tied to each other by the obligation of *rukun*. 'Streetside' subcontractors are at the mercy of anonymous and distant 'big brothers.' The stagnation in Yogyanese tourism has to be understood against the background of its tourism industry being basically a sector of branch offices, chain stores, sections, and subcontractors. Economic decisions affecting tourism in Yogyakarta are taken in Bali, Jakarta, Singapore, and even New York, while political decisions invariably emanate from Jakarta. The processes of political as well as economic decision making in these far-away places are out of touch with everyday practice in Yogyakarta. In contrast to current notions of the *kampung* economy representing the 'traditional,' backward, poor, and marginal sector, it seems that in Yogyakarta the *kampung* is the only place where product innovation can be expected to happen, as *kampung* tourism has largely withdrawn itself from stifling government intervention.

NOTES

1   The New Order government attempted to shift petty traders into multi-storeyed buildings and formalize trading arrangements (Guinness 1994), to demolish the squatter housing in Jakarta, and to banish pedicabs in many large cities in Java (Kartodirdjo 1981) and bemos from Jakarta (Jellinek 1991). Food sellers lost their businesses because of the authorities' reluctance to issue licences, and lottery sellers and street guides had to hide from frequent police raids (Dahles 1996, 1998b). The recent blows that tourism in Bali and Yogyakarta has suffered were blamed on the informal sector (Bras & Dahles 1998), leading to harsher government measures against hawkers, pedicabmen, foodstalls, and unlicensed guides. Outside the formal markets, petty economic arrangements still flourish and as soon as the police turn their backs, hawkers, lottery sellers, and street guides carry on as usual.

2   Sosrowijayan is the popular name of about two thirds of the *kecamatan* Gedongtengen that is composed of six *kampung*. First, there is Sosrowijayan Wetan, the busiest tourism *kampung* bordering the backyards of premises in Malioboro Street, Pasar Kembang, and Sosrowijayan Street as its southern border. Second, further to the east is Sosrowijayan Kulon; south of Sosrowijayan Street and north of Dagen street are the *kampung* Sosromenduran and Sosrodipuran, and further south are Jogonegaran and Pajeksan.

3   Homestays are most prominent in Bali, where locals began to take in foreign backpackers as early as the 1960s. By the late 1980s, these businesses formed a large and thriving sector in Bali's economy (Wall & Long 1996; Long & Kindon 1997; Van der Giessen & Van Loo; Van der Giessen, Van Loo & Bras 1999).

4   Mazur, who did a survey among young travellers in Sosrowijayan in 1989, reports that 70 per cent of his respondents intended to stay more than one month, 42 per cent more than two months (1993:150). A stay that extends

beyond two months implies that tourists have to leave Indonesia to acquire a new tourist visa to re-enter the country. A tourist visa cannot be extended in Indonesia.

5   All names of persons and *kampung* businesses are pseudonyms.

6   The *salak* growing region near Yogyakarta has been developed for domestic and international agritourism (cf. Telfer 1997). Other initiatives can be found in the brochures of tour operators marketing their products in terms of responsible tourism. They take small tour groups to villages, visit local industries, and offer overnight stays in the homes of local people.

7   This home, which is run by a local Non-Governmental Organization, is integrated into the programme of a Dutch tour operator. My efforts to introduce this tour operator to a local housing project for formerly homeless river flat dwellers established by a Jesuit priest failed for reasons unknown to me.

8   I came across this mistake in '*Yogya-in-a-week*,' the English-language weekly addition to the *Yogya Post*, an Indonesian-language newspaper. The addition was published over a period of eighteen months to support the Visit Indonesia Year campains. The edition of 29 November – 5 December 1991 promotes 'taking a rest in Yogya' and lists a number of attractions that should be explored by local means of transport such as *becak* or *andong*. Under the heading 'The Antiquities of Kotagede' it says: 'Kotagede is an old city, the former capital of Mataram kingdom during the glory of Panembahan Senopati. There are historical remnants found in Kotagede, like the Royal Mosque, the Royal Burial Ground of pamen bahan Senopati which is located in Kampung Kauman, and the foundation stones and the *banyan* trees of the castle in kampung Dalem.' The 'historical remnants' mentioned here are actually located in the *kampung* within the Kraton walls, not in Kota Gede, except for the Royal Burial Ground which is indeed situated in Kota Gede.

9   As far as initiatives to make the city more lively and entertaining are concerned, one has to take into account the presence of a large student population. Yogyakarta is a troublesome city politically speaking. Creating places of entertainment where many people come together could be construed as supporting political activism and creating potential unrest. Though it would be beneficial to tourism, the authorities prefer to concentrate entertainment in hotels rather than in public places in the city.

10   It is the habit of hotels to give gifts in money or in kind to the *kampung* at Idul Fitri and to contribute to larger *kampung* projects, like sports facilities for *kampung* youth or the construction of communal buildings.

11   This has been the case for the 'INTAN Pelangi Tours & Travel' agency which is associated with the INTAN Hotel Group with three-star hotels

all over Indonesia. Backed by this hotel chain, INTAN is able to make the most of the Japanese market which constitutes more than half of its customers. If Japanese tourists do not come to stay in Yogyakarta, they are flown in from Bali on a transit tour and lunch in an associated hotel. In this sense, the travel agent as well as the hotel benefit.

12   The Akademi Pariwisata Indonesia (API) regards itself as the pioneer among the Yogyanese tourism schools and claims to be the 'oldest' institute of higher tourism education in the city. It was established in 1971 before tourism started booming. The academy is a local initiative as the Yogyanese tourism industry required more and more trained labour. For eleven years the academy operated without accreditation; when this accreditation finally materialized in 1982, a great deal of autonomy (regarding the content of the programme) had to be ceded to national authorities (the Ministry of Education and more specifically the Polytechnic Education Development Center in Jakarta) which are in charge of all official training programmes. The school has 1,600 students, 60 per cent of whom are in the hospitality sector, the other 40 per cent in the tourism training section. API's most prominent competitor is AMPTA (Ambarrukmo Palace Tourism Academy). Founded in 1987, AMPTA is affiliated with the Ambarrukmo Palace Hotel. It has 800 students. The school co-operates closely with ASITA (as the hotel hosts many ASITA members) and is able to allocate two or three students with each ASITA member annually, offering 150 internships to its students. For airline training, Garuda Airlines is the exclusive partner. Tourism education is becoming such an interesting market that even Gadjah Mada University (UGM) is developing an educational programme in this field. UGM started a vocational programme in tourism in September 1994. At the time of the research (in 1996), the programme had not produced any graduates yet. It is established under the Faculty of Arts as language training occupies a major role in tourism education. Some of the students come directly from high school as well as from the Yogyanese Tourism Department and the provincial KANWIL office. The latter group come for upgrading, the former because they are attracted to a job in the tourism industry. The programme is multidisciplinairy: lecturers from different departments are hired to teach in the tourism programme. Moreover, guest speakers from the government and the tourism industry are invited to throw light on practical aspects of tourism entrepreneurship and policy and to serve as vehicles for arranging internships for the students. In contrast to the other tourism schools, the university does not possess facilities for practical training, such as a hotel kitchen or a ticket counter. The reason behind UGM's development of the tourism programme is the policy of the Ministry of Parpostel which is to concentrate in Yogyakarta

as a destination for MICE tourism. Building on its first-hand experience with large events on a national scale, UGM trusts that the Ministry will allocate money to this institute to build up expertise in this field.

13 A Diploma III certificate is roughly comparable to a diploma from a European polytechnic.

14 API receives about 1,000 applications per year, while there is room for only 500 new students of whom 350 are in the hospitality sector. The tourism programme of Gadjah Mada University admits 125 students per year, while there are hundreds of applications from all over Indonesia.

15 Students and staff of prestigious tourism academies are worried about these developments as an article in 'Pembaruan,' a magazine published by Akademi Pariwisata Indonesia (December Issue 1995, p. 6) shows. Under the title 'Quo Vadis Alumnus API,' the anonymous writer (probably the editors) raises the issue of inflation of tourism education in Yogyakarta in particular and Indonesia in general because of the proliferation of schools and programmes.

16 On that occasion, the Sultan composed a paper to pinpoint the objectives of such a provincial branch. The paper strongly emphasizes the need for niche marketing (cf. Hamengku Buwono X 1995).

17 As far as Borobudur is concerned, the idea is to create a show of water, light, and dance that depicts the life of Buddha. A famous Javanese choreographer has been contracted to implement this project. A similar performance is planned at Prambanan temple centring on the story of Loro Jonggran, the princess who according to legend was turned into a stone statue in the main temple of the complex (actually a statue of Siva) by a rejected suitor.

CHAPTER 5

THE POLITICS OF GUIDING

ENCLOSED SPACES AND CONTROLLED DISCOURSES

INTRODUCTION

Tour guiding constitutes a strategic factor in the representation of a tourist destination area and in influencing the quality of the tourist experience, the length of stay, and the resulting economic benefits. Tourism based on cultural heritage in particular, demands a specific body of knowledge and a high standard of tourist guiding. The emerging role of tourist guides[1] in conveying information, offering explanations, and developing narratives has become a current theme in the study of guiding in tourist areas. The industry, the media, and government officials are beginning to see that a tourist guide's role extends well beyond welcoming and informing visitors. The tourist guide is entrusted with the purest of public relations missions: to encapsulate the essence of a place and to be a window onto a site, region, or country (Pond 1993:vii).

Among the first to study tourist guides systematically was Holloway (1981). Starting from role-theory, Holloway regards tourist guides as information-giver and fount of knowledge, teacher or instructor, motivator and initiator into the rites of touristic experiences, missionary or ambassador for their country, entertainer or catalyst for the group, confidant, shepherd, and ministering angel, group leader and disciplinarian (1981:385-6). Cohen (1985) goes more deeply into the interpretative role of tourist guides. He distinguishes different styles of guiding in terms of 'pathfinding' and 'mentoring.' Pathfinders are guides who restrict themselves to pointing out the route and the attractions, without offering elaborate explanations. The pathfinder is a geographical guide who leads the way through an environment in which tourists lack orientation or through a socially defined territory to which they have no access (Cohen 1985:7). This category emerges mainly in literally inaccessible areas like mountains – less so in cities which, nonetheless, can be 'rugged' in a social and cultural sense. Besides finding the way in an unmarked territory, guides are faced with the necessity to ensure themselves of the goodwill and hospitality of the natives of an area. Gaining access to a remote social environment and making themselves and their party welcome is a difficult task that makes heavy demands on the guides' mediation talents which makes them the pivotal link in an encounter between total strangers. If they operate in a young, still underdeveloped tourist area, they are called pathbreakers, who literally select new objects of interest and make them accessible to tourism (ibid:25). The role of the mentor resembles the role of teacher, instructor, or advisor. The mentor points out the objects of interest, explains them, and tells the tourist where and when to look and how to behave. The mentor may select the objects of interest in accordance with their own personal preferences or tastes, their professional training, directions received from their employer or the authorities, or the assumed interest of their party (ibid:14). Their narrative may be interspersed with historical facts, architectural comments, or pieces of cultural information. The information part is considered to be a vital element in the mentor's task. This mentor-type of guide blossoms in mature tourist destinations where the transfer of information takes on an almost academic character. An extensive body of knowledge is required to establish the professional status of the mentor. The organizational, practical, and entertaining activities are of minor importance. In contrast to the pathfinder, the mentor focuses on organized mass tourism. Having had a formal education and being employed by a tour operator makes mentors work in the centre of the tourism system. Unlike pathfinders mentors work on established attractions and do not discover new sites or produce new narratives (ibid:26).

Cohen makes two points that are of interest here. First, he observes that the pathfinder/pathbreaker type of guide is predominant in young and as yet undeveloped tourist sites and in areas characterized by nature-based tourism. The mentor type of guide is commonly found in developed tourist areas, and especially in cultural tourism destinations. Therefore, in Yogyakarta we should expect to be dealing predominantly with the mentor, and less so with the pathfinder/pathbreaker. Secondly, Cohen argues that the role of the tourist guide is evolving and shifting from the logistical aspect to the facilitation of the travel experience, from the pathfinder to the mentor role, away from leadership towards mediating and away from outer and towards the inner-directed sphere with the communicative component becoming the centre of the professional role (ibid:21). Guides are becoming interpreters, not 'translators' of other cultures in the limited sense of the word, but mediators who enable tourists to experience the other culture; guides who encourage tourists not just to see, but also to hear, smell, taste, and feel the other culture (cf. Urry 1990). Pivotal to the interpreter's approach is the art of storytelling. In Urry's terms (1995:146) there is a shift away from the didactic legislator who instructed visitors where to look, what to look for, and when to look, towards an encouragement to look with interest at an enormous diversity of artefacts, cultures, and systems of meaning with the help of an expert whose role it is to interpret the different elements for the visitor.[2] In this context, Gurung et al. (1996) have come up with the distinction between tour management and experience management. The task of tourist guides necessarily involves both approaches to management: the organization of the itinerary and the selection and interpretation of sites in an interactive process with tourists. This implies that tourist guides are cultural brokers whose pivotal role is 'to influence the visitors' impressions and attitudes, as well as enhance their appreciation and understanding of their surroundings' (ibid:11). Guides in their role as brokers 'serve as a buffer, insulating many travellers from the difficulties and possibly, some delights of the visited culture (...) indigenous guides play an important role in building better host-guest relationships' (ibid:12).

Turning to Yogyakarta this implies several things. With the mentor-type of guide dominating the scene, it could be expected that tours are well-established and standardized, and that the art of storytelling is becoming more pronounced. This is somewhat precarious as the position of interpreter and communicator makes local guides extremely susceptible to outside intervention and manipulation. After all, decisions regarding the 'true' story or the 'most appropriate' interpretation are subject to relations of power and dependence. In many countries, tourist guides can go about their activities as they please as guiding does not constitute a well-established and formalized profession (Crick 1992, Pond 1993), but in Indonesia guiding is subject to government regulations in compliance with the tourism policy as outlined in previous chapters. Under the New Order, government intervention in tourism extended to the regulation of tourist guiding in terms of licensing, certification, training, pay and benefits, marketing and conducting tours, and the organization and professional ethics of guides. The New Order established formal training and the possession of a licence to be the criteria in deciding who may operate as a guide and who may not. In government terms the boundaries of the profession were well-defined and guides were organized and strategically used to serve political objectives.

Government regulation even extended to the content of the information and explanations provided by guides at the tourist sites. Processes of attraction building are complex exchanges of information and meaning between a number of agents, including the site, the local community, the state, the tourism industry, guides, and tourists. These processes are characterized by interests which are partly converging, partly conflicting and multivocal interpretations. As the preceding chapter has shown, different categories of local agents act as mediators of the culture and heritage industry in Yogyakarta, some representing the government-controlled 'quality' tourism sector, others operating in the locally-organized and partly informal *kampung* tourism. Although both act as social and cultural brokers between tourists and host society, they do so in very different ways, offer divergent tourist experiences and represent conflicting images of the local community. 'Street-side' tourism in Yogyakarta with its regulated and controlled tourist attractions supposedly offers a well-organized and professional guiding service. *Kampung* tourism, by contrast, can be expected to operate with more informally organized guides operating outside the government-controlled arena.

One aspect which the different theoretical approaches to guiding have in common is a strong emphasis on the mediation activities of tourist guides: mediation between hosts and guests, mediation between the tour operator/ travel agency and the tourists, mediation between the tour leader and the local tourist scene, mediation between the hotel sector and the tourist. The tourist guide is portrayed as someone who builds bridges between different groups of people through the deployment of money, services, access, and information. This applies to heritage sites in particular. As Gertler (1993) argues, tourist guiding becomes a genuine force in cultural tourism, since the motivation is to inspire the tourists' interest by digging more deeply into the culture itself. It is all well and good but this approach paints an idealized picture of guiding. That tourist guides in some way or other are intermediaries cannot be denied, but it is doubtful whether their work can be interpreted purely according to a harmony model of 'mediation,' of keeping all parties involved satisfied, and the tourism development in a specific area in balance. In tourism practice, the process of mediation is not as innocent and unproblematic as this perspective implies. As Bras (2000) points out, tourist guides are not altruistic mediators by vocation, nor can they be expected to submit blindly to government rules and regulations exacting them to tell pre-fabricated stories. Instead, they *sell* images, knowledge, contacts, souvenirs, access, authenticity, ideology, and sometimes even themselves. Their knowledge of the local culture is not limited to facts, figures, and *couleur locale*, it includes the art of building a network, of monopolizing contacts, a familiarity with the operations of the tipping and commission system, a notion of trends in tourism and of the characteristics of tourists and the countries they come from – all this converges to make the encounter with tourists as profitable as possible for the guides themselves. Successful guides know how to turn their social relations and narratives into a profitable enterprise. They act as profit-maximizing individuals, and therefore should be regarded as entrepreneurs (Dahles 1998a, Dahles & Bras 1999a, 1999b, Bras 2000).

From a political as well as economic point of view on guiding, two perspectives have to be added to the often-quoted 'mediation' role of guides: the entrepreneurial mode and the manipulative mode. The first perspective focuses on tourist guides as small entrepreneurs, i.e. autonomously operating and risk-taking individuals who benefit from their intermediate position in terms of income and contacts. The latter perspective tends to focus on the power relations within which these small entrepreneurs have to operate. It regards tourist guides as pawns who are being used as vessels to transmit the government-controlled image of a destination area. In this chapter, two related questions will be raised: firstly, what strategies does the Indonesian government apply to professionals and to control tourist guides in general and to what extent does *pancasila* tourism represent the ulterior motive behind the normalization of guiding in the Special Province of Yogyakarta in particular? Secondly, what are the modes of operation of local tourist guides in Yogyakarta in terms of small-scale entrepreneurship, and to what extent does government intervention constitute restrictions to and opportunities for their activities?

GOVERNMENT POLICIES ON TOURIST GUIDES: THE MANIPULATIVE MODE

During the last few years, tourist destinations in Indonesia have witnessed a proliferation of unlicensed guides, generally local young men, exhibiting a hustler style in approaching tourists. In the eyes of the authorities and the quality sector industry, these young men – the 'wild guides' (*guide liar*), as they dubbed them – represent a potential embarrassment. Their disturbing presence has been reported from areas as different as Bali (McCarthy 1994), South Sulawesi (Adams 1997), Lombok (Dahles & Bras 1999b, Bras 2000) and Yogyakarta (Dahles 1996, Dahles & Bras 1999, Schlehe 1997). The majority of these wild guides are young unemployed or underemployed men who seek their clients in restaurants, hotels, or in the streets frequented by tourists. Although a few of these young men are reputed to be hustlers overindulging in alcoholic drink and marihuana, for the most part they are entrepreneurs who have taught themselves one or two European languages and enjoy associating with foreigners. From the viewpoint of government officials and the industry's executives, wild guides are not only untrained, what is worse they are unprofessional. In the early 1980s when international tourism in Indonesia began to boom and the deregulation policy facilitated the establishment of what later came to be called 'quality' tourism, tourist guiding was a field that could be entered by anyone. There were no requirements as far as training, diplomas, and accreditations were concerned. This honeymoon period did not last long and the New Order government quickly began to formalize the as yet unregulated economic activities, among them was guiding. This concern with professionalism reflected the New Order's ideas about order and security: whereas wild guides were perceived as a threat to the state's carefully manufactured imagery of tamed cultural diversity, professionalism promised uniformity and central control (Adams 1997). In emerging tourist areas with a shortage of licensed guides and a growing demand for guided tours – like Lombok and South Sulawesi – upgrading measures were indeed offering opportunities to practising but as yet unlicensed guides to acquire professional status. In established tourist destinations like Yogyakarta, however, with their oversupply of accredited guides and a diminishing demand for guided tours, the government regulations became an instrument for protectionism in 'streetside' tourism. In Yogyakarta, the so-called professionalization of guiding contributed to a decline in opportunities for as yet unlicensed guides to enter the profession and to a stricter control of the practices of licensed guides. The way in which unlicensed guides operate in the margins of 'streetside' tourism in Yogyakarta will be investigated in the next chapter. In this chapter, the focus is directed to the ways in which government-controlled guiding is organized and licensed guides operate within the 'streetside' tourism in the city.

The first step towards more control on guiding was the establishment in 1983 of a national guiding association, *Himpunan Duta Wisata Indonesia*, renamed as *Himpunan Pramuwisata Indonesia* (HPI) shortly after. This national organization was constituted by provincial sections that were operational in those provinces in which there were a substantial number of tourist guides. The by-laws of the national organization were shared by the provincial sections which usually copied the text (including the philosophy, objectives, tasks, conditions of membership, organizational structure, etiquette, and ethical code), only to append a first page with the names of the members of the provincial board. In the by-laws of the HPI the *pancasila* state ideology naturally formed the basic philosophy (*anggaran dasar*) on which the organization was built. In both the guiding etiquette (*tata krama*) and the ethical code (*kode etik*) as defined in the by-laws, the first responsibility of the guide was towards the state, the nation and its culture, and adherence to the 'Guide to the Realization and Application of *pancasila*,' the '*P4*' programme (cf. Chapter 2).[3]

The HPI Yogyakarta was established in 1983 immediately following the inauguration of the national guiding association. The board serves a five-year term and the chairman is replaced after that period, although re-election is possible. The provincial sections are subdivided into 'language groups': guides are organized according to the language in which they conduct their tours. In Yogyakarta the largest group are the English guides followed by the Japanese and French guides, with the Japanese showing a rapid increase.[4] Usually the leader of the strongest group becomes chairman at new elections. According to the chairman of the Yogyanese section, the provincial association was not initiated by the tourist guides operating in the area, but by the *Diparda*. The provincial government introduced the HPI as an instrument to effectuate the new licensing regulations and to enforce their observance. The guides in the area were reluctant to become members of the HPI from the start. The fact that in 1996 about 450 guides were registered as members of the HPI in the Yogyakarta area was not because the association had proven beneficial to the guides, but that travel agencies (organized by ASITA) required HPI membership for guides to be employed. If they wanted to acquire and renew their licences, guides had to be members of the HPI, especially as the renewal of the guiding licence was effectuated through the HPI, which all goes to show that the government and the industry strongly promote the HPI among the tourist guides.

In the mid-1990s aspirant-members were required to pay an entrance fee of 25,000 *rupiah* to the HPI, and subsequently a contribution of 5,000 *rupiah* per month – the equivalent to about two hours guiding on a free-lance basis. Basically the money was to be used for running the head office (situated in a building on the premises of the Ambarrukmo Palace Hotel). However, the chairman said only about 20 per cent of the members paid their contribution; the others usually promised to do so when their licence was about to come up for renewal. According to the objectives as defined in the by-laws, the HPI organized monthly meetings for its members, except during the high season when the guides were fully employed and had no time to spare for meetings. The aim was to provide additional education, for example by inviting guest speakers from the industry or educational institutions as sophisticated as Gadjah Mada University. Only about five per cent of the members used to show up at these meetings. The disinterest displayed by guides in their association was disappointing to the chairman who accused his colleagues of a 'slave mentality':

> Bad guides having a bad relationship with travel agents and little employment want a strong HPI, but those with good relations and plenty of employment do not want the HPI at all! Only if things go wrong, like a guide getting sick and needing financial support, do they make a claim on the collective insurance that the HPI offers its members. But if they are healthy, they refuse to pay the insurance fee.

When it came to the employment of guides, the HPI claimed to have little impact, as the association did not function as a labour union. Guides had to maintain a network of their own to find travel agents willing to employ them. In fact, guides depended more on ASITA, the organization of their employers, than on their own interest group. It was the ASITA which established a pricing system to fix the guides' honorarium to be paid by the travel agent for whom a guide is conducting a tour. According to the official list (dated 1995), the maximum fee per hour was 5,000 *rupiah* (US$2.30 at the time of the research), but generally a free-lancer did not make more than about 3,500 *rupiah* per hour. Provided that a guide maintained good relations with local travel agencies, he could make about 15,000 – 20,000 *rupiah* per day. Although the HPI claimed to have no influence on its members' employment, it unwillingly served as a vehicle for its members to be selected for a job by local tour operators. The HPI issued lists with the names of its local members, their level of expertise or specialities and language proficiency. The names were arranged according to their level and 'quality.' This 'hit list' circulated widely among local tour operators who seemed to rely on the information given by the HPI and made their choice from this index. As travel agents usually do not have any guides permanently on their payroll but hire their services whenever required, having one's name on the list would be thought to be important to guides. In practice guides seemed to be unaware of this effect as they strongly criticized the association and contended that it was of no help whatsoever in boosting their employment opportunities.

Another crucial step towards the professionalization of tourist guides was the decree entitled *Keputusan Menteri Pariwisata, Pos dan Telekomunikasi,* issued by the *Depparpostel* in 1988, stipulating the requirements and responsibilities of tourist guides in Indonesia.[5] In accordance with the national government's guidelines, licensing procedures and guiding courses were established by the *Diparda* in many provinces to upgrade the knowledge and morals of young people aspiring to a career in tourist guiding and prepare them for an examination that had to be passed to acquire a licence. Basically, all Indonesian citizens with a minimum age of eighteen years with a permanent address and a secondary school diploma, able to speak *bahasa Indonesia* and at least one other foreign language fluently were eligible to become a professional guide. Provided that a person met these basic requirements, he or she could apply for admittance to a guiding course organized by the *Diparda* in the province where the person was registered as permanent resident. Upon passing the examination which concluded the course, the person acquired a certificate that gave access to the licence and the badge testifying professional status. These rules were enforced by the provincial Department of Justice and implemented, most strikingly, by the tourist police.[6]

The government makes a basic distinction between tourist guides and tour managers. Tour managers accompany roundtrips passing through a number of Indonesian provinces according to government rules. Tour managers are representatives of a tour operator; their presence is required on all tours organized for foreign tourists. They supervise transportation, lodging, sightseeing tours, excursions and other tourist activities and co-ordinate assistance in case of accidents. As tour managers operate at a trans-provincial level, they fall under the authority of the *Depparpostel* and the KANWIL in the different provinces. These provincial guides wear a red badge, the *cenderawasih,* the bird of paradise identifying the licensed guide. In the guides' jargon this badge is called a 'wing.' Tourist guides, on the other hand, are intermediaries between tourist objects within a specific province and the visitors. They fall under the authority of the *Diparda* and operate at different levels. Again, there are two basic categories: provincial tourist guides and local tourist guides.

Provincial tourist guides cover tours in the *Wilayah Daerah Tingkat I* (the provincial level) for which they have been authorized by the *Diparda*. Generally they are 'senior' guide or *pramuwisata madya*; they wear the yellow 'wing.' Local tourist guides operate at two levels. First, there is the general tourist guide who is authorized to guide visitors within the boundaries of a specific town or district (*kabupaten*, or *Wilayah Daerah Tingkat II*). These are 'junior' guides or *pramuwisata muda*, wearing the green 'wing.' Secondly, there are 'special' tourist guides or *pramuwisata khusus* operating on a specific tourist object, as for example in the Kraton or at Prambanan. They usually wear an identification badge of the specific attraction. In colloquial language the junior and senior guides are also called *guide umum* (public guide), to be distinguished from the 'special' guide who works in enclosed spaces. These different categories overlap, as some guides hold a number of licences. Tour guides combine the round-trip coaching with guiding tourists in the province where they live; and many special guides also hold the licence for general guide.

TOURIST GUIDE CLASSIFICATION

Tour manager	Tourist guide		
red cenderawasih	Provincial tourist guide, or	Local tourist guide	
	'senior' guide (*pramuwisata madya*) *yellow cenderawasih* (*guide umum*)	General tourist guide, or 'junior' guide (*pramuwisata muda*) *green cenderawasih* (*guide umum*)	Special tourist guide (*pramuwisata khusus*)

This classification system for guides corresponds to government-run courses preparing guides to pass the exam at different levels. Tour managers have to prove their competence at the KANWIL level conforming to the requirements set by the *Depparpostel*. Tourist guides, on the other hand, have to pass the *Diparda* examinations. Although it is the *Diparda* that is responsible for the content of the guiding courses for tourist guides, the *Depparpostel* issued a number of 'guidelines' in 1989 and again in 1991 that have to be observed by the *Diparda* division for Education and Training (DIKLAT, *Pendidikan dan*

Latihan).[7] These guidelines are compulsory in the sense that the authorization of the guides depends on whether they have successfully passed the subjects as defined by the *Depparpostel*. There is one remarkable exception to the rule, the guides in the Kraton of Yogyakarta. Here royal autonomy reigns: Kraton guides are not under the control of any governmental authority except the authority of the sultan. These guides receive a private training from Kraton instructors. All the other guides are subject to the government guidelines which prescribe three different clusters of subjects. The first are 'basic' subjects that focus on 'good citizenship': *pancasila*, the Indonesian language, HAN-KAMNAS (*Pertahanan dan Keamanan Nasional*, defence and national security), national history, culture and the arts. The subjects have to be taken by all levels, which means that a guide who goes for the senior level after having succeeded at the junior level, has to go through these subjects all over again. The second cluster focuses on 'main' subjects that vary with the level of education. For example, while the candidates for junior guides have to study the tourist objects at the district level, the candidates for senior guide have to expand their knowledge of tourist objects at the provincial level. The special guide has to learn the details about the tourist object where he will be guiding, while the tour manager has to be informed about the major attractions of Indonesia. Thirdly, there is a cluster of 'supplementary knowledge,' like traffic rules, hygiene, and sanitation, which again vary according to the level of guiding. One thing to bear in mind is that the government guidelines foresee a one year course split into two semesters to cover the considerable number of subjects.

The guidelines are one thing; the way in which they are implemented at the local and provincial levels are another thing. As Bras (2000) reports from Lombok, the *Diparda* course lasted only ten days, while Adams (1997) found in Sulawesi that crash courses for unlicensed guides were taught for one month. In Yogyakarta the course takes four months, said the head of the *Diparda* in 1996. However, a perusal of the course syllabus showed unequivocally that it took two months (July to September 1994). Nor was this course offered regularly (less than once in three years), access was restricted and subject to bribe, as will be shown below. Little effort was made by the government to provide more licensed guides in Yogyakarta. One of my informants, who contacted *Diklat* to obtain information about the course was told by an official that there was no demand for newly licensed guides. When my informant insisted, the official was very discouraging, telling him that candidates had to be at least twenty-five years old (my informant was twenty-three and the official guidelines said that eighteen is the minimum age), that proficiency in English was not enough but at least one other foreign language was required, and that people not born in Yogyakarta would not be accepted (my informant was born in North Sumatra, and the state guidelines only required local residence). Most revealing was the official's advice that my informant should not bother about the course and the licence, as he could operate as a guide anyway: 'Many people from outside of Yogya do so.'

The last guiding course in Yogyakarta was organized in 1994. Its target group was junior guides who could try for senior status. This implied several things. First, the 1994 course was an upgrade course for already licensed guides. It did not offer new opportunities to those young people with a high school and even university degree who looked for a job in professional guiding. Second, as no other course was planned until 1997 and it was still unclear whether that course would be at the level of junior guide or rather special guide or again senior guide, the opportunities for becoming a guide at all were extremely scarce in Yogyakarta. Third, it may well be asked whether a two-month course could provide all the knowledge and training that the task of senior guides requires. A brief glance at the list of subjects taught within the two months shows that the Yogyanese authorities attempted to put the minister's guidelines that were designed for a two semester course into these two months, plus piling in additional subjects focusing on matters typically Yogyanese (*Sub Dinas Diklat* 1994).[8] While the programme looked impressive, only a few hours were available to discuss the complex matters thrown up in the lectures. Quite a large amount of time was spent on field trips to the tourist objects in the area. Before candidates were admitted, an entrance-exam had to be passed, consisting mainly of questions about the *pancasila* state ideology. This examination freed the *Diklat* of the obligation to teach *pancasila* on the programme. Also part of the entrance-exam was an interview to test the candidates' ability to speak English. Candidates were expected to have at least three years experience in guiding if they were going for senior status. The competition was fierce. While the *Diparda* officials remained vague about the number of participants for the entrance-exam, guides who passed this procedure reported that there were about 200 people present at the intake-exam. In 1994, sixty were admitted, of whom fifty received the certificate and a licence.

The compulsory *Diparda* course was generally considered to be insufficient to obtain the required knowledge and skills to be a good guide. All the tourism-related institutions in Yogyakarta subscribed to this point of view: the HPI, the ASITA, the hotel managers and, most importantly, the guides themselves. Therefore, many actors in the tourism industry strongly favoured the establishment of additional upgrade programmes for guides. It is striking that the tourism academies and other educational institutions of higher tourism education, of which Yogyakarta accommodates many, were unable to deliver well-trained young people for guiding. As these institutions focused strongly on hospitality training and offered guiding only as a sub-subject in the tour and travel trajectory of their three-year programme with some basic training 'on the job,' there were only few graduates well prepared and motivated for a professional career in guiding. Highly dissatisfied, a number of private institutes either had established or were about to establish their own programme for upgrade guides.[9] To implement one of the pivotal recommendations of the UNDP/UNESCO team in the early 1990s, a guide upgrading programme was established by a private university, Sanata Dharma University, in 1993/4, as a follow-up to the needs assessment for cultural tourism development in 1991-2 (Amato 1991-2b, Spillane 1992, 1993).[10] The aim of this programme was to overhaul the current system of regulating tourist guides and to develop occupational skill standards under a new national vocational training system, test these standards, and then introduce new upgrade courses. All existing tourist guides would be upgraded, re-tested, and licensed anew if they managed to satisfy the requirements. The result would be to improve the standards of tourist guides across the country. Yogyakarta was chosen as a test case, as Sanata Dharma University submitted a proposal for the establishment of a centre for tourist guide training (Doswell 1992).[11] About twenty-five tourist guides from the provinces of Yogyakarta and Central Java enrolled in the course. The participation dropped considerably during the course as it turned out to be difficult to keep up the participants' motivation. The head of the programme claimed that the diminishing attendance could be attributed to the fact that the participants were volunteers who attended the lectures after work and often had to cover long distances to reach the university in the evening. Additional factors, not mentioned by the head of the programme, might have been the amount and complexity of the subjects and the style of teaching. The course material and lectures were in English, and some of the material was quite unpalatable.[12] Despite the ambitious approach, the high hopes, and the UNESCO support, this programme was not continued, like so many initiatives that emerged under the UNESCO programme to establish cultural tourism in the region.

The ideal guide in terms of New Order government regulations was educated in *pancasila* state ideology, operated only in the ASITA-organized quality sector, held the required certificates and licences, paid HPI membership, and renewed it in due time, attended HPI meetings and took upgrade courses, did not indulge in any jobs on the side, limited contacts with foreigners to a purely professional exchange and focused representation of Indonesia on the officially approved 'facts.' This all reveals that the government-approved guide in Indonesia is the mentor-type of guide rather than the interpreter. The guides themselves were instructed where and when to tell what and how to behave so as to be a worthy representative of the country and the nation. They were supposed to convey this image and information to the tourists without questioning it. By submerging them in a plethora of education, regulations, and licences, the interpretative role of tourist guides was minimized. Education in particular played a key role in the control of Indonesian tourist guides. As was the case with all educational and training programmes in Indonesia, every programme required government approval, and to acquire this approval a number of compulsory subjects had to be taught, including *pancasila* state ideology, the national language, culture and history, defence and national security, and *repelita*. Throughout a person's education, these were recurrent themes that gobbled up the time that could otherwise have been spent on subjects relevant to the discipline or job a person was trained for. In the two-month government guiding course almost two entire weeks were dedicated to these 'basic subjects.' In contrast to the often-heard argument that these subjects were mere rhetoric (cf. Chapter 2), the indoctrination with *pancasila* did have an effect on the way in which guides arranged their tours and discourses, as will be shown below.

Conditions of Employment:
The Entrepreneurial Mode

In this section a number of tourist guides will be introduced. They represent a selection of tourist guides I interviewed in Yogyakarta and followed on tours to one of the well-known tourist sites in or in the vicinity of the city. My analysis does not include tour managers as this category generally transfers tourists to local tourist guides upon arrival at Yogyakarta and it is the construction of Yogyakarta as a tourist destination that is pivotal to this book. I selected informants – all licensed or preparing for the *Diparda* exam or at least accredited to work at a particular attraction – who fitted one of the following categories: the professional guide working exclusively for one travel agent, the free-lancer scratching together tours from a large number of different travel agents, the trainee (the guide-to-be practising for the examination through training on the job) a special guide to Prambanan, and a Kraton guide. Below I shall briefly describe their career history, their acquisition strategies, their networks, the kinds of services they provide, and the tours they conduct. These five categories cover the basic modes within which licensed guides operate. For each I selected an informant who represents a specific mode, although it will inexorably emerge that guides often combine these modes or have passed through different modes in the course of their career.

THE PROFESSIONAL
Pak Rudi is in his early thirties. He is from Manado (Sulawesi) where his parents still live. He describes his family as upper-middle class, well-educated and well-to-do. His father was head of a secondary school, his mother comes from a landed family and his brother studies sociology in Cologne (Germany).

After graduating from high school, Pak Rudi attended teachers' college in Yogyakarta where he obtained a 'minor' in English and a 'major' in German. Although his parents planned his future as a high school teacher, Pak Rudi became interested in European literature and the arts without formulating any clear idea about a professional career ahead. He enrolled in a post-graduate programme on 'culture and civilization' at the *Universitas Indonesia* in Jakarta, but did not finish with a higher degree. Instead of becoming a teacher, he enrolled in the *Diparda* guiding course in 1988 and received his licence for senior guide. His language proficiency is excellent: he speaks German in a well-articulated and grammatically correct manner and English with a slight German accent. His speciality is guiding German tourists, one of the most important visitor categories in Yogyakarta. His becoming a professional guide caused much distress to his family. The relationship with his parents has not yet recovered, although he is married to a Yogyanese woman, has three children and is doing fine. His parents still think that he made the wrong choice, not because they reject his contacts with foreigners (indeed these contacts are highly valued among the educated urban middle classes, as Rudi notes), but because they are critical of his failure to provide a regular income for his family and to lead a regular life.

The regularity of his employment may indeed be somewhat precarious, but Pak Rudi is one of the happy few who has an 'almost' permanent job. He works exclusively for one Yogyanese travel agent who specializes in the German market and co-operates with one German agency that provides them with a permanent flow of tourists. Pak Rudi has some sort of monopoly of the German groups: he is the one who conducts these tours; only during high season when there tends to be a real flood of Germans, are additional guides hired. Besides Germans, the travel agent occasionally caters for Korean, Italian, and French tourists. If he happens to be at a loose end, Rudi guides these other tourists as well, speaking English. Pak Rudi does not have a formalized contract. Instead the relationship with his employer is based on a 'gentlemen's agreement.' Pak Rudi does not work for other travel agents, not even occasionally. Because of his agent's firm relationship with a German organization, it is possible to make some long-term planning which enables Pak Rudi to prepare his schedule. During high season (in the months of July and August) he is flooded with work, guiding tourists from early morning till late at night, working more than twelve hours per day, seven days a week. In the 'off months' (September to November and February to June) he is employed about three days per week, while in December and January he is out of work. As he is paid per tour – 'no tour no pay' – he has to save money during the good months to survive the bad ones. He has no insurance and no right to paid leave. Though an HPI-member, Rudi refuses to join their collective facilities. During the off season, he visits his agent's office every day, chit-chats with the secretary (it is she who gives him a call when there is an unexpected job to do) and hangs around to be seen by his employer. Other guides usually shop around, accepting all kinds of jobs, but Pak Rudi would not do so because if a guiding job comes up unexpectedly and he is not available, his boss may be disappointed and hire another guide who may become a serious competitor. If a guide gains a reputation as someone who shops around, travel agents will not rely on him and it will be more difficult to establish or maintain a permanent relationship with a travel agent. This seems to suggest that loyalty is a core strategy in securing employment.

Pak Rudi makes some additional money through commissions, but not as much as he would like to. He regrets to say that the firm relationship that his employer maintains with the German agency exacts its price: it is this German agency that makes the appointments directly with batik and silver factories in Yogyakarta for their tour groups to visit. As a consequence, the commission that is usually paid to the Indonesian travel agent, goes straight to the German agency, not to Rudi's boss, let alone to Rudi himself. Nevertheless he maintains friendly relations with art shops on his routes and he does not hesitate to encourage his groups to take a look at these shops as well. But he does so in an unobtrusive way, as he cannot afford to have the tourists complaining about him to the travel agency. If the tourists are interested and there is still some time left on a tour, they might stop at a shop where the commission goes straight into Pak Rudi's pocket. These occasions, however, are rare. Pak Rudi criticizes his colleagues who make earning commissions the major target of their job. In his eyes, a guide should focus first and foremost on the content of his job: how to present and explain cultural attractions to tourists. Guides should be true mediators and vehicles of culture contact. With their minds on the money, they become entrepreneurs, which Pak Rudi regards as treason to the 'true cause of guiding.'

THE FREE-LANCER

Ibu Yanik came to Yogyakarta as a twenty-year-old after she ran away from her parents' home in Cirebon (West Java). She found employment as a translator and secretary with a foreign lady who came to work in Yogyakarta for a couple of years. When her job finished, Yanik had saved enough money to enrol in a tourism programme at AMPTA, the Ambarrukmo Palace Tourism Academy, a highly reputed tourism school in Yogyakarta. But after two years the money was spent and Yanik had to find a job. With the last of her money she took the *Diparda* course, passed the exam, and acquired a guiding licence.

After obtaining her green wing, Yanik was given a job as a 'special guide' at Prambanan. At the time, the temple area was not yet under the control of the *P.T. Taman Wisata* and the guides were not organized. In the morning the Prambanan guides gathered under the big tree which still features as the obligatory photo-stop during the walk towards the temple, as from here there is a beautiful panoramic view. In 1990 when Yanik sat under that tree, she and her colleagues approached passing tourists soliciting them with: 'Hello Mister, want guide?' The guides applied social control in their own group and regulated whose turn it was to accompany tourists. One was lucky to have a group twice a day. With a tour lasting only one hour, the rest of the time was spent waiting. The guides offered their services for 5,000 *rupiah*, but tourists could bargain and often guides did the job for less money. Competition among the guides was fierce and the green wing provided nothing but the right to sit under that tree. Again, she turned to the *Diparda* to get her yellow wing as senior guide. With her new licence and her old network she attempted to establish herself as a free-lance guide in Yogyakarta. This was and still is not easy. She works irregularly with five travel agents and tries to maintain friendly relations with many others. She is an English guide and there are 125 other English guides in town and she is an unmarried woman: two good reasons why it is hard to survive in the guiding business. There is only one Yogyakarta-based travel agent who bothers to call her more or less regularly to conduct a tour. The others hire her only if she happens to be around when a guide is needed. Therefore, she visits them often and brings their staff small presents (*oleh-oleh* in Indonesian) from her tours.

Ibu Yanik is usually hired for tours to Borobudur and Prambanan. Other tours are hardly ever required. During high season she may go to Prambanan temple twice a day (first for the 'sunrise,' second for the 'sunset'), three or even four times a week. She is expected to finish a tour to either of the temples within four hours. As she gets paid per tour – she receives 20,000 *rupiah* for a trip to a temple – it is her own responsibility to stay within the set limits of time, as overtime is not paid. It is also her responsibility to see to it that the bus returns to the transport company in due time: any overtime means that her travel agent is charged for the additional time that the bus and the driver spend on a tour. Travel agents are extremely chary about hiring guides who notoriously exceed their time limits. Like Pak Rudi, Yanik has only limited opportunities to earn extra money through commissions. The shops and factories she visits on tours are contracted by her employers and commissions are paid directly to the travel agents. She has her own ploy to counter this. Yanik cautiously discourages tourists from buying souvenirs in those places to which she is forced to bring the tourists. 'If you want to buy real good batik for a good price, I know a better address,' she says. If tourists fail to react to this suggestion, she does not insist, as pushing the tourists could lead to complaints and loss of employment.

Yanik's relationship with her colleagues is strained. Her male colleagues especially treat her badly and spread rumours about her. Her unconventional appearance and behaviour is the root of her trouble. She is called 'Tom Boy' as she prefers to wear her hair short and to wear long trousers instead of skirts, a style that deviates completely from what is expected of a Javanese woman. Moreover, she is thirty-four years old and still unmarried. People think that her reputation reflects badly on the travel agents that are employing her. Despite her 'yellow wing' and years of professional experience, Ibu Yanik still cannot make a living from guiding. She needs an additional job to provide for her basic needs. For several hours a week she works at a children's day nursery where she is paid in kind: ten kilos of rice and five pounds of sugar a month. The job can easily be combined with her guiding, as her colleagues at the nursery understand her position and are flexible about standing in for her when she has a tour. Yanik is very keen to make friends among the tourists and to consolidate long-term relations with them. She hopes to meet another kind person, like the foreign lady, who will give her a job and a permanent income. For the time being, she has to be satisfied with occasional letters and gifts, mainly books to improve her English, that tourists send her from their home country.

THE TRAINEE

Amin, a young man in his early twenties, was my guide on several tours which I booked at the Sosro Tours office, Pak Djoko's successful travel agency in Sosrowijayan. Amin looks well-groomed with his neatly cut hair and well-dressed with dark trousers, shining shoes, and pilot-style shirt. He is a very serious young man who attempts to act as a professional, but he still is an apprentice guide. After finishing senior high school Amin worked as an odd jobber in a hotel and a restaurant for a short while, but soon dropped out as the jobs were not to his liking. Thanks to his brother's (who is a professional tourist guide) connections, he came into contact with Sosro Tours in Sosrowijayan. He has been working there for about one-and-a-half years now. Amin usually guides in English, but he is working on his French as he intends to become a French guide in his future professional career. He is aware of the fact that the competitive position of French guides is better than that of English guides. Amin is self-taught: he has taught himself English and French from books that he received after writing to the embassies of these countries and asking for dictionaries and grammar books. He was born in Klaten, a town between Yogyakarta and Solo. His father is a construction worker and his mother a housewife. The family later moved closer to Yogyakarta as his father was frequently hired by a contractor to work in the city. His family settled down in Prambanan Village, about fifteen kilometres east of Yogyakarta. They cannot pay for their son's vocational training as his younger sisters and brothers are still at school and school fees are a big burden on the family. The job at Sosro Tours is a great opportunity for him to provide for his family as well as preparing himself for the *Diparda* examination which he will take as soon as it is offered again – but nobody knows yet when that will be.

Amin usually accompanies the tours to Borobudur and Prambanan according to a set scenario. He has to show up at the office before six o'clock in the morning. This is when the office staff members have worked out the schedule for the day and instruct the guides which tour they are to take. As one of the youngest, Amin has to cover for colleagues who take a day off. He cannot prepare himself as he learns which tour he is scheduled for only five minutes before his bus leaves. Then he picks up the tourists at their hotel – Sosro Tours collects the guests from all over town, from 'streetside' as well as *kampung* accommodation. Upon arrival at the tourist site he hands 'his' tourists over to a 'special guide' as Amin himself is not authorized to accompany them on the temple site. Just to clarify matters: Amin does not have a licence and he is not supposed to present himself as a guide but as a 'tour leader.' This is his company's policy, which he adheres to strictly, which means he keeps a low profile while on the temple premises. Amin maintains friendly relations with the special guides at the sites and with other guides who, like himself, have to kill time while waiting for their guests to finish their guided tour. During these breaks Amin is busy maintaining his network, and this will recompense him handsomely as soon as he has his licence. He knows a number of special guides at the major tourist objects who began their career at Sosro Tours and through their friendship with other guides got a job at the *P.T. Taman Wisata*. For the time being he has to be satisfied with the fairly limited role he is playing.

During high season, Sosro Tours sends many buses to the major tourist objects without a guide. In these cases the driver takes the tourists to the ticket office, buys the tickets, and then hands them over to a special guide, only to pick them up again after the tour. In other words, Amin is an 'extra' which the travel agent can easily do without. But his boss, as we have learned in the previous chapter, is a man with a social conscience who wants to help young people to begin a career in tourism. That is why he is employing young unlicensed guides-to-be like Amin. While they can practise on-the-job, establish a network in the tour and travel business and earn some money, Sosro Tours itself is promoted from a transport company to a travel agency. As far as the payment is concerned, the information is ambiguous. While the owner of Jaya Tours and some of his employees state that the guides are paid per tour – as is the custom in the tour and travel branch, and long tours pay better than short tours – Amin claims to be paid per tourist on his tour. He did not want to tell me how much. Whatever the payment, full buses and frequent tours are good for Amin.

THE SPECIAL GUIDE

During one of my visits to Prambanan as an individual tourist (I came by public bus from Yogyakarta) I was asked by the staff at the ticket counter to wait for more 'walk-in tourists' (as individual travellers are called) to be taken to the site by Pak Hasan, one of the fifty guides working at the Prambanan. When the group finally consisted of five persons, Pak Hasan would lift his arm: 'Ladies and gentlemen, welcome to Prambanan temple, my name is Hasan, I'll be your guide today, please follow my umbrella.' Hasan can be easily identified as a guide as he wears a uniform: green trousers and a white and green shirt, and carries a green umbrella. The 'yellow wing' that decorates his shirt, immediately catches my eye. Most of his uniformed colleagues wear a name tag provided by the *P.T. Taman Wisata* instead of a 'wing.' Pak Hasan is a man in his forties. He lives with his wife and three children in Prambanan Village and teaches *bahasa Indonesia* at a junior high school. His salary as a teacher is not sufficient to support his family. Therefore he makes additional money as a guide whenever the school timetable allows. 'A teacher has a lot of empty hours,' Pak Hasan smiles. He has worked as a special guide at Prambanan temple six times per week since 1987, mostly in the afternoons because school finishes at one o'clock. This leaves him enough time to take two groups to the temple. During summer vacations he is a full-time guide: usually guiding six groups per day. Occasionally Pak Hasan covers for a 'friend,' an ASITA guide, and accompanies groups to other attractions in Yogyakarta and its vicinity. As a senior guide and an HPI member he is fully authorized to do so.

Pak Hasan started working at the temple years before the establishment of the *P.T. Taman Wisata*. At the time guiding was a self-regulating business. We have already learned from Yanik that the guides were organized as a loosely structured network and that they offered their services to tourists very much in the way street guides do. It was through the mediation of a friend that Pak Hasan joined the group under the tree. Since the establishment of the company in 1991, guiding on the temple premises has become a strictly controlled activity. First of all, guides are regarded as employees of the company. In 1996 there were one hundred guides under contract, fifty for each temple complex, Borobudur and Prambanan.[13] The *Taman Wisata* special guides are required to have the *Diparda* licence for 'special guide' and a letter of recommendation from the head of their regency testifying that they are persons of good repute. People unable to produce these two documents are not accepted as applicants. It still helps tremendously to have a friend who is already working for the company, but it is no longer the only precondition. New guides receive on-the-job training specifically tailored to one of the temple complexes; therefore Prambanan and Borobudur guides cannot take each others' place. This training is provided by historians, archaeologists, and local government officials. After passing the exam with good marks, the new guide receives a contract and a uniform: there is a different uniform for each day of the week ('Our guides should look fresh and neat every day,' says the director of *P.T. Taman Wisata*). Just like any other guide in the province, they are paid according to the principle 'no tour, no pay.' The company has established a price list in co-operation with HPI. It says that for small groups of up to five persons guides are paid 5,000 *rupiah* per tour. Groups from five to ten persons yield 7,000 *rupiah*, and groups larger than ten persons 10,000 *rupiah* (Sumaryanto 1993:53). When I visited the temples in the mid-1990s, it was the 'rule' that groups should consist of at least five persons. I had the impression that this rule was set by the guides themselves to catch the 7,000 *rupiah*, which for them made quite a difference. The guide's fee is included in the entrance fee that foreign visitors have to pay to be admitted to the temple. Guides walk around the temple about four to six times a day during the busy high season. In the off season the frequency declines to one or two tours per day. A tour takes about an hour at Borobudur and forty-five minutes at Prambanan. The guides usually leave the tourists at the temple to give them additional time to wander around after they have finished their explanation. In contrast to the *guide umum* the position of special guides leaves little room for additional income from tips and commissions. There are no souvenir shops in the temple area to which tourists can be taken; the only shops are souvenir and food-stalls that are licensed and thus controlled by the company. As far as tips are concerned, it depends on the boldness of the guide whether he dares ask for them. I met several guides who, at the end of the tour, frankly told the tourists they may be tipped if they liked their story. However, there are many guides who say goodbye to their group and then wait shyly to see whether anything will happen, and often they wait in vain. Pak Hasan is too proud a man to beg for a tip. When his tour is finished he thanks his audience for their attention, apologizes for his poor English, points out the direction to the exit, and then returns to the ticket counter to pick up the next group.

The majority of guides working for *P.T. Taman Wisata* are not fully employed in guiding. Like Pak Hasan they come to the temple to make some additional money. Often their first loyalty is to the other job(s) they hold. Some work full time as a guide during high season and switch to another occupation during low season. Others combine guiding with a shop, trading or teaching throughout the year. The motivations for becoming a special guide vary widely. For some, guiding tourists at the temples is one of the many jobs they undertake to make ends meet and they are quite content with the additional income they make. Visitor flows are stable throughout the year and there is always something to do; even in the low season they are never completely without work, in contrast to many of their colleagues working for ASITA agencies. But for some guides being a 'special guide' is only the start of their professional career. Many special guides proudly wear the 'green wing' of the junior guide and conducting tours at one of the temples is a good way to train their skills on the job and to prepare themselves for the *Diparda* exam to become a senior guide. Many special guides complain about the boredom that seizes them after a few months on the job. Telling the same story four times a day is not the most challenging job one can imagine. A number of guides cannot hide their frustration and trot out a routine performance that finishes within half an hour. They treat tourists with contempt, for example leaving them at the temple without showing them the way to the exit which causes visitors to roam the premises in panic on occasion. On the other hand, there are guides who use the routine to their advantage. While familiar with the logistics and the story-line, they concentrate on a good performance, telling jokes and involving the tourists in their narrative.

THE KRATON GUIDE

The Kraton area is an exception to the rule that major tourist sites in Yogyakarta are controlled by the government. The land behind the thick, white-washed walls in the very heart of the city is the private property of the Sultan and he rules this enclosed space. Ever since the palace opened up to tourists in 1972 visitor flows have been controlled by the *Tepas Pariwisata Keraton Yogyakarta*, the Tourism Organization of the Kraton Yogyakarta. The Kraton attracts hundreds of thousands of tourists every year: about half a million in the early 1990s (Yumarnani 1993:48). In the palace, guiding is organized in an almost military fashion. The tourists who show up at the ticket counter form two queues, one for foreign and one for domestic tourists. Foreign tourists are asked to name their nationality before receiving their tickets. This information is for the man with the loudspeaker who summons a guide who has mastered the specific language required to receive the visitors at the entrance gate. There the tickets are checked and the guide introduces him/herself to the tourists. In this way groups are formed with tourists speaking or at least understanding the same language. Of course English is the language most required, but the Kraton also provides guides who speak Dutch (many still do from the old times), French, Spanish, and Japanese. There is a lack of Italian- and Mandarin-speaking guides. If Italian or Chinese groups arrive, the rule that only Kraton guides may accompany tourists on the palace premises is broken and their tour guides are admitted.

In 1996 the Kraton employed eighty guides I was told by a knowledgeable informant.[14] Kraton guides do not need a *Diparda* licence. Instead aspirant guides – introduced by a staff member of the Kraton – receive an internal training from older Kraton guides. The training is conducted in the language of the candidate's choice, the language in which he or she intends to conduct the tours. The candidates have to have considerable knowledge, as they are not taught the facts about the Kraton (they are supposed to be knowledgeable already). What they are trained for is to develop narratives about the history of the palace, the vicissitudes of the royal family, the architecture and symbolism of the buildings, artefacts, and colours on the palace premises. There is something particular about employment in the Kraton. Official requirements so essential to jobs outside the Kraton walls like formal knowledge and education, certificates and diplomas obtained from educational institutions do not play any role. Working for the Sultan is a great honour that is bestowed only on people who belong to different echelons of the Javanese gentry and have 'traditional' ties with the royal family. The guides operating within the palace constitute a group of older, honourable people, well-educated and intimately familiar with the vicissitudes of the palace and its inhabitants. As a general rule there are many women among the Kraton guides as in contrast to being a *guide umum*, working for the Sultan is an honourable job for both sexes. Many Kraton guides have a background in teaching: many are (retired) teachers and university professors, some graduated from a tourism academy and one is a German lecturer from the Goethe Institute. As many aristocratic families consider teaching an appropriate profession for their children and as teachers are not well-paid, Kraton guiding is an honourable as well as lucrative occupation. Kraton guides take great pride in going to their work in the Kraton dressed either as a palace guard wearing a *keris* (Javanese dagger) or the uniform of the palace guide which is basically green, the colour of the sultan. Like the guides at the temples, Kraton guides wear uniforms that change according to a fixed sequence with the day of the week. These guides operate in the inner part of the palace where the Sunday dances take place and the museum is located: the royal central court. Here guiding is not left to any of the unqualified personnel who happen to be around as it is the case in the Pagelaran, where everybody who works for the sultan, cleaning staff and administrator alike, shows tourists around (cf. Chapter 6).

On one of the occasions when I visited the Kraton on a Thursday morning to watch the rehearsal for the Sunday Kraton dance, I was assigned to Ibu Minah, a seventy-year-old lady who is a senior guide at the Kraton and specializes in Dutch-language guiding, but is also fluent in English and German. Ibu Minah comes from an aristocratic family whose male members held high administrative positions in the royal administration. She has had a Dutch-language college education and worked for a Dutch publisher before the war. After independence she was employed by the Palace as a teacher to educate the children of Sultan Hamengku Buwono IX. When his eldest son became sultan, times changed: his children went to school with other Yogyanese children and she became redundant. However, in 1985 the sultan offered her another job, as senior tourist guide in the Kraton. She was released from the obligation to follow the training, as her knowledge and language proficiency were beyond doubt. She is very proud of her job and unwilling to give it up despite her somewhat advanced years.

Working as a Kraton guide undoubtedly has its advantages for the happy few who are admitted to the job. The job is very flexible. Guides decide themselves how many hours they want to work. Generally, working hours are from eight to one o'clock in the morning seven days a week, in accordance with the opening hours of the palace. Some of Ibu Minah's colleagues come in every day, others take one or two days off, and others again pop in occasionally. Unlike other work around the palace, guiding does not fall completely under the *ngindung* system (cf. Chapter 4). Guides are paid for their services, though considerably less than their *guide umum* colleagues outside the palace walls. Basically the guides are paid 2,000 *rupiah* for every day they show up, remitted at the end of the month. A full-time guide makes a maximum of 60,000 *rupiah* a month. Of course, nobody can live on such a low income. However, as Ibu Minah points out, there are several opportunities to increase this amount of money to 100,000 *rupiah*. The additional income is provided by the tour managers and *guide umum* who bring groups to visit the palace. The rule is that these guides transfer their guests to the Kraton guides and pay these guides directly for their services from their tour budget; how much depends on the personal agreement between the Kraton guide and their colleague from outside. The Kraton guides maintain friendly relations with a number of tourist guides. They are informed in advance when their 'friends' will arrive with groups and see to it that they are present. The tourist guides, for their part, come asking for a specific guide when arriving at the palace gates. This is what Ibu Yanik did when she took me and my friends to the Kraton. She introduced us to Ibu Anna as her dear friend who took over the guiding from her. This patronage by tourist guides is the reason Kraton guides prefer tourist groups instead of individual tourists: the former are brought by colleagues who pay for their services, the latter come by themselves. During low season, when there are few groups to visit the Kraton, the guides' income is meagre. It is obvious that the profession of Kraton guide does not provide enough money to support a family. This is why the vast majority of Kraton guides are women: they are satisfied with a flexible job that allows them to manage a household and earn some additional income.

All licensed tourist guides in Yogyakarta – whether fully authorized or as yet a trainee, junior or senior, special or *umum* – are heavily dependent on their personal networks to find enough tours to make a living from guiding. Those who are fortunate enough to be regularly employed by one single travel agent have to be loyal towards and available for this employer in good times and of bad. Other guides have to put a huge amount of effort into maintaining a network of potential employers; often they have to find additional sources of income as guiding does not provide them with enough money to make a living.

The latter is true of most guides. As tourism is subject to seasonal fluctuations, travel agents, even a large enterprise such as *P.T. Taman Wisata,* cannot afford to take on guides as permanent employees. Verbal agreements instead of written contracts are the rule. Under the New Order regime all guides in Yogyakarta are forced to undergo the government-organized indoctrination with *pancasila* rhetoric. Its effect on the way in which guides arrange their tours and discourses differs according to their employment conditions and level of professionalism. Almost all the guides I followed during my fieldwork in Yogyakarta tell the story of Yogyakarta from the *pancasila* perspective in one way or another, a story which they have basically learned by heart and repeat over and over again on every tour they conduct. This is equally true of the Kraton guides who, as members of the gentry, generally enjoy protected status under Kraton law. Nevertheless, they are expected to convey the image of the Kraton not only as a Javanese heirloom, but also as the stronghold of the revolution. However, the reproduction of the rehearsed narratives is never complete or devoid of deviation, as will be shown below.

VISITING BOROBUDUR: TWO NARRATIVES COMPARED

In this section I shall investigate the narratives current about one core attraction, the stupa of Borobudur. I shall compare two different situations: a 'fully organized' tour provided by a 'streetside' travel agent, accompanied by a senior guide, and the same tour arranged through a *kampung* agency, accompanied by a trainee, supported by an attraction-bound 'special' guide. I shall describe fragments of both tours. To structure the guides' narratives during the tour, I distinguish four consecutive 'acts': first the narrative during the trip to the stupa, second the introduction of the stupa on the spot, third the favourite story about the stupa, and fourth the climax at the top of the stupa. I shall compare the performances of the guides in these four acts focusing on the similarities and differences in their narratives which I shall relate to the diverging business cultures in 'streetside' and *kampung* enterprises. For this purpose I shall quote fragments of their explanation at length. These quotations are original spoken texts I recorded during the tours. The guides were not aware that they were being taped as I used a small dictaphone hidden in my pocket or daypack. The texts may convey incorrect information about the temple and other tourist objects along the road. I shall not dwell on these errors. No changes have been made in the way the guides use the English language. This is done to indicate the way they actually speak and in no way meant to insult them. It also reveals the difficulties the audience may experience in understanding them. The objective of this description is to point out the extent to which the control-system that is to enforce *pancasila* tourism in Yogyakarta puts a stamp on the working routine of the tourist guides and the extent to which *pancasila* state ideology has more impact on 'streetside' than on *kampung* guides.

ACT ONE: ON THE ROAD TO BOROBUDUR

To visit Borobudur temple with a streetside travel agent, I invited a couple of German tourists on a sunset tour (as the ASITA related travel agent refused to book for a single tourist) and I requested a German-speaking guide. This was how I met Pak Rudi.[15] He turned up at 2 p.m. sharp at my guesthouse situated in the Sosrowijayan area. He seemed astonished that a 'tourist' living in a budget accommodation booked a tour at an expensive 'streetside' agency. Although he felt out of place in this neighbourhood of 'ill repute,' his professionality got the better of him: he took the time to become acquainted with me and my party and briefly discussed the arrangement of the tour. He tried to establish whether we had special wishes, like a detour to a less-known site, to calculate possible time loss. And he mentioned shopping opportunities on our way back to Yogyakarta: 'There are some very interesting batik factories along the road.' After this introduction we took off in a neat air-conditioned *kijang* (large Indonesian jeep) provided with white headrests, plenty of space to stretch one's legs and a microphone for the guides' convenience. We never learned what the driver's name was.

The way in which I was picked up by Sosro Tours where I booked a 'Beautiful Morning at Borobudur' was very different. Whereas ASITA agencies arrange 'private' tours with bus, driver, and guide for one particular client, charging fixed prices per participant, Sosro Tours operates differently. This *kampung* agency collects tourists to the same destination and puts them all together on one bus and, therefore, the price differences between the ASITA and the *kampung* agencies are striking. The former charges twenty dollars (in 1996 about 40,000 *rupiah*) including the entrance fee of 5,000 *rupiah* for a tour to Borobudur, while Sosro Tours charges 15,000 *rupiah* excluding the entrance fee. At the office of Sosro Tours I was urgently requested to be ready by five o'clock in the morning. When the dilapidated minibus finally arrived – it was forty-five minutes late – it waited with its engine running at the entrance while Amin jumped out and urged me to get in quickly. The bus had eleven seats, all occupied. The air-conditioning was working full blast and my fellow travellers opened the windows to let some warm air into the cabin. While the bus was making its way through the narrow streets of the inner city part of Yogyakarta, Amin commenced the introduction using a microphone that tended to switch on and off. He finally decided to do without:

Okay everybody, good morning, welcome on this tour. You are on this tour we call the 'Beautiful morning at Borobudur.' This is not sunrise tour, because the sun will be up in the sky when we reach Borobudur temple. Sunrise impossible at Borobudur temple, because they open the gate only at six, and then the sun is up already. My name is Amin, means 'safe' in Indonesia.[16] Our driver is Pak Tui. We go now straight to Borobudur temple. No stop on the route. You can have snack on the way *(he starts distributing small packages containing a sandwich with butter and chocolate sprinkles, a banana, and a cup of water with a straw).* Okay everybody. Can you hear me? Can you understand me? Where are you all from? You people here in the front seat, where are you from?

This inquiry showed that there were three people from Holland, including me, two Japanese men, one Lebanese lady, a German couple, and three young Australians. The national background was about all we learned of our fellow passengers. Amin proceeded with a lengthy account of the political structure of Indonesia in general and the province of Yogyakarta in particular:

The province of Yogyakarta has of five regencies. Now we pass through the regency of Sleman, the others are Parangtritis in the south at the sea, Gunung Kidul in the east, Kulon Progo in the west and Merapi in the north. Merapi means mountain of fire: Javanese 'mer' and 'api.' Not to confuse with Merpati, which is a bird and an Indonesian airline. Yogya – we say Yogya, not Yogyakarta – is a small city, only 400,000 inhabitants, much smaller than Jakarta, big city which has three times more inhabitants. Yogya is situated in Java, Java is one of the 15,000 islands of the Republic Indonesia. These 15,000 islands are different but the same. They are united by one language, 'bahasa Indonesia.' Every region has its own language. Indonesia has twenty-seven provinces and many, many groups with their own language. And different religion. But all talk the same language, 'bahasa Indonesia,' means Indonesia language. Indonesia language in fact many languages at the same time, with words from Malaysia, Java, Dutch and English. Do you know wortel?

He suddenly addresses the Dutch tourists. *Wortel* is the Indonesian word for 'carrot' adapted from the Dutch language. In the meantime our bus has struggled out of the traffic jam of the Yogyanese suburbs and heads north. On our right is Mount Merapi, we pass the bridge that marks the border with the province of Central Java:

Okay everybody, this famous river. It comes from Mount Merapi. Is special river. Big but only little water. When Merapi spits lava, lava flows through riverbed to the sea. Lava and stones. Famous stones from Mount Merapi. Borobudur temple is built from these stones from Mount Merapi. This bridge is famous bridge. It is the border between the province of Yogyakarta and the province of Central Java. You can buy this stone, people make many statues from this stone. This area is famous for stone carving. Very cheap, if you can carry them home to your country (...)

The road we travel is decorated with yellow flags. One of the Dutch passengers inquires what this decoration is all about:

Oh, this is Javanese sign of prosperity and fortune, yellow colour good colour, and, eh, also of government party. These flags are from government party. Indonesia has three parties: the green party which is Muslim party, the yellow party which is government party, and the red party which is democratic party. (...) Okay, everybody, to the left you see hill with trees over there. This is Chinese graveyard. Chinese people always bury their dead on hills. But this graveyard different from graveyard in Yogya, in Kota Gede. You know Kota Gede? Silver city.

After passing through Muntilan, we reach the parking lot of the *Taman Wisata Borobudur*. We follow Amin and criss-cross through narrow pathways lined by souvenir sellers and foodstalls. The people running these stalls – mostly women – are getting ready for a long day, only a few were attracting the tourists' attention: 'Come see my shop.' We reach the ticket office and have to queue in front of the window for foreign tourists. Amin instructs us to buy a ticket and explains that the fee for foreigners is double the price that Indonesians pay, but the advantage is that it includes the entrance fee for the museum and the toilet. Indonesians have to pay extra if they want to use the facilities of the park. Amin steps through the gate, counts his eleven tourists, gathers them around him, takes his watch off his wrist and summons everybody to be back within fifty minutes. Some tourists complain: that would be too soon and it was decided to meet after one hour and five minutes. To stress the importance of our appointment, he taps on his wristwatch. In the meantime a young man in his twenties has joined our group, smiling. He, like the other special guides, wears dark green trousers and a light green shirt decorated with the 'green wing' of a junior guide, and carries an umbrella. Amin introduces him. While our small group sets out to follow our new guide, Amin strolls over to the place where the Borobudur guides use to gather and spend their break.

Our sunset tour to Borobudur with Pak Rudi and the anonymous driver offers an experience of a different kind. Before commencing with his well-prepared explanation of the temple, Pak Rudi dwells at length on the geography of the western part of Germany. My travel companions are from Düsseldorf, a medium-sized city at the River Rhine, and as Pak Rudi's younger brother lives in Germany to pursue his studies, he takes advantage of the situation to ask questions about all kinds of places that are situated in the area he had heard about through the letters and postcards his brother has sent him. When he finally resumes his task as our guide, we have left Yogyakarta behind and have entered the province of Central Java:

> You know, this is Central Java, different province than Yogyakarta. You know that Yogyakarta is city and province, both. This makes it special. But it is also special because it is ruled by a king, the sultan. The sultan is only responsible to the president, to nobody else. Because of the sultan and the palace – you know Kraton? – Yogya people are very proud of tradition. Yogya is short for Yogyakarta, actually it is Ngayogyokarto Hadiningrat, but nobody says so in daily talk. Borobudur temple is not in Yogyakarta province but in Central Java province. But both provinces are Javanese. They speak the same language: Javanese language. My language is Sulawesi, I am from Sulawesi, you know, Celebes. I had to learn Javanese when I came to live in Yogya. I could not understand the people. Well, of course we speak 'bahasa Indonesia,' our national language which unites all the Indonesian islands and all its cultures. But people on the street, the simple people, they do not speak bahasa Indonesia, even though they know and understand the language. They prefer Javanese(...) You see the sign over there: 'salak pondoh'? You know salak pondoh? Salak pondoh is a fruit, a very famous fruit, it is unique in the world. Salak pondoh is called snakefruit in English, I do not know the German word. Snakefruit because of its skin, it is brown and consists of tiny scales. If you peel them, the tasty white flesh appears, it tastes sweet-fresh. They grow salak in Bali as well, the fruit is bigger, the skin is lighter, but the flesh is not so tasty and the fruit rots away very quickly. They are the best from this area. So if you buy, ask for salak pondoh, the small, dark and firm fruit. Let's stop here and taste some. You do not need to buy. But if you want to, let me do the talking. I will bargain a good price.

Our jeep stops at a fruitstall and Pak Rudi addresses the vendor in Javanese. We are urged to taste some salak fruit and my travel companions decide to buy a kilo. After some bargaining we settle for two kilos for a 'good price' and continued our trip. Upon passing the Chinese graveyard, Pak Rudi resumes his role as mentor:

> You see this hill over there with the stones? These are tomb stones and the hill is a graveyard of the Chinese people. The Chinese believe that their deceased watch over the living, and so they bury them on an elevated place to make it easier for them to watch. They plant trees and bushes with beautiful flowers on the graveyard, flowers that smell sweet. You have seen the trees, the Cambodia

trees with the white flowers. They are popular with the Javanese people as well. We don't have so many Chinese people in this area, only in Yogya on Malioboro street. The Chinese are good business men and traders. Most shops are owned by Chinese people. They make much money, they are the rich people, Javanese are poor, they do not care much for money, they care concerned with spiritual things. (...) Ah, look at Mount Merapi, it shows only its top today. If you want to see Mount Merapi you have to get up very early, before sunrise. Later on it disappears behind clouds. It is still the most active vulcano of the world. It erupted only two years ago, killed and hurt many people, not with fire but with hot gas that escaped from the many holes on the slopes. They brought the people to the hospitals in Yogyakarta. But it is not dangerous in the city, Yogya is safe. They have scientists up there watching the mountain carefully. Have you climbed Merapi yet? No? If you do, take a sweater. It is very cold up there. And go with a good guide. They say it is easy to climb Merapi, but sometimes tourists get lost and there have been accidents. (...) You see those statues? Many people in this area are stone carvers. They make a living from the lava stone that is available here in abundance. People who come to see Borobudur temple, Indonesian people from all over the country, they like to buy these statues to put in their houses or gardens. You see, Merapi takes the life of some people, but gives a subsistence to others.

In the meantime we have reached the crossing where we leave the road north to turn west to the temple complex. Seven kilometres before the main temple we pass *candi* Mendut. Pak Rudi instructs the driver to drive slowly to enable us to have a good look at the temple, but we are not invited to get out of the jeep. As we pull up the parking lot of the main temple area, Pak Rudi gives some instructions to the driver. We get out of the car and follow Pak Rudi to the entrance. At the ticket office, he greets the controllers and guides in a friendly fashion. It is obvious that he comes here often. The formalities are quickly arranged. We do not have to buy tickets – they are included in the price paid to the travel agent. Pak Rudi is involved with some money transactions in the ticket office which I cannot see – I suppose he left some money for the 'special' guides, whose services we shall not use. Then we take off with him, walking through the park and heading towards the stupa which reveals itself at the end of the boulevard at the top of a hill. It is a breathtaking view.

ACT TWO: THE WORLD OF DESIRE

We climb the steps until we reach the terrace at the foot of the stupa. Here most guides gather their group to enable the tourists to catch their breath from the climb and to give some information about the history of the stupa. Pak Rudi directs us towards the low wall that marks the edge of the terrace; beneath it lies the park with its tropical flowers and tourist facilities.

Welcome to Borobudur. Maybe you know that Borobudur is one of the seven world wonders. Borobudur, the third of the trinity Mendut, Pawon and Borobudur symbolizes the Buddhist congregation, all the followers of Buddha and his teachings. Of the three temples this is the biggest. The name Borobudur is derived from the Sanskrit words biara and bidur. Biara means temple and bidur means hill: temple on the hill. Historically, the temple was built around the end of the eighth century, and it took about three generations to finish it and around two million blocks of volcanic or lava stone, the stone we saw the statues were made of when we came here. Originally the temple is built without any cement, any concrete, only the blocks were joined, a compact system. But UNESCO and the Indonesian government in between. When they discovered the temple it looked like a small mountain, because at the time the monument was covered with ashes from the volcano, ground and plants. For about 700 years it was buried, but not totally buried. The stupa on top of the hill was visible, at the time a broken stupa. It means that people here knew about the temple, but they didn't care. Only in 1813, Sir Raffles discovered the monument, and in 1835 the structure of the monument was nearly excavated by the Dutch. Now you can see the whole, but then the temple was broken (...) and mainly underground. In 1907 the Dutch engineer Van Erp supervised the restoration until 1911. Only a few years later the temple was ruined because the restoration did not make drainage system and also because of an earthquake. That's why in 1973 the Indonesian government in co-operation with UNESCO started the second restoration spending about 25 million US dollars. And there was twenty-eight countries, members of UNESCO, contributed to the restoration. Borobudur belongs to the world, not only Indonesia, especially the members of UNESCO. Around 55 per cent of the costs is paid by the members of UNESCO, the rest by our government. (...) Because after the main restoration is finished, we still maintain the temple every day. We use chemicals to protect the relief. And today the donation from UNESCO also finished. And for Buddhism that Borobudur has become symbol of the microcosms or little world, the congregation of believers. Buddhism divides the temple into three parts of life. In the lowest part at the base of the monument we call 'karmadatu,' 'karma' means desire and 'datu' means world, or the world of desire. In the second part of Borobudur consisting of galleries we call 'rupadatu,' is the world of thought (...) the people's mystery, your life. And then the third part consisting of three circles, we call 'arupadatu' or the world of spirits, we call 'nirvana' or paradise. Originally there were 505 statues of Buddha in this monument, but now you may find only 504 statues, that is the complete ones. One statue of Buddha from the big stupa, we call it the imperfect statue, because it was created not yet finished. And 200 Buddha statues are broken – broken by nature and people. Because of erosion many statues of Buddha fell down and they broke the head or arm. Others were taken as souvenir. Because according to Buddhism the temple is still a holy place, so it is very important to people. Thirty-three statues of Buddha are missing. And one statue of Buddha according to the legend is fortune or lucky Buddha. So for the people it is symbol of nirwana. If you believe it, but it's a legend only. Because there are many European, American, Australian, especially followers of Buddhism, like the Chinese, Korean, Indian. They come always and try to make a wish. Local Buddhists come to make an offering, bring many flowers, but that is special to the Buddhists, tourists don't make any offerings. But for you, you are lucky, you have long arm. For our people with the short arm, lucky Buddha is difficult to reach, lucky Buddha is only for people with long arm. This is why you European and American people are so lucky, you can touch the Buddha. Luck is not for people like us, Indonesian people.

With this undoubtedly unrehearsed and off-the-record complaint about the Indonesian situation, Pak Rudi proceeds closer towards the base of the temple to discuss the pictures carved in the stones of the relief:

And this is the lowest part as symbol of 'karmadatu.' Originally there were 160 relief around the temple of Borobudur, but today only four of them can be seen. 156 we had to be replaced, so this is all replacement, not original. Although you can see here only four panels, if you want to see more, go to the archaeological museum of Borobudur. You can find more pictures of the relief there, because in 1890 photos have been made of all the relief. Basically the themes have been taken from the 'karmadatu,' of the world of desire, of cause and effect, or the action and reaction of human life. So there is example of every action of human being, there is good and evil here, and be rewarded and punished, hell or heaven. All the relief are original, there is no replacement, though the colour is different, because the stone has been taken from different places of the volcano and because of that the colour is different. In Buddhism, people are not allowed to drink, especially no alcoholics. But people like to gamble, steal, even gossip and prostitution as well. So this is sin, that is not allowed in Buddhism. I have to inform you that this is not all the panel of 'karma,' because there are few panels, few relief of the way of life or the activities of the Indonesian people around 1200 A.D. in this corner. So here it is about the traditional healing, a method we call massage. You see here one man who drinks traditional medicine. Traditional medicine is made for many kind of treatment, what we call 'jamu.' It means that we can look here already at the traditional way which is still alive. 'Jamu' and massage already existed when this temple was built. If you go to the countryside, you still find many ladies doing like this, especially if a new baby is born in the 'kampung' or village, only three kilometres from here, you still find many ladies doing like this – the traditional medicine. There are two kinds of 'jamu': one for drinking, one for massaging that liquid.

The tour with the special guide, he introduced himself as Wawan, progresses according to an almost identical scenario, but with a different narrative. Wawan is not the solid mentor, but the entertainer. He likes to tell jokes and suggestive stories, but unfortunately his command of the English language is not good enough to put his message across. The group of eleven tourists from Sosro Tours follows Wawan who heads towards the stairs leading up to the Borobudur terrace at a steady pace. There is no time to marvel at the beautiful surroundings. As the temple appears and the tourists are totally charmed, Wawan wryly advises: 'You better take picture over there, better view.' As my fellow travellers complain about the pace, Wawan remarks that he walks this path four or five times a day and as a consequence does not look around very much. He does not talk very much either. All I learn of him is that he is from a village adjacent to Borobudur where he is a clerk in a government office. He has been guiding tourists at the temple since the establishment of the *P.T. Taman Wisata* in 1991 and spends more time at the temple than in the government office. Upon reaching the platform he plunges into his often-rehearsed narrative right away:

Borobudur was built in the eighth century by a king called Saratunga from Mataram kingdom, originally located in Yogyakarta in the city of silver. When this place was built in the first place means that Buddhists go here for praying and meditation. Second a centre for tourism. Some experts call it a dead monument because it is not for praying any more, but this is not true, because Buddhists come here to worship every year. The 'Waicak' ceremony, then a large procession that starts at Mendut temple and then to Pawon temple and ends here at Borobudur temple and behind that there are many altars. And this year we have it at the full moon in June, next month. And for this temple, I mean the temple of the name of Borobudur temple, Borobudur is not original name. According to an archaeologist from Java of the name of Professor Doctor Purwatjaraka, he has predicted that Borobudur consists of two words: 'biara' and 'beduhur.' 'Biara' means 'a holy place,' like Buddhist monastery. 'Beduhur' is a Balinese word, means 'berg.' So actually Borobudur means a 'holy place on a hill.' (...) It is not easy (...) Borobudur, Porobudur, even Budur (...) but I don't hope it will be shortened to 'Dur.'(...). Well, according to the architect (...) there are ten levels of which six of architectural wall like square, and four levels with a circular terras, a circular. But for the microcosms just divided by three levels: 'kamadhatu,' the world of desires; 'rupadhatu,' the world of shape; and 'arupadhatu,' the shapeless world – all from Sanskrit. The first two represent materialism, the third the situation like in 'nirwana.' So if we have come to the circular level, the 'nirwana,' we will have come to the heaven. So we will all go to the heaven. The Buddha statues are all incomplete. In Borobudur temple 500 Buddha statues – all incomplete. And why the Buddha statues not complete? There is a reason: the temple never appeared like a temple, but like a hill. The temple has been destroyed because of Merapi big eruption, and finally because of vandalism. After that there was discovered the ruin of stone that never appeared like a temple (...) not even by research. Then we get the first restoration which started in 1907 and was finished in 1911 by Theodorus Van Erp. After the first restoration was finished Borobudur temple was reconstructed because there was a reason. By the first restoration at the first stupa to look like an umbrella, but that umbrella not like mine, but made of stone and higher: more than forty meters. And like a stone umbrella it was broken by lightning and not possible to restore. The second restoration started at 1973 and was finished in 1983 and took more than ten years. (...) The Indonesian government and many co-operating subcountries, members of UNESCO, gave money for the second restoration.'

After this introduction Wawan takes us to the relief depicting the pleasures and shortcomings of the human 'world of desires.' These reliefs are very popular among guides and visitors, and Wawan explains why:

Here look at seventy-two Buddha statues, 'dharma chakra mudra,' turning the wheel of life: sometimes life is very happy, sometimes very sad. In nature we can enjoy nice panorama, nice view, or nice painting, like incarnation painting, Rubens painting, Van Gough painting (...) will be unsatisfied, empty money, eh, ya, empty money, empty honey, no money, no honey. This is philosophical meaning. The construction, the low construction, is not really the original foot, because the original foot must have kept 160 panel reliefs at the outside (...) here must be additional stone and original foot located inside like hidden foot for technical reason. According to some architects that Borobudur foot not strong enough (...) it will be destroyed. So the construction must be covered up with 15,000 cubic metres of lava stone. Another reason because many people believe that the original foot decorated with pornographic reliefs like 'kamasutra' (...) that must be covered up. But actually the original foot never showed the pornography. That relief just depicted the realism situation of life. The people in the eighth century were not different from us. Eighth century was the ancient time. At that time like a party and like Matahari supermarket. Over there is sitting a gentleman, eh, you know, but is normal. Okay, sometimes the pornography is more interesting than the other. And now I would like to show you the original foot that where we can find the pornography relief. Keep ready your camera and videocamera. Let's go to see the pornography. (...) So here the original foot, here the additional stone. (...) when this corner still open, now I have story that when Indonesia still occupied by Japanese soldiers, they just come here to see who make the pornography .. Playboy magazine and RTL-programme. (...) Here panel Number 19 on the right look like a segment who was surrounded by servants, perhaps one of them was a medication doctor because of his head, he got head aches. An old man just have traditional medicine(...). This segment sits next to his family. Actually this segment was a family, was a father of that family. At that time Indonesian family just have two children: one, two. But now in Indonesia in every corner you have KB, that means two children only! Number 12 depicted an ideal family with one kid only and many servants. But on the opposite segment are the cheaters, call it the badness. The badness can look like young people who get drunk, the badness of alcohol. Another one look like one who get flied by Marihuana. Because eighth century has not yet AA, anonymous alcoholics association, and abortion, abortus provocatus (...) they have panels to show badness(...)'

THIRD ACT: FAVOURITE STORIES ABOUT BOROBUDUR

One important theme at the second level is the different hand positions of the Buddha statues. Most guides love to elaborate on these positions – imitating them and sometimes encouraging the tourists to do the same – and to state their meaning. And so did Pak Rudi and Wawan. It makes no sense to present the fragments of the transcription here, because the explanation cannot be understood without visualizing the gestures. One reason for the popularity of Buddha's hand positions among guides is that they are rehearsed at length in the government's guiding course as well as in the training of special guides on the spot and even at the tourist academies in Yogyakarta.[17] Another core story that is brought up at this level of the temple is the Buddha's birth as depicted by the reliefs. Here follows Pak Rudi's version:

So this is the first relief I show you. This is the queen and the king, this is the parents of Buddha. King Suddhodana and Queen Maya. As we learned, Buddha was reincarnation of Boddhisattva, and before Buddha was a prince. He was born around 500 before Christ in the Kapilawastu kingdom in the north of India, Nepal. The story says that the king and queen have been married for a long time, for couple of years married, but they had no children. One day, King Suddhodana meditates. When he was meditating Boddhisattva knew that the king has been very sad. Then Boddhisattva descending on earth. On the way to release the man from suffering in all over the world. Before descending on earth, Boddhisattva in many reincarnations to become Buddha. So the couple, eh, like a good spirit, eh be sending to earth to see the holy lady or the future mother of Buddha, her name Dewi Maya. So when you see the film 'Little Buddha,' was made by Bertolucci from Italia, the story in the film is little bit different from Borobudur version. About 50-40 per cent is different, because mostly the film has a commercial background. And this is the famous relief in the monument with the sleeping lady. The story said that when Maya was sleeping in the palace, she had a strange dream. In her dream came the white elephant, and the white elephant walked around her in a clockwise direction(...) and the white elephant went inside her womb. Only Maya knew that the white elephant was inside her womb, and actually the white elephant was incarnation of Boddhisattva. (...) And this is (...) the white elephant on the Lotus flower. In Buddhism the Lotus flower is the symbol of purity. (...) And this is the most famous relief of the monument, later on you can see this picture on the postcard, on the book, even on the t-shirt. So this relief the Queen Maya or the future mother of Buddha on the way to her parents house after nine months pregnant. Even though nine months pregnant, but the womb does not look like you know, like a normal lady who is pregnant. Inside the womb is the incarnation of Boddhisattva. But in the film by Mister Bertolucci, when Maya pregnant like the real one with the big belly, and people carried her (...) This is the last important relief. So the story says that on the way to her parents house the queen felt tired and went to rest in the park or a garden. Maya or the mother Buddha was giving birth to the baby in standing position under the holy tree, holy and special tree, and the baby named Siddharta. The normal lady gives birth by lying down, but Maya in standing pose. There are people who say how the Buddha was born. One person would say that Buddha was born with a normal birth, another person would say that Buddha was born from the right side of Maya. Japanese and Chinese say that Buddha was born from the right side. And then few moments after baby born he can already stand up and walk. That's a miracle. You really can see that he is not normal person, but Boddhisattva. He can stand up and walk a few steps. And every step he left footprint and spring up Lotus flower, symbol of purity, because when he stood up on the Lotus, when he had meditation on Lotus flower. When Siddharta meditates under the holy tree in India, I mean .. Then he with a Lotus flower. And then he changed name into Gautama Buddha and he is named Siddharta Gautama Buddha. But during the life of Buddha Buddhism is a philosophical system. But after Gautama died the followers created a religion with Buddha as a leader. Until now there are people who say that Buddhism is a philosophy or a way of life. Then according to the Buddhism-Hinduists Buddha was a reincarnation of Wisnu – one of the gods of the Hindu. That is when Hindus say that Buddhism is part of Hindu religion. But today Hindus in Indonesia are less than Buddhism, because we have only one per cent of the population in the whole country are Hindus. You only find them in east of Indonesia. Here we have the temple of Buddha, but today there is no Buddhists here. They say that this place is a strange place. One of the biggest statues of Buddha in the world, but there is no Buddhist. We have around 1.5 per cent in Indonesia is Buddhist, and mostly the Chinese Buddhist. If you come here a few days ago, you might find a ceremony called Waicak ceremony, because thousands of Buddhists from this country and other countries come over here.

Whereas Pak Rudi takes the time to elaborate on the story of Buddha's birth and the religious meaning of this story, Wawan is pressed for time upon arriving at the second level, as he spent too much time in 'the world of desires' playing upon illusory pornographic images. Wawan's narrative on Buddha's birth is quite cursory:

> Every Buddha statue has to sit on the Lotus flower. Lotus is to describe the holy, even the purely. (...) here little angel on holy flower, little Buddha. Boddhisattva's life, a life biography of Buddha. Very famous reliefs. Even Bertolucci has made a famous film with the title 'Little Buddha.' Before he come into the world, after birth, after childhood and then after death in only 120 minutes. We call Boddhisattva our god. Here the little angel, the prehistoric situation in India. The symbol of the tree means before Buddha came into this world. Buddha as a boy, was to become famous as Boddhisattva. Over there another story with the name of Boddhisattva, the white elephant (...) Buddhism education (...) difficult to understand. Here more interesting than a lesson. And actually there have been carved many reliefs, but now just five (...)'

FOURTH ACT: IN PARADISE

After another climb up steep steps, we reach the circular galleries with the stupas, generally described as heaven or paradise by the guides. Wawan's enthusiasm has cooled down considerably. He is nervously looking at his watch. He has been on our tour for thirty-five minutes and it seems that his mind is on the next group of tourists waiting for him at the entrance gate. He gives us a very brief introduction to paradise:

> We enjoy to stay in heaven now because at five heaven will be closed. And here heaven is still divided. First layer called 'nirwana,' Sanskrit 'nirwana' and 'mahanirwana.' ' Maha' means superheaven, VIP heaven. We are living in economic heaven, but then we worried if we will go up to the spiritual heaven. And in this terrace are located seventy-three stupas. Stupa is the form of this whole monument. In every stupa is located a Buddha statue. All with a hand position like this (he imitates the gesture) called local life. Each stupa has many ventilation holes. But as the ventilation has form like this, the level in the second layer has different kind. Here at that level like diamond, other like square. (...)

166

I want to show you (...) in the right side to the west (...) here looking west (...) every Buddha statue has to be seated on the Lotus flower. Every stupa has been divided into three parts: the Lotus flower, then Buddha's bowl, Buddha's stick (...) And that's the main stupa. It's just hollow and not possible to go in (...). You have any questions for me? (...) Okay, no questions. You can stay in heaven until five if you want, but your bus is waiting. Thank you very much for your attention and forgive me for if my explanation was not clear because of my lacking English.'

Wawan leaves us behind in paradise and hurries towards the exit. Our group disintegrates and my fellow travellers wander off to take a look at the *stupas* and enjoy the scenery from the top of the temple. At the meeting point, down at the ticket office, our 'tour leader' Amin waits nervously for the arrival of his tour members who come trickling in slowly. His first concern being time management, Amin is totally occupied with the logistics. He roams the area in front of the ticket office and the parking lot to collect 'his' guests. It takes thirty minutes more than planned until everybody is back on the bus heading for Yogyakarta.

The private tour with Pak Rudi is much more relaxed. We spend a fair bit of time in 'paradise,' where the 'fortune Buddha' provides an entertaining climax to our visit:

Okay, and now I like to take you to the three circles of the symbol of nirwana. (...) And here the stupas and Buddha statue inside each one. But 70 per cent of the Buddha statues in the stupas broken, no head, no arm, because when the temple was neglected for many centuries, most stupas were broken. (...) So when people came here (...) they could take the head or the arm (...) it was free because nobody cared. Originally the temple had 1464 stupas, small ones. But today we have less than thousand, because many of the small stupas are broken or missing. And the whole form of this monument we also call stupa. Stupa is the body perfect or the Buddhist holy place. And the function of stupa are for meditating or sitting and keeping religion. But other Buddhists say that the monument is not real stupa because this temple is totally solid, you must walk around the hill, so there is no space, no room. The stupa or bell are symbolizing the three possessions of Buddha. So when you have been to a Buddhist country you know they always wear a saffron robe and mostly with the orange and the white, and they always holding the bowl for meal and water. And they are holding the walking stick. So the lowest part of the bell symbolizing the saffron robe, middle part of the bell symbolizing the bowl for the meal with its place on the roof and upside down, and the top symbolizing the walking stick. All stupas are decorated with the lotus flower. But according to the founder of the temple all of the stupas look like Lotus flower. Also the form of the Borobudur temple, because if you look at the temple from above, like from an airplane, you can see that the whole temple look like form of a lotus flower. Let's find a postcard to show. (...) And it was a Buddhist statue inside the big stupa, not a real Buddha. The Buddha from the big stupa is little bit slim, around ten centimetres taller. We call the imperfect statue because it was created not yet finished. According to the local people, that when the temple was built, the architect couldn't imagine how perfect Boddhisattva, how perfect a Buddha. That's why they created the statue unfinished. But before the architect made 504 statues except with the one, but they could not finish it, so they keep it inside. That's why stupa looks like solid one without any window hole like the small ones. So when Mister Van Erp found the Buddha statue in the big stupa, he found it by accident. Because nobody knew that inside the stupa was a Buddha. There is no space within. The stupas here – you can see the Buddha – without top are opened up to see. (...) Okay, now I like to see the fortune Buddha. Touch the right ring finger of the Buddha inside if you are a man, women at least the middle of the foot. You can take the fingers of the hand if you can reach them, men or women. Then you can make a wish, but not material wish, not the wish for money. You should make a spiritual wish. So good luck. Okay, we now go to the fortune Buddha. Touch the right finger, and one wish only, one visit for one wish only (...)'

After the three members of our little party have all made their wish under the gaze of many curious Indonesian visitors who were guessing what wish that could be, it is 4.30 p.m. The tour of the temple took exactly one hour. Instead of returning to the car, Pak Rudi invites us to take a seat at the top of *nirwana* and enjoy the view. The sun throws a golden glow over the landscape. Here and there charcoal fires have been lit and the smoke causes a veil of mist. After fifteen minutes sitting and marvelling at the beauties of the Central Javanese landscape, we get restless urging Pak Rudi to descend to the visitors' centre. But he refuses: 'We stay here until five. This is a sunset tour and we have to watch the sunset from the temple. This is what my travel agency requires me to do, otherwise I will get trouble with my boss.' So we keep on waiting until five o'clock, this is when 'paradise' closes, as is the rule set by *P.T. Taman Wisata*. As we finally start to descend, the sun is still shining, unimpressed by Indonesian government measures. It goes down at 5.50 p.m. as it has been doing since time immemorial.

In the guides' narratives there are more or less clumsy references to *pancasila* ideology, especially references that underline Indonesian nationhood and unity, the first and most pivotal of the five principles. For example, trainee Amin quoted at length from his *pancasila*-oriented course book on 'facts and figures' of the Indonesian nation state ('all different but the same'), in complete disregard to the tourists' interests, while the experienced senior guide Pak Rudi illustrated the making of an Indonesian citizen by means of his own biography: a man from Sulawesi being socialized in Javanese language to survive in his own national culture. And then there was Wawan attempted to arouse the interest of his audience by the promise of pornographic images from the eighth century, dwelling on the ideal Indonesian family, and appropriating pre-Javanese history as an early extension of national culture as orchestrated by the New Order. These general introductions to the 'modern developed nation,' I witnessed over and over again on the dozens of tours I took to the tourist sites in Yogyakarta. The issue of religion, of course, is a thorny one. The government guiding course instructs guides never to discuss religion or race. Needless to say this advice is difficult to keep to at a temple complex. The temples represent two of the five officially recognized religions (Hinduism at Prambanan and Buddhism at Borobudur) – and thus the fifth of the five 'pillars' of *pancasila*. The 'special' guide and entertainer Wawan, preferred to declare Buddha God which made him fit in with the 'one Lordship' of *pancasila* ideology. Senior guide Rudi had more problems with this. Is Buddhism a philosophy or a religion? And if it is a religion: who is Buddha? And what about Borobudur? A place of worship for the Buddhists from Indonesia and the rest of the world? Or a dead monument and theme park?

The elevation of the temple complexes to World Heritage sites transcends the cultural uniqueness to the level of a common civilized humanity, the second principle of *pancasila*. This theme is elaborated in the lengthy explanation about the process of restoration of the temples with international support. Without downplaying the role of UNESCO and the generous financial support of many countries ('Borobudur belongs to the world'), no doubt is left about the good stewardship of the Republic of Indonesia to which the world owes these sites. In Wawan's words, the rest of the world is reduced to 'subnations.' Cogently, the history of the restoration reveals the failure of the former colonial power to rebuild the temples, despite their alleged technical and scientific superiority. In all narratives the subsequent blunders in the process of restoration committed by well-reputed Dutch architects and archaeologists are dwelt on at length. The temples are also acknowledged as *pusaka*, sacred heirlooms, which are believed to confer good fortune and strength on the Indonesian people – the welfare of the nation being the fourth of the five pillars. However, in this respect, we learn from what Pak Rudi says that a lot remains to be desired in New Order Indonesia as the lucky Buddha is unreachable for Indonesians. Only Westerners have arms long enough to touch the Buddha's finger or toe to make a wish. If the 'short arm' of Indonesian people can be regarded as a metaphor for the failing political system based on a rather shaky third pillar of *pancasila* (the alleged 'unanimous consensus') remains the question.

CONCLUSION

Tourist guides in Yogyakarta come from various social and educational backgrounds, operate under different conditions of employment, and cherish divergent ideals and future perspectives. It is obvious that in the enclosed tourist spaces that constitute the attraction system of Yogyakarta, the parks of *P.T. Taman Wisata* and the walled Kraton area, the licensed guides do not act as pathfinders or pathbreakers. The 'paths' are generally well-developed roads leading to well-managed tourist objects, with fences, parking lots, visitor centres, toilets, and organized tourist guides. The guides operate in cultivated spaces and their performance is staged and routinized. Their role as 'mediator' of knowledge is quite limited. As the 'streetside' attraction system of Yogya-karta is neatly arranged and surveyable it allows for optimal control of the guides' performance. The authorities promote the mentor type of guide operating standardized and well-managed tours and reproducing well-rehearsed narratives. The art of storytelling is systematically curtailed. Acting as interpreter and communicator would make local guides extremely prone to outside intervention and manipulation. After all, decisions regarding the 'true' story or the 'most appropriate' interpretation are subject to relations of power and dependence. Direct control enforced by the tourist police and indirect control exerted through training and compulsory organization (under employers' associations and the HPI) have produced a striking uniformity in the way in which guides arrange their tours, select the objects of interest, and present these objects to tourists. The guides are always pressed for time, caught between the devil and the deep blue sea in their obligation to please their employers and the tourists, forced to make some additional money through tips and commissions, and subject to government regulations.

Government regulations tie the different categories of guides together in a system of subcontracting that imposes on them strict social control and mutual dependence. Because of the government policy of encouraging 'quality tourism,' the largest share of foreign tourism is channelled through ASITA-associated travel agencies that require their guides to acquire a government licence. Access to this licence is offered under the condition of passing a government exam and becoming a member of the government-controlled guides' association, the HPI. The employment of licensed tourist guides depends on the connections of mostly Jakarta-based travel agents with foreign tour operators organizing package tours to destinations in Indonesia. Upon arrival, every foreign group is received by an Indonesian tour manager who stays with the tour throughout their stay in the country. These are the red-winged 'national guides.' Their task has a logistical as well as political character. They see to it that the tourists are treated according to the principles of 'quality tourism.' It is the tour manager who safeguards the proper presentation of his country to the foreign visitors. At a local level, the branch offices of the Jakarta-based agencies arrange excursions for the package tourists to local tourist sites. The local branch offices select the senior guides who, in collaboration with their red-winged colleagues, take the tourists to the local attraction and provide the *couleur locale* as far as the situation permits. Finally, there are tourist objects so exceptional that they require 'special guides' with very specific training tuned to the specialized knowledge about this object. We met these special guides in the Kraton and at the world heritage sites in the vicinity of Yogyakarta. Local tourists guides – yellow or green-winged – are in charge of managing the tourists' experience.

This system of subcontracting carries different connotations. First of all it is a strategy to create employment opportunities for a vast array of guides. The 'red-winged' tour manager is not supposed to offer any explanations about local attractions – although he may be quite capable of doing so, he has to leave this task to his 'yellow-winged' colleague, a senior guide who is authorized to operate at the provincial level. At particular sites, the senior guide transfers his task to 'special' or 'green-winged' junior guides. Again there is no absolute necessity to do so, for senior guides often provide the guiding for their group anyway, as Pak Rudi did on our Borobudur tour. This system of subcontracting implies the transfer of money from the central to the local level. The senior guide is paid either by the travel agent or by the tour manager out of the tour budget; and the special guides are paid either by the senior guide from the tour budget or directly by the tourists. If the senior guide conducts the guiding – which often he does at the world heritage sites – he leaves a tip for the special guides. This system prevents the monopolization of benefits from 'quality tourism' at the national level and promotes the advantages of organized package tourism among the different echelons of the tourism industry. According to travel agencies, individual travellers are financially unattractive and difficult to manage, and according to guides 'walk-in visitors' yield less income than groups. These tourists are the leftovers for those colleagues who suffer the opprobrium of low esteem and are marginal in the guides' network. In this way the subcontracting system enforces and perpetuates 'quality tourism.'

Secondly, the system of subcontracting protects the guides against direct government intervention and arbitrariness, as it exhibits a number of in-built 'escape routes' from its manipulative mechanisms. By enforcing this system the government undermines its own means and measures of control. As the system requires the guides at different levels to co-operate, they also develop informal networks. For example, they warn and protect each other against the consequences of operating without a (valid) licence. 'Special' guides at the world heritage sites and Kraton guides are usually well-informed about planned raids by the tourist police and they tip off their friends among the local guides who do not have their documents updated or work without a (proper) licence. Moreover, the system enables a *kampung* agency like Sosro Tours to openly flout the government rules and operate with unlicensed guides. Where guiding by unlicensed guides is risky, this agency acts as a transport company and its guides as 'tour leader' which is not a protected profession. Operating with unlicensed guides is the rule rather than exception in 'open' public spaces, like the Dieng Plateau, Ratu Boko palace, Kaliurang, and the inner city of Yogyakarta. Here the guides of Sosro Tours act like professional guides. These tourist spaces are contested and the discourses are not controlled, as will be shown in the next chapter. In the enclosed spaces – which are the most visited in the Yogyakarta area and therefore the most lucrative ones to which to take tourists – unlicensed guides cannot work because of strict control mechanisms. These areas are the major assets where licensed guides work as professionals and make a living from guiding.

Thirdly, the subcontracting system enables guides to operate as entrepreneurs. It encourages and facilitates networking through their co-operative ties with other guides, and these ties support their efforts to find a job or be eligible for tours, covering for others and finally becoming a 'regular' guide at different travel agencies. The system helps to establish connections with shop owners other than those contracted by their employers to arrange commissions that go straight into their own pockets. The more secure the guides' job positions – like Pak Rudi's – the less they act as entrepreneurs. The more 'footloose,' the more they depend on their network; Ibu Yanik is a good example of this. The less experienced a guide, the smaller his network, the less successful he is as an entrepreneur. Amin illustrates this point: completely absorbed with the logistics of his job, he fails to take tourists to the shops and earn money through commissions.

There seems to be plenty of leeway but the system of subcontracting enforces the dependence of local actors in tourism on their Jakarta-based patrons. The consequences of this dependence for Yogyakarta as a tourist destination have been discussed in the previous chapter. In this chapter, I have dwelt on the impact of this dependence on the guides' narratives. The system of subcontracting enforces uniformity and standardization of the narratives. The rather striking consensus about which objects to select, what details to elaborate on, and which jokes to tell is not solely enforced by the *Diparda* compulsory guiding course, but comes about in the job routine. The different categories of guides regularly meet at the core attractions, during high seasons several times a day, and witness each other's performance, sharing information, gossip, and criticism. The guides know each other well, like or despise each other, support or thwart each other, but most of all watch each other jealously. By the obligatory division of tasks, local tourist guides are guaranteed a protected position in the system. They hold the exclusive right to conduct the guiding in and provide the authorized narrative at specific tourist spaces, but they are expected to do so in the spirit of state ideology. As has been shown, the five principles of *pancasila* are intertwined with their narratives, especially as far as the theme of 'national unity' and 'belief in one superior being' are concerned. Their presentation of the *couleur locale* has to materialize within the national context. However, there are significant limits to the extent that their narratives can be policed. The insinuations and jokes that often exhibit a hidden political message point to insecurities in the existing government-controlled discourses. As Thomas (1994:45) points out, where a discursive object, and its possible values and uses in a description or story are secure such that departure from these authorized uses is unintelligible and confusing, one might say that such a discourse is effectively policed. However, if narratives are disorganized and incoherence can be found even in conventional genres, then policing may be more conspicuous in its effort than in its effect. It seems that the stringent efforts by the New Order government to enforce *pancasila* ideology in the tourist presentations of Yogyakarta only partly pay off; the creativity of tourist guides is stimulates them to sprinkle their narratives with subversive elements.

NOTES

1 There are several synonyms for tourist guide (a term commonly used in Europe and many other parts of the world), like tour guide, city guide, and step-on guide. Other terms with slightly different connotations includes tour manager, escort, tour escort or tour leader (cf. Pond 1993:17). In this book I shall use the terms tourist guides, tour guides, guides or specific concepts to distinguish particular tasks and functions of guides.

2 Volkman (1990:106) gives a number of examples of the creation of representations in Sulawesi: 'The selection, compression and revision of ritual elements parallels the process by which tourism constructs its object and itinerary (...) Tour guides (...) faced with the 'whole' of Toraja culture must select, compress, interpret, and arrange their guests' experiences into some kind of narrative frame, often in just a day or two.'

3 Cf. Dewan Pimpinan Daerah Himpunan Pramuwisata Indonesia, Daerah Istimewa Yogyakarta, 1991.

4 The increase in the number of Japanese guides is noteworthy: it reflects the shift towards the Asian market. In 1990, English guides largely outnumbered the Japanese guides by more than 100 per cent (125 English versus 57 Japanese guides) (Amato 1991-2:13). In 1993 there were 148 English and 112 Japanese guides; in 1994 191 English and 158 Japanese guides (Sub Dinas Diklat 1994). But in 1994 for the first time, more

Japanese than English guides participated in the Diparda course. French guides maintain their market share with a steady third position throughout the years.

5   Decree nr. KM.82/PW.102/MPPT-88, cf. (Depparpostel 1991-2).

6   The tourist police, a body which was established as a branch of the local police force in 1991 basically to counter petty crime directed against tourists, was occasionally invited by the Department of Justice to participate in a so-called 'sweeping,' that is a raid at a tourist site. While these raids were popularly believed to be directed against unlicensed guides who were not entitled to take tourists to these attractions, the actual aim was to check on the guides working for ASITA-associated travel agencies to see whether they held valid licences. Guides on the job who failed to produce a valid licence faced a trial on the spot, as the Department of Justice usually sent an ambulant magistrate along with the raid. A special bus was equipped to hold these trials. The guides caught without a licence were brought immediately before this judge, interrogated, sentenced to pay a fine, and sent home, while the travel agent had to send another guide to pick up the tourists who were left behind. The local newspapers reported these sweepings, quoting the names of the judge and the defendants in full. It goes without saying that neither the HPI nor the ASITA or the guides approved of these methods of enforcing the law. In *Bernas* (March 27, 1996) I found a detailed description of such a raid and trial under the heading: 'Tak Bawa Izin 'Guide,' Didenda Rp 15,000' (caught without guiding licence, 15,000 *rupiah* fine).

7   Cf. Depparpostel (1989, 1991, 1991-2): 'Departemen Pariwisata, Pos dan Telekomunikasi. Direktorat Jenderal Pariwisata. Keputusan Direktur Jenderal Pariwisata. Nomor: KEP-17/U/IV/89 Tentang Pedoman Pembinaan Pramuwisata dan Pengatur Wisata'; 'Keputusan Menteri Pariwisata, Pos dan Telekomunikasi nomor: KM.105/ PW.304/MPPT-91 Tentang Usaha Jasa Pramuwisata'; and 'Surat Direktur Jenderal Pariwisata nomor: 51/D.2/XI/91 Perihal Petunjuk Pelaksanaan Usaha Jasa Pramuwisata'; in: Usaha Jasa Pramuwisata (1991-2).

8   There are forty-two subjects taught by forty-two different lecturers recuited from Gadjah Mada and other universities and academies, from provincial government departments, and tourism organizations like the ASITA, the HPI and the hotel sector. The first cluster conforms to the minister's guidelines regarding education in *pancasila* state ideology and related fields (like the national language, defence and security, national history, Indonesian culture and arts, and *repelita*). The second cluster also reflects the ministerial guidelines on tourism education (the provincial tourism objects, guiding technique, Indonesian customs, Indonesian trade,

Land and People, geography, tourist packages, tourism industry and organization). However, the third cluster, that is liberally dedicated to 'additional' subjects, is characterized by a large number of subjects added to the list by the Yogyanese authorities to meet the needs of the special features of the province. Tourism in Yogyakarta, the special provincial tourism objects, Yogyanese society, human relations, local history, etc. are among the subjects taught in this cluster.

9 At the time of the research, the ASITA intended to organize its own programme for guides who were employed by its members, and *P.T. Taman Wisata* wished to take the training of the special guides operating on Borobudur and Prambanan into its own hands.

10 The course was given under the heading 'Cultural Tourism Development Central Java – Yogyakarta.' Upgrading course for Licensed Tourist Guides. 13 September – 18 December 1993 at Sanata Dharma University (in collaboration with UNESCO and the International Labour Organization).

11 The course that figured as a test case consisted of two weekly lecture hours over sixteen weeks and was directed at tour managers, or the national guides in Indonesia. The objective was to enhance their knowledge and skills so they would be better prepared for cultural tourism. However, the question has to be raised whether it was wise to invite tour managers rather than senior guides specialized in the province where cultural tourism development was being strongly promoted. Besides *pancasila*, Indonesian language and military science – compulsory subjects indispensible to receiving official approval of an educational programme – the course covered subjects like history, geography, archaeology, Indonesian arts, handicrafts, flora and fauna, religion, human communications, lands and peoples, ethics and etiquette, first aid and health, customs and immigration formalities, foreign languages, guiding techniques, public speaking and fieldtrips to tourist objects.

12 Like a series of country summaries copied from *The Economist World Atlas and Almanac* and the *Encyclopedia Britannica* in the series about 'Lands and People.'

13 Although the company is in charge of the Ratu Boko complex as well, Ratu Boko is an exception as this site is in the process of being developed and visited by only a few thousand tourists per year, there are no special guides yet. Tourists coming to this place are guided by their own tour leader.

14 In 1991 the Kraton employed seventy-six people specifically for tourism, of whom nine were involved in the administration, four at the ticket

175

counter, and sixty-eight (twenty-two men and forty-six women) as guides (Yumarnani 1993).

15 The tour was conducted in German, the native language of my guests and myself. The subsequent fragments of Pak Rudi's narrative were translated into English in a way that imitates the typical usage of German by the guide.

16 This translation is not correct as 'safe' is *'aman'* in Indonesian. It is obvious that this is a white lie to make the tourists feel comfortable.

17 During my visit to Akademi Pariwisata Indonesia at the outskirts of Yogyakarta, I caught sight of a wall in the garden on which a Buddha with his six hand positions is depicted.

CHAPTER 6

BLURRING THE BOUNDARIES

CONTESTED SPACES AND COMPETING DISCOURSES

INTRODUCTION

Malioboro Street, the tourist *kampung* Sosrowijayan and Prawirotaman and the streets in the Kraton area swarm with young men offering their services to passing tourists. According to the 'streetside' entrepreneurs these men represent the 'unqualified,' 'unorganized,' and permanently 'unemployed' people who constitute the informal sector of the tourist industry. However, it is also true that many of them are students, shop assistants, hotel personnel, taxi drivers, and office clerks, even civil servants and teachers with more or less permanent jobs. They call themselves 'friends,' never 'guides.' The actors in 'streetside' tourism refer to them as 'unlicensed guides,' 'informal guides,' 'street guides,' 'batik guides,' and *'guide liar'* (*liar* is the Indonesian word for 'wild'). Other less favourable names are guide liar ('guides that lie'), nuisances and criminals. Every day unlicensed guides are strategically positioned at tourist meeting points: at the post office and the *wartel*, in shop doorways, in and outside cafés, on street corners, at the market, near hotels, at the McDonalds restaurant, in the shopping mall, at the central station, at the bus terminals, in front of attractions, even in museums and on the streets in the main tourist area.

> 'Hello Miss, how are you today?'
> 'Hello Misses, you look happy today!'
> 'Excuse me Miss, where are you from? Holland? Oh Holland. I know Holland.
> I have friend in Holland. Want to see my exhibition? Last day, Miss, close tomorrow.'
> 'This is Kraton, Miss, you see Kraton? I will show you, I'm your friend.'
> 'I like your sunglasses, where you buy?'

These and other related modes of address are typical of the way in which unlicensed guides address tourists. These men are pretty skilled at catching the eye of individually travelling tourists and engage in 'tactics talks' (Crick 1992). They try to find out what the tourist wants: visiting a specific attraction? The guides will show the way. Peeping into backyards? The guides take tourists to a *kampung*. Buying batik paintings or silverwork or puppets? The guides know where to find a shop or local factory. Finding an inexpensive place to eat where the locals meet? Drinking excessively? Buying joints? Visiting a prostitute? The guides know the right place and the right person. Catering to the whims of the tourists, street guides are no *mentors*, but *pathfinders* in the rugged surroundings of the untamed public space in downtown Yogyakarta. The street guides do not offer explanations, they make arrangements of different kinds. As pathfinders they ease access to local culture in a practical sense: they 'mediate' between tourists and the local tourism industry, especially the *kampung* businesses. Here, unlicensed guides act as touts and obtain an income from this 'mediating' role. Pathfinders are small entrepreneurs in local tourist services. Their assets are not of any financial kind, but consist of wits and time. They have to seize the opportunities as and when they occur. Tourists, on the other hand, have economic resources to spend, but they possess very little knowledge of the local language, price levels, or local customs. This is particularly the case with the individual travellers who cannot rely on the all-in packaged services created for the 'quality tourists' by tour operators, travel agents, hotels, and professional guides. Individual travellers have to arrange everything by themselves and this makes them easy prey to the street guides' intervention.

In addition to being pathfinders, unlicensed guides make excellent storytellers, but not in the sense of the academic performers to whom the tourism experts allude when defining their repertoire as consisting of profound knowledge of the local and regional history, architecture, religious and social practices, and the local attractions (Amato 1991-2, Holloway 1981, Urry 1990, Pond 1993). Being such an academic performer would imply the mastery of the dominant discourse (Holloway 1981:399) like that in which the licensed guides are trained. Unlicensed guides have no access to this dominant discourse or purposefully avoid the tourist spaces which require this knowledge. Being marginal to the dominant attraction system, unlicensed guides remain flexible, ready to cater to the needs and expectations of the tourists. However, very much like academic performers, they master at least the 'tourism vernacular' of different foreign languages and they do understand the art of storytelling. If necessary they invent a story on the spot. As storytellers – or rather storymakers – they develop their own style which is tuned to pleasing the tourist. They understand human nature, they know how to read a social situation and have general conceptions about tourist motivations, national stereotypes, and tourist types which they turn to their advantage (cf. Crick 1992).

Anybody can become an unlicensed guide in Yogyakarta, and, in fact, almost everybody in the main tourism areas does, permanently or occasionally. Some men make a living solely from 'street guiding,' others do so in combination with a multitude of other jobs, and a few grab the opportunity whenever it arises and leave their jobs occasionally to cater for tourists. In general, the dealings of unlicensed guides have to be understood in terms of small-scale entrepreneurship of a particular kind, i.e. small-scale peddling. It is a *pasar* style of making a living which has been characterized by Clifford Geertz (1963) as highly competitive, individualistic, and *ad-hoc* acts of exchange. Public space being their domain, unlicensed guides grasp occasions for gain as they arise spontaneously, benefiting in every possible way from the diffuse flow of individual tourists passing by. The growth of international tourism in Yogyakarta poses a challenge to the vast number of (mostly) young males with a low income and gloomy future perspectives. With tourists in town, the chances of making a quick windfall are bigger, but the stakes are higher – not only economically speaking. Doing business with tourists involves selling goods and strategically exploiting personal networks – as is characteristic of the *pasar* mode of making a living. Many young men in Yogyakarta's tourist areas combine work as a street guide with different kinds of economic activities. They frequently work as touts for several shops, restaurants, guest-houses, and bars on a commission basis. Some sell toys, ice cream, or cold drinks in the street; others work incidentally as barkeepers, waiters, security guards, bellboys in guesthouses, taxi drivers, and even pedicab men. Some-times they invest money in bulk buying to resell the goods at a profit. Other times, they walk the streets with samples of fake Rolex watches or perfume, trying to sell these products on a commission basis. Most of the time, they do all these things.

The most marked aspect of the street guides' work, accompanying tourists, is merely a strategy to earn some money. Only a few street guides generate a substantial income from guiding as such. They have to be satisfied with tips from tourists, a meal, a drink, or cigarettes. If they are lucky, they receive gifts of some value: western consumer goods like wrist-watches, walkmans, radios, leather jackets, an invitation to accompany the tourist to the next destination, or even a ticket to the tourists' home country. If a tourist is reluctant to buy souvenirs and does not tip, the guide has no other choice than to walk away, since he has no right to charge a fee. Windfalls are taken, but they may go for days without any business. Street guides cherish high hopes and expectations of the tourists, and try to keep the relationship going even after the tourist has left for the next destination or returned home. A recurrent theme among street guides is their effort to enter into a sexual relationship with a female (and occasionally male) tourist. Although a relationship emerging from these arrangements is of a transitory and instrumental nature, it can acquire other than purely financial characteristics. The chances of acquiring money and gifts, of having a good time, and, for the very lucky ones, a free ticket and an invitation to stay in Europe, America, Australia, or Japan constitute an enormous attraction. But because it is never certain whether a relationship will turn out that way, guides tend to spread the risk of an eventual break-up by being engaged in several relationships at the same time. A great deal of time is invested in that one love that promises to take them on a trip to her homeland. This is basically the street guides' hope for the future.

While unlicensed guides figure prominently in Yogyakarta's street life, they live on the margins of the city's tourism industry. They operate almost exclusively in *kampung* tourism, as it is the *kampung* where they live, where they have their business coalitions, and where they approach most of the tourists. 'Streetside' tourism is largely inaccessible to them and the actors in 'streetside' tourism look down their noses at unlicensed guides. However, opinions about the unlicensed guides differ widely. Entrepreneurs in the 'streetside' tourism industry tend to play down the impact of unlicensed guides, if only for the sake of impression management *vis-à-vis* the foreign researcher. In a similar vein to the disdain they display about the competition that emanates from *kampung* businesses, they contend that unlicensed guides are part of a different reality that does not touch upon their lives. The *kampung*, including the tourists who frequent it, are perceived as a world apart. 'They are no bad boys, they are harmless, but they can pass on cholera,' says one travel agent. 'Little scoundrels and thieves,' says a hotel manager. This opinion is shared by the licensed guides who do not wish to regard street guides as competitors for assignments from 'streetside' travel agents. The occasional involvement of unlicensed guides with language proficiency in an exceptional language is a strategy to maintain lucrative contacts with customers and to secure employment opportunities rather than jeopardize them. The boot is on the other foot if incidents occur in which tourists are injured or killed: licensed guides are quick to accuse *guide liar* of being involved. Even the stagnation in tourism growth is blamed on unlicensed guides as they 'give Yogyakarta a bad reputation.'

The government shows more overt concern about the negative impacts emanating from the activities of unlicensed guides. Cheating on tourists and local entrepreneurs, harassment, theft and other petty crime, drug abuse, sexual misbehaviour, and even murder are among the accusations with which government officials saddle *guide liar*. In the government-controlled Tourism Office, visitors are presented with a flyer (available in English, French, German, and Japanese) that warns tourists not to accept the offers of young men in Malioboro Street to take them to an exhibition of graduates from Yogyanese art schools, as this would be a tourist trap that results in the purchase of an overpriced piece of batik.[1] At a more personal level, on the notice board in the Tourism Office a letter is pinned apparently written by German tourists warning their fellow-countrymen against the practices of street guides. Considering the linguistic blunders in this 'letter,' it is obvious that it has not been written by Germans. Most probably it was composed by local government officials or licensed guides as propaganda against the *guide liar*. Discouraging, even frightening tourists away from encounters with street guides is one of the strategies used to exert more control on unlicensed guides. Another strategy is to police the street vendors and shops in the inner city to prevent unlicensed guides from conducting their business there. Theoretically, the Tourist Police is supposed to go after the shop keeper and the guide if tourists complain about being cheated and arrange for tourists to receive their money back. Curtailing unethical business practices in the tourist areas is among the measures taken to control the informal (tourism) sector. There are occasional campaigns to bar *becak* men from Malioboro Street and street vendors and street artists from particular tourist areas and to close down bars and restaurants in the downtown area. As far as these measures affect the tourism sector, they have to be understood against the background of the policy of 'quality' tourism. From the government's perspective, the informal tourism sector in general and the unlicensed guides in particular undermine the carefully constructed attraction system of Yogyakarta and the policed spaces and controlled discourses of *pancasila* tourism. Unlicensed guides largely withdraw from the influence of the government. They make themselves invisible in the eyes of the law. They operate in public spaces and avoid calling themselves guides. They act as harmless citizens who come to the help of tourists who seem to need assistance. In view of their marginal position and their low-profile in the tourism industry of Yogyakarta it could be argued that the government's fear of the detrimental impacts of the so-called shennanigans of the unlicensed guides is exaggerated. How could these poor and powerless *kampung* dwellers possibly represent a threat to the carefully constructed and systematically controlled tourist spaces and discourses that constitute Yogyakarta's *pancasila* tourism?

The latter question will be dealt with in this chapter. On the basis of an analysis of the practices of *guide liar*, this chapter attempts to provide a better understanding of the ways in which different categories of unlicensed guides operate in the *kampung* tourism economy and in the attraction system of Yogyakarta. After a brief discussion of the peculiarities of the informal sector in the tourism industry, three interrelated questions will be raised: firstly, what modes of operation are employed by the unlicensed guides in Yogyakarta in terms of small-scale '*pasar*-style' entrepreneurship? This question will be answered by an analysis of the following aspects of their daily life: their approach to and dealings with tourists; their economic strategies in the city's tourist industry, especially their relationship with local shopkeepers, artisans and other street guides; their spending patterns; and their future prospects and perspectives. Secondly, to what extent does government intervention constitute restrictions on and provide opportunities for their activities? And thirdly, in what way do *guide liar* pose a challenge to *pancasila* tourism?

THE '*PASAR*'-STYLE OF ENTREPRENEURSHIP

While Indonesia has one of the largest informal sectors in the world (Evers & Mehmet 1994), the New Order government refused to regard informal businesses as a force in economic development, in general, or in tourism development in particular. Instead they were seen as an obstacle to the development orchestrated by the New Order regime (Clapham 1985). It seems that the tolerance towards informal economic activities declined towards the end of the New Order. The informal service sector particularly underwent a process of formalization. The ease of entry into this sector was reduced by being hedged in by a multiplicity of permits and licensing required by various levels of government authorities. Paradoxically the labour-absorption capacities of the informal sector in Indonesia in general declined during the 1980s and 1990s, stifled by the sixth national Five-Year Development Plan (*Repelita* VI) that theoretically at least aimed at the increase of the productivity and income levels of informal sector participants (Evers & Mehmet 1994). As a consequence, the position of informal businesses in Indonesia has changed. They have had to reconcile themselves to operating under harsher conditions and in conformity with a proliferation of government regulations, or face destruction.

In tourism, which is basically a service industry, much of the employment is in the form of self-employed, small-scale entrepreneurship. The petty enterprises establish a vigorous and visible element in the tourist sector, employing a large proportion of the labour force. The employment effects of this small-scale sector are often excluded in the assessment of tourism employment, because official employment data fail to measure the labour-absorption capacities of informal businesses accurately (Cukier 1996). Owing to all kinds of interlinkages between formal and informal sectors, it is difficult to identify what and who constitutes the informal economy as such. A broad range of jobs is found both in the formal and informal sectors. While many authors associate small-scale economic activities with the informal sector (Cukier 1996, Long & Kindon 1997, Timothy & Wall 1997), it should be noted that it is often the lack of an official licence and the withdrawal from the taxation system that classifies an economic activity as informal, not its scale, organization, or function (Drakakis-Smith 1987:68, Evers 1991:34). The boundaries between the formal and the informal are constantly shifting, as they in particular are succumbing to ever-changing regulations that are the outcome of power struggles between the government and the private sector (Boer 1989). Despite these shifting boundaries, the distinction between the controlled and uncontrolled small-scale sector is of vital importance as the Indonesian government pursues a supportive policy towards small-scale enterprises in general, provided that these enterprises operate under government control.[2]

The tourism-related sector is particularly illustrative of the manifold economic relationships that encompass formal as well as informal modes of employment. As Timothy and Wall (1997:323) have pointed out, it is as much an oversimplification to dichotomize the tourism industry into two distinct sectors, as it is for any other economic activities. In Indonesia, jobs in the tourism sector continue to grow and diversify as the tourism industry develops (Cukier 1996:55). As tourism is seasonal and changeable being subject to volatile consumer preferences, petty businesses may make incidental windfalls, but the individual entrepreneur may go without income for days or even weeks during the low season. However, the informal tourism sector cannot be associated exclusively with poverty since many tourism-related activities provide higher incomes than the lower paid formal jobs do. Making a living in the tourism sector may involve long working hours, unpaid labour by household members, accumulated experience on the job rather than formal training, protected access to working areas as well as unprotected labour and competitive markets, reliance on personal networks and patronage, and the flexibility to switch between activities responding to changing demands in the market. People involved in the tourism sector may combine formal and informal-sector activities, i.e. stable part-time or temporary wage work with self-employment, they may work on a wage or commission basis, they may belong to the skilled, semi-skilled, or unskilled workforce (Timothy & Wall 1997:323). Over and above this, there are both backward and forward linkages between formal and informal activities. The former refer to the purchase of products and services from the formal sector by informal enterprises, the latter occur when informal-sector entrepreneurs supply goods or services to other informal businesses and even to formal enterprises. The boundaries between formal and informal activities in the tourism industry are blurred at both the individual and the collective level: the individual easily slips in and out of all kinds of jobs and there are many inter-sectoral linkages. Jobs created and performed on the boundary between the formal and informal tourism sector are numerous and their conditions, organizations, and functions are differentiated. Therefore we need concepts that characterize the activities of petty entrepreneurs in tourism more clearly than the distinction between formal and informal economy.

It may seem to be obvious that tourism is thriving and absorbing many people who would otherwise be unemployed (Timothy & Wall 1997), but in terms of economic growth and development as envisioned by the New Order government, it is important to differentiate between employment opportunities on the one hand and entrepreneurial activities on the other. As a sector that provides occasional and seasonal jobs, tourism is of vital importance to vast numbers of less-educated and less-qualified local people. As a sector that provides interesting prospects for entrepreneurial initiatives, the significance of tourism is less clear. Entrepreneurship, according to the classical economic definition, is an instrument for transforming and improving the economy and society, as entrepreneurs are regarded as persons who build and manage an enterprise for the pursuit of profit in the course of which they innovate and take risks, as the outcome of any innovation is usually not certain. Boissevain (1974:147-62) distinguishes between two distinct types of resources that are used strategically by entrepreneurs, first-order and second-order resources. The first includes resources such as land, equipment, jobs, funds, and specialized knowledge which the entrepreneur controls directly. The second are strategic contacts with other people who control such resources directly or who have access to people who do. Entrepreneurs who primarily control first-order resources are called *patrons*; those who predominantly control second-order resources are known as *brokers*. While patrons strategically deploy private ownership of means of production for economic profit, brokers act as intermediaries, they put people in touch with each other directly or indirectly for profit. They bridge gaps in communication between people. Entrepreneurs can become brokers if they occupy a central position which offers them a strategic advantage in information management. To understand the way in which petty entrepreneurs in the Indonesian tourism industry operate, we have to distinguish two categories: independent patrons and network specialists.

If we classify small-scale tourism businesses in Yogyakarta in terms of Boissevain's distinction between patrons and brokers, we find that most of the local owners of small businesses act as patrons, while many of the categories of people that mediate between them and their clients usually combine patronage with brokerage, exploiting a combination of first- and second-order resources. Local owners of small-scale tourism businesses such as accommodation and restaurants, the tour and travel and transport sector, the souvenir, beauty, fashion, and entertainment businesses, act as patrons since they control first-order resources. They own land, real estate, money, equipment, and other means of production. The small enterprises are established without large capital investments, sometimes in collaboration with foreigners, often on a provisional basis, operated by no or only a few employees, preferably family members, and not always equipped with the requisite licences and government permits. These enterprises are easily combined with several other economic activities providing the owner with considerable flexibility to move in and out of the sector, as has been shown in the previous chapter.

Other people operate as brokers, making a living exclusively by manipulating second-order resources. Individuals occupying a central position in the local tourism sector can become brokers provided they possess considerable amounts of second-order resources, flexibility in terms of time, space, and social contacts. Brokers are in the middle of the action. They have free access to tourists and to the businesses in the local tourism industry. They use constantly updated information about where and when tourists arrive, where and how long they stay and where they will go next. They anticipate the tourists' activity patterns, their expectations and needs, and their spending power. It goes without saying that they have to be familiar with the local market and the opportunities to match demand with supply in a way that enables them to make a profit. There are several categories of entrepreneurs which fit this profile. Taxi-drivers, pedicab men, lottery sellers, street vendors, and informal guides are the most flexible and mobile people in a tourist area. They move around town constantly and have access to a vast network and up-to-date information. Others are more limited in their freedom because of permanent or part-time jobs tying them down, but nevertheless have free access to tourists and connections in the local tourism industry that enable them to operate as brokers. Brokers are frequently employees of small accommodation and travel agencies, waiters and bar-tenders, formal guides, shop assistants, and security men. Many brokers combine a number of 'informal' jobs to expand their network.

Turning to unlicensed guides in particular, it may be obvious that their way of operating, maintaining and expanding their networks and making a profit from their interactions with tourists is essentially the approach of a *pasar* trader to business which is of an economic as well as emotional nature. As Geertz (1963) has shown, the *pasar* trader focuses on the individual two-person transaction to get as much as possible out of the deal immediately at hand. He is perpetually looking for a chance to make a smaller or larger killing, is not interested in attempting to build up a stable clientele or a steadily growing business. He sees his activities as a set of unrelated exchanges with a wide variety of trading partners and customers which form no over-all pattern and build towards no cumulative end. Petty traders tend to think of their business career as a series of cycles in which one oscillates, more or less rapidly, between being ahead of the game and being behind it, between being well off and being bankrupt (Geertz 1963). While this description may not capture the business strategies of traders in a market place with a stable clientele, it does typify the outlook of brokers in the tourism sector. The relationships between 'seller' and 'buyer' in the tourism market are of an incidental and passing nature. Tourists come and go, and the chances of ever encountering the same tourist ever again are small. Therefore, overpricing goods and services, offering products of inferior quality, even cheating tourists do not have any consequences for the individual entrepreneur. He is not called upon to feel morally responsible for establishing a fair bargaining relationship. As a collectivity local tourism entrepreneurs may suffer from this strategy in the long run, because tourists may become fed up with the constant hassle and stay away from a site altogether.[3]

Pasar traders become emotionally involved with their trade: failing to make customers buy – failing to get tourists involved – makes them feel depressed: they feel that they have had their chance and have failed to capitalize on it (Geertz 1963). This emotional aspect of their trade may explain why street guides feign friendship, affection and – in the case of female tourists – even love right from the start: they try to maximize their chances. Although their relationships with fellow-entrepreneurs as well as tourists may be dyadic and individual, they are never exclusive and singular. As *pasar* traders they spread themselves thin over a wide range of deals rather than plunge deeply into any one (Geertz 1963). In the tourism industry, which is a precarious trade, it would be foolish to put all of one's eggs in one single basket. Therefore, street guides engage in a myriad of commissioned jobs and maintain multiple business relationships. Small-scale peddling and guiding tourists are flexible jobs which allow for strategic use fitting in with busy tourist seasons and calm off-season trade. To illustrate how the *pasar*-style mode of network specialists operates, the next section will present an in-depth analysis of the strategies of different categories of unlicensed guides.

Life as *Guide Liar*

Despite the fact that government officials and actors in 'streetside' tourism lump together all self-employed people who frequent the streets of Yogyakarta's tourism areas under the name of *guide liar*, there are important differences in their style of doing business and their future prospects. These differences justify a more refined approach that allows for a subcategorization of unlicensed guides. For many young males, taking advantage of passing tourists represents an additional, though irregular, source of income and excitement. They leave their jobs temporarily and at short notice to earn some money by taking tourists to shops. People operating on this ad-hoc basis can be found among the hotel and restaurant staff, shop-keepers, office clerks, workshop employees, museum staff, and travel agents. I shall term them 'occasional touts.' Individuals constituting this category are more or less permanently employed and are tied down to a specific locality to perform their jobs. Those who deal with tourists directly, like receptionists, waiters, and bar tenders, have a privileged position. A second category I call 'odd-jobbers' is constituted by individuals with occasional employment that requires considerable mobility, like taxi drivers, *becak* men, street vendors, and lottery and ticket sellers. These people have all kinds of jobs and businesses that are often tourism-related and that can easily be left behind for a while to engage in more lucrative deals with tourists. Commissions, tips, and gifts, and perhaps long-time financial and personal commitments from tourists are important sources of income for the 'odd-jobbers.' The infamous 'Taman Sari guides' may be classified under this heading. Finally, there are young men who maintain an almost professional outlook on street guiding. I call them 'professional friends.' They regard street guiding as their profession and tune their lives to dealing with tourists in a way that generates a reasonable income. Most of them operate in small groups and concentrate on taking tourists to the shops as directly as possible. Others work individually and conduct informally arranged guiding tours. Like the odd-jobbers, both the group-based and the individual 'friends' depend on commissions, tips, gifts, and the particular commitments of tourists, but unlike the odd-jobbers, professional *guide liar* do not have additional sources of income. A characteristic of all these young males is their keen interest in romantic and sexual encounters with female tourists. Elsewhere I have coined the phrase 'romantic entrepreneur' to describe (young) males who put much effort into the establishment of romantic relationships with female tourists, with the aim of being supported by these females or of acquiring a ticket to follow them to their home country (Dahles & Bras 1999b). These categories will be discussed in detail in the following parts.

CATEGORIES OF 'GUIDE LIAR' IN YOGYAKARTA

Occasional tout	*Odd-jobber*	*Professional friend* self-employed	
Permanent employment in other businesses	Self-employed, temporary jobs and trades Taman Sari guides	Group-based	individual
Romantic entrepreneur Female tourist as source of income, provider of investments or 'escape'			

The occasional tout[4]

As there are numerous occasions when tourists require services that will bring in extra money, 'occasional touts' can be found almost everywhere in Yogyakarta's tourist areas. Working as a street guide is popular among underpaid teachers as well as among schoolboys, students, truants, and dropouts. Language teachers, privileged by their proficiency in foreign languages, are among those who approach tourists. They compete with (their) students and others who claim to be students. They all try to make some extra money by taking tourists to shops and restaurants. Some are attracted by the money and glamour associated with tourism to such a degree that they throw up their studies to focus completely on some petty jobs in the tourism sector. Yogyakarta is known as the 'city of education' with dozens of universities and countless institutions for vocational and professional training. In the afternoon, after the lectures and lessons are finished, the number of street guides increases significantly in the city, especially in Malioboro Street and Beringharjo market. The same is true of other tourism objects, even at the strictly-controlled temple complexes. People from the villages in the vicinity of Prambanan and Borobudur know how to find their way onto the temple premises without passing through the entrance. Others who do not know where to find the hole in the fence, come to the temple with public transport or on their motor bike, buy a ticket and once on the temple premises look out for tourists who are not provided with a guide. As has been described in the previous chapter, the official guides at the temples are reluctant to take on groups smaller than five persons and there are also many tourists who wander off from their group. These tourists are an easy prey for the unlicensed guides. Sometimes, unlicensed guides from Yogyakarta bring tourists to the temples and enter the premises as paying visitors (making the tourists pay their entrance fee). These unlicensed guides may see to it that 'their' tourists are not guided by one of the official guides, but by a local *guide liar*. There are networks of unlicensed guides from Yogyakarta and the temple complexes sharing the income from tourists' tips. In that case, the unlicensed guide from the city pays his local counterpart. It is amazing that the networks of unlicensed guides extend to these strictly controlled and well-managed tourist objects, raising questions about the effectiveness of government control. It seems that the enclosed tourist sites are fairly contested spaces where a myriad of employees and entrepreneurs compete for the tourists.

In one of Yogyakarta's four-star hotels I met Ali (23). As a graduate of a sport academy he is responsible for the recreational programme of the hotel. Sometimes, after playing tennis or supervising fitness training, tourists ask him whether he could arrange a tour for them. It is the hotel's policy to transfer requests like this to the in-house travel agent, but if Ali likes the tourists and feels like having a good time with them, he arranges transport through his own network and acts as the guests' guide. Ali's employer is aware of this, but as the guests' satisfaction has absolute priority, the management turns a blind eye and allows the company's policy to be violated. Another occupational group that occasionally engages in tourist guiding is composed of people employed in transport services. Taxi-drivers taking tourists to their accommodation from the airport or train station usually ask about their passengers' programme for the days to come. They try to sell a private tour in their taxi to one of the tourist objects in the vicinity of Yogyakarta. For an occasion like this, taxi drivers use their company car for their private business interests.

Another category interested in tourists are the pedicab or *becak* men. Pedicab men have traditionally been entrepreneurs in local transport, but, with tourism booming in Yogyakarta, those working in the tourist areas have increasingly been involved in the transport and entertainment of foreign visitors. Taking them to the major tourist objects in town, especially the Kraton and Taman Sari and, most of all, to the Ramayana performance at the Purawisata and to batik shops and silver factories, now constitutes an important source of income for *becak* drivers. The emergence of tourism has created opportunities to earn considerably more money through overcharging, commissions, and support by the local tourism industry. The enormous attraction exerted by tourism areas on *becak* men from all over Yogyakarta has generated the establishment of organizations among the pedicab men in Sosrowijayan and Prawirotaman. Without the social control and discipline imposed by the organizations, the tourist areas would turn into battlefields with hordes of *becak* drivers competing for customers.[5] As these organizations do not cover all the tourist spaces in the city, many streets remain contested spaces where pedicab men compete for tourist customers, sometimes in a pretty aggressive way.

Finally there is the personnel of museums and art galleries who are constantly exposed to tourism in their everyday work. When I visited the Sonobudoyo Museum in the Kraton area on a quiet morning, I was welcomed by a bunch of males hanging around the ticket office. One of them, a man in his thirties, addressed me in English with the usual interrogation. He turned out to be employed as a curator by the museum. Without being asked, he elaborated on his biography, telling me about his being a graduate from Gadjah Mada University and that he was a historian. He was lucky to find this job in the museum as employment for historians is hard to find. Despite his acknowledged good fortune, he hastened to add, he earned little money, and one had to be smart to make some extra *rupiah* (tipping his forehead with his right forefinger). Uninvited he accompanied me on my tour through the museum, not acting as mentor, but as a salesman. There was virtually nothing that could not be purchased; not the original of course, but an excellent copy: books, gamelan instruments, prehistoric artefacts, ritual objects, pottery, jewellery, masks, batik, puppets, and so on and so forth. As I lingered in the hall with the puppets, my self-appointed guide concluded that I was interested in Javanese *wayang* and willing to buy. He offered to take me to the workplace of the museum where historical puppets were restored. He had a friend there and I could have one or two of these authentic Yogyanese puppets for a good price. I explained that I was not interested in buying any puppets, but that I would like to take a look at the workplace. After some more attempts to convince me of the uniqueness of this opportunity and countered by my continued refusal, the focus of our conversation took a sharp turn towards my private life. He asked whether I was married, had children, what my profession was. On realizing that he was dealing with an unattached professor in anthropology, he became his charming self. Upon reaching the exit, he offered me a chair and refreshments and sat down to talk. He asked me whether I could arrange a job for him in the Netherlands or at least a scholarship. He would show himself very grateful and I could always count on him as my assistant. He understood that I would need some time to think about it and said: 'I will come to your hotel tonight and we can talk things over.'

The odd-jobber

Many street guides are migrants from less prosperous and less touristic areas of Java and even from other islands of the archipelago. Attracted by the city as an economic and cultural centre, these men try to find a niche in petty trade. They make a living as street vendor, pedicab man, taxi driver, or lottery seller. Among the marginals it is possible to find young men with an excellent education, with diplomas from polytechnics and universities, who cannot succeed in finding appropriate work. A good example is Udin (44), a university graduate from Surabaya. He has worked abroad in the oil-drilling sector on a contract basis for Pertamina, the state-owned oil company. After his wife died, he was left with three children to take care on his own. He can no longer accept well-paid jobs overseas and has to find other employment until his children can stand on their own feet. Udin is not interested in a career as a licensed guide: employment in tourism is always insecure and dependent on networks. He would prefer to return to his profession as a technical engineer. For the time being, he is a 'serial' odd-jobber accepting temporary jobs in factories where his technical expertise is required for a specific project. Then again, he goes without a job for several weeks and months turning to batik selling. His working area is Yogyakarta's Beringharjo market. He has a silent agreement with several vendors that he receives a ten percent commission on sales that are settled through his mediation. So he hangs around the market and approaches Western tourists. 'Hello, where you from?' is his usual mode of address. He cooperates with another informal guide, a man of his age whom he 'trusts from the bottom of his heart' and with whom he shares on an equal basis. Udin claims it has become impossible to operate alone. In the market and Malioboro Street 'gangs' comprising ten to twelve members collaborate to direct the tourists to 'their' shops and galleries. The competition has become cut throat. The section of Malioboro Street adjacent to Beringharjo market which is teaming with batik shops is called *Jalan* Gaza, the Gaza Strip, alluding to the heavily patrolled buffer zone between Israel and Egypt. 'Spot the tourist, target, and hit,' is the motto of the unlicensed guides operating in this area. 'There is a war raging between the gangs, everybody is after the tourist,' says Udin, thereby providing a striking example of how the battle for the tourists in public space unfolds.

A different example of an odd-jobber is Dulah (25). He re-migrated from Sumatra where his father, originally from East Java, relocated when he was a young man. Dulah thought it would be better to live in urban Java as life in rural Sumatra did not appeal to him at all. Dulah finished senior high school and settled in Yogyakarta where he had a friend running a school for typing and stenography. At first he was a substitute teacher at this school and a waiter in downtown Yogyakarta. He wanted to be in touch with tourists and improve his English. Not for the money, he hastens to add, but to 'know about other cultures.' But he did not enjoy his two jobs as teacher and waiter. He preferred to work as a tout for a batik gallery and as a street vendor selling *kampung*-made batik postcards. This is what he still does occasionally, but he has expanded his business activities with one or two lucrative jobs. One is guiding: if the opportunity arises, he takes tourists on sight-seeing trips. This is not a way to get rich, but it brings him in some extra money, an opportunity to speak English, and have a good time. His most profitable business, however, is illegal lottery selling. He is totally devoted to soccer and runs pools on all Cup Finals, the Olympic Games, and the Italian and English soccer league. He works in Malioboro Street where he has all his contacts and where he uses his card selling as cover. Dulah has hundreds of regular customers, and when there is a major soccer event he sells thousands of tickets. During the Eurocup (in 1996) he had a turnover of seven million *rupiah*. This lottery selling amounts to 60 per cent of his income; the rest is from tourism. He gets 'friendly' with tourists in Malioboro Street, first trying to sell them some batik cards, generating a conversation, asking for his picture to be taken together with his new 'friends,' then suggesting some good shops to buy more batik. His demeanor is modest, even shy. He seems to have little in common with the shrewd street guides that dominate the area. Tourists trust him easily. He has established ongoing business relations with a couple of tourists. He is into batik bulk buying and ships his merchandise to Europe where his 'friends' sell it. This gives him a nice commission.

There are men who combine a job in the sultan's palace – being a gamelan player, dancer, singer, security man, cleaning man, or formal guide – with incidental street guiding. This applies to men from Yoganese families who enjoy the privileges of living in the Kraton area (under the *ngindung* system) and being counted among the personnel of the sultan. Working for the sultan is not paid in money but in kind, and the employees can walk away from their task whenever required by other obligations. Being formally employed at the palace means that they possess ID which makes them trustworthy and knowledgeable in the eyes of tourists. Happily for them, they are first in line when it comes to entering into a friendly conversation with foreign tourists, as the Kraton makes an excellent hangout. Their working area is the Pagelaran, the former assembly hall of the sultan's army and the place where the sultan held public audiences. Here we find an unstructured exposition of artefacts related to the royal family. Access to this area requires the payment of a small entrance fee, but is not organized as it is in the inner palace area. At the ticket office of the Pagelaran tourists are received by the palace personnel. The men hang around the entrance and watch the tourists arriving. One of them breaks away from the group to show newly-arrived tourists around. Indonesian visitors who flock to the palace in abundance, are left to their own devices. Western tourists are the targets. Whenever I went to the Pagelaran, even after many weeks and months in Yogyakarta, I was guided by one of the workers. Their knowledge about all the artefacts is impressive. The architecture and the interior, colours and styles of the Pagelaran, detailed knowledge and gossip about the royal family, the wall painting and costumes of representatives from all over Indonesia, gamelan instruments and ritual objects – all these things provided the material for lengthy explanations. Without exceptions my guides spoke respectfully about the sultan. All of them are from Yogyanese families which have served the palace for generations. Many are members of the Javanese nobility, like Amat (20), who bears the title of *raden* (laureat title of the Javanese nobility). His family has lived in the Kraton area for generations and his father worked as a clerk in the sultan's administration and played the gamelan at the palace all his life. His father is now retired from his administrative job, but still plays the gamelan. He has not missed one Sunday concert in the palace. Amat has inherited his father's privileges, though he is not employed in the administration. For the time being, it is his task to clean the floors in the Pagelaran before it opens its gates to visitors. In return he secures the free living quarters for his family; Amat's opinion is that is a good bargain for his humble job. Amat is a student at Gadjah Mada University; economics is his discipline. He dreams of becoming a palace administrator after finishing his studies, and perhaps he will succeed with his father's connections. After the tour of the Pagelaran, Amat wishes me a nice day, turns around and leaves, ignoring the *rupiah* notes that I try to hand him. This is merely making time because as I pass the gate, Amat is back asking me whether I would care to look at a 'royal workshop' where puppets are made. He seems to suggest that the puppets are made to be used for performances in the palace. I follow him criss-cross through the narrow streets of the Kraton area. We end up in a puppet workshop in the Taman Sari area, one of the many tiny shops in which two or three people produce hand-made leather puppets. Their product is for sale, not for royal use. As I buy an (overpriced) puppet representing Arjuna, one of the heroes from the Mahabharata, Amat smiles contentedly: 'You made a good choice, Miss. Arjuna is a strong and handsome man.'

Upon entering the Kraton area at one of the four gates, a tourist will almost immediately be addressed by a 'local':

'Hello Mister, palace close today because of ceremony. But Watercastle open. You know Watercastle? Taman Sari? Want see?'

Without waiting for an answer, the 'local' considers himself responsible for taking the tourist to the Taman Sari. Many of these local men also hang around the back entrance of the Kraton, where they attempt to attract the attention of foreign visitors: 'Pssst, Mister, want see puppet play, Javanese dance? Come, I show you!' With this tactic they hope to lure the tourist away from the palace and into the Taman Sari area. The tourist will not find any puppet play or dance, but lots of shops selling puppets and dance masks. One of my informants, Suparman (36) who is now a full-time batik seller in Malioboro Street, used to enter the palace through this back entrance to approach tourists. According to Suparman – who claims to be of noble descent, which his friends deny and ridicule – many *guide liar* enter the palace as they have friends or family among the Kraton staff. Again, an enclosed and controlled tourist space turns out to exhibit an amazing permeability for local people with local networks. Suparman attracted the tourists' attention by offering them a free class in Javanese dance. On Sundays, after the Palace dance, tourists would follow him eagerly. He took them to one of the *pendopo* (open veranda) on the southern *alun-alun* that have fallen into decay. There he would introduce himself as a teacher of Javanese dance and demonstrate some basic figures and hand positions to the tourists. He did this for fun, not for the money. He never demanded any money from the tourists, but he would tell them about the costumes and the masks that dancers wear. After the free class, tourists would ask him where they could buy these accessories, and he would guide the way to the shops.

A slightly different approach was taken by the young man who came running out of a garage for motor cycles when I passed by on my way to the birdmarket adjacent to the Watercastle. He was dirty from tinkering with the engines, cleaned his hands on his t-shirt and introduced himself: 'Hi, I'm Mike from Bali. I'm here for holiday with my family. Me tourist like you.' He really expected me to believe this obvious lie. Mike manoeuvred me through the narrow alleys of the birdmarket pointing out birds, bird food, chained monkeys, bats ('drink blood, good for cold'), pigeons, and the big lizard kept as a pet in a tiny pool with a rope around its middle. In less than ten minutes we have left the birdmarket to climb the stairs to the old palace that is now crumbling into ruins. Mike starts the conversation: 'Where you from? Holland?' Like so many other unlicensed guides he has a sister in the Nether-lands. 'Van Basten, Gullit,' he utters smilingly to prove that he is familiar with the Dutch soccer heroes. 'Where you stay? How long in Yogya? You married? You stay here alone? Me also alone.' Forgotten is his family with whom he had claimed to be staying here on a vacation just a couple of minutes ago. Mike skips the view from the old palace's roof, which is beautiful in the morning when Mount Merapi is still visible to the north. Asking him about the building we are in, he mumbles something about the 'king's stables where they kept the horses.' Other unlicensed guides assert that the building served either as the sultan's living quarters, or as a dance hall, the guards' quarters, or storage. We leave the palace and enter the adjacent living area where a myriad of tiny workshops produce batik paintings, silver jewellery, leather puppets, and other popular tourist gadgets.

We proceed to the entrance gate of the pool area of the old palace complex. Here, Mike is addressed by the ticket seller in Javanese. I pay my fee and pointing to Mike I say: I guess he is allowed in for free (which is the custom for unlicensed guides in this area). The ticket seller is affirmative: 'Yes, he my good friend.' Mike looks disturbed. Upon entering the pool area, he admits to living in the Kraton area close to the garage where he picked me up. He is married to a woman from East Java. She is a trader. He is doing all kinds of jobs, but likes to take tourists to the Watercastle 'to get away from my job for a while,' he says trying to look innocent. In the past he worked in a hotel in Bali, this is why he says that he is from Bali. His exposure leaves him demotivated. He does not feel like spending more time on sightseeing with me. 'These two swimming pools here for sultan family; there is another one over there (he points, but has no intention going there) for sultan and his wife. This building (again pointing) is watch tower, upstairs sultan's bedroom.' On other occasions, guides treated me to a lengthy explanation with fruity details of the sultan's sex life. A favourite story that consists of as many different versions as there are unlicensed guides, is about the sultan's forty wives – either naked or wearing underpants trimmed with lace – who did nothing but bathe and frolic in the pools all day. The sultan, who did nothing else but spy on his wives from behind his bedroom window, was said to have picked out two every evening to spend the night with up in his tower. For the palace administration, the happy two had to deliver their lace pants in a stone bowl that was emptied by the palace servants: 'Yogya sultan strong man, many children.' Disconcerted by his unmasking, Mike is not in the mood to make up an appealing story. He soon directs me towards the central court planted with big pleasantly-smelling trees. Here, a batik gallery is so strategically accommodated that almost no tourist manages to pass by without entering. In this gallery a historic map of the Taman Sari area is displayed as it was in the eighteenth century. 'Want see map?' is the usual question asked by unlicensed guides. Many tourists, having heard the stories and having been guided through the confusing ruins, like to eye the map, trying to figure out their present location. They have no idea where they are. Once in the shop (there is indeed a copy of an old map) the tourists are invited to have a look at the batik paintings. These paintings are similar to all the others that can be purchased in town, although the owner likes to claim that his 'artists' produce the paintings after an original and unique design that he created himself. On this occasion, his artists are two young women painting the bamboo trees with birds that are quite popular among local guesthouse owners who like to hang them in their rooms. 'My sister and my wife,' the owner smiles. Mike asks me whether I want to buy batik. If so, I should not buy at this place. Mike knows a better place: better quality and cheap price. On our way to his address he starts complaining about his life: it is no fun sitting at home unemployed and being dependent on his family. His family turns out to consist of artists, everybody is a highly talented batik painter. Actually, the shop for which we are heading is run by his mother. She sells family-made pieces of art. As we enter his 'family's' shop, I have a *deja-vu* experience. I was taken to this shop before, by another Taman Sari guide, who introduced me to the owner as 'his older sister.' This time the same woman, who sidles forward reluctantly, figures as Mike's 'mother.' I am offered tea and a photobook is presented, a book I have seen before. The time before my guide claimed that these pictures were taken by his sister on her European trip. Indeed, the book does contain pictures of a number of Indonesian people posing in front of well-known European tourist objects, such as Big Ben in London, the Eiffel Tower in Paris, buildings in Vienna, Salzburg and a number of Italian cities. 'My sister, she lives in Germany,' Mike never gives up and tries another story.

The professional friend

While many street guides operate on their own, there is a trend towards the establishment of small, loosely structured groups of friends, controlling a hangout, handling the tourists, and sharing the profits. In this part I shall introduce two friends, Timo and Mustafa. Both have known each other for many years and both make a living exclusively from guiding tourists. Both work in the Malioboro area, but they do not work together. Timo is a loner, he runs his own one-man business and he operates in a way similar to a professional guide taking tourists on sight-seeing trips. Mustafa joined a group a few years ago. As a team this group approaches tourists to direct them straight to the batik shops. I shall now compare the strategies of both 'professional friends,' starting with Mustafa.

Mustafa is *Yogya asli* and his family lives in a *kampung* west of the city centre. His father is a day-labourer, his two younger brothers are still at school, and his sister is attending law school. She is the brightest of the children, Mustafa admits. He himself went to university after senior high school to study English, but he failed his first exams and dropped out. 'I am studying at the Taman Sari Academy,' he says challengingly. To earn some money he worked as a shop assistant in a batik gallery in the Taman Sari area. Tiring of this after a couple of months he decided to start his own business and move to Malioboro Street. Mustafa established co-operative relations with a number of shop owners in Malioboro Street and its back alleys. They agreed that he would bring foreign tourists to their shop and would receive a commission in return. A *guide liar* cannot work exclusively for one shop, as he never knows where exactly he will meet tourists. He needs a network of shops. The next thing Mustafa did was to look for business partners who would support his activities in the street. It took him two years to find reliable allies. He met them at the hangouts where he usually looked for tourists. These hangouts are monopolized by males working nearby and attracting 'friends.' The best hangouts – bus stations, post offices, restaurants, shops, discotheques, and other tourist spots – are controlled by young men who occupy a relatively powerful position in the world of street guides. In some places, power might come from being a member of a local family, in other places from being of Javanese origin. Being involved with a girl working as a shop assistant or being related to the security guard or parking lot attendant enhances one's chances of being tolerated on the doorstep.

Mustafa and his group do not depend on a permanent hangout, but are constantly on the move, patrolling their business area. 'It's like the difference between an angler and a fly-fisherman,' Mustafa explains. 'Many people are anglers, they wait for the fish to come to them, but we are into fly-fishing, we go out looking for our prey.' The four of them are out in the street working independently but not far from each other. When they spot foreign tourists they first screen them: only new tourists make interesting victims. New in town are those who carry a map, look for street names and other landmarks, and walk slowly or hesitantly. Others, like the anthropologist living in the area for months and strolling to the post office in a relaxed manner, are 'no-buy-targets.' The tourists who seem to represent an interesting business opportunity are addressed casually by one of the group members. 'Good morning, Mister,' he would say, in the afternoon to a tourist lady. 'I am not stupid,' says Mustafa, 'but pretending that I do not know the right words tempts tourists to correct me. And then the ice is broken, we have a conversation going.' Even if tourists get angry, there is some interaction. It's better than being ignored. To understand the tourists' needs, the street guide requires some information about their background: Where you from? Where you going? Where you been? Have you seen Kraton? How long you stay? Where you stay? Are you married? Have boy/girlfriend? Children? How many? Boys or girls? What's your profession? You like Yogya? You like puppets? Batik? Silver? This investigation produces the necessary information to classify the tourist: is he rich? Is he/she travelling alone or with group? Will he spend a lot of money on souvenirs? What kind of souvenirs? During this conversation Mustafa or his co-workers attempt to direct the tourists towards one of their associated shops. He gives advice: 'If you buy something real good, you have to go to Matahari batik gallery, they are not commercial, but real art, for good price. But you have to go now, they are open only until twelve in the morning.'

Mustafa knows that business has to be done quickly. The tourists spend only a few hours shopping, then they are off to the temples or to their next destination. Hesitant tourists are lost as prospective buyers because of the oversupply of shops in Yogyakarta. To accelerate the tourists' decision making, he will point out that he has no personal interest in their buying batik, and to stress this point he shows them the direction to the gallery but refrains from taking them there. He pretends to have other business to attend to and leaves them at this point. In the meantime they are followed by the other group members and upon the departure of Mustafa, a colleague takes over. He walks past the tourists who have only recently been left by Mustafa and starts the same kind of conversation, recommending exactly the same gallery as Mustafa did before. 'If they hear it from two completely independent sources, they start believing it,' says Mustafa. The next move is very sensitive and depends on a number of conditions. On a busy day when many other unlicensed guides are in the street, the second co-worker will stick with the tourists to take them to the gallery, as there is a chance of losing them to competitors. On a quiet day, they may let the tourists go to the gallery on their own only to be met by a third man at the door.

Within groups there is a loosely structured division of tasks. Success in the 'tourist hunt' is largely dependent on communicative abilities, outward appearance, and proficiency in foreign languages. Group members scoring high on these criteria usually take the initiative in approaching tourists. If they are successful, they receive the biggest share of the profit. If they fail, other group members try to step into the breach. While the tourist experiences a series of approaches by different young men, these men belong to the same group. If one of the group 'has a bite' the others follow him and his guest at a distance, observing which restaurants or shops are visited, what souvenirs are bought, and how much money is spent. After the tourists and their 'guide' have left, group members enter the shop, guesthouse or restaurant to collect the commission, which will be divided amongst them, even those who had no part in earning it that day. Mustafa comments: 'Sometimes, when you have a real good day making lots of money, it is really hard to share. Then you think about what you could do if all the money was yours. But then when you are broke, you are so happy that the others share with you.' It is not uncommon that street guides try to cheat on their group members, but if discovered they run the risk that their co-workers will turn to their competitors and take their contacts with shops and galleries with them. The smart and handsome guides break away from the group if they become successful, and start working for themselves, as we shall see below.

It is extremely difficult to establish good business relations with shops and galleries in Yogyakarta. The big batik and souvenir shops in Malioboro Street, with a few exceptions refuse to pay any commission. Their location in the busiest shopping street in town guarantees a constant flow of customers making the services of *guide liar* superfluous. Businesses in the streets and alleys behind Malioboro street and in the tourist *kampung* of Sosrowijayan and Prawirotaman depend on the guides' services as they are intractable for tourists and because there are many shops of the same kind competing for customers. The better the location, the lower the commission. Mustafa and his group serve one shop in Malioboro Street where they receive ten percent of the amount of money their customers spend. Other addresses in the *kampung* pay fifteen to twenty per cent. Additional money can be made if the shop owner complies with the strategy of overpricing. In that case they ask 300 per cent of the normal price. The tourist is granted a small bargaining margin, still leaving the shop owner with about 200 per cent profit, 30 to 40 per cent of which may disappear in Mustafa's pockets. This is risky business though. If the tourists find their purchase for less than half the price in another shop, they might complain to the Tourist Police; and the police may investigate this case and fine the shop keeper and the tout. Mustafa hastens to add that this would be quite exceptional, as in Yogyakarta the Tourist Police is reluctant to fine business people for overpricing. They have learned that it is much more attractive to share the profits. It has become the habit for policemen off-duty to join the groups of *guide liar* to make some additional money, says Mustafa.

Mustafa is involved exclusively in batik selling; in terms of local government officials, he is one of the batik guides against whom they fulminate. At the beginning of his 'career' he used to take tourists to all kinds of tourist objects as far away as Borobudur, Prambanan, Dieng, and Mount Bromo! However, he learned the hard way that this is not a good strategy to make a living from tourism. He often spent half a day or even a whole day with the tourists who, after the trip, would turn around and walk away, some without even saying thank you – leaving him with empty hands. As an unlicensed guide he has no right to demand any money from them. The most difficult part of being a street guide, Mustafa points out, is to control your emotions. When he started out he wanted to be liked and accepted by the tourists. He could not stand being ignored or even chased away. He wanted to make new friends and establish ongoing relations through an exchange of addresses and letter writing. Therefore, he preferred to approach tourists of his own age. The problem was that young people have no money and regard his efforts as an expression of the 'wonderful Javanese hospitality.' Mustafa had to learn a more business-like way of thinking about tourists, differentiating between his business interests and his emotions. His successful new strategy is to concentrate on middle-aged European couples, preferably Swiss, as they tend to spend generously. But unfortunately the Swiss form only a fraction of the tourists in Yogyakarta, so he goes mainly after the Dutch, French and

Italians. 'I don't waste time any more on young tourists, and certainly not on Americans and Australians; they don't buy, just talk.'

Mustafa's business-like approach to life in Malioboro Street also has an impact on his future. Only a few years ago his street guiding strategy was to chase after tourist women. He dreamt of a fantastic future in Europe, where he intended to go with a female tourist who would be madly in love with him. He plunged body and soul into all kinds of romantic adventures. He himself got seriously involved two or three times with young women from Europe, and was seriously hurt when they broke off the relationship 'just because their holiday was over,' Mustafa remarks bitterly. He had to accept that young women do not represent any future investment. Older women do have the money to support a young man like Mustafa, but they would not regard him as a serious partner. 'I look as if I am only sixteen. These women find me cute, for one or two nights, but they would not introduce me to their friends as their new boyfriend.'

A very different outlook on life as a 'professional friend' is characteristic of Timo (25). He comes from a village in North Sumatra. His parents were blessed with ten children. His father is a clergyman of the Protestant church, and Timo was brought up with strong Christian values. He still goes to church on Sundays and prays regularly. He does not smoke or drink and is modest in everything he does. He is a serious and ambitious young man who wants to succeed in life. This is why he left the village after finishing senior high school, as there was no future there for him. He went first to Jakarta to find a job and enrol in a university programme, but he could not survive in that city. In Yogyakarta he felt at home immediately, but he soon learned that jobs are hard to find and, after paying his rent and food, there is no money left to enrol in a programme at a university or vocational school. Timo turned to tourism to make a living. However, he is not a businessman like his friend Mustafa. Timo cannot differentiate between his personal feelings and his business. Not that he gets involved with female tourists. His Christian values do not allow him to be casual about love and sex; he even finds it difficult to talk about these things, but he wants the tourist to like and trust him. He cannot understand why people whom he addresses with a friendly and open mind, ignore or even scold him. He honestly wants to be their friend and help them to have a good time while in Yogyakarta. And if tourists are nice to him, expectations begin to grow in his heart. First, there is hope that they will give him a good tip, and he does everything in his power to coax them into a happy mood. Second, there is the anticipation that these tourists may become true friends who will come back to Yogyakarta and perhaps help him to pay for an education. It makes him depressed that friendship with tourists is hard to strike up. Other *guide liar* like to boast of their contacts abroad producing business cards from and address books filled with the names of foreigners whom they call their friends. These tokens are used strategically to establish contacts with new tourists in the street. Having many friends abroad makes street guides appear more trustworthy and knowledgeable and there seems to be a common point of reference with a guide who 'knows' the place where the tourist comes from. What the tourists do not know is that the *guide liar* mostly copy the addresses from the guestbooks at the art galleries.

Timo started his career as an unlicensed guide as a member of a group of six. What Timo and his friends did was basically guiding: they accompanied tourists on their sight-seeing trips. A visit to the shops was a welcome interlude, but not the only thing on their minds. To distinguish themselves from their competitors, they created a city walk, a guided tour, which they tried to sell to tourists, like travel agents sell trips to the tourist attractions. The group had a number of very enthusiastic customers – Timo shows me some letters of recommendation written by satisfied tourists – but the initiative failed. One reason for this failure were the restrictions on operating clandestinely. The six tried to promote their city walk with flyers which they hung on notice-boards in hotels and guesthouses, but these flyers disappeared: 'Removed by our competitors, the travel agents,' Timo said. Another reason for the failure was the attitude of some of his group members. Two of the six would share their income without contributing their fair portion of work. This caused tensions in the group and finally led to its break up. Ever since Timo has preferred to operate alone. His favourite target group are 'older' tourists, people of thirty years or more. He certainly appeals to this category of visitors with his neat outward appearance and good manners. His target group reacts favourably when Timo addresses them: 'You like Yogyakarta, don't you?' Older tourists take more time to get acquainted with the city and its people, listen well, are interesting to talk to, they like Timo and are willing to exchange addresses and sometimes send him postcards and even gifts from their home country. Unfortunately these people are hard to find as they are more likely to travel in a group. The young people who frequent the streets of Yogyakarta in abundance, are not kind to Timo. He finds them indifferent, disinterested, and arrogant. They carry their Lonely Planet travel guide book and want to find their way ('to the cheapest restaurant and the cheapest accommodation,' Timo remarks bitterly) on their own. They do not want to become friends and do not want to buy souvenirs either. Going after them is a waste of time.

In Mustafa's terms, Timo is an 'angler.' He has his regular hangout, the main post office, where he is sitting on a bench waiting for tourists who 'need his help' to show up. Timo is well acquainted with the security guards at the post office. They tolerate him and discuss new faces that show up at the office regularly with him. When the post office is closed, as on Sundays, Timo either visits the Kraton (many tourists attend the Sunday dances) or the hotspots in

Malioboro Street (a number of tourist cafes and the shopping mall). During high seasons Timo is able to meet enough tourists to conduct about three city walks per day, in the low-season about one or two per week. A walk takes about three hours. At the end of such a tour Timo suggests to visit a batik, silver, or puppet shop, but if his guests are not interested, he does not pressurise them. The same applies to his fee. Timo is too shy to charge them money. He hopes 'in his heart' that tourists will pay him. He does not fail to mention that he is jobless and has to make a living, but this is as far as he will go. Often his hopes are fulfilled and tourists give him a generous tip. In that case Timo is happy, the more so if the tourists have also done some shopping. This entitles him to a commission which he collects immediately after departing from his guests, but before leaving them he usually asks about their programme for the next day: perhaps he can take them to the temples or even Dieng Plateau. Discouragingly he can walk with them for hours, but they show no sign of souvenir buying or of interest in his life. Then he has no other choice but to walk away.

Timo's guided tours presuppose current knowledge of the local tourist objects. After all, he has to fill three hours with explanations, stories, and entertainment. Timo is well-prepared for this job. When he arrived in Yogyakarta five years ago, his first tactic was picking the brains of other guides, licensed as well as unlicensed. He went to the sultan's palace to listen to the Kraton guides talking about the history and architecture of that place and the royal family. He learned about the significance of the items exhibited there. Most importantly, he studied how the guides presented their stories and dealt with the tourists. Comparing different guides, he soon found out which were the good techniques to copy. He travelled to Borobudur and Prambanan and observed the guides on the spot. He asked tourists to leave him their used travel guide books and he studied the explanations about the tourist places. And finally, he acquired a basic knowledge of the most important tourist languages. Whereas Mustafa speaks only English, besides Timo has an amazing proficiency in German and Italian, and he knows enough French, Dutch, and Japanese to make contact with tourists. '*Goedemorgen, hoe gaat het met u? Alles goed?*'[6] were his words in immaculate Dutch with which he addressed me when I first met him at the post office. Timo learns the languages from guide books which he reads in the original language, and then practices his newly-acquired knowledge in the streets. Therefore, his language proficiency appears almost perfect as long as the conversation revolves around the topics that are elaborated on in the guide books. The crunch comes if other themes are brought up and the conversation stagnates. this does not matter much as in everyday tourist encounters there is little room for in-depth conversations. Timo determines where to go and what to talk about. He stages a perfect performance. Usually he takes tourists to the Kraton in the morning.

He enters with his guests and conducts the guiding, transgressing the rules of the palace, but the Kraton guides let him proceed: 'He brings guests, he does not chase them away,' *Ibu* Minah, one of the guides, comments. Upon leaving the palace, Timo likes to take his visitors on a walk through a *kampung*, preferably the *Kauman kampung*, a traditional Muslim neighbourhood, and then to the birdmarket and Taman Sari. If there is more time, he will go by public bus or taxi (depending on his guests) to the housing project by the Code river, where Yogyanese homeless people established their own homes and organized a neighbourhood on the riverflat. On their way back to the city centre, he and his guests may come across a cockfight in a *kampung*, and they may pay a brief visit to a *dukun* to attend to a minor ailment of one of the tourists. Timo's approach to Yogyakarta is a genuine one, unequalled by the 'streetside' travel agents. During these walks, the factual information that Timo conveys is limited. He points out objects of interests and reproduces some of the material presented by the tourist guide books that he has studied. However, he succeeds in setting the stage for a unique experience: first, because he combines visits to the tourist highlights with a look behind 'backstages': a *kampung*, a local market, a squatter area, even his own humble home; second, because he has mastered the art of storytelling. Buildings and artefacts become alive in Timo's stories. He tells tourists about local people attending sermons at the mosque and then enters a mosque demonstrating how the prayers are performed. He leads them to a Chinese temple and cajoles the attendant into throwing the tourist's 'lucky number' and predicting their future. He makes them taste local fruit and spices at the market. He explains the names of plants and trees, demonstrates the use of equipment and the production of food stuffs. These encounters are not staged for the tourist, but made accessible by Timo who maintains a wide network and is popular with many local people.

Timo does not intend to remain an unlicensed guide for the rest of his life. He wants to continue his education and to enter a respectable profession. He is not sure about which profession, but he would like to study languages and literature. 'And perhaps become a licensed guide,' I suggested. Timo has considered acquiring the government licence and entering 'streetside' tourism. He has carefully weighed up the pros and cons of this option. Becoming a formal guide undoubtedly implies more status and the remuneration of belonging to a professional community and, with a large network, a guaranteed reasonable income. With his fluency in German and Italian he would easily find travel agents willing to employ him regularly. There is a reason he is reluctant about taking the plunge. Timo has experienced some discouraging encounters with officials of the *Diparda*, where he went to inquire about the requirements for obtaining a licence. They were not only chary about coming forward with this information (making him come back several times), but also made it clear that he – not being *Yogya-asli* – would have to make more effort to be accepted for the obligatory *Diparda* guiding course. In other words, they expected Timo to pay them a bribe. Timo: 'They make up their own rules telling me that as being born in Sumatra, I cannot become a guide in Yogyakarta. The course and the licence cost 250,000 *rupiah*, however, to be admitted, I would have to pay 300,000.' Besides the bureaucratic perils, Timo is struggling with the 'loss of freedom' that working in the 'streetside' tourism sector entails. Like many of his friends in the same position, Timo perceives any obligation, such as a steady job or a marriage that ties them down – as a loss of freedom. As he is wont to say: he wants to be free like a bird in the sky, not captive like a fish in a pond. Like so many of his friends, he hopes for a windfall, an exceptional business opportunity or a generous tourist who is willing to 'adopt' him and pay for his education. He contends that a few of his friends were lucky enough to be supported by a tourist for some time. Timo alludes to the so-called *orang tua angkat* (adopted parents) phenomenon. It happens that after a pleasant stay to which the local guide has contributed significantly, tourists express the desire to stay in touch with their new friend. Older couples without children of their own sometimes decide to 'adopt' a local guide. They send him letters and presents, support his family, pay for his studies, and sometimes even invite him to their home country. Although some tourists regard this as an act of charity or private aid, often they expect some favours in return, like taking care of their business interests in Indonesia, attending to private property they purchased in Yogyakarta, or sexual services. Timo has thought about the option that many of his friends are after, acquiring the money he needs through an intimate relationship with a female tourist. He finds this acceptable only if 'true love' and an 'exclusive and permanent' relationship evolved with a female tourist, but he is not ready to get married yet.

The romantic entrepreneurs
One of the most important motives for young men to operate as street guides, an aspect that adds glamour to this 'profession,' is the ever-present chance of entering into a sexual relationship with a tourist. Offering sexual services is an important ingredient of the street guide-tourist relationship, and all categories of street guides as described above are willing to take a chance with a female tourist. Regarding the strict cultural codes for the public behaviour of women – Indonesia is a Muslim country after all – females offering their services as guides or friends are immediately associated with prostitutes. Only a small number of the street guides are females, and some of the women working as street guides actually are prostitutes. Others operate as an unlicensed guide for a brief period of time. Their backgrounds are different but their objectives are identical, to meet a foreign man and marry him.[7]

As far as the male guides are concerned, offering sexual services to female travellers is quite common. It is not surprising that one of the first questions addressed to a female tourist is: 'Are you married? Have boyfriend?' A negative answer almost immediately encourages the young man to make romantic overtures. These overtures may consist of soliciting openly and directly. It is mostly in cafes, restaurants, and hotel lounges that the first romantic overtures are made. Waiters, receptionists, bellboys, and other hotel personnel – occasional touts – are actually in the best position to approach female tourists, and they do take advantage of this privileged position. However, many street guides – odd jobbers and professional 'friends' – hang around in these places, cultivating friendly relations with the personnel to share their access to the constant flow of newly arrived tourists. Introducing oneself as a guide, a promise of a ride on the motorbike or a trip to a remote beach (like Parangtritis) have proved to be successful strategies for coming into contact with the ladies. In Yogyakarta, where tourists stay for only one or two nights, street guides have to be fairly explicit about their intentions. Telling lies about their activities, their names, and marital status is part of their tactics to secure the attention and lasting interest of the female tourists. Many beach boys and street guides like to adopt popular English names and prefer pseudonyms that sound more familiar to the tourists' ear. To establish even more familiarity, they show business cards or letters they have received from tourists originating from the same country as the woman they are approaching. They usually claim to have many friends in her country to make her feel more comfortable. Others introduce themselves as local (village) boys who never have left Yogyakarta and who never had an affair with a Western woman before. Some women are totally taken in by this 'authentic' image.

When a street guide in Yogyakarta is becoming friendly with a female tourist, he will take her to 'romantic' places, like Taman Sari, to tell stories about the virility of previous sultans and to praise the virility of Yogyakarta men in general. He will try to take her to the tombs of Imogiri or to Parangtritis beach: both well-known but quiet attractions, as they are situated away from the main tourist routes, allowing for a romantic interlude.[8] As Mustafa recalls:

> My most beautiful experience with a woman happened when I met this Italian girl. Her name was Carmen. If I think of her, I see her body, as beautiful as a Spanish guitar. She had white skin and her hands and legs were covered with soft hair. We went to Parangtritis and on the beach we made love like husband and wife.

If such a romantic interlude leads to a relationship, the street guide might leave his various jobs for a while, make travel arrangements for the remaining days or weeks the tourist will spend in Indonesia and accompany her on her trip. The tourist is supposed to pay for all his expenses.

Although the relationship emerging from these arrangements is generally of a transitory and instrumental nature, it can acquire more than purely financial characteristics. The relationship can become intense, as tourists can become an entry to the good life for the guide. Tourists give gifts of both money and kind to their young friends, and take them along on excursions, visits to night clubs, and other leisure activities. It is understandable that the chances of acquiring money and gifts, of having a good time, and, for the very lucky ones, a free ticket and an invitation to stay in Europe, America, Australia, or Japan are an enormous attraction. But because it is never certain whether a relationship will turn out that way, guides tend to spread the risk of an eventual break-up by being engaged in several relationships at the same time which can lead to complicated situations whenever those female 'true loves' plan their holidays in the same period (cf. Cohen 1986). The guides tell their prospective partners that, unlike all the other boys, they were after a one and only 'true love.' Though the boys prefer girls of their own age, they do understand that older women often find themselves in a more secure economic position with better purchasing power which makes them highly attractive as sexual partners promising a ticket to a better life in the West. Female tourists in their thirties, forties and older find themselves 'courted' by boys in their teens and early twenties. 'I do prefer older women,' one of my informants (24) used to say, 'they are more mature and patient, they understand how my heart feels.' It is not that he prefers older women, but they usually have more money than young ones who are still at school or college.

There is one desire that all of them are cherishing, the desire to acquire a ticket to one of the 'promised lands' where their ever-changing 'true loves' come from. A wealth of time is invested in that one love that promises to take them on a trip to her homeland. This is basically the guides' goal. Meeting female tourists travelling individually they do not beat about the bush: they offer their services as lover, servant, housekeeper, cook, and they want to fulfil these tasks without any payment, just for board and lodging in the tourist's home country. Some street guides succeed in being invited to follow their tourist friends to their home country. However, for many, life in the West turns out to be disappointing. Ill-informed they expect to lead a prosperous and leisurely life, they soon find that working-life is exhausting and boring, jobs are hard to find, and lifestyles are different. Their relationship breaks up and they become incurably homesick. Provided with some savings, they finally return to Yogyakarta, to play the big spender for a short while, buying drinks all round and throwing parties. When all the money is spent, they are back on the street again. Isman (26), a Taman Sari guide, got involved with a girl from Austria. When she got pregnant, both decided to live together in Yogyakarta. But they split up as Isman would not give up his life socializing with his friends, using drugs, and spending the girl's money. She left for Austria and took their little boy with her. Isman could not live with this separation. He went to Austria to start a new life with his family there. Uprooted he felt isolated, lacking friends and money. He took money from his girlfriend and hiked through Europe. He returned to his girlfriend broke and remorseful. Then as his visa had expired, the police put him on a plane back to Jakarta. Isman is back in Taman Sari. He is sad that he failed as a father and drowns his pain in rice wine. All the street guides who have gone through that kind of disillusioning experience in the 'promised land' regard their return as a failure. They keep yearning for a better life in the West and advise their friends to seize their chances whenever they arise, be smarter, and become a successful businessman abroad. Street guides who are growing older without being able to realize their dream, change their tune. They begin dreaming of accumulating enough money to start their own enterprise: a shop, cafe, restaurant, *losmen*, boutique, or *atelier* to become a 'boss' in the backpacker area of the city, preferably through marrying a 'rich' tourist. The few examples of mixed couples (consisting of a former *guide liar* and a female tourist) who successfully run a guesthouse or restaurant in Sosrowijayan or Prawirotaman have an enormous impact on the future goals of the young males.

Street guides spend part of their income on maintaining their social network. Those operating in groups are in particular obliged to share windfalls with their friends from the street and the tourism industry. At night, the pubs in Pasar Kembang, Sosrowijayan, and Prawirotaman are crowded with the 'wild' guides, drinking beer, smoking *ganja* and flirting with female tourists. Their lifestyle is an imitation, not of Western tourists but of the *Kuta cowboys*, the infamous Balinese beachboys, who set the fashion in the world of guides. Many street guides in Yogya boast of having visited Kuta in Bali to see both the 'bare breasts' on the beach as well as the Kuta beachboys. Young men inspired by their Bali counterparts aspire to a career as a musician in a local (reggae-)band.

'Ask a local in a third world tourist destination [what tourism means to them], and they may well tell you that it's about selling: selling their environment, their culture and their services to the guest,' comments an Australian journalist on this subculture of male youth in Bali – the so-called 'bad boys,' 'Kuta cowboys,' 'gigolos' (by other people), or 'guides' (their own term), 'whose peripheral yet lasting flirtation with the West has left them with a taste for drugs, alcohol, and one night/one month relationships with tourist girls. ... Maybe a life of shallow, temporary relationships, on the fringes of the tourists' largesse is better than the alternatives (Wolf 1993).

These alternatives entail leading the life of a rice-cultivating peasant, a factory worker, and the head of a large family in a situation of dire poverty. One may argue that this condition characterizes what sociologists have defined in terms of prostitution: emotionally neutral, indiscriminate, specifically remunerated sexual services. As Cohen (1971, 1982, 1986, 1993) and Crick (1992) have observed in various cultural contexts, the concept of prostitution does not adequately convey the meaning of the relationships emerging from sexual encounters between tourists and locals as described here. The term *gigolo* – male prostitute – is not quite a literal one here. These boys are not paid for their services as such, but relationships with tourists entail an improved degree of financial security. Perhaps prostitution is not the right concept to characterize these relationships, but love is not the right concept either. It is true that the young man underplays the commercial side of the relationship from the beginning, feigns affection, changes his identity and, if necessary hides other emotional or even marital obligations. The street guides' flirtations have to be understood as their being risk-taking small-scale entrepreneurs who have to seize their opportunity under pressing limits of time. Tourists visiting Yogyakarta usually stay in town for too short a period of time to 'develop' a relationship. Within this short span of time the young men strive to benefit as much as possible from this relationship and as long as it remains beneficial, they are willing to continue for weeks, months and perhaps even years. But when the profit drops, they break off the relationship easily and enter into another one without hesitation when the opportunity arises. Usually they keep a number of relationships going simultaneously taking great pains to keep them concealed from each other, but boasting about it among friends. Street guides act like Geertz' *pasar* traders even when it comes to amorous relationships. They are also entrepreneurs in romance which is among the myriad economic strategies, albeit a rather exciting one, to make a living.

CONCLUSION

The unlicensed guides of Yogyakarta constitute a prominent feature of the city's streetlife. As brokers they benefit from relationships of patronage with business people who depend on the unlicensed guides to provide a constant stream of customers. Despite these ties, their position is insecure, their income is irregular, mostly commission-based and dependent on tips and gifts received from their tourist friends. They have to spend some of their money on the tourist lifestyle in which they must to some extent participate and some of it has to go to their peer group in an effort to live up to their role models, the Kuta cowboys, which have proved to be the most successful presentation of self in the field of romancing the tourist. Having money entails the obligation to share it, to spend it on parties, drinks, and drugs with other guides. Generally, unlicensed guides do not save money and they do not invest in any long-term scheme to improve their situation permanently. They perceive any obligation, such as a steady job or a marriage that ties them down as a loss of freedom. As one informant used to say: they want to be free like birds in the sky, not captive like fish in a pond (Dahles 1998a). The street guides rely mostly on their contacts within their own peer group or operate independently.

Their *pasar*-style of entrepreneurship represents both a reservoir of hidden unemployment and an overt innovative and enterprising forces. It absorbs a labour force that would otherwise be unemployed, but also constitutes a vital force in the Yogyanese tourism sector. In contrast to the image held by actors in 'streetside' tourism and among government officials, unlicensed guides operate neither in the margin of the tourism industry nor of the centralized state bureaucracy. They form an integral part of this industry. The competition generated by the entrepreneurial activities of unlicensed guides is under-estimated by the 'streetside' tourism industry. They do not operate in a world of their own, segregated from the 'streetside.' Very much in the picture, the *guide liar* compete for the attention of the very category of tourists that is classified as the target group of the government-controlled 'quality' tourist, i.e. the middle-aged and middle-class visitor. The more this tourist category relinquishes package tours and turns to individual travel, the more its members come within reach of the unlicensed guides. Therefore, *guide liar* cannot be categorized as representatives of a traditional, informal economy, set in contrast to the modern, formal, capitalist sector. They participate in both economies. As brokers they mediate between both types of economy for economic benefit. Unlicensed guides are supreme examples of network artists (Dahles 1996). They depend heavily on loosely structured relationships with a vast variety of people in the local economy and beyond, based on personal friendships, family relations, ethnic ties, and religious bonds. These networks constitute more meaningful units than formal organizations and state-controlled associations – which are not accessible to *guide liar*. Unlicensed guides are enterprising, inventive, and creative in the exploitation of new niches in the market. As *pasar*-traders they are extremely flexible in turning changing consumer preferences to their advantage. They benefit from the disorientation and ingenuousness of the unorganized tourists, their need to find a place to sleep and to experience 'authentic' local life in a *kampung* or one or the other. As 'pathfinders' they are innovative daring to take risks in the exploitation of means of orientation. They explore all kinds of approaches and techniques to extract money from tourists. Once a strategy has been proven successful, everyone is keen to share in the success and imitates it. This is the principle of *ikut-ikutan* (imitation), which is well established in all sectors of the Indonesian economy. Therefore, tourists encounter only limited variation in address and approach by unlicensed guides, as these guides act within certain parameters defined by the entrepreneurial culture on which they depend.

In the field of the government policy, no measures should be expected to improve the position of the unlicensed guides. Local authorities in Yogyakarta exhibit ambivalent attitudes and policies towards this category. In contrast to what is happening elsewhere in Indonesia where increasing government intervention forces self-employed people into formal organizations, the local authorities in Yogyakarta exclude unlicensed guides from their efforts to formalize the local economy. If an unlicensed guide attempts to obtain a licence, he meets with discouragement, including the necessity to bribe the officials. As a consequence, unlicensed guides are rather suspicious of government measures. Training programmes and a more liberal licensing system to become a formal tourist guide will not appeal to them immediately as they suspect the government of trying to exert just another form of control by means of such measures. Moreover, their idea of 'being free as a bird' inclines them towards looking for 'a ticket to a better life' instead of making efforts to establish themselves in 'streetside' tourism. The evidence presented in this chapter seems to confirm that unlicensed guides either figure as convenient scapegoats for things that go wrong in the urban tourism sector or as a source of additional income as officials press them to share part of their revenues to secure their working area.

The Yogyanese authorities do not make any efforts to upgrade and professionalize, and thus control, unlicensed guides as happens in other Indonesian provinces like South Sulawesi (Adams 1997) and Lombok (Stam & Ter Steege 1997). They seem simply content to define them as a danger to tourism development in particular and public order in general. Local government officials and people in the 'streetside' tourism industry regard *guide liar* as criminals. The case studies presented above seem to support this view. Cheating tourists (through overpricing) and pressurizing shop owners (claiming commissions) are an integral part of their business strategies. These strategies, not the guiding of tourists, are essentially the unlicensed guides' mode of making a living from tourism. Quite apart from this, *guide liar* are occasionally involved in drug dealing, pimping, and illegal lotteries. And the outward appearance and behaviour of some of them – which is not necessarily 'criminal' but 'indecent' in terms of cultural norms and values – undoubtedly contributes to their bad reputation. Modelling themselves on the Kuta Cowboys, some wear their hair long and dress in 'hippie clothes' or walk about 'half naked,' they smoke *ganja*, drink beer and rice wine, and frequent 'sinful' places like bars and discos.

While illegal dealings and 'indecent' behaviour are not the exclusive domain of unlicensed guides, these are part of a whole range of activities that undermine the image of the 'decent nation,' as Indonesia was constructed by the New Order government (cf. Chapter 2). Unlicensed guides position themselves outside the system that reinforces this image. By no stretch of the imagination could it be said that they constitute any force of political significance. On the contrary, their mode of operation being highly individualized and clandestine, they cannot possibly be suspected of any organized or planned subversive activities. They even refrain from making political jokes. Intent on maximizing their economic opportunities, unlicensed guides shy away from controversial subjects like politics and religion, as their foremost aim is to please the tourists. Uttering a political opinion entails the risk of offending or putting off potential customers. Their whole attitude is utterly pragmatic. They obtain the knowledge and skills required to deal with tourists 'in the street' by the imitation of other unlicensed guides and from books that are left behind by tourists. They learn their vocabulary and practise their language proficiency 'on the job.'

In contrast to the curriculum of the government and the tourism school's guiding courses designed for the education of formal guides, the activities of *guide liar* unfold uncontrolled by the authorities and go unscreened for their *pancasila* content. This withdrawal from state control does not imply that the life of unlicensed guides is anarchic, a charge government officials level against them when they declare them a threat to public order. As has been shown, the public space that serves as the working area for unlicensed guides is closely guarded by the guides themselves, as they jealously watch over their business opportunities. Those who share such an area – security guards, parking assistants and shop assistants – are intimately familiar with each other. A new face is immediately identified and the whereabouts of this person are examined. New individuals are not easily accepted at a hangout; they need an introduction from a regular 'member' of this loosely structured web of stakeholders. This close social control of the public space in Yogyakarta enhances overall security rather than threatens it. And this security extends to tourists, as nobody wants tourists robbed or molested at his hangout; incidents are detrimental to business.

Here a paradox emerges. It seems that public space in the Yogyakarta tourism system which remains largely uncontrolled by the government is safer and better guarded and organized than the enclosed and regulated tourist spaces that fall under the auspices of the state authorities. Local people force entry into the enclosed tourist sites. Fences are either physically violated or strategically surpassed. Personal networks extend beyond artificial boundaries as the ties of friendship, family, and ethnicity that link actors in 'streetside' and *kampung* tourism are stronger than government-imposed regulations. Unlicensed guides in particular are not under any obligation to make themselves subservient to these regulations. They remain largely beyond the control of the authorities. *Guide liar* manage to enter the 'controlled' tourist spaces of the Kraton and the temple complexes. Their networks extent beyond the public space of Yogyakarta's inner city and into the protected areas managed by the *P.T. Taman Wisata*. For *guide liar* Borobudur is a 'very old temple' that carries the promise of a good tip and the Kraton is the 'place where the king lives' and where a reasonable commission can be earned on batik sales. The measures designed to clear these areas of the presence of *guide liar* obviously fail. While the *P.T. Taman Wisata* pretends to control tourism through a regulated 'guiding system,' the premises of Borobudur and Prambanan swarm with unlicensed guides receiving the tourists brought by their friends from outside. They succeed because those people who represent the government and are paid for enforcing state regulations on these premises are willing to turn a blind eye if remunerated accordingly. In other words, the unlicensed guides not only withdraw from government control, they even challenge it by showing up its failures. Paradoxically, private entrepreneurial interests in 'contested' public space generate 'informal' social control that is more effective than state-orchestrated regulations in 'enclosed' areas. The latter seems to arouse the urge to indulge in subversive activities among the local people, making the 'enclosed' areas as contested as public space.

Characteristic of the narratives of *guide liar* is the lack of a *pancasila* content. As has been shown, unlicensed guides are excellent storytellers, but the stories they tell are largely devoid of historical and cultural, let alone political and ideological, 'correctness.' Unlicensed guides reproduce and invent stories to please the tourists, to consolidate the relationship with their potential clients, and to extract money from them. As a consequence, a myriad of partly converging and partly conflicting narratives of Yogyakarta emerge, coloured by the unlicensed guide's personal definition of the situation. These guides do not reproduce the *pancasila*-proof narrative of Yogyakarta as the heart of central Java, with its polished objects of national pride and friendly population proud of Javanese tradition. Instead, the unlicensed guides' narratives convey the image of Yogyakarta as a city of migrants from all over Indonesia, struggling to make a living under harsh conditions and enjoying themselves while engaging in partly illicit trade and leisure activities. Whereas the '*pancasila*-ized' narratives present Yogyakarta as a homogeneous Javanese community, a city walk with unlicensed guides shows that this place accommodates many different cultures and religious beliefs that may not fit the *pancasila* ideology. Many of the migrants who live in *kampung* came to Yogyakarta to try to escape sheer poverty and still live on the margins of poverty. Often the story of the guides' personal lives, a story that is shaped and reshaped to arouse the tourists' pity, adds to this image, as does a visit to the housing project of the riverflat people. The presence of the homeless and the poor in the inner city is not even noticed by these tourists whose stay is organized by the 'streetside' tourism industry. The efforts to stage prosperity, Javanese serenity and harmony so prominent in the state-orchestrated narratives are destroyed by the unlicensed guides' intervention.

One threat to *pancasila* tourism emanates not only from the uncontrolled narratives by unlicensed guides, but also from the contested spaces to which these young males take the tourists. Often, they end up in *kampung* where foreigners are not supposed to go. *Guide liar* make the so-called 'backstages' that tourists are so keen to visit accessible. As Dean MacCannell suggests in his much-quoted book 'The Tourist' (1976), tourists seek to encounter the 'real' life of the people they visit, pursuing 'authentic' experiences that reveal, even allow the sharing of, some aspects of the daily life of the host community. MacCannell used the term 'backstage' to describe the physical setting that allows tourists to have such an 'authentic' experience. State-controlled 'quality' tourism denies tourists access to backstages. Instead such backstages are constructed in a contrived and artificial manner by the tourism authorities to meet the requirements of *pancasila* tourism. In Yogyakarta tourist spaces are organized around what MacCannell terms 'staged authenticity' (1973). Performances of the Ramayana ballet, English-language puppet shows, and Javanese dance and gamelan music in tourist theatres feature among such staged events. Formal tourist guides, trained by the government in politically and ideologically correct narratives and demeanour, play a pivotal role in staging backstages. They verbally construct tourist attractions and maintain the carefully established boundary between tourist space and local community. The formal guides act as buffers between tourists and the social environment. They reduce the opportunity for interaction between tourists and locals. As Holloway (1981) observes, on a guided tour the tourists' attention is directed inward towards the guide rather than outward towards the setting. The tourists not only view and interpret local sites through the words of the tour guides, they are made to experience the environment according to the way in which the guides construct and represent it. Licensed guides in New Order Indonesia were not supposed to facilitate access to back regions at all. Instead they were instructed to control the front regions properly and direct tourists to staged backstages. After all, tourism planning under the New Order was about concentrating tourists in certain areas or resorts made specially available to them and to demarcate their frivolous holiday behaviour from the everyday life of Indonesian people 'unaffected' by tourism.

Although unlicensed guides constitute an integral part of the modern tourism economy, their activities threaten the image of Indonesia as a modern developing nation, at least in the eyes of the government. Associating unlicensed guides with the traditional, informal economy, as a token of backwardness they seem to be solid living evidence of the imperfections of the New Order's policy of *pembangunan*. According to conventional wisdom, the informal sector is the negation of economic growth and prosperity, an indication that the bureaucracy is unable to control the market. Although the Indonesian economy is largely dependent on the so-called informal sector for jobs and incomes for its masses of underemployed and unemployed, it is unacceptable for the government to admit this weakness in the presence of an international audience of visitors. These visitors are supposed to take home with them the bright and shiny image of a prosperous modern nation. To make matters worse, *guide liar* act as vehicle for access to the 'ugly backstages' of this nation characterized by poverty, lack of infrastructure, unemployment, prostitution and drug abuse, and ethnic and religious conflict, a backstage that should be hidden from the eyes of the international visitors' eye.

A final aspect that explains why unlicensed guides are a thorn in the flesh of the Indonesian government is their celebration of Western consumer culture. Most of these young men adore the way young people from Western countries dress and style themselves, and they eagerly copy them. Therefore, they desire blue jeans, leather jackets, designer t-shirts, 'cool' sunglasses, Nikes, walkmans, and ghetto blasters. With these consumer goods goes the long hair, the preference for fast food, a taste for alcohol and even drugs, and for promiscuous relationships. Politicians and religious leaders fulminate against Western 'consumerism' and the forsaking of 'Indonesian' products and values in the media and in public appearances. Those Indonesians who are exposed to tourism in particular are supposed to radiate their love of and commitment to Indonesian culture towards foreign visitors. More specifically, Yogyanese people are supposed to behave as worthy representatives of the most prominent 'peak culture' of Indonesia, Javanese culture. Untrammeled by such scruples licensed guides, however, act neither as dignified Javanese nor as patriotic Indonesians. The reverse is true. For the young males who are attracted to Western consumer culture, tourists enact the dream of Western consumerism. As Yogyakarta is having to cede its position as the second tourism area in Indonesia, but at the same time is ever more dependent on tourism, it may well be that the future prospects of small entrepreneurs in tourism are gloomy. Therefore it is not surprising that in Yogyakarta young men are preoccupied with the desire to get away and to establish a better life in a Western consumer paradise. Their quest for the female tourist or for generous, adoptive Western parents to be used as vehicles for realizing this dream makes painfully clear that their greatest desire is to leave the country for a better future in the West. These young entrepreneurs voting with their feet are not a good promotion for Indonesia.

NOTES

1   In the back alleys of the tourist *kampung*, groups of young men have established batik galleries selling the typical mass-produced pieces available in the less expensive shops all over town. However, the paintings in these galleries are generally overpriced, and touts are employed to attract inexperienced tourists who are eager to obtain an 'authentic piece of art.' These are the terms under which the merchandise of the galleries is promoted by the touts that hang around the places frequented by tourists in Malioboro Street and the Kraton area. They usually approach tourists spinning the yarn that there is a unique exhibition by young artists from the famous Yogyanese arts academy (many tourists have read about this academy in their guide books); but unfortunately this exibition will close this afternoon to be moved to Jakarta; there is a last chance to have a look (no buy, no problem) at this unique work. This strategy works quite well; many tourists are willing to take a look. At the 'gallery' (often a badly-lit room in a *kampung* shack), the tourists find themselves engaged in bargaining for one of the common batik paintings by a group of young men who turn out to be street guides instead of artists. They refuse to take 'no' for an answer and many tourists end up paying too much money for an inferior batik painting just to get away unharmed.

2   Since the first Five Year Development Plan (*Repelita* I), starting in 1969, the Indonesian government has given high priority to small industries in particular and small enterprises in general. During *Repelita* V (1979-84), the Directorate General of Small Industries was created within the Ministry of Industry and billions of dollars have been made available to develop household and cottage industries (employing up to five persons) and small industries (employing six – nineteen persons) (Suhartono 1988:51). The micro and small-scale service sector with less than five employees, however, does not fall under this agency and as a consequence does not benefit from the funding schemes.

3   There is no evidence that abuse by local entrepreneurs has ever caused tourism decline in a specific area. Indonesian authorities claim that temporarily decreasing visitor numbers from Australia in Bali in the mid-1990s were related to the misbehaviour of street and beach vendors (cf. Bras & Dahles 1998).

4   In this section some random examples from my fieldnotes are presented. The encounters described took place during several fieldwork periods extending over three years.

5   For a detailed description and analysis of the activities of pedicab men in Yogyakarta's tourism areas please refer to Van Gemert & Van Genugten (1996); Van Gemert, Van Genugten & Dahles (1999).

6   Translation: 'Good morning, how are you? Is everything okay?'

7   For example Ana (22), former student of Akademi Pariwisata Indonesia. She dropped out, operated as an unlicensed guide in the Prawirotamen area, met an Australian man, got married and lives alternately in Indonesia and Australia. Or Tuti (22), from a village south of Yogyakarta. She used to accompany small groups of backpackers as far as Bali and Sumatra. On one of these trips she met a Dutch policeman, they got married and she lives in The Netherlands. Nani (28), an English teacher, has been less fortunate. She has been looking for a foreign man to marry for many years. In addition to her job at a junior high school, she lectures in Indonesian at a language school for foreigners and she occasionally works as an unlicensed guide. After a number of disappointing love affairs she is on the verge of losing faith. But every time she starts a new class with foreign students, her hopes are high. Finally, Irma (23), who is still at university. She studies management and occasionally shares a hangout with a group of unlicensed guides. She had a relationship with one of her group members, but they broke up when it became clear that she was carrying on a correspondence with a Swiss man whom she met during his vacation in Yogyakarta. The last thing I heard of her was that this man sent her a ticket and that she was about to leave for Switzerland.

8   Schlehe (1999) points out that Parangtritis beach is a site where locals meet for religious and recreational purposes. The emergence of beach tourism bringing foreign tourists to this beach has contributed to its attraction to locals as watching and romancing the tourists has become an exciting leisure activity.

CHAPTER 7

LOCAL IDENTITY AND NATIONAL CULTURE

CONCLUSIONS

Post-developmentalists insist that modernization strips people and countries of their human and historical places. It makes them homogenized and stereotyped. However, many countries in Southeast Asia that have enthusiastically subscribed to the modernization ethos, have either successfully avoided, and in some cases actively challenged, the assumption that development should also embody homogenization according to Western models (Rigg 1997:45). In Chapter 1 we have dwelled at length on strategies of diversity management in various Asian countries which advocate their own way to modernization. The policies of China and Singapore towards their ethnic groups allow for narrow margins of expression of cultural differences under strict state control. These policies of cultural diversity resemble in many ways the approach applied by Indonesia under the New Order. To obtain a better understanding of the ways in which the New Order government attempted to accomplish both economic development and national unity against the background of the potential threat of ethnic upheaval and secession movements emanating from its much celebrated cultural diversity, this book offers an analysis of the dynamics of cultural tourism development under the New Order regime. The politics and policies of tourism represent an arena in which conflicting interests and diverging agendas regarding 'culture' compete with each other. The concept of cultural tourism clearly dominates the New Order's discourse on tourism development in Indonesia. Other forms of tourism (nature-based ecotourism, marine tourism, adventure tourism, etc.) are developed to diversify culture-based tourism to attract new 'market segments' and to enhance the visitors' length of stay, but they remain additions to the 'core-product,' culture.

The marketing terminology employed in the New Order vernacular describing culture in terms of 'product' and people in terms of 'market segments' and 'consumers' reveals what tourism is basically about: making money. In the Indonesian economy the state and its bureaucrats are key players. The accumulation of investment capital within Indonesia has, until recently, been derived from oil taxes and foreign loans channelled into the country (and the elite's pockets) through the state. Consequently, the state managers and those who politically control the terminals of economic decision making had the power to allocate these resources and determine priorities. Middle-class and domestic capitalists have continued to be dependent upon the state as the engine of employment and investment (Robison 1997:82). When tourism was propelled to compensate for lost oil revenues, this sector – especially the Jakarta-controlled 'quality' tourism – was employed to provide the bureaucratic elite with an instrument to channel foreign investment capital into the country. Therefore, the foreign revenue-generating 'quality' tourism was developed under strict government control.

The unaccountable nature of the bureaucracy's authority in economic matters has been legitimized in the *pancasila* state ideology which stresses the organic nature of society and the role of officials as pursuing the 'common good' and the 'national interest' over and above the forces of particularist vested interest. Nevertheless, the state's absolute monopoly of political and economic power and of the authority of bureaucrats has been eroded during the last decades. This process of erosion has accelerated since the fall of oil prices in the 1980s and the resulting increased reliance on private sector investment. Combined with the need to raise non-oil revenues and establish non-oil foreign earnings is the more recent pressure to become internationally competitive and more integrated into the international economy. Deregulation of the financial sector has facilitated a dramatic growth of private sector activities during the last decade (Robison 1997:83).

Governments and industries all over the world legitimate the development of tourism in terms of the revenues and employment opportunities that emanate from this sector. In many countries tourism policy and planning ranges under the ministries of economic affairs, which most clearly testifies to the role that it is expected to play. In New Order Indonesia, tourism was first under the ministry for transportation as the logistic problems that large flows of visitors posed for a still underdeveloped country with a lack of infrastructure were first to be solved. However, in the 1980s when a political reshuffling of the national bodies of decision making took place, tourism was accommodated by a new ministry, the Ministry of Tourism, Post and Telecommunications. This affilia-tion gives a clue about the goals and ambitions that the New Order government invested in tourism. Tourism became a vehicle for modernization and for the connection of the country with the global market. As a field that involves national image-making, tourism was strategically used to present 'politically correct' images of the Indonesian nation-state to the international polity. As Wai-Teng Leong (1997:72) points out: 'Elements of tourism are at the same time the ingredients of nationalism: the identification with a place, a sense of historical past, the revival of cultural heritage, and the national integration of social groups.' Moreover, tourism was used by the New Order government to communicate images of Indonesia as a culturally sophisticated and economically advanced nation. The flamboyant personality of former Director General and subsequently minister of tourism, Joop Avé, acted as the perfect ambassador of these objectives. With tourism as Indonesia's 'number one economic sector,' the concept of development had been invested with much more than the improvement of infrastructure, housing, education, and health of the country's citizens: development became the vehicle for obtaining the recognition and esteem from the international community and a role of considerable significance in the international political arena.

Under the New Order cultural tourism was regarded as the most appropriate form of tourism to direct the world's attention to the 'endless cultural diversity' of the country, a diversity which was well-organized and marketed in a national as well as global market. As has been argued in the previous chapters, the New Order regime adhered to a product approach of culture in its promotion of cultural tourism. In this approach, culture could easily be quantified in terms of numbers: the numbers of attractions available or still to be developed, the number of visitors and the amount of revenues received. Reduced to a 'quantity' in easy-reference graphics and tables, culture seemed easily manageable and used for planning and for legitimizing tourism developments. The product approach to culture enhanced its controllability and thus suited the New Order's concept of *pembangunan*. This concept carried connotations of planning and control, guidance and support, the implication being that development could not be achieved without the helping hand of the State. It emphasized the 'need for guidance' by those with power and knowledge, in this case the government officials who elaborated the notion in the first place. Over time, the New Order had, as it were, appropriated *pembangunan* so that the identity of the state had become intimately associated with the word (Rigg 1997:46-7). In selecting *pembangunan*, the Indonesian state rejected other terms which suggested spontaneous growth or progress. It had been widely suggested that the legitimacy of the New Order was based on the achievement of healthy economic growth. This created an explicit link between state legitimacy and modernization (Rigg 1997:49).

In this perspective cultural tourism in Indonesia, and in particular its planned and controlled product, quality tourism, showed a strong resemblance with phenomena described in terms of 'McDonaldization,' a metaphor that indicated that the principles of the fast-food restaurants are permeating all areas of modern life (Ritzer 1993). In Western countries the modernization process based on formal rationality brings about increasing efficiency, calculability, predictability and control. Implications are that modernization in terms of growing rationalization will inevitably result in a homogenization of the economy and culture world-wide under Western hegemony. Turning to cultural tourism development under Indonesia's New Order, one cannot overlook the strong resemblances with the process of 'McDonaldization.' Notwithstanding the fact that the regime advocated Indonesia's own path to modernization, preference was given to a 'rationalized' approach to tourism development. Cultural tourism as a strategy of development first of all had to be calculable: the growth of the number of international arrivals and the revenues were defined, targeted, and preferably surpassed. It had to be controllable; hence the complex and elaborate master plans, development schemes and government-initiated bodies and organizations that monitored and implemented these plans. Cultural tourism had to be predictable and efficiently organized. Therefore resort development and package tourism was strongly favoured, whereas cultural tourism in its conceptual form, gazing at everyday life, glimpsing at backstages, and soaking up the atmosphere, or even experiencing ethnic culture, did not figure in the Indonesian government's approach to tourism. Tourists mixing freely with local people, communicating with them without the intervention of a tourist guide, spending their money in the local economy, designing their own images, and locals developing their own spontaneous discourses and narratives – situations characteristic of ethnic tourism (Wood 1984), were regarded as threatening by the New Order. One could say that the Indonesian government was involved in the 'McDonald-ization' of both cultural tourism and national culture, Taman Mini Indonesia Indah being its ultimate expression (Hitchcock 1997).

This point requires further elaboration. For as far as 'McDonaldization' is associated with processes of homogenization, the homogenization that emerges under government control in Indonesia is not synonymous with 'globalization,' 'Westernization' or 'Americanization.' The impact of both local/ethnic and global elements on 'Indonesian' cultural tourism was strictly controlled under the New Order. Only those cultural performances and products that could be ascribed to the so-called 'peak' cultures were admitted to be incorporated into cultural tourism. Education constituted a key factor in the dissemination of the culturally and politically correct images and narratives. Being an important component in nation-building, the state engaged in the cultural construction of citizens through its control of education, inculcating loyalty to that conception of the nation to which it publicly adhered. By making education a common cultural currency, of which people could have more or less, the state created hierarchy (cf. Hannerz 1996:71). In Indonesia, more formal education tended to be synonymous with a greater involvement with metropolitan culture, as was reflected in the tourism industry. Those who play key roles in the representation and communication of this tourist product are carefully selected, educated, trained, and licensed as to guarantee their ability to mediate the core values of national unity to the vast audience of visitors both foreign and domestic. Hence the strong emphasis on *pancasila* state ideology in the educa-tion of the Indonesian youth in general and employees in the tourism industry in particular. National schooling altered the outlook of the new generation, orientating it towards Jakarta rather than to their own cultural environment. An analysis of the narratives of tourist guides has shown that the indoctrination with state ideology throughout the curricula had far-reaching effects on the guides' presentations. Whereas *guide liar* threatened the image of tamed cultural diversity and of the citizen proud of his Indonesian identity, the licenced guide is supposed to be a re-creation of the national character, the exemplary *'pancasila ,'*person,' who embodies the true Indonesia and adhered to a lifestyle that is plain and unpretentious. Homogenising effects on culture in Indonesia emanated from this enforcement of national unity. Therefore, 'McDonaldization' of culture in Indonesia did not imply an increasing rationalization Western style, but ,''nationalization,' 'Indonesianization' of local or ethnic cultures. The state as a nation legitimized itself by means of the 'imagination' that its inhabitants, of whatever class, represent a solid cultural community, a 'good' or 'decent' society. This community was imagined to be constituted by selected and cultivated ethnic groups whose culture 'exemplify the uniqueness of our people,' as formulated by the director of the national museum in Jakarta (as quoted in Schefold 1998:275). These 'unique' elements of traditional culture deserved to survive; others, by contrast, 'truly do not need to be preserved any longer' (ibid). The problem remained that the pan-Indonesian component of the national culture could rely on the obviousness of primordial attachments that are so typical of ethnic groups. Therefore, the uniqueness was either stretched or cut back to fit the territory of one Indonesian province to create regional cultures. What had been called localization was in fact the regionalization or provincialization of culture under the control of the national government. This leads to a re-evaluation of everything that has been achieved jointly in the Indonesian setting: the glorification of the pre-colonial past, the remnants of which had been meticulously reconstructed, the political and artistic achievements of these eras, the history of the struggle for Independence and its heroes, the creation of a national language, and all this cemented together by the national ideology of *pancasila* (Schefold 1998:276).

In the Special Province of Yogyakarta which establishes the regional focus of this book, these common national achievements found their symbolic expression in the cultural heritage of the region. Representing the common history, revolutionary spirit, national pride, and the defeat of the colonial power, Yogyakarta had been designed as an obligatory place to visit for Indonesians to experience both 'Indonesianness' and 'Javaneseness' and for foreign tourists to be lectured about Indonesian national identity. Therefore it is argued here that Yogyakarta had been created as the centre of *'pancasila* tourism.' A visit to Yogyakarta, particularly for domestic tourists, bears elements of a national pilgrimage, with an emphasis on cultural continuity. However, Yogyakarta was not one of those 'peak' cultures that had been domesticated by the New Order to become a worthy representative of national culture. Yogyakarta embodied national culture during the struggle for Independence when it was the capital city of the young republic. It was only after the defeat of the colonial power and the return of the administration to Jakarta that a cultural cleavage emerged between Yogyakarta and Jakarta. This cleavage is defined by Yogyakarta being the heroic city in a revolution which was led by prominent persons of what would later be dubbed the Old Order regime, and by the ambitions of the sultan to establish Yogyakarta as an independent kingdom in a federative Indonesion alliance of provinces (Woodward 1989). Although the role of Yogyakarta in the struggle for Independence is uncontested, the New Order regime showed an ambivalent attitude towards this old centre of Javanese culture. In New Order representations of Indonesian national identity the role of Sukarno and the Old Order was deliberately downplayed in favour of the role and stature of Suharto (Maurer 1997). The strife for autonomy of the sultanate had been turned down in the political arena, in the cultural arena Yogyakarta maintained its own expressions of Javaneseness.

This expression of Javaneseness is not the stuff that Indonesian national culture is made of. As Maurer (1997) points out, many Javanese features, like gamelan, wayang kulit, Javanese dance and costume, have been accepted as Indonesian, but it would be misleading to conceive of this as evidence of Javanization. What is being created is a Javanese-Indonesian culture, 'a synthesis of Javanese and other Indonesian elements combined with elements introduced from outside' (Hitchcock & King 1997:14). This New Order culture emerged in the national capital of Jakarta and quickly surpassed the old centre of Javanese culture in Yogyakarta. In Jakarta an Indonesian 'superculture' emerged which was generated by an endless flow of the images and simulations of government propaganda (Mulder 1994). In this hyper-reality the real and the imaginary were confused to become even more real than reality. Images and rhetoric of Indonesianess became intertwined with strong references to a contrived version of Javaneseness. That this newly-invented version to become the dominant discourse on Javaneseness implied that Yogyakarta had to be ascribed a different role in this hyper-real national culture. Therefore, Yogyakarta came to be constructed as the cradle of the history and heritage of the Indonesian nation. In fact, Yogyakarta had been modelled as the heritage centre or historic theme park of Indonesian national culture, constructed to offer 'authentic' remnants of the past in 'frozen images' that never change.

Cultural tourism in its 'product approach' constitutes a perfect medium to disseminate these frozen images of the past. The New Order regime adopted a twofold strategy to cultural tourism development in Yogyakarta. First, culture was moulded for tourism and tourists and, second, tourism and tourists were moulded for culture. The former entailed the development of specific products such as tourist art or tourist-oriented festivals, like the Kraton festival. The latter entailed modifying tourist sites, like the 'heroic' museums in the city to celebrate the struggle for Independence. Indonesianization was given first priority in the formation of sites, performances, images, and discourses to be presented to a domestic and international audience. In its role as frozen image of a common past, the Javanese culture of Yogyakarta itself had also come to be regarded as a remnant of the past. The image of Yogyakarta as a 'big village' almost untouched by modern life, where lifestyles are relaxed and people are fiercely proud of their ancient traditions was paramount to the process of making Yogyakarta a living museum. Notwithstanding the self-image of Yogyanese people as 'truly' Javanese, the Javanese culture they represented became a thing of the past in the eyes of the Jakarta power elite. Yogyakarta's place in state ideology was that of the cultural heritage of the New Order regime. Modern versions of Javaneseness were enacted not in Yogyakarta, but in the province of Central Java. Therefore, Central Java came to be defined as the representative of Javanese culture as 'peak' culture. Whereas people in Yogyakarta experienced the rise of its neighbouring province as a tourist destination as unfair competition and the allotment of the new international airport to Solo as the outcome of a corrupt political game, the development of Central Java in terms of cultural tourism was the logical consequence of the cultural policy of the New Order. As has been pointed out in one of the previous chapters, this cultural policy reflected the personal ambitions of former President Suharto, or rather the ambitions of his wife, who traced her genealogy to the sultan of Surakarta. Pemberton (1994) suggested that the favourable treatment of the province of Central Java did not stem from his wife's 'primordial' loyalties towards her agnates (the sultan of Surakarta refrained from relating to the Jakarta power elite), but rather from the Yogyakarta court refusing to acknowledge the aristocratic claims of the president's wife.

The presidential manipulations were at the basis of a government-led reshuffling of cultural relations in Java. The consequence was that ever since the regional culture of Java has been represented by the province of Central Java, its historical version by the Special Province of Yogyakarta and the national superculture by the capital city of Jakarta. As for the people of Yogyakarta, one may argue with Hannerz (1996:58), that they did not only possess culture, but they were also possessed by it: they were constructed out of its materials of meaning and expression – in this case a construction orchestrated by the New Order. Safeguarding Yogyakarta as the New Order's cultural heritage, the national government had to make sure that Yogyanese culture was preserved as a living entity, and the people's 'right to their own culture' was turned into a duty to that government-orchestrated version. This duty was captured in the slogan 'Yogyakarta, the heart of central Java.' This slogan explains why Yogyakarta remained a political as well as economic backwater. After all, modernization had to be tempered so as not to destroy the living museum.

However, the 'frozen images' showed signs of wear in the 1990s after decades of playing a prominent role in the national propaganda of the New Order – as the regime itself showed signs of weariness that culminated in the showdown of May 1998. In Chapter 3 I have dwelled at length on the stagnation that hit the tourism economy of Yogyakarta in the mid-1990s. Among the many factors and trends that threatened tourism development in Yogyakarta, was the Indonesian government's adherence to the distinction between high and popular culture, obviously because the former was its own construction, thoroughly Indonesianized and *pancasila*-ized. Popular culture is multivocal by definition, unpredictable, difficult to control, and often afflicted with Western consumer culture. The threat that emanated from popular culture became visible in the domain of tourism. The increased interaction between Indonesian people and the millions of tourists, an interaction resulting from the heavily promoted tourist sector was hard to control and brought about the influx of particular elements of Western culture (Persoon 1998:301). Where tourist-host interaction was limited to the state-orchestrated resort enclaves and staged performances of national culture, the impacts were minimized. Planning for cultural tourism, therefore, provided cultivated spaces where well-developed roads led to, and well-managed tourist objects, with fences, parking lots, visitor centres, toilets, and organized tourist guides whose performance was staged and routinized and whose narratives were well-rehearsed. As the 'streetside' attraction system of Yogyakarta was neatly arranged and surveyable, it allowed for optimal control on the guides' performance. 'True' stories and 'appropriate' interpretations reproduced by the guides were modelled by government officials or experts loyal to the regime.

However, in the popular versions of tourist narratives, in which the experience of local culture established the predominant element, 'uncontrolled' local discourses posed a threat to *pancasila*-tourism. Popular versions emerged for domestic as well as foreign tourists. It seemed that domestic tourists were particularly attracted to 'Westernized,' 'Disney-style,' amenities, while foreign tourists were especially attracted to local life. Starting from this distinction, two trends in the New Order 'tourist product' emerged: first, a 'Disneyfication' of leisure facilities and tourist sites in Indonesia, and second a process of 'ethnification' of tourist attractions. 'Disneyfication' describes the process by which people that have taken on the identity of consumers, approach resorts, theme parks, museums, shopping malls, and other leisure locations in the knowledge that the spectacles offered are simulations, and accept the montaged world and hyper-reality for what it is (Urry 1988, Featherstone 1990). The quest for authenticity, i.e. the search for a genuine pre-simulational reality, that according to MacCannell (1976) constitutes the motivation of 'modern' tourists to travel to far-away places, is lost. In contemporary tourism it seems that the quest for authenticity does not figure any more. It is a distinct characteristic of Disneyfication that consumers have the capacity to enjoy surface sensations and spectacular imagery without nostalgia for the real (Featherstone 1990:60). Research on upper middle-class lifestyles in Jakarta (Van Leeuwen 1997) has shown that Indonesians exhibit this 'disneyfied' fun-mentality fed by amenities of global culture. The Indonesian middle-class spends much of its leisure time in shopping malls or mega-amusement parks like *Taman Mini*, *Ancol* and *Dunia Fantasia* (fantasy land). These are truly McDonaldized places, air-conditioned, safe, and clean, where control is optimal. Instead of being spearheads of world-wide homogenization of culture through Westernization, these places represented the basic principles of the New Order. Similar trends could be observed in the visitor parks that surrounded the large temple complexes of Borobudur and Prambanan that increasingly took on characteristics of attraction-parks. As has been argued in Chapter 3, it seems that Central Java was in a better position than Yogyakarta to cater to both Disneyfication 'Indonesian-style' and representation of New Order culture. With its new marinas, adventure and amusement parks, Central Java attempted to emulate the success of Jakarta's middle-class leisure facilities. Yogyakarta as the 'heritage theme park' of the New Order had been designed for 'edutainment' instead of mere fun. Therefore it had to offer entertainment with a 'mission': the Kraton festivals and Kraton-related fun-fair and markets, the attractionparks of the Taman Wisata company.

Culture as process unfolded before tourists visiting *kampung* which partially withdrew from direct government intervention because of its social cohesion and marginality. In *kampung* like Sosrowijayan and Prawirotaman 'international communities' emerged consisting of expats, long-term travellers, backpackers, *kampung* dwellers, students, and migrants from all over the Indonesian archipelago, embedded in the partly informal economy. The very unorganized diversity and spontaneity of these communities countered the 'McDonaldization' of cultural tourism that characterizes the product approach. These communities emerged in an unplanned and uncontrolled manner, and their economy showed the 'irrationalities' of the informal market. They exhibited the inefficiency, incalculability, unpredictability, and uncontrolla-bility that created the chaotic and colourful street life that foreign tourists expected to find in an Indonesian downtown neighbourhood. This situation appealed to different categories of tourists for different reasons. Domestic tourists were attracted to these tourist areas because the accommodation was inexpensive and offered a glimpse at tourist culture. To watch foreigners eat and engage in leisure activities, even talk to them and giggle about their clothing style and demeanour, enhanced the attraction value of a place for Indonesian visitors. Foreign tourists were attracted to these areas because they found both Western amenities and local life. For as far as 'Indonesian' culture reveals itself in an undisguized and unmediated way, it is in the tourist *kampung* that 'authentic' experiences emerge – authentic in the eyes of the tourists. Tourists were unaware of *kampung* life being as little or as much 'Indonesian' as the Ramayana dance performed at the Open Air Theatre at Prambanan temple. Tourists do not know that *kampung* represent one specific layer of local culture, i.e., the lower classes. Moreover, *kampung* in a city like Yogyakarta is a mixture of cultural and ethnic elements from all over Indonesia, and tourist *kampung* which accommodates visitors and expats from all over the world, constitutes a truly creolized cultural setting. In terms of the New Order classification of culture, there was little cultural 'peak' to be found in a setting like this and there was nothing to be domesticated by the government. These 'international communities' and the 'spontaneous' encounters with street guides, with which the streets and sites of many popular tourist areas were swarming, formed examples of situations that the New Order government defined as highly undesirable. But there was little the authorities could do about it. The only solution that had occasionally been suggested by government officials (and shared by the streetside tourism industry) was to destroy the *kampung* to clear the land for resort development. However, there was a dilemma to be solved first. As the *kampung* tourism economy flourished, it attracted a constant flow of tourists and offered employment to large numbers of people who would otherwise be unemployed. Although *kampung* tourism undermined *pancasila* tourism, it was less disruptive than masses of urban poor might be. As recent instances of political unrest have shown, dissatisfied and distressed, these masses posed a much more serious threat to the Indonesian government (that derived its legitimacy from promises of economic growth and prosperity) than the 'half-naked and dirty hippies' that allegedly constituted the majority of guests in the *kampung* area. Streetside entrepreneurs and their government representatives feared that the impoverished people would find support among the well-educated youth that were produced by the many educational institutions that have given Yogyakarta the name of 'city of education.'

Kampung is the place where popular versions of Yogyanese culture were designed and reproduced. Here, versions of tourism emerged in which the experience of local culture formed the predominant element, and where uncontrolled local discourses posed a threat to government-orchestrated tourism. These narratives were no threat in an immediate sense as they did not contain politically subversive messages. Instead, they were threatening in the eyes of the government because they conveyed images of and provided access to Yogyakarta's backstages that did not fit the concept of the 'New Order heritage.' As has been shown in Chapter 6, the self-designed narratives about Yogyakarta were devoid of any *pancasila*-content, they were unplanned

225

constructions to please and entertain the tourists and to extract money from them. Moreover, their celebrating Western consumer culture jeopardized the image of *pancasila*-man, the patriot and dignified representative of Indonesia's most prominent 'peak' culture, i.e. Javanese culture. Informal guides in pursue of the tourists' money unwillingly blurred the carefully established boundaries between frontstages and backstages, between the 'cradle of modern Indonesia' and *kampung* life, and between tourist space and local community. In contrast to the formal guides who were supposed to act as buffers between tourists and backstage communities through reducing the opportunity for interaction between tourists and locals, informal guides acted as vehicles for 'tourism culture' to penetrate the local community. The ultimate threat to the state emanating from this 'tourism culture' is the 'escape' it provided to withdraw from the government's manipulative mechanisms. The emerging 'tourism culture' of which unlicensed guides were a prominent exponent undermined the government's policy of demarcation that allowed for the tourism sector to contribute to *pembangunan* while leaving the everyday life of Indonesian people 'unaffected.'

It has become clear that by enforcing formalization in all areas of tourism, the government undermined its own means and measures of control. As for the tourist guides the system required co-operation at different levels giving rise to informal networks that comprised of streetside and *kampung* businesses, formal and informal guides, frontstage and backstage attractions, 'enclosed' and public space. As has been noted in a previous chapter, the situation in Yogyakarta's tourism sector was paradoxical. Government control of 'enclosed' areas and 'rehearsed' narratives was considerably less effective than the efforts exerted by the state leads one to suspect. Private entrepreneurial interests in 'contested' public space generated 'informal' social control that was more effective than state-orchestrated regulations in 'enclosed' areas. Public space, the domain of the 'informal' tourism economy that remained largely uncontrolled by the government, was more closely guarded and better organized than the enclosed and regulated tourist spaces that ranged under state authorities. Local people depending on public space for their subsistence developed their own mechanisms of control that had their own logic and operated independently from government intervention. On the other hand, strict control as exerted on many tourist objects aroused subversive activities by local people rendering the 'enclosed' areas as contested as public space. Local people forced an entry to the enclosed tourist sites. Fences were either physically violated or strategically surpassed. Personal networks extended beyond the artificial boundaries as friendship, family, and ethnic ties that link actors in streetside and *kampung* tourism were stronger than government-imposed regulations. Unlicensed guides in particular remained largely beyond the control of the authorities as they managed to obtain access to the 'controlled' tourist spaces. On the other hand, formal guides took the opportunity of face-to-face contact with tourists to express their discontent with their own lives and the political and economic situation of their country. Strikingly, they conveyed more politically sensitive information by playful variations on their well-rehearsed texts than informal guides in their spontaneous stories. Even though the criticism expressed by formal guides were largely ventilated in guarded terms, their position as spearheads of Indonesian 'quality tourism' injects their words with much more power than those articulated by an informal guide. Being meticulously modelled on the ideal of *pancasila*-person, the disloyalty of formal guides to the system mercilessly reveal the failure of the New Order.

Seen in an international perspective the adherence to Jakarta-constructed high culture did not fit the trend of de-differentiation that characterized the production and consumption of culture in Western societies. As has been argued in Chapter 1, one of the characteristics of post-modern culture is the fading of distinctions between 'high' and 'low' or 'popular' culture. As the boundaries between 'high' and 'popular' culture evaporate, so the consumption of popular entertainment becomes part of the cultural tourism sphere as well (Richards 1996:26). As the Indonesian tourism planners failed to acknowledge these trends, Indonesia lost its position in the global market. The government had not been insensitive to the demands of the market. High government officials recognized that tourism trends in the 1990s indicated that many travellers were seeking alternatives to large-scale resorts which required small-scale projects to be supported, especially in still underdeveloped destination areas. This implied several things. First, the tourism policy did not undergo profound changes as small-scale projects would always be subsidiary to large-scale projects. Second, the existing resorts in established tourism areas like Bali would not be affected. Third, the small-scale projects involved local people and ethnic groups that were supposed to play key roles in tourism development to accomplish the development objective of the national tourism master plan. Fourth, small-scale developments outside or opposing the national master plan would not be tolerated. The violent destruction of small tourism-related enterprises on the island of Gili Trawangan (Kamsma 1996) illustrated how the government reacted to local people that got in its way. Therefore, much of the debates about tourism contributing to sustainable developments remained rhetoric to perform well before international audiences. Initiatives to diversify the tourist product, as reported from Yogyakarta where *kampung* entrepreneurs started tours to agritourism areas, housing projects, home industries, and caving and trekkings in the vicinity of the city, were absorbed by the streetside tourism industry if they proved to be successful. The streetside travel agencies entered the market when projects began to yield profits and re-organized the tours as to fit the 'quality' tourism policy by involving star-rated accommodations, licenced guides and expensive means of transport. The attempts to integrate *kampung* initiatives showed that the *kampung* tourism economy was regarded as a real threat to streetside tourism. The denial by streetside actors that *kampung* tourism was a serious competitor, had to be seen as impression management in the face of the foreign researcher. This denial also showed that the government underestimated *kampung* tourism in regarding it as a mere nuisance that could be cleared away by police raids and bulldozers.

Instead of guaranteeing a bright future ahead, the role as the nation's heritage centre became Yogyakarta's predicament. The area's problem was its being a 'national' heirloom. Local diversity as made subservient to *pancasila* state ideology, it was not strategically used to establish the city centre as a meeting place of a variety of cultural flows. It was this failure that had its repercussions on international tourism in Yogyakarta, as the international cultural tourist was not satisfied any more with a presentation of 'frozen images' but demanded a more conceptual approach to culture. This approach was offered by the much maligned *kampung* tourism. To an increasing degree, *kampung* entrepreneurs turned to the localization of their cultural tourist product. Visits to 'undeveloped' rural areas, villages, home industries and even the dwellings of the *gelandangan*, the homeless people and street children of Yogyakarta, entered their repertoire of tour programs. Undoubtedly, this repertoire appealed to the changing tastes of Western tourists who seemed to become more and more interested in the imponderabilities of everyday life. Streetside tourism, on the other hand, attempted to find the solution to the more and more pressing problems of the declining appeal of Yogyakarta to the tourist masses both domestic and foreign in the 'McDonaldization' and the 'Disneyfication' of their product. Streetside entrepreneurs argued in favour of a metropolitan image of Yogyakarta and turned to resort and amusement park development. Undoubtedly their strategies appeal to Asian and domestic tourists whose tastes are tuned to large-scale leisure and tourist facilities. There may be a shift in the tourist market to more intra-Asia travel, like other tourist destinations in Asia are experiencing. This trend may be beneficial in economic terms, but at the same time detrimental to the position of Indonesia in the global arena. After all, Thailand and the Philippines became major intra-Asian destinations only after their reputation was ruined (in terms of prostitution, environmental damage, and political unrest) and arrivals from Western countries declined (cf. Go & Jenkins 1997).

Finally, the symbolic construction of national unity through the domestication of cultural diversity, the establishment of a national 'superculture' and the invention of cultural heritage has turned out to be a double-edged sword. Whereas the involvement of the bureaucratic elite in nation-building entrepreneurship aimed to enforce national unity, it actually contributed to creolization of the newly-created national culture. As Hannerz (1996:75) points out, the very idea of the nation-state is itself in part an item of global cultural diffusion; it encompasses a standardized inventory of forms, to be given local and contrastive, as well as culturally resonant, content. This inventory may have been developed in nineteenth century Europe, but in the twentieth century it is used almost everywhere. States in other parts of the world, like Indonesia, are creations of the international system, built from the top down rather than from the bottom up. Pursuing this line of thought derived from Hannerz (1996:76), one might go as far as to argue that the Indonesian state, as it promoted messages of nationhood, was itself a creolized local culture. The Indonesian state produced new culture by inserting selected indigenous meanings and symbols into an imported matrix, to which they had in some ways to be adapted. Yet this is a creolization which the state could hardly celebrate itself, but had to define away, in its pursuit of cultural integrity and authenticity. Its national culture as discursive object was and still is fiercely contested, as is powerfully illustrated by the ethnic and religious upheavals surrounding the post-New Order political crisis. Narratives on Indonesian nationhood that emerge in the setting of cultural tourism are disorganized and incoherence can be found even in conventional genres, because their objects of knowledge are imperfectly recognized by the 'imagined national community.' Therefore the state control exerted on the discourses has been more conspicuous in its effort than in its effect.

CHAPTER 8

EPILOGUE

In September 1997, when the economic and political crisis was teetering on the brink, then minister of tourism, post and telecommunications, Joop Avé, published the brochure 'Tourism 21', which presented the 'Vision and Mission of National Tourism in the Twenty-First Century' (Avé 1997:v). At the time designed as the path to a prosperous future, this document became Avé's political will. In this document Avé makes a plea for national unity, anchoring tourism development in the 1945 Constitution and *pancasila*, and calling on the support of major religious and societal organizations, which reflect the *pancasila* ideology: *Majelis Ulama Indonesia, Parisada Hindu Dharma Indonesia, Perwalian Umat Budha Indonesia, Persekutuan Gereja-Gereja di Indonesia, Konperensi Wali Gereja Indonesia, Badan Pembinaan Pendidikan Pelaksanaan Pedoman Penghayatan dan Pengalaman Pancasila Pusat*, and *Dharma Wanita Pusat*. What is striking about the political embedding of tourism in Indonesian state ideology is the intensity with which Avé warns against threats emanating from tourism development without specifying these threats. Instead, he emphasizes that tourism plans must be implemented 'without sacrificing any national interests' (Avé 1997:32). On the threshold of a stormy phase in the country's history and unmistakably echoing the desintegration of the New Order regime that was underway, Avé pleaded for:

> (...) the continuing existence of the Republic of Indonesia as a unitary state as well as the ongoing unity and integrity of the nation; and, most importantly, the success, continuation, and sustainability of national development (Avé 1997:32).

Ever since, the department of tourism has seen many changes. In the subsequent cabinets of the post-Suharto area, tourism has changed ministries several times. The strategic use of tourism by the bureaucratic elite for ideological purposes was highlighted once again by the position of the tourism portfolio in the reshuffled cabinet of post-New Order President Habibie. Tourism was integrated with its corollary in the new Ministry of Tourism, Art and Culture - representing the heritage of the New Order tourism policy.

In the democratically elected cabinet of President Wahid, tourism is the responsibility of the state minister for 'tourism and the arts'. When the role of tourism in present-day Indonesia is discussed in public, references to national unity are conspicuously absent. It is tourism's contribution to the national economy that is of major concern. Although President Wahid has confirmed the importance of tourism to the Indonesian economy on several occasions, the fact is that tourism collapsed because of the political unrest during and after the May events of 1998, and has failed to recover because of ongoing ethnic and religious unrest in various provinces. Tourism statistics show that the number of foreign visitors dropped from five million in 1997 to 3.76 million in 1998. In 1999 there was only a slight increase in visitor numbers to 3.92 million. Earnings from international tourism have declined by almost 50 per cent since 1997. Many countries, including major tourism markets such as Japan, Australia and the United States, have reportedly issued travel warnings to their citizens discouraging visits to Indonesia. To increase the numbers of foreign visitors, Indonesian policy makers have recently turned to a tourism market which for the past decades has been left unexplored for political reasons: the People's Republic of China. The New Order regime's suppressive policies towards the Indonesian Chinese minorities had its corollory in the neglect of the Chinese market. China was not included in the list of nationalities visiting Indonesia. Following the recent visit of President Wahid to China, the government announced plans to provide Chinese tourists with 'on arrival visits'. This reorientation to China as a tourist market illustrates above all else the winds of change that have been blowing through the Archipelago since 1999.

APPENDIX 1

THE YOGYAKARTA DECLARATION ON NATIONAL CULTURES AND UNIVERSAL TOURISM

Gadjah Mada University, Yogyakarta, Indonesia, 16 November 1992

Recognizing that universal tourism has become a major global activity and the third most important international trade and therefore has tremendous potential impact on all aspects of life.

Recognizing the national cultures and universal tourism are interdependent because all forms of tourism exercise a cultural effect on tourists and the host countries.

Recognizing that universal tourism can have both beneficial and harmful impacts on the cultural life of a community.

Recognizing that cultural tourism in particular also enhances our insight into cultural pluralism as a manifestation of human existence.

Recognizing that we are all stewards of our common heritage having a responsibility to sustain it for future generations.

We, the participants in the International Conference on Cultural Tourism held at the Gadjah Mada University in Yogyakarta, Indonesia on 24-26 November 1992.

Resolve that

1. The relationship between tourism and the natural and cultural environment must be managed so that the environment is sustainable in the long term. While recognizing that tourism can be a positive activity, it must not be allowed to damage the resource, prejudice its future enjoyment, or bring an unacceptable impact.

2. In any location, harmony must be sought between the needs of the visitor, the place and the community.

3. Tourism development should be guided by a planning process involving broad community participation which ensures a proper balance between economic, social, cultural, and human objectives.

4. The success of any proposed action is dependent on the interrelationship of government, the host communities, and the tourism industry.

Urge

1. Governments to introduce and enforce legislation which will ensure the protection of national cultures while facilitating the optimum development of suitable forms of tourism activity.

2. Governments to give priority to education which leads to national cultural awareness at all levels in the community, including the teaching of comparative religion as part of the understanding of other cultures.

3. Members of the Tourism Industry to train their staff and prepare their clients to be sensitive to and respectful of the national cultures of host countries.

4. Members of the Tourism Industry to sustain natural and cultural resources by investing in programs of conservation, preservation, and interpretation.

5. Educational institutions at all levels to understand that sustainable tourism development requires a high level of skills in many interrelated disciplines and that adequate resources be allocated for programs to this end.

6. Host communities including young people working in special interest groups and Non-Governmental Organizations to participate actively in the tourism development process and advocate action that sustains the balance between national cultures and universal tourism.

Copied from the original (see also Nuryanti, 1993).

APPENDIX 2

NUMBER OF FOREIGN VISITORS TO INDONESIA AND REVENUES
1969-96

Year	Number of visitors	% Growth	Revenues (in US$ mln.)	% Growth
1968	52,400			
1969	86,100	64.00	10.80	
1970	129,319	50.20	16.20	50.00
1971	178,781	38.25	22.60	39.51
1972	221,195	23.72	27.60	22.12
1973	270,303	22.20	33.80	48.19
1974	313,452	15.96	54.40	33.00
1975	366,293	16.86	62.30	14.52
1976	401,237	9.54	70.60	13.32
1977	433,393	8.01	81.30	15.16
1978	468,614	8.1 0	94.30	15.99
1979	501,430	7.00	188.00	99.36
1980	561,170	11.92	289.00	53.72
1981	600,151	6.94	309.10	6.96
1982	592,046	-1.35	358.80	16.08
1983	638,855	7.91	439.50	22.49
1984	700,910	9.71	519.70	18.25
1985	749,351	6.91	325.30	1.08
1986	825,035	10.10	590.50	12.41
1987	1,060,347	28.52	954.30	41.86
1988	1.326.800	22.70	1.060.80	22.69
1989	1.625,965	24.97	1.284.00	24.98
1990	2.177,566	33.92	2.105.30	63.89
1991	2.964.000	18.02	2.522.00	19.80
1992	3.205.000	19.23	3.278.20	29.98
1993	3.403,138	11.06	3,987.60	21.64
1994	4,006,312	17.72	4.785.30	20.00
1995	4,324,229	7.94	5,228.30	9.26
1996	5,034,472			

Source: Indonesia. Tourism Market Data Base 1996. Directorate General of Immigration, Parpostel and Biro Pusat Statistik.

APPENDIX 3

NUMBER OF VISITORS (FOREIGN AND DOMESTIC) TO YOGYAKARTA
1973-95

Year	Foreign tourists	Domestic tourists	Total
1973	44.265	53.468	97.733
1974	40.453	56.833	97.286
1975	48.111	88.234	136.345
1976	72.460	111.737	191.247
1977	75.821	186.426	262.247
1978	60.478	84.854	145.332
1979	74.148	83.013	157.161
1980			
1981			
1982	58.962	176.732	235.694
1983	60.913	239.506	300.419
1984	70.099	359.104	429.203
1985	74.598	330.127	404.725
1986	93.512	343.279	436.791
1987			
1988	113.091	235.716	348.807
1989	180.896	483.520	664.416
1990	188.549	398.636	587.185
1991	216.051	492.048	708.099
1992	256.192	561.224	817.416
1993	299.433	610.818	910.251
1994	323.194	640.801	963.995
1995	344.265	837.265	1.181.530

Source 1973-1979: Duta Citra Design Consult 1980
Source 1982-6 Rencana Induk Pengembangan Pariwisata DIY 1987
Source 1989-95 Statistik Parpostel Daerah Istimewa Yogyakarta, KANWIL, 1995

NUMBER OF VISITORS (FOREIGN AND DOMESTIC) TO THE CORE ATTRACTION SITES OF YOGYAKARTA KRATON, PRAMBANAN AND BOROBUDUR
1989-95

Year	Kraton		Prambanan		Borobudur	
	Foreign	Domestic	Foreign	Domestic	Foreign	Domestic
1989	120.126	280.887	95.362	511.172	123.107	982.626
1990	144.770	324.794	118.012	522.066	212.688	1.553.826
1991	167.132	276.785	124.889	797.611	227.172	1.613.023
1992	204.929	266.434	146.490	661.745	594.030	1.396.176
1993	205.619	297.357	219.294	800.382	215.508	1.743.022
1994	230.824	283.592	277.759	755.595	257.416	1.784.097
1995	211.590	347.922	279.435	883.749	284.149	2.053.488

Source: KANWIL 1994, KANWIL 1996

GLOSSARY

alun alun	big square usually in the centre of town
alun alun lor	the northern square (here: the big northern square in front of the Yogyakarta Kraton, traditionally used for gatherings and ceremonies)
andong	horsecart
ASITA	Association of Indonesian Tour and Travel Agencies
bahasa	language
bahasa Indonesia	Indonesian language
bakpia	Local snack made from green beans
bapak angkat	lit. adopted father, i.e. subcontracting relations between a large and a small business
BAPPEDA	*Badan Perencanaan Pembangunan Daerah*: Agency for Regional Development
becak	pedicab
benteng	fortress
BPHN	*Badan Pusat Hotel Negara*: National Hotel Association
candi	'temple'
Depparpostel	*Departemen pariwisata, pos dan telekomunikasi*: the ministry of tourism, post and tele-communications
Diparda	*Dinas pariwisata daerah*: the provincial tourism department
Garebeg	one of the three major Muslim religious festivals, the 'day of sacrifice'
gelandangan	homeless people
gunung	mountain
gunungan	mountain-like figure; here: 'rice mountain' distributed among the people during one of the Muslim religious festivals
homestay	small-scale accommodation
HPI	*Himpunan Pramuwisata Indonesia*: Indonesian guide association
ibu	mother, married woman, mode of address: 'mrs.'
Idul Fitri	last day of the month of fasting, ramadan
ikat	a method of weavingtie-dye material

ikut-ikutan	lit. going along with whatever happens to be the prevailing view
jalan	street
jamu	herbal medicine
kampung	(low-class) neighbourhood
kampungan	backward lifestyle
kabupaten	regency, administrative unit below the province
kantor pos	post office
kanwil	*kantor wilayah*: provincial government office
lesehan	nightly street restaurant in Yogyakarta
liar	wild, unlicensed
long-termer	foreign travellers staying for weeks or even months
losmen	bed and breakfast accommodation
mandi	Indonesian bath: water is taken from a basin with a dipper and poured over the body
Maulud	one of the three major Muslim religious festivals: Mohammed's birthday
melati	jasmin flower
ngindung	honourable services paid by the Yogyanese gentry to the Sultan
orang tua angkat	adopted parents
Pagelaran	assembly hall in the front part of the kraton
paguyuban	association
pak, bapak	father, or respectful mode of address: 'mister'
pancasila	the 'five pillars' of the state ideology
pasar	market
pembangunan	development; key concept of New Order politics and policies
pencak silat	system of self-defence
pendopo	veranda
pengelola	management
penginapan	lit. lodging for the night; small pension
pondok wisata	accommodation with less than five rooms
pos	post
priyayi	Javanese gentry
PT.	*perseroan terbatas*: Inc., Ltd.
repelita	*rencana pembangunan lima tahun*: 5-Year Development Plans
repelitada	*rencana pembangunan lima tahun daerah*: 5-Year Regional Development Plans
rupiah	Indonesian currency; in 1995/1996 1,000 rupiah was worth about US\$ 0.45

Sekaten	festival held in Yogyakarta (and Solo) in honour of the Prophet Muhammed's birthday
streetside	concept borrowed from Patrick Guinness (1986) to characterise the built environment and the people establishing the commercial middle-class in Yogyakarta
stupa	dome enshrining a relic of the Buddha
tempe	fermented soybean cake
wartel	*warung telpon:* commercial telecommunications office
warung	food stall
wayang	puppet theatre
wayang kulit	leather puppet
wisma	guesthouse

REFERENCES

Abram, S., J. Waldren and D.V.L. Macleod (eds) (1997) *Tourists and Tourism. Identifying with People and Places*. Oxford/New York: Berg.

Adams, K. (1990) 'Cultural Commoditization in Tana Toraja, Indonesia,' *Cultural Survival Quarterly* 14/1, pp. 31-4.

– (1997) 'Touting Touristic "Primadonas": Tourism, Ethnicity, and National Integration in Sulawesi, Indonesia,' in: M. Picard and R.E.Wood (eds) *Tourism, Ethnicity and the State in Asian and Pacific Societies*. Honolulu: University of Hawai'i Press, pp. 155-80.

– (1998) 'Domestic Tourism and Nation-Building in South Sulawesi,' in: *Indonesia and the Malay World* 26/75, pp. 77-96.

Aditjondro, G.J. (1995) *Bali, Jakarta's Colony: Social and ecological impacts of Jakarta-based conglomerates in Bali's tourism industry*. Asia Research Centre of Murdoch University, Perth, Australia. Working Paper no. 58.

Amato, E. (1991/92) Tourist Guide Review. Activity Report no. 3. Cultural Tourism Development. Central Java - Yogyakarta. Directorate General of Tourism. UNESCO/UNDP.

Anderson, B. (1991) *Imagined Communities. Reflections on the Origin and Spread of Nationalism*. Revised Edition. London, New York: Verso.

Antweiler, Ch. (1995) 'South Sulawesi: Towards a regional ethnic identity? Current trends in a "hot" and historic region,' in: I. Wessel (ed.) *Nationalism and Ethnicity in Southeast Asia*. Proceedings of the Conference 'Nationalism and Ethnicity in Southeast Asia' at Humboldt University, Berlin, October 1993. Berlin: Fakultätsinstitut für Asien- und Afrikawissenschaften, Humboldt Universität, pp. 107-36.

Anwar, D.F. (1997) 'Participatie van het volk. De agenda voor de ontwikkeling van de politieke demografie,' *Reflexie*. Forum Nederland-Indonesia 1/1, pp. 4-13.

Appadurai, A. (1990) 'Disjuncture and Difference in the Global Cultural Economy,' in: M. Featherstone (ed.) *Global Culture. Nationalism, Globalization and Modernity*. London: Sage, pp. 295-310.

Avé, J. (1997) *Tourism 21*. Department of Tourism, Art and Culture. Republic of Indonesia.

Basuki, P., H. Sigit and M.P. Gunawan (1993) *INDONESIA. Environment and Heritage*. Jakarta: Directorate General of Tourism.

Bernas (1996) 'Tak Bawa Izin "Guide", Didenda Rp. 15.000,' *Bernas*, 27-03-1996.

Boer, L. (1989) 'Duistere schakels: Relaties tussen de formele en informele economie,' in: P.J.M. Nas, J.W. Schoorl and B.F. Galjart (red.) *Aanzetten tot een schakelingenperspectief in de ontwikkelingssociologie.* Leiden Development Studies 9. Leiden: Culturele Antropologie en Sociologie der Niet-Westerse Samenlevingen. Rijksuniversiteit Leiden, pp. 133-52.

Boissevain, J. (1974) *Friends of Friends. Networks, Manipulators and Coalitions.* Oxford: Basil Blackwell.

Boissevain, J. (ed.) (1996) *Coping with Tourists. European Reactions to Mass Tourism.* New Directions in Anthropology 1. Providence/Oxford: Berghahn Books.

Booth, A. (1990) 'The Tourism Boom in Indonesia,' *Bulletin of Indonesian Economic Studies* 26/3, pp. 45-73.

– (1992) 'The Service Sector,' in: A. Booth, *The Oil Boom and After. Indonesian Economic Policy and Performance in the Soeharto Era.* Singapore: Oxford University Press, pp. 283-300.

Bowman, G. (1992) 'The politics of tour guiding: Israeli and Palestinian guides in Israel and the Occupied Territories,' in: D. Harrison (ed.) *Tourism and the less developed countries.* London: Belhaven Press, pp. 121-34.

Bras, C.H. (1999) Lombok and the Art of Guiding. The Social Construction of a Tourist Destination in Indonesia. Ph.D. Thesis. Department of Leisure Studies. Tilburg University.

Bras, K. (1997) 'The "real" story about *Dusun* Sade: Local tourist guides, the regional government and the (re-)presentation of a tourist attraction on the island Lombok, Indonesia,' in: Proceedings of the Conference 'The Battle for the tourist,' Eindhoven, June 8-10. Technische Universiteit Eindhoven and European Institute of Retailing and Services Studies, pp. 1-13.

Bras K. and H. Dahles (1998) 'Women Entrepreneurs and Beach Tourism in Sanur, Bali: Gender, Employment Opportunities, and Government Policy,' *Pacific Tourism Review* 1/3, pp. 243-56.

Britton, S. (1991) 'Tourism, capital, and place: towards a critical geography of tourism,' *Environment and Planning D: Society and Space* 9, pp. 451-78.

Clapham, R. (In co-operation with Reiner Strunk, Heinz G.H. Schaldach, Gisela Clapham) (1985) *Small and Medium Entrepreneurs in Southeast Asia.* Research Notes and Discussion Paper 49, Institute of Southeast Asian Studies. Singapore.

Cohen, E. (1971) 'Arab Boys and Tourist Girls in a Mixed Jewish-Arab Community,' *International Journal of Comparative Sociology* 12/4, pp. 217-33.

– (1982) 'Thai Girls and Farang Men: The Edge of Ambiguity,' *Annals of Tourism Research* 9/3, pp. 403-28.

– (1985) 'The Tourist Guide: The Origins, Structure and Dynamics of a Role,' *Annals of Tourism Research* (Special Issue) 12/1, pp. 5-29.

– (1986) 'Lovelorn Farangs: The Correspondence Between Foreign Men and Thai Girls,' *Anthropological Quarterly* 59/3, pp. 115-27.

– (1993) 'Open-ended prostitution as a skillful game of luck. Opportunity, risk and security among tourist-oriented prostitutes in a Bangkok soi,' in: M. Hitchcock, V.T. King and M.J.G. Parnwell (eds) *Tourism in South-East Asia*. New York/London: Routledge, pp. 155-78.

Craik, J. (1997) 'The Culture of Tourism,' in: Ch. Rojek and J. Urry (eds) *Touring Cultures. Transformations of Travel and Theory*. London/New York: Routledge, pp. 113-36.

Crick, M. (1992) 'Life in the informal sector: street guides in Kandy, Sri Lanka,' in: D. Harrison (ed.) *Tourism and the less developed countries*. London: Belhaven Press, pp. 135- 47.

Cukier, J. (1996) 'Tourism employment in Bali: trends and implications,' in: Richard Butler and Thomas Hinch (eds) *Tourism and Indigenous Peoples*. London: International Thomson Press, pp. 49-75.

Dahles, H. (1996) '"Hello Mister!": De rol van informele gidsen in Yogyakarta,' *Derde Wereld* 15/1, pp. 34-48.

– (1998a) 'Of Birds and Fish. Streetguides, tourists and sexual encounters in Yogyakarta, Indonesia,' in: M. Oppermann (ed.) *Sex Tourism and Prostitution*. New York: Cognizant Communication Corporation, pp. 30-41.

– (1998b) 'Tourism, government policy, and petty entrepreneurs in Indonesia,' *South East Asia Research* 6/1, pp. 73-98.

Dahles H. and K. Bras (1999b) 'Entrepreneurs in Romance. Tourism in Indonesia,' *Annals of Tourism Research* 26/2, pp. 267-93.

Dahles H. and K. Bras (eds) (1999a) *Tourism and Small Entrepreneurs. Development, National Policy and Entrepreneurial Culture, Indonesian Cases. Tourism Dynamics*, edited by Valene L. Smith and Paul F. Wilkinson. New York: Cognizant Communiction Corporation.

Dahles, H. and T. van Meijl (eds) (1999) 'Local perspectives on global tourism in the Asia-Pacific region,' *Newsletter of the International Institute for Asian Studies*, special issue, no. 19. Leiden, the Netherlands.

Dalton, B. (1991) *Indonesia Handbook*. Moon Publications.

De Graaf, H.J. (1947) 'Beknopt overzicht der geschiedenis van het sultanaat Jogjakarta,' *Historia. Maandblad voor Geschiedenis en Kunstgeschiedenis* 12/12, december 1947, pp. 275-85.

Depparpostel (1988) Departemen Pariwisata, Pos dan Telekomunikasi. Keputusan Menteri Pariwisata, Pos dan Telekomunikasi. Jakarta: Depparpostel.

– (1989) Departemen Pariwisata, Pos dan Telekomunikasi. Direktorat Jenderal Pariwisata. Keputusan Direktur Jenderal Pariwisata. Nomor: KEP-17/U/IV/89 Tentang Pedoman Pembinaan Pramuwisata dan Pengatur Wisata.

– (1991) Keputusan Menteri Pariwisata, Pos dan Telekomunikasi nomor: KM.105/PW.304/MPPT-91 Tentang Usaha Jasa Pramuwisata; and Surat Direktur Jenderal Pariwisata nomor: 51/D.2/XI/91 Perihal Petunjuk Pelaksanaan Usaha Jasa Pramuwisata, in: *Usaha Jasa Pramuwisata* (1991-1992).

– (1991/92) Decree nr. KM.82/PW.102/MPPT-88. *Usaha Jasa Pramuwisata*, Direktorat Jenderal Pariwisata, Proyek Peningkatan Industri Pariwisata.

Dewan Pimpinan Daerah Himpunan Pramuwisata Indonesia (1991) *Dewan Pimpinan Daerah Himpunan Pramuwisata Indonesia*. Daerah Istimewa Yogyakarta.

Dharmaputera, E. (1988) *Pancasila and the search for identity and modernity in Indonesian society. A cultural and ethical analysis*. Leiden: E.J. Brill.

Diponegoro University (1995) Tourism Development in Central Java. Presented in the workshop on Tourism, Culture, Economy, Environment, Goldcoast, Queensland, 10-15 April 1995. Diponegoro University, Central Java Tourist Office, Semarang Municipality Tourist Office. Semarang.

Discover Indonesia (1992) *Discover Indonesia. A Travel Guide to the Indonesian Archipelago*. The Official Guidebook of The Indonesia Tourist Promotion Board (ITPB) Jakarta, Indonesia. Published by Bali Intermedia in co-operation with ITPB.

Doswell, R. (1992) National Tourist Training Standards and Programmes. UN/UNDP/ILO/UNESCO. Unpublished manuscript.

Dove, M.R. (1988) 'Introduction: Traditional Culture and Development in Contemporary Indonesia,' in: M.R. Dove (ed.) *The Real and Imagined Role of Culture in Development. Case studies from Indonesia*. Honolulu: University of Hawai'i Press, pp. 1-40.

Drakakis-Smith, D. (1987) *The Third World City* (Routledge Introductions to Development). London and New York: Routledge.

Erlina, B. (n.d.) Urgent! Penyajian informasi pariwisata yang meluas dan berkesinambungan. Unpublished manuscript.

Evers, H.-D. (1991) 'Shadow Economy, Subsistence Production and Informal Sector: Economic Activity Outside of Market and State,' *Prisma* 51, pp. 34-45.

Evers, H.-D. and O. Mehmet (1994) 'The Management of Risk: Informal Trade in Indonesia,' *World Development* 22/1: 1-9.

Featherstone, M. (1990) *The Paradox of Culture and the Globalization of Diversity*. Utrecht: ISOR.

Final Report 1991/2 Cultural Tourism Development. Central Java – Yogyakarta. Second Phase. Final Report. UNDP/UNESCO. Directorate General of Tourism and UNDP/UNESCO.

Friedman, J. (1990) 'Being in the World: Globalization and Localization,' *Theory, Culture and Society* 7/2, pp. 311-28.

Geertz, C. (1963) *Peddlers and Princes. Social Development and Economic Change in Two Indonesian Towns*. Chicago and London: University of Chicago Press.

– (1973) Thick Description: Toward an Interpretive Theory of Culture,' in: C. Geertz, *The Interpretation of Cultures. Selected Essays*. New York: Basic Books, pp. 3-30.

Gellner, E. (1983) *Nations and Nationalism*. Oxford: Basil Blackwell.

Gertler, L. (1993) 'Linkage Between Past, Present and Future,' in: W. Nuryanti (ed.) *Universal Tourism. Enrichring or Degrading Culture?* Proceedings on the International Conference on Cultural Tourism. Gadjah Mada University Yogyakarta, Indonesia, pp. 11-19.

Giddens, A. (1990) *The Consequences of Modernity*. Cambridge: Polity Press.

Go, F.M. and C.L. Jenkins (eds) (1997) *Tourism Development and Economic Development in Asia and Australasia*. London and Washington: Pinter.

Graburn, N. (1995) 'Tourism, Modernity and Nostalgia,' in: A. Ahmed and C. Shore (eds) *The Future of Anthropology. Its Relevance to the Contemporary World*. London and Atlantic Highlands, NJ.: Athlone.

– (1997) 'Tourism and Cultural Development in East Asia and Oceania,' in: Shinji Yamashita, Kadir H. Din and J.S. Eades (eds) *Tourism and Cultural Development in Asia and Oceania*. Bangi: Penerbit Universiti Kebangsaan Malaysia, pp. 194-211.

Guinness, P. (1986) *Harmony and Hierarchy in a Javanese Kampung*. Singapore: Oxford University Press.

– (1989) '"Social Harmony" as Ideology and Practice in a Javanese City,' in: Paul Alexander (ed.) *Creating Indonesian Cultures*. Sydney: University of Sydney, Oceania Publications, pp. 55-74.

– (1991) 'Kampung and the Street-Side: Yogyakarta under the New Order,' *Prisma. The Indonesian Indicator* 51, pp. 86-98.

– (1994) 'Local society and culture,' in: Hal Hill (ed.) *Indonesia's New Order. The Dynamics of Socio-economic Transformation* (pp. 267-304). London: Allen and Unwin.

Gunawan, M.P. (1997a) 'National Planning for Indonesia's Tourism'. Country Reports. *Pacific Tourism Review* 1/1, pp. 47-56.

– (1997b) 'Tourism in Indonesia: Past, present, and future,' in: John Minnery, Myra P. Gunawan, Michael Fagance and Darryl Low Choy (eds) *Proceedings on the training and workshop on Planning sustainable tourism*. Bandung: ITB, pp. 17-28.

Gurung, G., D. Simmons and P. Devlin (1996) 'The evolving role of tourist guides: the Nepali experience,' in: Richard Butler and Tom Hinch (eds) *Tourism and Indigenous Peoples*. London: International Thomson Business Press, pp. 107-28.

Hailin Qu and Hanquin Qui Zhang (1998) 'The projection of international tourist arrivals in East Asia and the Pacific,' in: F.M. Go and C.L. Jenkins (eds) *Tourism and economic development in Asia and Australasia*. London and Washington: Pinter, pp. 35-47.

Hamengkubuwono, X, Sri Sultan (1993) 'Revitalization of Cultural Heritage Within the Context of Tourism,' in: W. Nuryanti (ed.) Universal Tourism. Enriching or Degrading Culture? Proceedings on the International Conference on Cultural Tourism. Gadjah Mada University Yogyakarta, Indonesia, pp. 20-9.

– (1995) Re-orientasi pengembangan pariwisata Daerah Istimewa Yogyakarta. Sarasehan Pembentukan Badan Promosi Pariwisata Yogyakarta (BPPY) 17 april 1995.

Hannerz, U. (1992) *Cultural Complexity. Studies in the Social Organization of Meaning*. New York: Columbia University Press.

– (1996) *Transnational Connections.Culture, people, places*. London, New York: Routledge.

Harrison, D. (1992) 'Tourism to less developed countries: the social consequences,' in: D. Harrison (ed.) *Tourism and the less developed countries*. London: Belhaven Press, pp. 19-34.

Hartono, F.M. (1997) 'Towards sustainable tourism development: A policy planning perspective,' in: John Minnery, Myra P. Gunawan, Michael Fagance and Darryl Low Choy (eds). *Proceedings of the training and workshop on Planning sustainable tourism*. Bandung: ITB, pp. 39-52.

Hatley, B. (1993) 'Constructions of "Tradition" in New Order Indonesian Theatre,' in: V.M. Hooker (ed.) *Culture and Society in New Order Indonesia*. Kuala Lumpur: Oxford University Press, pp. 48-69.

Hellman, J. (1998) 'The use of "cultures" in official representations of Indonesia: the fiftieth anniversary of Independence,' in: *Indonesia and the Malay World* 26/74, pp. 1-12.

Hewison, R. (1987) *The Heritage Industry: Britain in a Climate of Decline*. London: Methuen.

Hitchcock, M. (1996) *Islam and identity in Eastern Indonesia*. Hull: The University of Hull Press.

– (1997) 'Indonesia in Miniature,' in: M. Hitchcock and V.T. King (eds) *Images of Malay-Indonesian Identity*. Kuala Lumpur: Oxford University Press, pp. 227-35.

– (1998) 'Tourism, Taman Mini, and National Identity,' in: *Indonesia and the Malay World* 26/75, pp. 124-35.

Hitchcock, M. and V.T. King (1997) 'Introduction: Malay-Indonesian Indenti-
ties,' in: M. Hitchcock and V.T. King (eds) *Images of Malay-Indonesian
Identity*. Kuala Lumpur: Oxford University Press, pp.1-17.

Hitchcock, M., V.T. King and M.J.G. Parnwell (1993) 'Tourism in South-East
Asia: introduction,' in: M. Hitchcock, V.T. King and M.J.G. Parnwell
(eds) *Tourism in South-East Asia*. London: Routledge, pp. 1-31.

Hobsbawm, E. (1983) 'Introduction: Inventing Traditions,' in: E. Hobsbawm
and T. Ranger (eds) *The Invention of Tradition*. Cambridge: Cambridge
University Press.

Holloway, J.C. (1981) 'The Guided Tour. A sociological Approach,' *Annals
of Tourism Research* 8/3, pp. 377-402.

Hooker, V.M. and H. Dick (1993) 'Introduction,' in: V.M. Hooker (ed.)
Culture and Society in New Order Indonesia. Kuala Lumpur: Oxford
University Press, pp. 1-23.

Howes, D. (1996) Introduction: Commodities and cultural borders,' in: D.
Howes (ed.) *Cross-cultural consumption. Global markets, local realities*.
London and New York: Routledge, pp. 1-16.

Hughes-Freeland, F. (1993) Packaging dreams: Javanese perceptions of
tourism and performance,' in: M. Hitchcock, V.T. King and M.J.G.
Parnwell (eds) *Tourism in South-East Asia*. London and New York:
Routledge, pp. 138-54.

Hutajulu, R. (1994) The Creation of Ethnic Tourism: The Impact of Tourism
on Toba Batak Ceremony Paper: Leiden: KITLV.

Indonesia Tourism Market Data Base (1996) Indonesia Tourism Market Data
Base. Visitor Arrivals to Indonesia by Country of Residence and Expenditure in Indonesia, Pelita I - Pelita VI. Directorate General of Immigration, Depparpostel and Biro Pusat Statistik, 1996, p. 79.

Jansen, F. (1997) 'Urban Tourism in Bandung,' in: M.P. Gunawan (ed.)
Pariwisata Indonesia. Berbagai Aspek dan Gagasan Pembangunan.
Bandung: Pusat Penelitian Kepariwisataan, Lembaga Penelitian, Institut
Teknologi Bandung, pp. 107-20.

Jellinek, Lea (1991) *The wheel of fortune. The history of a poor community in
Jakarta*. Sydney: Allen and Unwin.

Kadir Din (1997) 'Tourism and Cultural Development in Malaysia: Issues for
a New Agenda,' in: Shinji Yamashita, Kadir H. Din and J.S. Eades (eds)
Tourism and Cultural Development in Asia and Oceania. Bangi: Penerbit
Universiti Kebangsaan Malaysia, pp. 104-18.

Kagami, H. (1997) 'Tourism and National Culture: Indonesian Policies on Cultural Heritage and its Utilisation in Tourism,' in: Shinji Yamashita, Kadir
H. Din and J.S. Eades (eds) *Tourism and Cultural Development in Asia
and Oceania*. Bangi: Penerbit Universiti Kebangsaan Malaysia, pp. 61-82.

Kamsma, M.J. (1996) 'Grof geweld in het Paradijs,' *De Volkskrant,* 23 november 1996.

Kamsma, Th. and K. Bras (1999) 'Gili Trawangan: Local Entrepreneurship in Tourism under Pressure,' in: H. Dahles and K. Bras (eds) *Tourism and Small Entrepreneurs. Development, National Policy and Entrepreneurial Culture. Indonesian Cases. Tourism Dynamics,* edited by Valene L. Smith and Paul F. Wilkinson. New York: Cognizant Communiction Corporation.

KANWIL (1994) Statistik Pariwisata, Pos dan Telekomunikasi. Daerah Istimewa Yogyakarta Tahun 1993. KANWIL VIII, Departemen Pariwisata, Pos dan Telekominukasi. Daerah Istimewa Yogyakarta.

– 1996 Statistik Pariwisata, Pos dan Telekomunikasi. Daerah Istimewa Yogyakarta Tahun 1995. KANWIL VIII, Departemen Pariwisata, Pos dan Telekominukasi. Daerah Istimewa Yogyakarta.

Kartodirdjo, S. (1981) *The Pedicab of Yogyakarta. A study of low cost transportation and poverty problems.* Yogyakarta: Gadjah Mada University Press.

King, V.T. (1993) 'Tourism and culture in Malaysia,' in: M. Hitchcock, V.T. King and M.J.G. Parnwell (eds) *Tourism in South-East Asia.* London: Routledge, pp. 99-116.

Kipp, R.S. (1993) *Dissociated Identities: Ethnicity, Religion, And Class in an Indonesian Society.* Ann Arbor: University of Michigan Press.

Kodhyat, H. (1992) 'Strategies for the Development of Tourism in Indonesia,' *The Indonesian Quarterly* XIX/30, pp. 216-23.

– (1996) *Sejarah Pariwisata dan Perkembangannya di Indonesia.* Jakarta: PT Gramedia Widiasarana Indonesia.

KOMPAS (1999) 'Setelah Pemilu, Industri Wisata DKI akan "Booming",' *Kompas,* Rabu, 31 Maret 1999, Jakarta.

Kumorotomo, W. (N.d.) The Key Issues In Cultural Tourism Management in Bali - Indonesia. Unpublished manuscript.

Lanfant, M.-F. (1995a) 'Introduction,' in: M.F. Lanfant, J.B. Allock and E.M. Bruner (eds) *International Tourism. Identity and change.* London: Sage, pp. 1-22.

– (1995b) 'Tourism, Internationalization and Identity,' in: M.F. Lanfant, J.B. Allock and E.M. Bruner (eds) *International Tourism. Identity and change.* London: Sage, pp. 24-43.

Lanfant, M.-F., J.B. Allock and E.M. Bruner (eds) (1995) *International Tourism. Identity and change.* London: Sage.

Lenhart, L. (1994) 'Ethnic Minority Policy and National Development,' in: I. Wessel (ed.) *Nationalism and Ethnicity in Southeast Asia.* Proceedings of the Conference "Nationalism and Ethnicity in Southeast Asia" at Humboldt University, Berlin, October 1993. Berlin: Fakultätsinstitut für Asien- und Afrikawissenschaften, Humboldt Universität, pp. 87-106.

Leong, L. Wai-Teng (1997) 'Commodifying Ethnicity: State and Ethnic Tourism in Singapore,' in: *Tourism, Ethnicity and the State in Asian and Pacific Societies*. Honolulu: University of Hawai'i Press, pp. 71-98.

Liddle, R.W. (1997) 'Coercion, Co-optation, and the Management of Ethnic Relations in Indonesia,' in: M.E. Brown and Šunit Ganguly (eds) *Government Politics and Ethnis Relations in Asia and the Pacific*. Cambridge: MIT Press.

Long, V.H. and S.L. Kindon (1997) 'Gender and tourism development in Balinese villages,' in: M.T. Sinclair (ed.) *Gender, Work and Tourism*. London and New York: Routledge, pp. 91-119.

MacCannell, D. (1973) 'Staged authenticity: arrangements of social space in tourist settings,' *American Sociological Review* 79, pp. 589-603.

– (1976) *The Tourist - A New Theory of the Leisure Class*. New York: Shocken.

– (1992) *Empty Meeting Grounds. The Tourist Papers*. London and New York: Routledge.

Marjatmo (1996a) Perkembangan Wisata Minat Khusus dan Optimalisasi Biro Perjalanan Wisata. Sekretariat Forum Koordinasi Pengembangan Pariwisata Budaya Jawa Tengah dan Yogyakarta. Januari 1996.

– (1996b) Pengembangan Daya Tarik Wisata. Makalah Untuk Seminar Dalam Kerangka Pekan Pariwisata Yogyakarta. 12 Maret 1996.

Maurer, J.-L. (1997) 'A New Order Sketchpad of Indonesian History,' in: M. Hitchcock and V.T. King (eds) *Images of Malay-Indonesian Identity*. Kuala Lumpur: Oxford University Press, pp. 209-26.

Mazur, W. (1993) *Aspekte tourismusinduzierten Wandels in Entwicklungsländern unter besonderer Berücksichtigung des Individualtourismus. Dargestellt am Beispiel eines Wohnquartiers in Yogyakarta (Indonesien)*. Europäischer Verlag der Wissenschaften: Europäische Hochschulschriften Reihe XXXI. Politikwissenschaften. Bd. 245, Frankfurt am Main:Peter Lang.

McCarthy, J. (1994) *Are Sweet Dreams Made of This? Tourism in Bali and Eastern Indonesia*,' Indonesia Resources and Information Program (IRIP) Australia.

McGrew, A.G. (1992) 'Conceptualizing Global Politics,' in: A.G.McGrew and P.G. Lewis (et al.) *Global Politics. Globalization and the Nation-State*. Cambridge: Polity Press, pp. 1-28.

McGrew, A.G. and P.G. Lewis (et al.) (1992) *Global Politics. Globalization and the Nation-State*. Cambridge: Polity Press.

McTaggert, W.D. (1977) 'Aspects of the tourist industry in Indonesia,' *The Indonesian Quarterly* 4, pp. 62-74.

Michaud, J. (1997) 'A Portrait of Cultural Resistance: The Confinement of Tourism in a Hmong Village in Thailand,' in: M. Picard and R.E.Wood (eds) *Tourism, Ethnicity and the State in Asian and Pacific Societies*. Honolulu: University of Hawai'i Press, pp. 128-54.

Moertjipto and Bambang Prasetyo (1993) *Borobudur, Pawon dan Mendut*. Yogyakarta: Kanisius.

Mulder, N. (1994) *Inside Indonesian Society. An interpretation of cultural change in Java*. Bangkok: Editions Duang Kamol.

Nas, P.J.M. (1998) 'Global, National and Local Perspectives. Introduction,'. *Bijdragen tot de Taal-, Land- en Volkenkunde*, special issue 'Globalization, Localization and Indonesia,' edited by Peter J.M. Nas, 154:2, pp. 181-92.

Oakes, T.S. (1997) 'Ethnic Tourism in Rural Guizhou: Sense of Place and the Commerce of Authenticity,' in: M. Picard and R.E.Wood (eds) *Tourism, Ethnicity and the State in Asian and Pacific Societies*. Honolulu: University of Hawai'i Press, pp. 35-70.

OCTA (1974) *Republic of Indonesia: Central Java and Yogyakarta Area: Tourism Development*. Tokyo: Overseas Technical Cooperation Agency.

Pangasti, I.A. (1992) Pengaruh usaha pariwisata terhadap keadaan social ekonomi kampung Sosrowijayan Weten. Studi kasus: kampung Sosrowijayan Wetan. Sripsi Diajukan Untuk Memenuhi Salah Satu Syarat Memperoleh Gelar Sarjana Pendidikan Program Studi Pendidikan Ekonomi Koperasi Jurusan Pendidikan Dunia Usaha. Fakultas Pendidikan Pengetahuan Sosial. IKIP Sanata Dharma, Yogyakarta.

Parapak, J. (1995) Opening Speech. Education and Training for Industry Growth Conference, Jakarta, Indonesia, 17-18 July 1995.

Paribud Ekoling (1995) Tourism, Culture, Economy, Environment. A Joint University of Diponegoro/Griffith University Programme. Seaworld Nara Resort, Gold Coast, Queensland, 10-12 April 1995.

Parnwell, M.J.G. (1993) 'Tourism and Rural Handicrafts in Thailand,' in: M. Hitchcock, V.T. King and M.J.G. Parnwell (eds) *Tourism in South-East Asia*. London: Routledge, pp. 234-57.

Peeters, S. and J. Urru (1996) *Homestays: Een glimp van het echte Javaanse leven? Een onderzoek naar de budget-accommodatie sector in Yogyakarta, Indonesië*. M.A. Thesis, Department of Leisure Studies, Tilburg: Tilburg University, unpublished.

Peeters, S., J. Urru and H. Dahles (1999) 'A home away from home? The production and consumption of budget accommodations in Yogyakarta,' in: H. Dahles and K. Bras (eds) *Tourism and Small Entrepreneurs. Development, National Policy and Entrepreneurial Culture: Indonesian Cases*. An edition in the series 'Tourism Dynamics,' edited by Valene L.

Smith and Paul F. Wilkinson. New York: Cognizant Communication Corporation, forthcoming.

Peleggi, M. (1996) National Heritage and Global Tourism. *Annals of Tourism Research* 23(2), pp. 432-48.

Pemberton, J. (1994) *On The Subject of 'Java'*. Ithaca and London: Cornell University Press.

Penduduk Indonesia (1994) *Proyeksi Penduduk Indonesia per kabupaten/-kotamadya 1990-2000*. Jakarta: BSP Biro Pusat Statistik.

Periplus (1991) *Java*. Berkeley/Singapore: Periplus Editions.

Persoon, G. (1998) 'Isolated groups or indigenous peoples, Indonesia and the international discourse,' *Bijdragen tot de Taal-, Land- en Volkenkunde*, special issue 'Globalization, Localization and Indonesia,' edited by Peter J.M. Nas, 154/2, pp. 281-304.

Picard, M. (1990) '"Cultural Tourism" in Bali: cultural performances as tourist attraction,' *Indonesia* 49 (April) pp. 37-74.

– (1993) 'Cultural Tourism in Bali: national integration and regional differentiation,' in: Michael Hitchcock, Victor 'T. King and Michael J.G. Parnwell (eds) *Tourism in South-East Asia*. London: Routledge, pp. 71-98.

– (1995) 'Cultural Heritage and Tourist Capital: Cultural Tourism in Bali,' in: M.F. Lanfant, J.B. Allock and E.M. Bruner (eds) *International Tourism. Identity and change*. London: Sage, pp. 44-66.

– (1997) 'Cultural Tourism, Nation Building, and Regional Culture: The Making of a Balinese Identity,' in: M. Picard and R.E. Wood (eds) *Tourism, Ethnicity and the State in Asian and Pacific Societies*. Honolulu: University of Hawai'i Press, pp.181-214.

Picard, M. and R.E. Wood (eds) (1997) 'Preface,' in: *Tourism, Ethnicity and the State in Asian and Pacific Societies*. Honolulu: University of Hawai'i Press, pp. vii-xi.

Philip, J. and D. Mercer (1999) 'Commodification of Buddhism,' *Annals of Tourism Research* 26/1, pp. 21-54.

Pond, K.L. (1993) *The Professional Guide. Dynamics of Tour Guiding*. New York: Van Nostrand Reinhold.

Real Demand Study (1991) Real Demand Study. Final Report. YUDP - Yogyakarta Urban Development Project. Elektrowatt Engeneering Services LTD Switzerland, in association with Hasfarm Dian Konsultan Indonesia.Directorate General Cipta Karya, 15 June 1991.

Rencana Pengembangan (1987) Rencana Induk Pengembangan Pariwisata. Daerah Istimewa Yogyakarta. Buku I + Buku II Rencana Pengembangan. Pemerintah Propinsi Daerah Istimewa Yogyakarta. Dinas Pariwisata. Proyek Pengembangan Penyuluhan dan Perencanaan, Pariwisata Daerah Istimewa Yogyakarta. Berkerjasama dengan Pusat Penelitian Perencanaan Pembangunan Nasional, Universitas Gadjah Mada.

Richards, G. (ed.) (1996) *Cultural Tourism in Europe*. Oxon: CAB International.

Richter, L.K. (1989) *The Politics of Tourism in Asia*. Honolulu: University of Hawai'i Press.

– (1992) 'Political instability and tourism in the Third World,' in: D. Harrison (ed.) *Tourism and the less developed countries*. London: Belhaven Press, pp. 35-46.

Rigg, J. (1997) *Southeast Asia. The human landscape of modernization and development*. London and New York: Routledge.

Ritzer, G. (1993) *The McDonaldization of Society. An Investigation Into the Changing Character of Contemporary Social Life*. Thousand Oaks/-London/New Delhi: Pine Forge Press.

Ritzer, G. and A. Liska (1997) '"McDisneyization" and "post-tourism": Complementary perspectives on contemporary tourism,' in: Ch. Rojek and J. Urry (eds) *Touring Cultures. Transformations of Travel and Theory*. London/New York: Routledge, pp. 96-109.

Robertson, R. (1990) 'Mapping the Global Condition: Globalization as the Central Concept,' in: M. Featherstone (ed.) *Global Culture. Nationalism, Globalization and Modernity*. A Theory, Culture and Society special issue. London: Sage, pp. 15-30.

Robison, R. (1996) 'The middle class and the bourgeoisie in Indonesia,' in: R. Robison and D.S.G. Goodman (eds) *The New Rich in Asia. Mobile phones, McDonald's and middle-class revolution*. London, New York: Routledge, pp. 79-104.

Rosyidie, A. (1995) Tourism Development: Economic, Social, and Environmental Impact. Case Study: Indonesia. Ph.D.Thesis, Institute of Social and Economic Geography. Faculty of Social Sciences. Katholieke Universiteit Leuven.

Rotge, V.L. (1991) Addressing Regional Development and Rural Employment Creation in the Context of Rising Rural-Urban Linkages. Second country seminar on regional development in the special province of Yogyakarta. September 3-6, 1991, Yogyakarta, Indonesia.

Sammeng, A.M. (1995) Tourism as a Development Strategy. Plenary Address. Plenary V: International Tourism, Development, and Policy Making. The 1995 Indonesian-Swiss Forum on Culture and International Tourism. Universitas Gadjah Mada, Yogyakarta, Indonesia.

Schefold, R. (1998) 'The domestication of culture. Nation-building and ethnic diversity in Indonesia,' *Bijdragen tot de Taal-, Land- en Volkenkunde* 154/2 special issue 'Globalization, Localization and Indonesia, edited by Peter J.M. Nas, pp. 259-80.

Schlehe, J. (1997) Interkulturelle Geschlechterbeziehungen im Tourismus. Paper. Frankfurt, Tagung der Deutschen Gesellschaft fuer Voelkerkunde, 5-10 Oktober 1997.

1999 'Tourism to holy sites and pilgrimage to hotel rooms in Java,' in: H. Dahles and T. van Meijl (eds) Local perspectives on global tourism in the Asia-Pacific region. *Newsletter of the International Institute for Asian Studies*, no. 19. Leiden, the Netherlands.

Schmidt, C. (1979) 'The Guided Tour: Insulated Adventure,' *Urban Life: A Journal of Ethnographic Research* 8/4, pp. 441-68.

Selosoemardjan (1962) *Social Changes in Jogjakarta*. Published under the auspices of the Modern Indonesia Project Southeast Asia Program, Cornell University. Ithaca, New York, Cornell University Press.

Selwyn, T. (1993) 'Peter Pan in South-East Asia. Views from the brochures,' in: M. Hitchcock, V.T. King and M.J.G. Parnwell (eds) *Tourism in South-East Asia*. London and New York: Routledge, pp. 117-37.

Silver, Ch. (1994) 'Urban Tourism Development: A Case for Indonesia,' *Jurnal Perencanaan Wilayah dan Kota*. Edisi Khusus, nomor 13, juni 1994, pp. 45-52.

Shields, R. (1990) *Places on the margin. Alternative geographies of modernity*. London/New York: Routledge.

Smithies, M. (1986) *Yogyakarta. Cultural Heart of Indonesia*. Singapore/-Oxford/New York: Oxford University Press.

Soedjarwo, A. (1991) Social Aspects of the Special Province of Yogyakarta. Some important issues to be considered in the Urban Development and Planning of the Special Province of Yogyakarta.

Second country seminar on regional development in the special province of Yogyakarta. September 3-6, 1991, Yogyakarta, Indonesia.

Soelarto, B. (1993) *Garebeg di Kesultanan Yogyakarta*. Yogyakarta: Penerbit Kanisius.

Sofield, T.H.B. (1995) 'Indonesia's National Tourism Development Plan,' *Annals of Tourism Research* 22/3, pp. 690-94.

Soekmono (1973) *Satu abad usaha penyelamatan candi Borobudur*. Yogyakarta: Kanisius.

Soemarwoto, O. (1992) *Candi Tourism*. Activity Report no. 81. Cultural Tourism Development. Central Java and Yogyakarta. UNDP/UNESCO.

Spillane, J.J. (1992) Proposal. Upgrading Courses for National Tourist Guides and Tour Managers in Indonesia. Economics Faculty at Gadjah Mada University, Sanata Dharma Research Center, Steering Committee, Cultural Tourism for Central Java and Yogyakarta. Yogyakarta: February 1992.

– (1993) Laporan Hasil Penelitian Hibah Bersaing. Judul: Needs Assessment Untuk Meningkatkan Mutu Pemandu Wisata Daerah Istimewa Yogyakarta: Suatu Studi Kasus di Daerah Istimewa Yogyakarta. Direktorat Jenderal Pendidikan Tinggi. Departemen Pendidikan dan Kebudayaan. Pusat Penelitian. IKIP Sanata Dharma Yogyakarta. Februari, 1993.

Stam, S. and K. Ter Steege (1997) A Travel Survival Kid. The interaction between mountain guides and nature-based tourists in North Lombok, Indonesia. Unpublished M.A. Thesis, Tilburg: Tilburg University.

Statistik Pariwisata (1995) Statistik Pariwisata, Pos dan Telekomunikasi, Daerah Istimewa Yogyakarta Tahun 1995. Diterbitkan oleh: KANWIL VIII Departemen Pariwisata, Pos dan Telekomunikasi. Daerah Istimewa Yogyakarta.

Statistik Kunjungan Tamu Asing 1995 (1995) Biro Pusat Statistik, Jakarta.

Statistik Wisatawan Internasional di Indonesia (1996) Pengumpulan Data Statistik Kunjungan Tamu Asing. BPS Biro Pusat Statistik, Jakarta.

Sub Dinas Diklat (1994) Laporan Penyelenggaraan Pendidikan Pramuwisata Budaya/Umum. Propinsi DIY. Sub Dinas Diklat. Dinas Pariwisata Propinsi DIY. Buku 1 dan Buku 2.

Sudarmadji, S. (1991) Enhancing Industrial Development in the Special Province of Yogyakarta. Second country seminar on regional development in the special province of Yogyakarta. September 3-6, 1991, Yogyakarta, Indonesia.

Suhartono R.B. (1988) 'Small and Medium-Scale Industries in Indonesia,' *Asian Development Review* 6/2, pp. 41-69.

Sullivan, J. (1991) Inventing and imagining community: the modern Indonesian ideologies. Monash University, working paper 69.

– (1992) *Local Government and Community in Java. An Urban Case-Study*. Singapore: Oxford University Press.

Sumaryanto (1993) Perkembangan Fasilitas dan Perkembangan Jumlah Pengunjung. Studi kasus pada objek wisata Candi Prambanan, Kabupaten Sleman, Yogyakarta. Jurusan Pendidikan Dunia Usaha. Fakultas Pendidikan Ilmu Pengetahuan Sosial. IKIP Sanata Dharma, Yogyakarta.

Telfer, D. (1997) *Agrotourism: A path to community development?* Paper presented at the ATLAS International Conference, Viana do Castelo, Portugal, 4-6 September.

Theobald, W.F. (ed.) (1994) *Global Tourism. The next Decade.* Oxford: Butterworth-Heinemann Ltd.

Thomas, N. (1994) *Colonialism's Culture. Anthropology, Travel and Government.* Cambridge: Polity Press.

Timothy, D.J. (1998a) Cooperative Tourism Planning in a Developing Destination. *Journal of Sustainable Tourism* 6(1), pp. 52-68.

– (1998b) 'Incremental Tourism Planning in Yogyakarta, Indonesia,' *Tourism Recreation Research* 23/2, pp. 72-4.

– (1999) 'Participatory Planning. A View of Tourism in Indonesia,' *Annals of Tourism Research* 26/2, pp. 371-91.

Timothy, D.J. and G. Wall (1995) 'Tourist Accommodation in an Asian Historic City,' *The Journal of Tourism Studies*, 6/2, pp. 63-73.

– (1997) 'Selling to Tourists, Indonesian Street Vendors,' *Annals of Tourism Research* 24/4, pp. 322-40.

Tjokrosudarmo, S. (1991) A Brief Outline of the Approach to Tourism Development. Second country seminar on regional development in the special province of Yogyakarta. September 3-6, 1991, Yogyakarta, Indonesia.

Tsuchia, K. (1984) 'Yogyakarta in a Time of Transition,' in: K. Tsuchiya (ed). *'States' in Southeast Asia. From 'tradition' to 'modernity'*. Kyoto University: Center for Southeast Asian Studies, pp. 209-10.

Turner, L. and J. Ash (1975) *The Golden Hordes*. London: Constable.

Turner, P., B. Delahunty, P. Greenway, J. Lyon, Ch. McAsey and D. Willett (1995) *Indonesia, a Lonely Planet travel survival kit*. Hawthorne/-Australia: Lonely Planet Publications.

Urry, J. (1988) 'Culture change and contemporary holiday making,' *Theory, Culture and Society* 5, pp. 35-55.

– (1990) *The Tourist Gaze. Leisure and Travel in Contemporary Societies*. London: Sage.

– (1995) 'Tourism, Travel and the Modern Subject,' in: *Consuming Places*. London and New York: Routledge, pp. 141-51.

Van der Giessen, E. and M.-C. van Loo (1996) *Bali, a 'paradise ' with two faces. A study of low-budget accommodation in Kuta and Ubud on the island of Bali in Indonesia*. M.A. Thesis. Tilburg: Tilburg University, unpublished manuscript.

Van der Giessen, E., M.-C. van Loo and K. Bras (1999) 'Homestays, *Losmen* and Guesthouses: Doing Business in the low-budget accommodation sector in Kuta and Ubud, Bali,' in: H. Dahles and K. Bras (eds) *Tourism and Small Entrepreneurs. Development, National Policy and Entrepreneurial Culture: Indonesian Cases*. An edition in the series 'Tourism Dynamics,' edited by Valene L. Smith and Paul F. Wilkinson. New York: Cognizant Communication Corporation, forthcoming.

Van Gemert E. and E. van Genugten (1996) *Tukang Becak. A Study of becak drivers who operate in the tourist sector of Yogyakarta, Indonesia*. M.A. Thesis. Tilburg: Tilburg University, unpublished.

Van Gemert, E., H. van Gemert and H. Dahles (1999) 'Tukang Becak: Tourism and the pedicab men of Yogyakarta,' in: H. Dahles and K. Bras (eds) *Tourism and Small Entrepreneurs. Development, National Policy and Entrepreneurial Culture: Indonesian Cases.* An edition in the series 'Tourism Dynamics,' edited by Valene L. Smith and Paul F. Wilkinson. New York: Cognizant Communication Corporation, forthcoming.

Van Leeuwen, L. (1997) *Airconditioned Lifestyles. De nieuwe rijken in Jakarta.* Amsterdam: Het Spinhuis.

Vatikiotis, M.R.J. (1993) *Indonesian Politics under Suharto. Order, development and pressure for change.* London and New York: Routledge.

Volkman, T. (1990) 'Visions and revisions: Toraja culture and the tourist gaze,' *American Ethnologist* 17/1, pp. 91-111.

Wai-Teng Leong, L. (1997) 'Commodifying Ethnicity: State and Ethnic Tourism in Singapore,' in: M. Picard and R.E.Wood (eds) *Tourism, Ethnicity and the State in Asian and Pacific Societies.* Honolulu: University of Hawai'i Press, pp. 71-98.

Wall, G. (1995) People outside of the plans, Address to the Indonesian-Swiss Forum on Culture and International Tourism, Yogyakarta: Gadjah Mada University.

– (1996) 'Perspectives on Tourism in Selected Balinese Villages,' *Annals of Tourism Research* 23/1, pp. 123-37.

– (1997a) 'Indonesia: The impact of regionalization,' in: F.M. Go and C.L. Jenkins (eds) Tourism and Economic Development in Asia and Australasia. London and Washington: Cassell, pp. 138-49.

– (1997b) 'Linking Heritage and Tourism in an Asian City: The Case of Yogyakarta, Indonesia,' in: P. Murphy (ed.) *Quality Management In Urban Tourism.* Chichester: Wiley, pp. 137-48.

Wall, G. and V. Long (1996) 'Balinese Homestays: an indigenous response to tourism opportunities,' in: R. Butler and T. Hinch (Eds) *Tourism and Indigenous Peoples.* London: International Thomson Business Press.

Warren, C. (1989) 'Balinese Political Culture and the Rhetoric of National Development,' in: P. Alexander (ed.) *Creating Indonesian Cultures.* Sydney: Oceania Publications, pp. 39-54.

Waters, M. (1995) *Globalization.* London and New York: Routledge.

Wessel, I. (1994) 'State Nationalism in Present Indonesia,' in: I. Wessel (ed.) *Nationalism and Ethnicity in Southeast Asia.* Proceedings of the Conference 'Nationalism and Ethnicity in Southeast Asia' at Humboldt University, Berlin, October 1993. Berlin: Fakultätsinstitut für Asien- und Afrikawissenschaften, Hunboldt Universität, pp. 33-48.

Wiendu Nuryanti (ed.) (1993) *Universal Tourism. Enriching or Degrading Culture?* Proceedings on the International Conference on Cultural Tourism. Gadjah Mada University Yogyakarta, Indonesia.

– (1996) 'Heritage and Postmodern Tourism,' *Annals of Tourism Research* 23/2, pp. 219-60.

– (1998) 'Tourism and regional imbalances,' *Indonesia and the Malay World* 26/75, pp. 136-44.

Wijono, D. (n.d.) *Taman Sari. Community Tourism Development Project.* Yogyakarta: Unpublished manuscript.

Wolf, Y. (1993) 'The World of the Kuta Cowboy. A growing subculture of sex, drugs and alcohol is evident among male youth in the tourist areas of Bali and Lombok as they seek an alternative to poverty,' *Inside Indonesia*, June, pp. 15-17.

Wood, R.E. (1984) 'Ethnic Tourism, the State, and Cultural Change in Southeast Asia,' *Annals of Tourism Research* 11, pp. 353-74.

– (1993) 'Tourism, culture and the sociology of development,' in: Michael Hitchcock, Victor T. King, Michael J.G. Parnwell (Eds) *Tourism in South-East Asia*. London and New York: Routledge, pp. 48-70.

– (1997) 'Tourism and the State: Ethnic Options and Constructions of Otherness,' in: M. Picard and R.E. Wood (eds) *Tourism, Ethnicity and the State in Asian and Pacific Societies*. Honolulu: University of Hawai'i Press, pp. 1-34.

Woodward, M.R. (1989) *Islam in Java. Normative Piety and Mysticism in the Sultanate of Yogyakarta*. Tucson: University of Arizona Press.

Yogya-In-A-Week (1990/1991) 'Yogyakarta In A Week' - Weekly Special Issue in English of the newspaper *YOGYA POST* published from October 5, 1990 to December 27, 1991.

Yumarnani, M. (1993) Perkembangan Pariwisata di Kraton Yogyakarta dari tahun 1981-1991. Fakultas Pendidikan Ilmu Pengetahuan Sosial. Jurusan Pendidikan Dunia Usaha. IKIP Sanata Dharma Yogyakarta.